W9-CCY-474

Tales, Then and Now

Tales, Then and Now

More Folktales as Literary Fictions for Young Adults

Anna E. Altmann

Gail de Vos

2001
Libraries Unlimited
A Division of Greenwood Publishing Group, Inc.
Englewood, Colorado

SIENA COLLEGE LIBRARY

Copyright © 2001 Anna E. Altmann and Gail de Vos
All Rights Reserved
Printed in the United States of America

No part of this publication may be reproduced, stored in a retrieval
system, or transmitted, in any form or by any means, electronic,
mechanical, photocopying, recording, or otherwise, without the
prior written permission of the publisher.

LIBRARIES UNLIMITED
A Division of Greenwood Publishing Group, Inc.
P.O. Box 6633
Englewood, CO 80155-6633
1-800-237-6124
www.lu.com

Library of Congress Cataloging-in-Publication Data

Altmann, Anna E.
    Tales, then and now : more folktales as literary fictions for young adults / Anna E.
Altmann, Gail de Vos.
        p. cm.
    Includes bibliographical references and index.
    ISBN 1-56308-831-2 (softbound)
    1. Folklore in literature. 2. Literature and folklore. 3. Young adult fiction--History and
criticism. 4. Tales--Adaptations--History and criticism. I. De Vos, Gail, 1949- II. Title.

PN56.F58 A45 2001
398.2'0835--dc21

                                                                                    2001038274

SIENA COLLEGE LIBRARY

PN
56
.F58
A45
2001

To my siblings,
Toni, Urs, Barbara, and Erik,
who share the journey.
AEA

To Taryn and Lawrence,
who are beginning their "happy ever after" story.
GdV

Contents

ACKNOWLEDGMENTS

We gratefully acknowledge the fine work of our research assistant, Tami Oliphant, and the grant from the Faculty of Education, University of Alberta, that allowed us to hire her. We also thank the far-flung network of libraries that made the material we needed available to us through interlibrary loans.

INTRODUCTION

Folktales for Today's Readers: Tried, Tested, and New

In spite of a great deal of evidence to the contrary, most adults and teenagers think of folktales as children's stories. Certainly we usually encounter them first in childhood, most often in picture books: *The Three Little Pigs, Little Red Riding Hood, Hansel and Gretel, Jack and the Bean Stalk, Cinderella.* But the extraordinarily durable threads of folktales run through our daily adult lives as well. An internationally respected Canadian newspaper, *The Globe and Mail*, is wooing readers with a banner advertisement on the front page that reads: "Cinderella had a fairy godmother./globeandmail.com/Your competitive edge." A variation on this ad points out that "The third pig had bricks" as his "competitive edge." Then there are the television ads for the Ford Windstar. One shows the three little pigs hustling into the vehicle and slamming the doors on the big bad wolf. Another has Grandma pulling up in her Ford in the nick of time to save Little Red Riding Hood. One of the widely syndicated "Bizarro" cartoons (January 14, 2000) showed "GOLDILOCKS & THE SURVIVING MEMBER OF THE ORIGINAL 3 BEARS RENUNION TOUR," and another, published just before Christmas 1999, showed Hansel and Gretel's gingerbread house behind a chainlink fence with a big sign in front of it: "CONDEMNED BY THE FOOD AND DRUG ADMINISTRATION. Coming Summer 2000, BRAN MUFFIN TOWNHOMES."

Folktales are common currency in today's adult world, not only in the allusive or parodic snippets I've just cited from mass media, but in films, television programs, poems, novels, short stories, stage musicals, operas, and ballet. We're in the middle of a folktale boom, and the new versions come in all shapes and in all types of media. In the year 2000, for example, at one end of the range was the most beautiful book of traditional tales I have ever seen, *Fairy Tales,* written by Berlie Doherty and illustrated by Jane Ray. The stories are well-crafted retellings of a selection of folktales from a number of sources. The illustrations by Jane Ray are extraordinarily lovely and make the book worth buying no matter how many collections you already own. At the other end of the range is the live-action television mini-series *The 10th Kingdom*, which was broadcast on NBC during prime time in the winter of 2000 and came out as a book written by Kathryn Wesley shortly thereafter. It reworks just about every folktale motif anyone might ever have come across into one extended, action-packed quest story that is as heavily intertextual as it is suspenseful. (Neither work is included in this book, because the Doherty book is a collection of retellings rather than reworkings, and *The 10th Kingdom* isn't a reworking of a single tale.)

Among the new versions of folktales appearing in every possible narrative genre, there are many aimed specifically at a teenage audience. Francesca Lia Block's collection of short stories, *The Rose and the Beast: Fairy Tales Retold*, came out in 2000. So did Ellen Datlow and Terri Windling's collection of stories for young adults, *A Wolf at the Door and Other Retold Fairy Tales*. The recent young adult novels include Donna Jo Napoli's *Beast*, Robin McKinley's *Spindle's End*, and Philip Pullman's *I Was a Rat*. In 1999 Paradox Press put out *The Big Book of Grimm: Truly Scary Fairy Tales to Frighten the Whole Family*, "the original, uncensored bedtime stories in all their grim glory." It's a comic book collection, 191 pages long, with a splash of blood on the cover and a skull in the initial "O" of "Once upon a time." The back cover warns, "suggested for mature readers."

There are also many new versions of folktales that are published for adults but easily find a young adult audience, especially in the genres of fantasy and science fiction, where teenagers commonly read across the age division implied by shelving in book stores and libraries. For example, Tanith Lee's *White as Snow* and Orson Scott Card's *Enchantment* (a reworking of "Sleeping Beauty" from the Jewish prince's point of view) are books that teenagers will read because they're already hooked on these writers.

And then there are the picture books, usually relegated to the children's section because of their physical format, that also should have young adult readers. Some of these picture book folktales tell their stories seriously. Most retell the tales with an irony and clever wit ideally suited to adolescents. Jon Scieszka's *The Stinky Cheese Man and Other Fairly Stupid Tales*, *The True Story of the Three Little Pigs by A. Wolf*, and *The Frog Prince Continued* are obvious examples.

Many of the contemporary reworkings of folktales, for whatever audience, are parodies, a form of humor particularly suited to teenagers. Parody is one of the first stages of achieving critical distance. It plays with conventions in an easily recognizable way, challenging and examining the norm. It can be used to turn accepted meaning or form upside down, just for fun or as an acid critique. Whether simply hilarious or wickedly cutting, it is always subversive. And because as metafiction it declares some sort of detachment, it is "cool."

When new versions of folktales aren't parodies, they are usually quest stories, like the traditional tales on which they are based. A quest is a process of initiation, of transition from one stage of life to another. The heroes of folktales are always isolated, separated by difference or distance from their home communities. They must survive tests that bring them self-knowledge and prepare them for a new place in society. They also have to be open to the wide, "wonder-full" world from which unexpected helpers come to their aid. The initiatory scenario of the quest story is likely to have particular resonance for teenagers, who face a number of important transitions all at once: leaving home, choosing a trade or profession, entering into adult sexuality, and taking on responsibility for themselves. Often feeling isolated, they are preoccupied with who they are and who they will become, with choosing a path into the unknown.

Some contemporary reworkings of the old quest tales are fat, complicated novels that only an avid reader would greet with joy. But there are also dozens of slim novels, scores of short stories, and a number of films that are accessible to a more reluctant teenage audience. The choices include fantasy, realistic fiction, horror, science fiction, adventure, farce, and romance. There's bound to be something for everyone. This book is intended to help you find it.

Scope and Organization of the Book

Our subject is the contemporary reworkings of classic folktales that have been written for or would interest teenage readers. By reworkings we mean versions that are more radically changed than simple retellings. In its concept and organization, *Tales, Then and Now* follows the pattern established in our earlier book, *New Tales for Old: Folktales as Literary Fictions for Young Adults*, which was published by Libraries Unlimited in November 1999.

New Tales for Old, which can be used as a companion to this work, deals with reworkings and critical interpretations of eight popular folktales, all from the oral tradition and all retold by either the Brothers Grimm or Charles Perrault or both: "Cinderella," "The Frog King," "Hansel and Gretel," "Little Red Riding Hood," "Rapunzel," "Rumpelstiltskin," "Sleeping Beauty," and "Snow White." This volume addresses a more diverse group of tales: three major folktales outside the Grimm and Perrault traditions and five literary fairy tales by Hans Christian Andersen. The folktales are "Beauty and the Beast," "Jack and the Beanstalk," and "Tam Lin" and "Thomas the Rhymer." All three have inspired a large number of reworkings that would interest teenagers and have attracted a substantial body of critical interpretation. "Beauty and the Beast" was first shaped as a French literary fairy tale, albeit from old folk motifs. The origins of "Jack and the Beanstalk" are difficult to sort out. There are actually two Jack tales that get mixed up together, and although both are part of the English folk tradition, the oldest known versions are definitely literary. "Tam Lin" and "Thomas the Rhymer" are two Scottish ballads often interwoven. They are the only ballads we know that have given rise to numerous reworkings in prose.

We deliberately excluded the literary fairy tales of Hans Christian Andersen from *New Tales for Old* as one way of setting workable limits on our material. Andersen is the name most commonly associated in the popular imagination with the term "fairy tales," even more commonly than that of the Brothers Grimm, but most of his stories are his own inventions rather than versions of traditional folktales. However, "Beauty and the Beast," because of its literary origin and the hugely successful animated movie version by Disney Studios, opens the door to Andersen's "The Little Mermaid." In addition, Andersen's "The Wild Swans," a version of a folktale from the oral tradition that also appears in the Grimms' collection, came to our attention when three new novels based on the story were published in 1999. So we looked for other Andersen tales that have given rise to a notable number of reworkings. We found far fewer than we expected. There are plenty of retellings and new translations, but only "The Little Mermaid," "The Snow Queen," "The Wild Swans," "The Emperor's New Clothes," and "The Princess on the Pea" have enough reworkings by our definition to warrant inclusion.

Diverse though this second group of tales is, they are all wonder tales, as are the eight stories in *New Tales for Old*. They all fit into the AT (Aarne-Thompson) tale type range 300–749, classified as "tales of magic." "The Snow Queen" and "The Little Mermaid" don't actually have tale type numbers because they are literary fairy tales: as of 1961 they hadn't given rise to enough folk variants to be included in the Aarne-Thompson classification. But they definitely belong in the "tales of magic" category.

The last chapter of this book is an update of *New Tales for Old*. It is an annotated list of reworkings that have been published in the last three years and also includes some earlier titles that we inadvertently missed the first time. It's a substantial list, because the fairy tale boom is still swelling. In the process of our research, we inevitably came across reworkings of tales that aren't included in either *New Tales for Old* or this book. It seems a shame not to make them available for readers who want to pursue this kind of gathering for other tales, so we have included citations for them in an appendix. They are reworkings of Child ballads, folktales, and Andersen tales, arranged within these categories by title of the tale. There are no annotations, but we do indicate the genre.

The organization of this book follows that of *New Tales for Old* as closely as possible. For each tale we first give the tale type and motifs from the Aarne-Thompson classification of folktales.[1] Only "The Little Mermaid" and "The Snow Queen" do not have an AT tale type number. These two long stories, although both contain folk motifs, are Andersen's own inventions and have never made their way into the oral tradition.

The tale type and motifs are followed by a brief synopsis of the tale and an account of its history as a book folktale. Then we give an overview of critical interpretations of the tale, arranged in chronological order from the earliest to the most recent. This section is followed by the heart of each chapter: a summary and discussion of each of the reworkings of the tale that we have found. The reworkings are arranged first by genre and, within each genre, by date of publication. Suggestions for use of this material by teachers and librarians working with young adults appear at the end of each chapter. Web sites identified in this book were last checked in August 2001.

As in *New Tales for Old*, each of us has written in her own voice, and we have divided the chapters between us according to our own interests. (Gail, of course, claimed "Tam Lin" because of Dianne Wynne Jones's *Fire and Hemlock*, and I bagged "Beauty and the Beast" because of Robin McKinley's *Beauty*, the two books that started us on this project some years ago.) However, we shaped the book together, and as a whole it is our joint responsibility.

Purpose

We planned this book for the same diverse audience that has found *New Tales for Old* useful or interesting: storytellers; librarians; researchers; and teachers in high schools, colleges, and universities who deal with folktales in their classrooms. The original purpose was to bring to the attention of teachers and librarians the large and steadily increasing number of folktale reworkings that would appeal to teenage readers. We set out to group, list, and describe them in a way that would provide both an overview of the body of material and easy access to individual titles or to a variety of reworkings based on a particular tale. Folktales are closely related to fantasy, and the best of these reworkings are fantasy. Although fantasy is popular with young adults, teachers and librarians often know too little about it. So we wanted not only to provide access to these stories but also to publicize them, to introduce them to the adults who need to become better acquainted with this type of literature. The heart of these two books, therefore, is the annotated lists of reworkings.

The tale type numbers and motifs of the original tales are given because they are essential information for storytellers and folklorists. The early literary history of each tale and the summaries of critical interpretations that the tale has provoked have a double purpose. First, they make each chapter a convenient, single source of the most important background information on the folktale in question and provide leads for deeper exploration depending on the need or pleasure of readers. Second, they make it very clear that there is no one correct version and no one definitive meaning for a given folktale.[2]

The classroom extensions suggest ways of thinking about the structure and possible meanings of one or more of the reworkings of the traditional tale with a group of students, exploring them as crafted works of a writer's imagination. Many of our suggestions can easily be adjusted from one tale to another and adapted for further study or comparison between tales. The suggestions can be used for classroom discussions or debates or as themes for reports or term papers. Retellings of folktales are a gift to language arts teachers. The type of story will be familiar to most students, no matter what their background, because such tales are common in cultures around the world. Further, the traditional tale is short, with a clear, formulaic structure and a strong plot. The reworkings in the form of short stories, picture and comic books, and poems are also relatively short texts that don't take long to read in their entirety. The young adult novels, although longer, are very accessible because they were written to entice and absorb today's readers. Such manageable texts can give reluctant readers confidence. There is no need to slog through a dauntingly large number of pages to participate actively in discussions or assignments. Best of all, readers can become interested in the comparative analysis even when they don't much like the texts in question. Students who seldom look voluntarily for the pleasure of immersing themselves in fiction can discover the different pleasure of a removed, critical reading. Because the traditional tales are so porous and their reworkings so clearly sets of individual choices, they have many surprises to offer. We learn best from surprise.

Sorting Out the Labels: Folktales and Literary Fairy Tales

Different things must be called by different names. The term "fairy tale" is used so loosely that it isn't very informative as a label. For example, one of the standard German works on literary fairy tales (Mayer and Tismar) includes in a single historical progression the works of Straparola, Basile, Perrault, the Grimms, Andersen, Wilde, Dickens, Thackeray, and Carroll, along with a number of other writers. This is slippery territory indeed. The main distinction that must be made within the broad category of stories generally called fairy tales is between tales that were or are alive in an oral tradition, the common property of many tellers, and those known as the invention of a single, identifiable author.

We use the term "folktale" in this book, as we did in *New Tales for Old*, for stories that come from the oral tradition. Because ours is a literate rather than an oral culture, each of the stories we think of as the classic folktales has a family tree of written versions going back through several centuries. All of these versions are literary in the sense that they were polished, embellished, and revised by writers to please their anticipated readers. Even the Brothers Grimm, who set out with scholarly intention to record the oral tales of German folk culture, cut and expanded and rewrote the stories they collected to make them fit their own idea of what the German folktale should be and what their audience would find attractive. But versions of these tales existed before the Grimms got hold of them, and other versions continue to exist. The bones of the folktale are shaped and preserved in popular oral culture.

"Literary fairy tale" is the term established by usage for stories that imitate folktales in structure, style, and subject matter but are the product of one individual's craft and creative imagination. A literary fairy tale has one original, and therefore definitive, version. Literary fairy tales are not as porous as folktales, not as open to variation and interpretation by later tellers.[3] The personal history, beliefs, and cultural context of the author are more firmly glued into the literary fairy tale than they are into any version of a folktale. The details invented by a particular teller of a folktale, the slant one teller chooses to give the story, are usually easily replaced by those of another. There are exceptions: Perrault's glass slipper and pumpkin and fairy godmother were such successful inventions that they were carried back into the oral tradition of "Cinderella" and have become enduring elements of the story; the Disney animated film version of "Snow White" may turn out to have had the same effect.

The border between literary and oral traditions is permeable in both directions. Literary variations on a folktale become part of the folk tradition, and authors of literary fairy tales make use of folktale motifs. A literary fairy tale can become a folktale: "Beauty and the Beast" is an outstanding example of such a story. Some tales, like "Jack and the Beanstalk" and "Jack the Giant Killer," have histories in which the folk and literary traditions are so mixed that scholars cannot agree on an origin. But that very lack of agreement proves them to be folktales in practice. They have been retold and reworked so often that they can no longer be identified as one person's inspiration.

The five Andersen tales represented in this book are an interesting mix of examples. Two of them, "The Princess on the Pea" and "The Emperor's New Clothes," might be called captured folktales. They have earlier folk sources, but Andersen's retellings became the dominant versions of the stories. "The Wild Swans" is a folktale still known in other versions, including that of the Grimms, so Andersen's retelling is one among many. "The Little Mermaid" and "The Snow Queen" were Andersen's creations from the start and are still firmly identified as his, the Disney animated movie version of "The Little Mermaid" notwithstanding. They have remained literary fairy tales.

Generally speaking, because the folktale is open to variation in a way that the literary fairy tale is not, folktales have more reworkings than literary fairy tales do. The surprisingly small number of reworkings we found of Andersen's tales, among a large number of retellings and adaptations for children, goes a long way to prove the point that folktales and literary fairy tales are different things.

How Reworkings Work

The authors of the reworkings included in this book take approaches that range from the playfully or critically humorous, through the ponderously serious, to the genuinely profound. In every case, the writers work with and within the traditional framework of the story, and, if they do it cleverly, the reader's pleasure is a mix of recognition and surprise. The surprise can be achieved in a number of different ways. One way is to decenter the story, to shift the focus from the traditional hero to one of the hero's antagonists. Gary Maguire, Patricia Galloway, and Donna Jo Napoli use this mechanism. Another way is to write a sequel to the traditional story. Philip Pullman's *I Was a Rat* and most of the poems based on "Beauty and the Beast" are examples of this technique. A third way is to change the expected outcome of the story. Some of Emma Donoghue's stories, and Margaret Haddix's novel *Ella Enchanted,* are examples of this tactic. A fourth way is to replace the magic with rational explanations. All of the science fiction and realistic fiction versions necessarily work this way. A fifth way, and the most subtle one, is simply to fill the gaps in the folktale, to invent the motivations, the character development, and the specific setting that the traditional tale lacks, while staying within the realm of fantasy. Robin McKinley's novels are outstanding examples of reworkings of this kind. Each of these mechanisms or techniques permits both humorous and serious approaches to the original story. None of them guarantees the success of the result.

Not all reworkings are created equal. They all have the advantage of the recognition value of the traditional tale, but what they make of it depends on the quality of the writer's craft and creative imagination. Reading yards of contemporary reworkings gives one a sharp eye for the poor or mediocre, of which there is a great deal. There are two types of reworkings that most quickly become tedious: the humorous parody and the wonder tale turned fable. The parodies have an initial shock value that soon wears off. Traditional folktales are easy to parody because their form is so highly stylized and they are so well known. The second type, the fairy tale turned fable, is written to teach something in a narrow, culturally specific context. The aim is reform or revolution, and the wonder of the fairy tale is replaced with the closed, ideological agenda of a fable.

The charm of any reworking lies to some extent in the taste and experience of the reader. For that reason we have included in this book every reworking we could find. Our own preferences have undoubtedly influenced the annotations we've written. Certainly we have exercised our critical judgment in our commentary. But any omissions are the result of oversight, and we would be glad to hear of titles we have missed.

Endnotes

1.   The classification of tale types was developed by Antti Aarne, a Finnish folklorist, and was revised and enlarged by Stith Thompson. Thompson's 1961 edition of *The Types of the Folktale* is an indispensable tool for people who work with folk narratives. Stith Thompson defines a tale type as follows: "A type is a traditional tale that has an independent existence. It may be told as a complete narrative and does not depend for its meaning on any other tale. It may consist of one motif or many" (1977, 415). Thompson defines a motif as "the smallest element in a tale having a power to persist in tradition" (1977, 415) and identifies three classes of motifs: the actors in a tale such as witches, fairies, the youngest child, or the cruel stepmother; items in the background of the action, such as magic objects or particular customs or beliefs; and single plot incidents, which make up the largest class by far. A tale like "The Princess on the Pea," which is made up of a single incident, is both a type and a motif.

2.   The first chapter of *New Tales for Old*, "Folktales and Literary Fictions," sets out to correct these misconceptions at some length.

3.   For a discussion of the porousness of folktales, see *New Tales for Old*, Chapter 1, "Folktales and Literary Fictions."

References

The Big Book of Grimm:Truly Scary Fairy Tales to Frighten the Whole Family!, by the Brothers Grimm as Channeled by Jonathan Vankin & Over 50 Top Comic Book Artists. 1999. New York: Paradox Press.

Block, Francesca Lia. 2000. *The Rose and the Beast: Fairy Tales Retold.* New York: Joanna Cotler Books.

Card, Orson Scott. 1999. *Enchantment.* New York: Del Rey.

Datlow, Ellen, and Terri Windling, eds. 2000. *A Wolf at the Door and Other Retold Fairy Tales.* New York: Simon & Schuster Books for Young Readers.

de Vos, Gail, and Anna E. Altmann. 1999. *New Tales for Old: Folktales as Literary Fictions for Young Adults.* Englewood, CO: Libraries Unlimited.

Doherty, Berlie. 2000. *Fairy Tales.* Illustrated by Jane Ray. Cambridge, MA: Candlewick.

Lee, Tanith. 2000. *White as Snow.* New York: TOR.

Mayer, Mathias, and Jens Tismar. 1997. *Kunstmärchen.* 3d Auflage. Stuttgart: Metzler.

McKinley, Robin. 2000. *Spindle's End.* New York: G. P. Putnam's Sons.

Napoli, Donna Jo. 2000. *Beast.* New York: Atheneum Books for Young Readers.

Pullman, Philip. 2000. *I Was a Rat!* New York: Knopf.

Scieszka, Jon. 1989. *The True Story of the 3 Little Pigs.* New York: Viking Kestrel.

———. 1991. *The Frog Prince Continued.* Illustrations by Steve Johnson. New York: Viking.

———. 1992. *The Stinky Cheeseman and Other Fairly Stupid Tales.* New York: Viking.

The 10th Kingdom. 2000. Directed by David Carson and Herbie Wise. Screenplay by Simon Moore. Hallmark Entertainment.

Thompson, Stith. 1961. *The Types of the Folktale: A Classification and Bibliography. Antti Aarne's Verzeichnis der Märchentypen,* translated and enlarged by Stith Thompson. 2d revision. FF Communications, no. 184. Helsinki: Suomalainen Tiedeakatemia.

———. 1977. *The Folktale.* Berkeley: University of California Press, 1977. [1946. Holt, Rinehart and Winston].

Wesley, Kathryn. 2000. *The 10th Kingdom.* New York: Hallmark Entertainment Books.

CHAPTER 1

BEAUTY
AND THE BEAST

Throughout this historical buffeting, the literary tale thrives, sometimes in its simplest form, sometimes vastly expanded, but always as recognizable as it seems malleable. (Hearne 1989, 57)

"Beauty and the Beast" began as a literary folktale for adults and then made its way into the oral tradition. From its first appearance in 1740, it has always been popular with both adults and children. The Opies called it "The most symbolic of the fairy tales after Cinderella, and the most intellectually satisfying" (1980, 179). There is, of course, no Perrault version of it, because it didn't exist at the time that Charles Perrault wrote, although a related story, "Riquet with the Tuft," appeared in his *Histoires, ou contes du temps passé,* published in 1697. The Grimms did not include it in their collection, undoubtedly because of its known French literary origin, but a number of their tales, including "The Lilting, Leaping Lark," the "Frog Prince," and "Snow White and Rose Red," are close relatives. A very useful short overview of the history of the tale and of its relatives may be found under "Beauty and the Beast" in *The Oxford Companion to Fairy Tales* (Zipes 2000). Anyone interested in learning about "Beauty and the Beast" is in luck. Betsy Hearne's *Beauty and the Beast: Visions and Revisions of an Old Tale* (1989) traces the history of the tale in folklore and literature, analyzing its structural elements and representative examples from different historical periods. Hearne's book is a very rich resource, and this chapter owes a great deal to her work. She introduces the tale as follows:

> This is a story with levels of meaning for all ages. Its audience has always fluctuated between children and adults. Children absorb the symbolic dimensions through the literal, while both aspects offer possibilities for elaboration that attract sophisticated adults. Although some versions clearly are created for children

and others for adults only, the broad age appeal is an important aspect of the tale's popularity with readers and its perpetuation by writers and artists who find it challenging. (Hearne 1989, 2–3)

❧ ───

A rich merchant has three lovely daughters. The youngest is the most beautiful of all, loving, and kind. The merchant loses his wealth when his ships are lost at sea. After some time he hears that one ship has returned safely and, having first asked his daughters what he should bring back for them, he makes a journey to settle his affairs. The two older sisters want dresses and jewels, but Beauty asks only for a rose. On his way back, not much better off than before, he gets lost in a storm and finds shelter for the night in a mysterious, magical palace. As he leaves the next morning he picks a rose from the garden for Beauty. At once a horrible Beast appears and tells the merchant that either he must pay for the theft of the rose with his own life or send the Beast one of his daughters. When the merchant returns home with his story, Beauty insists that she be the one to go back to the Beast. At the Beast's palace she is surrounded by every comfort, and as time passes she loses her fear of the Beast and comes to enjoy his company. But she misses and worries about her father, and when she discovers that he is gravely ill the Beast gives her permission to go home, on the condition that she return within a set time. Her sisters persuade her to stay longer than she should, and when she finally returns to the palace she finds the Beast dying from grief for her. She discovers that she loves him, and tells him so, thus breaking the enchantment that made him a beast. He turns into a handsome prince, and the two marry.

Tale Type: AT 425C

Tale type 425 is *The Search for the Lost Husband*, within section 400–459, *Supernatural or Enchanted Husband [Wife] or Other Relatives. Beauty and the Beast*, AT 425C, is summarized as follows: "Father stays overnight in mysterious palace and takes a rose. Must promise daughter to animal (or she goes voluntarily). Tabu: overstaying at home. She finds the husband almost dead. Disenchants him by embrace. (No search, no tasks)" (Thompson, 143). Tale type 425C is quite narrowly identified, with fewer variations than many other tale types. This specificity is undoubtedly due to the fact that "Beauty and the Beast" began as a literary tale that made its way into the oral tradition in Europe after its publication. The original literary tale clearly contains folktale elements and seems to have had tale type 425A, *Cupid and Psyche*, as one of its sources. Where "Cupid and Psyche" emphasizes the tasks of the bride, "Beauty and the Beast" emphasizes the Beast and its transformation. The analysis of tale type 425 that applies to 425C is the following (143):

I.   *The Monster as Husband.* (b) he is a man at night. (c) a girl promises herself as bride to a monster or (d) her father promises her (d¹) in order to secure a flower (lark) his daughter asked him to bring back from journey, (d²) to pay a gambling debt, or (d³) to escape from danger.

II. *Disenchantment of the Monster.* (a) The girl disenchants the monster (dwarf, bear, wolf, ass, snake, hog, hedgehog, frog, bird, or tree) by means of a kiss or tears, or (b) by burning the animal skin or (c) by decapitation or (d) by other means

III. *Loss of the husband.* (c³) But she loses him because she has broken the prohibition by staying too long at home.

V.   *Recovery of Husband.*(b) She disenchants him by affectionate treatment.

Motifs that occur in versions of the story examined in this book are in the following list. Future versions may include others from the list of motifs for tale type 425, and readers will need to consult Thompson to identify them.

Motifs:

L221: Modest request: present from the journey

S228: Daughter promised to monster as bride to secure flower (bird) she asked for

S221.1: Bankrupt father sells his daughters in marriage to animals

S222: Man promises (sells) child to save himself from danger or death

L54.1: Youngest daughter agrees to marry monster; later her sisters are jealous

D735.1: Beauty and the Beast. Disenchantment of animal by being kissed by woman (man)

D766.3: Disenchantment by tears

C761.2: Tabu: staying too long at home

A History of "Beauty and the Beast"

"Beauty and the Beast" is based on an ancient folktale with variants that have turned up in Asian, African, European, and Native North American cultures. Indeed, Graham Anderson traces it back to the Greek myths of "Europa and Zeus" and "Kallisto and Zeus" (70). The many related tale types feature a broad variety of Beauties and Beasts of both genders. Because the tale under discussion here is a relatively recent variant that has a known, published original, it usually keeps "Beauty and the Beast" as its title. It both entered the oral tradition and gave rise to new literary versions, and so flourished as folktale and literary tale at the same time. The first "Beauty and the Beast" was "La belle et la bête," written by Madame Gabrielle de Villeneuve and published in 1740 as a story in her *La jeune américaine, et autres contes merveilleux.* It is a convoluted romance, 187 pages long (in some editions 200 pages), written for aristocratic and bourgeois adult readers. Jack Zipes describes it as "a discourse on true love and class difference in marriage" transcribed "into a classic fairy tale" (1999, 45). Almost half of the story is an explanation of the Beast's enchantment and of Beauty's family history.

The most influential version was that written by Madame Le Prince de Beaumont,[1] published in 1756, and only 17 pages long. It was closely based on de Villeneuve's story, but very much shorter and intended for girls between the ages of 12 and 18. The work by de Beaumont in which it appeared was translated into English in 1759 with the title *The Young Misses Magazine, Containing Dialogues between a Governess and Several Young Ladies of Quality, Her Scholars.* "Beauty and the Beast" turned out to be the only memorable story in this didactic collection. De Beaumont's story became the classic model for most later works, including those for adults. Eighteenth-century literary versions that follow de Beaumont's story include a play by the Comtesse de Genlis in 1785 and an opera by Jean François Marmontel and André Modeste Grétry in 1788.

de Villeneuve

Because de Villeneuve's story is foundational for this tale, it is summarized here. The shortest and clearest way to present it is through an abbreviated version of the plot outline worked out by Hearne (1989).

1. Father's loss of wealth
2. Beauty's request for the rose
3. Father's journey to recover wealth
4. Storm and Beast's castle
5. Father's plucking of the rose and Beast's demand for retribution
6. Beauty's journey with father to the castle and father's departure
7. Beauty's first dream of a recurring series
8. Palace life and Beast's nightly proposals
9. Beauty's two-month leave at home
10. Beauty's return and revival of Beast
11. Queen mother's arrival
12. Prince's story told with Dream Fairy's help
13. Arrival of King of the Happy Isles (Beauty's real father)
14. Beauty's story, told by Dream Fairy
15. Beauty's Fairy Queen/mother's appearance, with story
16. Beauty's stepsisters' and their husbands' arrival from the hunt
17. Beauty's merchant/adoptive father's arrival
18. Marriage and dispersal to various duties
19. Adoptive family given work at court

Beauty's adoptive sisters are unkind to her, and she easily outshines them. She insists on returning to the Beast with her father to take his place. The Beast is not only ugly (de Villeneuve's description is limited to mentioning that he is huge and has a trunk like an elephant) but must appear to be stupid as well. At the palace, Beauty is visited in her dreams by the prince the Beast was and will be again; she falls in love with him. The Beast asks every night whether she will marry him. After she revives the dying Beast, Beauty agrees to marry him, and they watch three hours of celebratory fireworks. The Beast is not transformed until the next morning, when Beauty wakes to find her dream prince in her bed. She tries to kiss him awake, but he sleeps soundly on until the noise of his mother's arrival wakes him.

The arrival of the prince's mother creates a new crisis. She doesn't want her son marrying a mere merchant's daughter, and Beauty volunteers to give him up because she isn't worthy of him by birth. The Dream Fairy, who appears throughout to explain things to the characters (and thereby the readers) and make the many morals of the story very clear, argues that virtue matters more than social class, but the problem disappears when Beauty's biological father appears and explains that she really is a princess. The deception of appearances, that virtuous behavior is true beauty, the importance of gratitude, and the need to put duty before love are among the lessons the Fairy explicates. A full translation of the tale can be found in Zipes's anthology *Beauties, Beasts and Enchantment* (1989). Hearne worked from Ernest Dowson's 1908 translation, which differs in some important details from Zipes's. I have used the Zipes translation here.

de Beaumont

Madame de Beaumont took her story from de Villeneuve but left out the long descriptions of Beauty's entertainments at the Beast's palace, the appearances in Beauty's dreams of the prince and the fairy, and the stories of Beauty's and the Beast's backgrounds. Beauty is the merchant's own daughter, with three brothers and two sisters. There is no mention of a mother. Although Beauty's brothers are kind and loving, Beauty's sisters are gadabouts who laugh at her for spending so much time reading good books. They marry, one for good looks and the other for wit, and both are miserable with their husbands, who have nothing else to recommend them. Beauty herself has refused several very eligible suitors, saying that she is too young to marry and prefers to stay at home with her father for a few years yet. De Beaumont added to Beauty's virtues a good education, which she makes use of by spending her free time reading, playing the harpsichord, or singing while she spins. Appropriately, the Beast provides her with a large library, a harpsichord, and several music books in her room at his palace. And Beauty discovers her new independence (away from her family in which she is the dutiful daughter) through the inscription in the first book she opens in there (de Beaumont, 188):

> Welcome Beauty, banish fear,
> You are queen and mistress here:
> Speak your wishes, speak your will,
> Swift obedience meets them still.

The Beast, as in de Villeneuve's story, was transformed by a wicked fairy for no fault of his own, and was also obliged to conceal his intelligence if the curse was to be lifted. All he has to persuade Beauty to marry him is his good temper.

Beauty "sincerely loved" the Beast, writes de Beaumont, but a few lines farther down the page we are told what a limited love hers is. She has overstayed the week with her family and dreamt of the Beast dying in his garden and reproaching her with ingratitude. In tears, she reflects on her wickedness:

> Is it his fault if he is so ugly and has so little sense? He is kind and good, and that is sufficient. Why did I refuse to marry him? ... It is true, I do not feel the tenderness of affection for him, but I find I have the highest gratitude, esteem and friendship; I will not make him miserable, were I so ungrateful I should never forgive myself. (de Beaumont, 193)

"Tenderness of affection" undoubtedly is a suitably modest euphemism for passionate love that encompasses sexual desire. Beauty has given up hope of finding that in marriage and feels that she must settle for kindness and goodness and be grateful to have that. She intends to marry to oblige the Beast rather than because she herself desires the marriage. Beauty's self-sacrifice pays off. She gets romantic love and the perfect husband.

The dream fairy appears only twice, once on the night before Beauty and her father journey to the palace to reassure Beauty that she is doing the right thing and again at the end of the story to explain the morals and turn Beauty's two sisters into stone statues at the palace gate. The explicit morals are that virtue is to be preferred before either wit or beauty, that virtue is rewarded, and that evil (in the persons of the two sisters) will be punished. As statues at Beauty's palace gates, the sisters are condemned to watch her happiness. They will remain statues until they admit to their faults, which will never happen. "Pride, anger, gluttony, and idleness are sometimes conquered, but the conversion of a malicious and envious mind is a kind of miracle," says the good fairy who arranges their punishment. Beauty and the Beast marry, "and their happiness as it was founded on virtue was compleat" (de Beaumont, 195).

The magic elements in de Beaumont's story are: the ring the Beast gives Beauty, which brings her back to the palace after her visit home; the blooming roses in the palace garden when it is winter outside the walls; the Beast's magic chest, which sends the merchant home with gold and Beauty with the clothes and jewels that make her sisters jealous so that they tempt her to overstay her promised return to the Beast; and the mirror in which Beauty sees her family. In the palace, she hears music without seeing anyone play. Food appears on the table for the merchant and Beauty, but no invisible servants are mentioned.

Nineteenth-Century Versions

Hearne finds that nineteenth-century versions of "Beauty and the Beast" were largely stable, keeping the characters, narrative structure, and key elements established by de Beaumont. Although the tone and style of these stories vary, many of them emphasize "the importance of Duty, Fate, and Nature" (1989, 56). In contrast, didactic moralizing is absent from the enormous number of versions of the tale produced from 1900 to 1950 for children and adults. During this period the story became what Hearne calls "multi-traditional" as writers, illustrators, and notably Jean Cocteau in his 1946 film *La belle et la bête* began to rework the tale. The versions for children and those for an adult audience formed two distinctly separate streams as writers developed more complex interpretations of the tale. In the latest period covered by Hearne's study, 1950 to 1985, "the publications and media productions of 'Beauty and the Beast' multiplied dramatically but ephemerally" (1989, 90). Most of them were mediocre, and many trivialized the tale by caricaturing it or by reducing it to its lowest common denominator to reach the widest possible market. But a few strong and interesting versions, both for children and for older readers, had staying power. Among them is Robin McKinley's young adult novel, *Beauty: A Retelling of the Story of Beauty and the Beast*, the first version published specifically for young adults since de Beaumont's foundational story. The best-known of the recent versions is Disney's film, which came out in 1991 and is loved by viewers of all ages.

By Hearne's count, more than 250 publications, films, and recordings of "Beauty and the Beast" have appeared since 1740, most of them from Great Britain, France, or the United States. Twentieth-century versions include opera, dance, film, radio and television productions, drama, poetry, novels, short stories, and picture books (Hearne 1989, 3).

Overview of Critical Interpretations of "Beauty and the Beast"

The single most important scholarly resource for this tale is Betsy Hearne's *Beauty and the Beast*. There is also much valuable material in Marina Warner's *From the Beast to the Blond* (1994). In addition, most of the studies of folktales that are cited in the other chapters of this book consider "Beauty and the Beast."

1878: W. R. S. Ralston, exploring the elements of folklore in "Beauty and the Beast," concluded that it "is evidently a moral tale, intended to show that amiability is of more consequence than beauty" (Hearne 1989, 12–13).

1975: For Bruno Bettelheim, "Beauty and the Beast" is a story about satisfactory resolution of the natural Oedipal connection between a father and his daughter. Bettelheim interprets the rose Beauty's father brings her as symbolizing both his love for her and the impending loss of her virginity. Both father and daughter are likely to fear this event as a "beastly" experience for her. But if, as the daughter matures, her attachment to her father loosens and is transformed as it becomes concentrated on a lover, sex no longer seems a frightening and ugly thing, but beautiful.

> Our Oedipal attachments, far from being only the source of our greatest emotional difficulties (which they can be when they do not undergo proper development during our growing up), are the soil out of which permanent happiness grows if we experience the right evolution and resolution of these feelings. (308)

1980: Derek Brewer points out that the rose Beauty asks her father to bring back is analogous to the twig Cinderella asks her father for in some versions of that story. The father, therefore, is a "split" figure. Although he tries to keep her at home and causes her to come home because he is ill from grieving for her, he is also the one who gives Beauty the opportunity to leave home, to set out on her path to independence and maturation. According to Brewer, both aspects of the father are projections of Beauty's feelings about him. She knows he will help her, but she also feels guilty about growing up and leaving him. Brewer notes that the theme of "Beauty and the Beast" can be found in a number of popular literary fictions. "The story illustrates the willingness of the heroine to go out and get her man, once given an opportunity, as do the heroines of *Pride and Prejudice* and *Jane Eyre*" (39). Both Mr. Darcy and Mr. Rochester have strong touches of the Beast in them.

1989: Sylvia Bryant reads Angela Carter's two versions of "Beauty and the Beast"—"The Courtship of Mr. Lyon" and "The Tiger's Bride"—against Jean Cocteau's film *La belle et la bête*. Carter's short stories shatter "the controlling narrative paradigm" (440) of male desire, whereas Cocteau's film reinscribes it. Bryant apparently has no understanding of folktales. She begins with an attack on folktales for their "inherent binarism of desire" and "seemingly un-self-conscious gender bifurcation," and for denying "the presence of any narrative—any personal, individual story—to the characters at all" (439). She further states that the folktales offer a "social scenario of reward based on essential goodness" (439). Her reading of Carter and Cocteau is more reliable, although I disagree strongly with her description of "The Courtship of Mr. Lyon" as "a hip, contemporary '60s style parody" (441).

1989: According to Betsy Hearne, in the eighteenth century, "Beauty and the Beast" was about romantic, courtly love. In the classic pattern of such courtship, the Beast serves Beauty as best he can, Beauty continues to refuse him despite his efforts, the Beast suffers to the point of death for his lady, and Beauty finally says yes. In the tradition of courtly love, Beauty always has a choice, and the insistence of the eighteenth-century writers on this choice was revolutionary, a protest against daughters being given away in marriage to husbands of their father's choosing. Beauty initially chooses not to marry to stay with her father. She chooses to go to the Beast in her father's place, is free to reject the Beast's proposals of marriage, is requested rather than required to return to him, and breaks the enchantment inadvertently when she realizes that she loves him. When Beauty comes to the Beast's palace, he asks whether she came of her own free will and tells her repeatedly that everything there is at her command. Hearne points out that this matter of choice is a key difference between "Beauty and the Beast" and the closely related "Cupid and Psyche." Whereas Psyche is required to be blindly obedient to succeed, "Beauty's is a test of the perception of heart and mind" (16). There is no question of Beauty's obedience to a male.

Beauty is attracted to the Beast but is still tied too strongly to her family, especially her father, to willingly make her life with him. She resolves her inner conflicts of her own free will, moving forward into a new stage of her life. The Beast is the passive character, waiting patiently to be rescued by any woman who comes along and decides she wants him. About the Beast Hearne makes a memorable comment: "The ancient power of the Beast's presence, controlled by a gentle nature and respect for another individual, makes 'Beauty and the Beast' appealing to modern readers. Irrepressible instincts allied with good intentions are so palatable" (16).

Hearne points out that Beauty's education and her love of reading are significant in de Beaumont's version. As a governess, de Beaumont discovered that girls have a much larger capacity to learn, form arguments, and make solid judgments than society allowed them at the time. Beauty's sisters have no sensible or useful occupations. They waste their days waiting for a suitable husband to propose himself, and when they marry, they choose very badly. As a consequence they are miserable and are finally petrified in their unhappy state, while the bookish Beauty has chosen wisely for herself.

According to Hearne, whereas the eighteenth- and nineteenth-century versions moralized in a straightforward didactic way about duty and the deception of appearances, those published in the first half of the twentieth century looked more deeply for meaning. They found in the story the possibility of exploring the struggle for balance between "personal dualities of light and dark, reality and fantasy, animal and spiritual, male and female, alienation and reconciliation" (89). The huge number of versions that have appeared in the second half of the twentieth century make dominant themes for the period harder to pin down. But the successful resolution of the Oedipal triangle, the need for self-acceptance and reconciliation with the Other, the conflict between spiritual values and materialistic values, and the recognition that only love can bring about resurrection are all themes to be found in "Beauty and the Beast" that seem to have relevance in our time.

After looking at variations of this tale over three centuries, Hearne pulls out the images, objects, and symbols that are retained in every version. They may be more or less fully developed, but they are the stable elements that form the core of the tale and make it recognizable as "Beauty and the Beast," no matter what changes a particular reteller has introduced. It must be noted that Hearne's book was published two years before the Disney film came out in 1991, so she was not able to take the film and its influence on later versions into account in her analysis.

The seasonal cycle is one of the enduring elements of the story. Winter signifies defeat or death. The merchant, whose hopes of the one returned ship are unfulfilled and who was unable to find a rose for Beauty, is caught in a snow storm. When he stumbles onto the Beast's palace, the gardens around it are in the full bloom of summer, which Hearne suggests is the season of courtship (1989, 125). These same gardens are dying and the season is turning to winter when Beauty finally returns to the Beast's palace, almost too late. The movement from city to country to the hidden enchanted palace of the Beast deep in the forest is a second basic element. Journeys are the frame for the plot, and the physical journeys are metaphors for Beauty's inner journey. A third constant element is a rose, which traditionally signifies love. In most of the versions, Beauty asks her father for it, and it brings her to the Beast. In some there is a second rose, given to Beauty by the Beast when she returns home, that stands for the Beast's life. That life is now in Beauty's hands because of his love for her. Hearne gives us Thomas Mintz's reading of the rose "as representing both the Beast's masculinity and Beauty's femininity, the thorns signifying the former, and the seeds and color of menses/defloration the latter" (Hearne 1989, 126). The reading of the rose in the Disney film and in the teenage romance that borrows from it must, of course, be a different one. Here the rose is meaningful only in relation to the Beast and is a measure of the time he has left before his chance for redemption expires.

The Beast's garden is a fourth stable element, a natural environment for growth on Beauty's part, a place of amazing loveliness in which cultivation and nature come together. The garden flourishes in the Beast's magic field, and magic is the fifth enduring element. It is necessary to transform the prince into the Beast in the first place, and the way magic plays with time and space is perhaps a catalyst for Beauty's self-transformation. It shakes loose her accustomed way of seeing the world and herself in it. Its strangeness is like the human subconscious world of dream in that it is full of significance without being rational. But magic plays no active part in releasing the Beast from the enchantment.

Hearne's look at the stable elements of the tale confirms the analysis of the style of the folktale developed in the first chapter of this book. She finds that the narrative voice is the element of the story that varies the most, and "represents an individual author's primary contribution" (1989, 129). The narrative structure is simple, as in every folktale, and allows a great deal of variation within the frame of the journeys without weakening the story. Although the cast of supporting characters changes from version to version, the three essential characters are Beauty, the Beast, and the father. Like all folktale characters, their essential role in the story is as carriers of the action, or actants, so they may be developed in many different ways. Beauty may be vacuous, pliant, determined, feisty, a tomboy, or a model of femininity, but she is always isolated in some way. The father may be strong or weak. The Beast is really the central character in that he is pivotal to all the events of the plot, and therefore changes in the development of the Beast affect the story most strongly, as the Disney film demonstrates. In all the versions Hearne studied, the Beast is capable of love and has learned wisdom through suffering. He can only wait and try to persuade Beauty to love him.

Together, the two of them have complementary imbalances. The Beast waits for an outward transformation that depends on Beauty's inner growth:

> "Beauty and the Beast" offers the promise that for all our human ugliness and brutality, we can be acceptable, even lovable, to another human being. The continued relevance of "Beauty and the Beast" as a modern theme stems from this fearful knowledge that we are each beastly, juxtaposed with the hopeful knowledge that we are each beautiful. (Hearne 1989, 133)

1991:   Irene Gad gives a Jungian reading of the tale, beginning with the premise that each character in a fairy tale "represents an aspect of the hero or heroine" (31). Because Beauty is too closely connected with her father, is his "anima carrier," she is separated from her own femininity and her personality cannot mature. The time in the forest (the Beast's castle is reached through a forest) is "time for transformation" (42) in which Beauty can contact "repressed forces" within herself and find her "inner truth" (43). She is attracted by the caring and nurturing (feminine) qualities of the Beast because she never had a mother's warmth and support. The Beast is ugly because Beauty is afraid to change; she projects onto her partner the lost parts of herself that she does not want to face. In any couple, the partner may be "a mirror we are too scared to look into" (43). But both Beauty and the Beast are able to change. "Fairy tales teach us that curses can be lifted. What is needed is a capacity to love, a willingness for sacrifice, and a patient acceptance of the inevitable pain" (46).

1992:   In *Off with Their Heads!*, Maria Tatar discusses daughters sacrificed to beasts in a chapter titled "Beauties and Beasts: From Blind Obedience to Love at First Sight." Tatar puts "Beauty and the Beast" in the context of other variants of tale type 425, *The Search for the Lost Husband,* and compares 425 to 400, *A Man on a Quest for His Lost Wife.* She points out that recent versions of tale type 425 "highlight the importance of obedience, self-sacrifice, and self denial, even as they downplay the courage it takes to put these virtues into practice" (143). She gives Angela Carter's "Courtship of Mr. Lyon," published in 1979, as an example of such versions. Tatar suggests that where the heroes of folktales in the oral tradition act with courage or intelligent diplomacy, book folktales and literary folktales tend to replace these qualities with virtues like obedience and humility (147). But folktales are not meant to be moral tales, and the attempts of literary retellers to build in lessons often create internal contradictions. For example, the rose that Beauty asks for out of modesty or because she wishes to spare her father's purse gets her father into terrible trouble. "Beauty and the Beast," however, seems to be more adaptable than most folktales as an instrument of socialization. "That moves in the direction of self-sacrifice are invariably rewarded . . . remains one of the enduring sad facts of this extraordinary tale" (158).

1994:   Barbara Fass Leavy's book is about "the interplay between stories about a fairy captured by a mortal man and forced into a tedious domestic existence and, obversely, about a mortal woman courted by a demon lover who offers her escape from that same mundane world" (11). She looks at folktales from all parts of the world. In chapter 4, "The Animal Groom," some of the discussion includes "Beauty and the Beast." The motif of the animal's coming close to death when the woman stays away too long "may reflect exogamous marriages in which the bride is sent away to join her spouse among alien people" (109). The trauma of the separation may cause her to see her new husband as a beast and "she will come to see him as human only as the psychological if not literally physical distance between her former and present home widens" (116–17). The problem is not one of Oedipal attachment, but of what may seem to her "expulsion from the parental home" (116). Although some interpreters have suggested that the happy ending of these tales is achieved because the bride "liberates her personality from the father-image (superego) in an act of self-assertion," Leavy argues that the benefit is more often not really to the woman but to society: "[T]he heroine . . . plays her part by elevating man above the level of beast," usually by accepting her subservience to him and becoming "properly 'womanly' as her people define that attribute" (152).

1994:   Marina Warner looks at folktales as stories told by women: old wives (as in the dismissive phrase "old wives' tales"), Mother Goose, nursery maids and grandmothers, the French aristocrats like Madame d'Aulnoy who brought folktales into the literary salons at the turn of the seventeenth century, and the governesses like Madame Le Prince de Beaumont who rewrote Madame de Villeneuve's novel as a short story for young girls. As women's tales, they speak about the patterns of women's lives in the time they were told. They both reflect and subvert these patterns. Warner is always interesting, but it is difficult to pull together entirely coherent interpretations of a particular tale from this work. Her analysis of "Beauty and the Beast" is complicated by the fact that she treats "Cupid and Psyche" both as the immediate ancestor of "Beauty and the Beast" and as a parallel version. This conflation of the two tales confuses a reading of "Beauty and the Beast" alone.

  Warner suggests that because it is a story told by women, the usual pattern of the chivalrous quest of the male lover for an unknown or mysterious female beloved is reversed in "Beauty and the Beast," and the woman is the active figure while the man is forced to wait patiently and passively for rescue. At the heart of the story is the frightening transition for a young woman from a familiar life, her family and home, to the unfamiliar territory of marriage. Until recently, choosing a husband was the most important decision of a woman's life, and for the first century or so of the story's popularity, the decision was one she was seldom allowed to make for herself. Usually she was given, bartered, or sold by her father, who might take into account only the advantage of the union to himself or the family, not the happiness of his daughter. Her husband might well be a brute in some way, perhaps unsympathetic, most likely unknown. The bride would become the possession of this stranger, and Warner suggests that in the story of Beauty and the Beast a female audience could grapple with the fear that a marriage of this kind would raise. The Beast wears a mask created by that fear. When Beauty faces the fear and accepts her duty as a wife, the mask dissolves, revealing the perfect husband. The perfection of the prince behind the Beast's mask is both romantic and practical reassurance, according to Warner. The bride leaves the protection of her family to become a powerless outsider in her husband's family, and her husband will be her best ally, if he is so inclined. "The issue is not sex, but love, and the pledging of mutual life-long attachment" (219). In the development of such a mutual attachment, the wife is the civilizing force that smoothes the rough edges and brings out what is good and noble in her husband. The eighteenth-century Beauty learns to be a loving wife.

Warner sees one dominant trend in the changes "Beauty and the Beast" has gone through in its different versions from the seventeenth century to the present.

> At first, the Beast is identified with male sexuality which must be controlled through *civilité*, a code chiefly established by women, but later the Beast is perceived as a principle of nature within every human being, male and female, young and old, and the stories affirm beastliness's intrinsic goodness and necessity to holistic survival. (280)

Changing depictions of the Beast, of the narrator's attitude to the Beast, reflect society's understanding of what it is to be human, of the difference and relationship between humans and animals, and (where the Beast is male) of the nature of men.

In de Villeneuve's and de Beaumont's stories, Beauty pours water on the dying Beast to revive him, and in de Beaumont's version it is at this point that he becomes a prince again. Warner reads this act as a parallel to the sacrament of baptism, washing the Beast clean of beastliness (not of any evil he committed as a man, for he was blameless, but of the taint of his animality) so that he may be human. In the eighteenth-century versions, the Beast is not only hideous but also inarticulate, stupid, and clumsy. Only the good heart hidden beneath a furry or scaly exterior can recommend him to Beauty, and his redemption depends entirely on her good will and kindness. In later versions, the Beast becomes a more attractive character, a shift that is in part due to our changed attitude to nature (Warner includes in chapter 18 an interesting analysis of the development of the teddy bear as a cuddly children's toy) but also due to men's adoption of this material and the introduction of what she calls special pleading on their own behalf. She notes that the versions in which Beauty resists the arrangement her father has made gradually fall out of circulation, and attributes the prevalence of a willing, even eagerly compliant Beauty to the fact that most printers, publishers, editors, and writers were themselves fathers and husbands who didn't want to be cast as tyrants. Warner points to Cocteau's film as a particularly effective example of special pleading for the Beast. In *La belle et la bête*, Beauty seems passive and uninteresting compared to the Beast. It is Beauty who has to change to be a fit match for the Beast, who needs the Beast. "He no longer stands outside her, the threat of male sexuality in bodily form, or of male authority . . . but he holds up a mirror to the force of nature within her, which she is invited to accept and allow to grow" (Warner, 307). In fact, in some recent versions it is the Beast himself, rather than the man within the Beast, whom Beauty loves and, most important, desires, and the Beast never turns back into a man at all.

1994: According to Jack Zipes, the major theme of both de Villeneuve's and de Beaumont's "Beauty and the Beast" is that civilized behavior demands the taming of unruly feelings, and that Beauty is a model of virtuous self-denial. The code of civility these two stories hold up as desirable maintains the power of an elite class and patriarchal rule. De Beaumont's story is ambivalent. She is campaigning for education for women, but doesn't want to change their place in the family or in society:

> Furthermore, *Beauty and the Beast* has been especially instrumental in rationalizing male domination, gender polarity, and violation because of its formation in the eighteenth century when the middle classes were restructuring family and society in specific patterns that would be internalized through literary socialization. (Zipes 1994, 36)

The fact that Beauty's mother is long dead leaves Beauty with only male models of authority. She has already learned to make her father's desires her own, and when she agrees to fulfill the Beast's desire to marry her, she merely gives up one master for another. According to Zipes, the gentleness and consideration the Beast shows Beauty are actually manipulation and emotional blackmail to win her submission. Presumably in this ideological reading, although Zipes does not say so, the library, harpsichord, and music books that the Beast has waiting for Beauty at the palace would be bribes to make Beauty accept her captivity rather than gifts that recognize and encourage her intellectual and aesthetic development; the verse inscribed in the book that tells her she is queen and mistress here in the palace would be the old patriarchal ploy of keeping women contented with their powerlessness in public life by giving them the illusion of authority in the domestic sphere. Zipes points out that the traditional elitist and patriarchal messages of "Beauty and the Beast" have, of course, been challenged by alternative versions. He cites a verse parody by Albert Smith published in 1853, and another by Guy Wetmore Carryl published in 1902, in which Beauty's dissolute father loses her to the Beast in a card game (an idea that Angela Carter developed in "The Tiger's Bride" in 1979). In Carryl's poem, Beauty is clever and feisty enough to deliberately drive the disagreeable Beast to suicide (Zipes 1994, 41). There have been many other versions since then, including some that treat the material seriously, that have made meanings out of the tale quite different from the traditional one.

1997: Cristina Bacchilega raises an interesting question about the Beast's transformation into a handsome prince: "Is the Beast's metamorphosis desirable, then? And whose desire is at work?" (80). Bacchilega points out that in de Beaumont's story Beauty is not immediately enraptured by the prince who appears at her feet: "Though this prince was worthy of all her attention, she could not forbear asking where Beast was" (de Beaumont, 195). In a collection of folktales adapted and illustrated by Margaret Tarrant for children in 1920, Beauty cries out poignantly, "But where is my Beast? I do not know you. I want my beast, my lovely Beast!" (Hearne 1989, 76). In Cocteau's film, when Prince Ardent asks Beauty if she is happy, she answers: "I'll have to get used to this" (Hearne 1989, 82). Bacchilega refers to Jacques Barchilon's conclusion that when Beauty accepts the Beast she abandons her childhood fantasies and accepts reality. But when her fear vanishes, so does the Beast. Barchilon calls this turn of events a "charming irony" (Bacchilega, 81). Bacchilega suggests that perhaps the transformation of the Beast is not so charming for Beauty. It is a happy ending for the Beast/prince, but a trick played on Beauty, who loses what she had come to know and to desire. (Certainly I have found the obligatory prince a disappointingly conventional replacement for the mysterious and powerful Beast in versions of the tale that develop his complexity.) De Villeneuve avoided disappointment for Beauty by introducing the prince to her in advance as a dream lover. Some later revisions have explored the interpretive possibilities of not taking the transformation for granted. Bacchilega looks at four of these. In Ron Koslow's TV series (1987) the Beast cannot change physically, but his inner transformation is heavily emphasized. In Tanith Lee's science fiction story (1983), the Beast is perfect as he is, and Beauty only has to come to see that perfection. Angela Carter's "The Courtship of Mr. Lyon" (1979) suggests that it is not the Beast's physical transformation but Beauty's vision of herself that is at issue. Most unusually, in Carter's "The

Tiger's Bride" (1979), Beauty rejects her father's view of her and turns into a beast herself.

1998:   Vigen Guroian's understanding of what the tale can teach is based on versions in which Beauty's sisters are vain and selfish. Although she is called "Beauty," the emphasis of the story is not on her loveliness of appearance but on her beauty of character. Because she is good herself, Beauty is able to see the essential goodness of the Beast. "The paradoxical truth that the story portrays is that unless virtue is present in a person she will not be able to find, appreciate, or embrace virtue in another" (22). Another moral truth conveyed by the story is that our choices make us who we are. The sisters are unhappy because they chose their husbands for looks and wit; Beauty finds happiness, wealth, and social power with the Beast, all the things her sisters wanted and didn't get, because she chose the Beast for his virtue.

Reworkings of "Beauty and the Beast" in Novel Form

Robin McKinley's two superb books stand out in this list of 11 novels. Four of these reworkings are fantasy, four are realistic fiction, and two are science fiction. Timpanelli's novella is perhaps historical fiction.

Beauty: A Retelling of the Story of Beauty and the Beast

1978. McKinley, Robin. **Beauty: A Retelling of the Story of Beauty and the Beast.** New York: Harper & Row. [1993. Harper Trophy].

McKinley's book was published as a young adult novel in 1978. It was included in both the "ALA Best Books for Young Adults" and "Notable Children's Books" lists for that year and continues to be widely read. It was most recently reissued as a Harper Trophy paperback in 1993.

This is a greatly expanded version of de Beaumont's "Beauty and the Beast." The core elements of the story—the father's financial loss, the move to the country, the father's stealing the rose from the Beast's garden, the Beast's magic, Beauty's decision to go back to the Beast in her father's stead, her pleasant life with the Beast, her visit home (which she overstays), her declaration of love for the Beast, and the Beast's transformation—are all there. So is Madame de Beaumont's most delightful invention, Beauty's excellent education and her love of reading. These traditional elements have all been made new with skillful and engaging elaboration. But McKinley also makes some significant changes in the traditional story that shift its meaning.

First, Beauty's real name is Honor, and she is not beautiful. She asked to be called Beauty when she was five years old and didn't understand what Honor was. She's a thin, undersized tomboy with big hands and feet who is only interested in books and horses. Her closest companion is her horse, Greatheart, whom she takes with her to the Beast's palace. Beauty works hard, but so do the rest of her family. Her two older sisters are good, loving, and capable. Her father loves her but doesn't depend on her, and he has a romance of his own after the family moves to the country. When Beauty makes the nearly fatal visit home it is for a sister's rather than her father's sake. McKinley has dismantled the Oedipal triangle entirely. Beauty's attachment is to her family and to a childish self that she is ready to outgrow.

The meaning of Beauty's name, Honor, is not easy to read, although the Beast gives us some help. On her first night at the Beast's castle, he tells her that if her father had come back to the Beast alone, the Beast would have sent him home unharmed. Beauty asks, "You mean that I came here for nothing?" But the Beast answers:

> No. Not what you would count as nothing. He would have returned to you, and you would have been glad, but you would also have been ashamed, because you sent him, as you thought, to his death. . . . In time it would have ruined your peace and happiness, and at last your mind and heart. (115)

Honor is what one owes oneself. The *Concise Oxford Dictionary* defines it as "high respect; glory; reputation, good name; nobleness of mind; allegiance to what is right or to conventional standard of conduct; (of a woman) chastity, reputation for this." Traditionally, a woman's honor is her chastity, but that isn't McKinley's concern here. Reputation and a good name are external qualities, but the Beast points us toward a sense of inward rightness, high respect for oneself, which is the only sound basis for honor. A Latin dictionary gives three meanings for honor: "repute, office, and beauty." To be beautiful, then, is to have an inward rightness and to live accordingly.

The other names McKinley chooses have significance as well. Beauty's sisters are called Hope and Grace. Hope is one of the three theological virtues, a quality or state of being essential for a life that is properly open to change and development. Grace is a pleasing quality of appearance or manner. More important, it is also mercy or a privilege that cannot be earned or claimed as a right but is freely given. Beauty's horse is called Greatheart. He was given to her after the family's fortunes collapsed by the man who bred and trained him, simply out of affection for both the girl and the horse because the two love each other. Greatheart is enormous, a noble descendant of the huge chargers that armored knights used to ride into battle. For Beauty and her family he willingly pulls a cart or a plow. Beauty and Greatheart are a working team, and Beauty takes him to the Beast's castle, where he stays as her comfort and only companion other than the Beast.

McKinley's novel is definitely Beauty's story, although the Beast is very important in it. Like Cocteau's Beast, he is a noble figure, but he is resigned to his beastliness rather than tormented by it. He has had 200 years of being enchanted to learn to accept the limitations and implications of his physical form. His struggle with himself took place before the book begins. Beauty's door is locked at night because, as the Beast explains, "I am a Beast, and I cannot always behave prettily, even for you" (132), but Beauty is safe with him. He is wise, benevolent, always beautifully dressed. He was changed into the Beast because his overpious and overzealous family had long irritated the local magician, and the young man the Beast used to be gave the magician his first chance to make a curse stick (240–41). Early on in Beauty's stay at the Beast's palace, she looks at portraits of generations of a noble family. One of them particularly catches her attention. It is, as we can guess, a portrait of the Beast as he was two centuries ago. In this way McKinley mitigates the shock and possible disappointment caused to both Beauty and the reader by the Beast's transformation at the end of the book, her equivalent of de Villeneuve's dream lover. It helps that the handsome man who appears in place of the Beast has hair streaked with grey, and that Beauty recognizes his voice the moment he speaks.

It is Beauty, not the Beast, who struggles and learns in this story. The Beast's world expands her perceptions, asks and allows her to grow into herself. It is another kind of education for her, and very different from the Greek and Latin she has learned. She shoots up seven inches in the seven months she spends with the Beast, a physical parallel to her inward growth. She also grows up beautiful, although right to the end she tries to deny the fact, insisting that she is "a dull drab little nothing" (241). There are no mirrors in this Beast's castle. Beauty steadfastly resists the attempts of her invisible servants to dress her in fine clothing, and these are wonderfully funny scenes, but in the end she faces her physicality, recognizes her own beauty, and is able to release the Beast.

The magic needs a little explanation, because I think McKinley's version of it must have been an influence on the Disney film and yet has an entirely different effect. There is no magic for its own sake; what is there has meaning. It is a rather domestic magic, entirely benevolent. For example, the magic rose is supplemented by a packet of rose seeds the Beast sends home with her father for Beauty. She plants them in the frozen ground, and in the month before she has to leave home to go to the Beast they grow out of the spring mud, up the walls of house and stable and smithy, and bloom on her last night there. They are a reassuring earnest of the Beast's good intentions. At the Beast's castle there are invisible servants, but the effect is nothing like the highly serious chiaroscuro of Cocteau. The two unseen beings who wait on her, whom she thinks of as breezes, are brisk and decisive and try to bully her for her own good. Their names are Bessie and Lydia, and they serve as a kind of Greek chorus for both Beauty and the reader. Their conversations between themselves give clues and partial explanations of the Beast's situation. Tables walk up to Beauty, and doors open and close of themselves. The magic is endearing and amusing rather than mysterious or awe-inspiring, but it is never cute.

The tone of the book is homely, comfortable, and wholesome. That description may make it sound dull, but it is entirely absorbing. There is tension in it, but the magic and magnificence are in delightful balance with the pleasant dailiness of fried potatoes and onions, cleaning tack, and the satisfactions of hard work. Although no country or time period is identified, the once-upon-a-time of the folktale is so grounded in a world McKinley makes entirely particular that much of the book reads like the best historical fiction.

Kristin and Boone

1983. Rose, Karen, and Lynda Halfyard. **Kristin and Boone**. Boston: Houghton Mifflin.

This young adult novel is an undistinguished piece of realistic fiction. Kristin is a beautiful 14-year-old actress who lives with her divorced mother. She desperately wants to win an Emmy award. She is Beauty, both thematically and in a television movie of *Beauty and the Beast* which is in the process of being filmed. The movie is science fiction. Boone is the brilliant director of the movie, and a dwarf; he suffers physically from dwarfism. He is the physical part of the Beast. Keith, the gorgeous young actor who plays the Beast in the movie, is the courtly lover part, and Kristin's no-good father, a failed actor who abandoned her and her mother, is the beastly Beast. The plot is both over-obvious and muddled, and the ending tells it all. Kristin wins an Emmy for the performance Boone has bullied and coaxed out of her, but she misses the presentation because she has chosen to be with Boone as he dies in hospital. Keith accepts the award for her. She also decides she doesn't really need the father she spent so much time fantasizing about and looking for. The story could be summed up by a captionless cartoon that appeared in *The New Yorker* a few years ago. It showed Barbie (the ever-popular doll) in full wedding regalia standing in front of an altar with Barney (the cuddly purple dinosaur of children's television).

Roses

1984. Cohen, Barbara. **Roses**. New York: Lothrop, Lee & Shepard.

Barbara Cohen's *Roses* is a young adult novel, and also realistic fiction. In this version of "Beauty and the Beast," the Oedipal triangle is the focus of the story. Beautiful 17-year-old Izzy's mother died when Izzy was five years old. Izzy's father, a commodities broker who is having a bad year, remarried some time ago. The stepmother is nice, and so is Izzy's older sister, but Izzy and her father are especially close. Izzy, beautiful and talented, doesn't have a boyfriend. She is afraid to love anyone other than her father, because you lose the people you love; after all, her mother died and left her. One day Izzy's father goes to a flower shop and, unable to get service, breaks off a rose from a bush for Izzy. The irate owner appears—enter the Beast. His name is Mr. Lyon, and he is hideously disfigured by burns from a car accident. Izzy gets a job, ridiculously overpaid, in the flower shop, and becomes Mr. Lyon's friend. He especially wants her because she reminds him of the young actress who was killed in a car accident with him 20 years before, and he wants to make amends. Izzy, meanwhile, is being courted by Rob, the most popular boy in her class. Rob is understanding and generally wonderful, and, as it turns out, the brother of the dead actress. In the end, Izzy lets herself love Rob, and Rob persuades Mr. Lyon to have plastic surgery at last; he has suffered enough.

Having the Beast split into two roles is moderately interesting. The story is coherently worked out, and Izzy's maturation is reasonably convincing. It is not a bad young adult novel, but one misses the magic. The folktale is visible behind the novel, but it has been reduced to allegory, with the novel making its meaning explicit. Allegories aren't porous. They have a single, limited purpose.

Beauty and the Beast

1989. Hambly, Barbara. **Beauty and the Beast**. New York: Avon. Based on the series created by Ron Koslow.

Like the television series on which it is based, this version of the tale carries echoes of the Phantom of the Opera and Robin Hood. Vincent, the Beast, lives in a utopian underworld of the rejected, a benevolent community of outcasts who hide in the tunnels under New York City. He is a big, strong man, but his face is strangely unhuman. He is also remarkably well read. Hambly gives the bookishness that is usually Beauty's to the Beast. Catherine, the Beauty, is frittering her life away as a corporate lawyer, defining herself as her father's beautiful daughter. They meet when Vincent saves Catherine from a savage attack that nearly kills her and ruins her beauty, at least temporarily. The rescue is psychological as well as physical. Catherine leaves her father's law firm and becomes a public defender. Vincent and Beauty develop an emotional connection of extraordinary sensitivity, so strong that Catherine is even able to call Vincent back from death.

A sequel, *Beauty and the Beast: Song of Orpheus*, published in 1990, is mentioned by Clute and Grant in their entry on the television series (99), but I have not seen it.

Beauty and the Beast: Night of Beauty

1990. Pini, Wendy. **Beauty and the Beast: Night of Beauty**. Chicago: First Publishing. Based on the television series by Ron Koslow.

In this graphic novel, Catherine (Beauty) is dead, but the Beast cannot let her spirit go. With the help of a "seeress," he makes the mystical journey to the other side of death so that he can lead Catherine out of a sort of limbo to the light. They have to accept their final separation; he cannot go with her. Pini explains in her "Reflections" at the end of the book that she drew her inspiration from Jean Cocteau's film *La belle et la bête*, from Rainer Maria Rilke's poem "Requiem for a Friend," and from Anton Grosz's interpretation of the Tibetan Book of the Dead.

The Fire Rose

1995. Lackey, Mercedes. **The Fire Rose**. Riverdale, NY: Baen.

This novel was published in hardcover in 1995 and as a paperback in 1996. The fact that it came out first in hardcover is a clear indication of Lackey's commercial success as a writer of fantasy and science fiction. Her books are published and sold as adult novels, but she is widely read by teenagers, and *The Fire Rose* was reviewed very positively in *VOYA*. The *VOYA* reviewer gave it 4 out of 5 for quality, 5 out of 5 for predicted popularity, and suggested a high school readership. However, a devoted 15-year-old Mercedes Lackey fan I know who read it hot off the press was disappointed by the book.

The story is set in San Francisco in 1905, the year of the great earthquake. The Beast is Jason Cameron, a firemaster, a magician who can control the elements of fire. There are a fair number of magicians around, masters of earth, air, fire, or water, all of whom use their magic primarily to become rich businessmen. This particular firemaster got himself stuck part way through a spell that was intended to turn him into a wolf temporarily. Because he can't read properly any more with his wolf eyes or turn pages with his wolf hands, he needs someone fluent in various medieval languages who can read his magic books to him so that he can figure out how to reverse the spell. He wants a young woman with no relatives, so that she will be helpless and entirely in his power. With the help of his familiar, a salamander, he finds Rose Hawkins, who is the Beauty to his Beast. She is destitute but learned, and an orphan. She wants to be a medieval scholar, but gender prejudice at the university and her father's bankruptcy and death kept her from getting her doctorate.

Jason writes to Rose pretending that he needs a governess for his children, and out of desperation she takes the job. But when she arrives at his mansion, she discovers that there are no children, and that her employer will communicate with her only through a speaking tube in the wall of her room. She is never to see his face. Her task is to read to him from the books he has delivered to her room. The traditional rose figures in the story as Beauty's name and in the roses that decorate the watch Jason gives her so that he will be able to track her movements. Jason has a magic mirror, and there are a number of other mirrors in the house, but they have nothing to do with the traditional theme of perception. Rose and the world think she is plain, and although Jason recognizes her beauty hidden by glasses and cheap clothing when he first sees her in his magic mirror, Rose never changes her opinion of her looks.

Rose first sees Jason when the salamanders call her to Jason's room to save his life. He has tried another spell to undo the one that keeps him half wolf, and something has gone seriously wrong. Rose had been away, but had broken no tabu by overstaying her time, and his near-death is not connected with her in any way. Rose is shocked at first by Jason's appearance, but soon comes to think him handsome. When she realizes that she has fallen in love with him, she begins to hope that he will never be able to undo the wolf spell, for his unusual appearance is the only thing that could bridge the social gulf between a rich railroad baron (Jason) and a poor, plain, orphaned scholar whose father died under a cloud of debt and disgrace. Jason falls in love with Rose also, but he hides his love from her. He is afraid that he will revert entirely into a wolf and kill those he loves. In the meantime, Rose begins to take magic lessons from Jason and discovers that she can also be a magician, and that her element is air.

The plot is complicated by Jason's apprentice, Paul Du Mond, who is a thoroughly nasty piece of work. He wants to acquire his magic the easy way, through the use of drugs and sadistic sex, rather than through arduous tests and discipline, and he has some very unpleasant plans for Rose as a part of his process. The number of pages spent on his sadism, which Lackey dwells on at some length, seems to me to be gratuitous. Rose's possible fate at his hands could have been hinted at just as effectively, and he doesn't serve as a useful foil for Jason because although Jason's outer form is that of an animal, Paul's perversions are thoroughly human. Besides, Rose loves Jason just as he is and detests Paul, so she has nothing to learn from the juxtaposition of the two.

When Paul tries to abduct Rose and the salamanders call Jason to help her, Jason acts like a wolf and tears Paul's throat out. Rose goes into shock at the sight and flees to the city. Here another magician in competition with Jason for power tries to bribe Rose to kill Jason for Jason's own sake, to put him out of his misery and prevent his being shot down like a beast once he begins to kill like one. In the end, Rose refuses to betray Jason, the two of them meet each other again trying to help contain the damage of the San Francisco earthquake with their magic powers, Jason gives up trying to change himself back into a man, and Rose and Jason are married by a Presbyterian minister.

There is a great deal more in the plot than this summary covers, but even a more detailed analysis would fail to pull a coherent interpretation of "Beauty and the Beast" out of Lackey's novel. *The Fire Rose* contains many of the motifs from the folktale, but they are not used in a meaningful way. The ending tries to convince the reader that Rose has transformed Jason inwardly, given him back the human warmth that was taken from him by accident and disaster as a child. Perhaps; but that part of him was restored simply by his loving Rose, not by her acceptance of him. Does Rose become more fully herself because of her time with Jason? She does discover her true calling as a magician. She describes her feelings after her first try at working magic: "How did it feel? . . . As if I was born to do this, as if nothing in the world was more natural or right for me. There was a joy, a feeling of completion a feeling of coming home" (358). But she would also have been a first class medievalist, given the chance. The novel is a muddle of folktale motifs, historical fiction, series romance, and modern fantasy.

The Rose: A Novel Based on Beauty and the Beast

1996. Baker, Jennifer. **The Rose: A Novel Based on Beauty and the Beast.** New York: Scholastic.

This book was published in a Scholastic series of teenage romances based on well-known folktales. The series is called Once Upon a Dream, and the back cover of the book states: "Once Upon a Dream . . . where wishes really do come true." The series title is an accurate signal of the book's content, for while the phrase "Once upon a time" is mythic, "Once upon a dream" is simply wish fulfillment. Baker's novel follows Disney's *Beauty and the Beast* so closely that it is almost a spin-off from the movie, but it is nowhere near as much fun. The setting has been changed to an American fishing town named Land's End sometime in the 1990s. Beauty/Belle's name is Bonnie, a variant spelling of "bonny," which means comely or healthy looking. Her father is a poor, hard-working fisherman (and inventor in his spare time), originally from Portugal, named Antonio Oliviera. Her dead mother was a Land's End native. Bonnie works with her father on his boat when she's not in school. Like Belle, she reads a great deal and wishes she could travel.

The Beast's conditions of enchantment and his character are the same as those in the Disney film, but he has none of the Disney Beast's physical magnificence. He has "little beady eyes," a "furry pointed face," and Bonnie sees him as a "sad, spoiled house pet" (133). He dresses in clean jeans and a polo shirt, and he admires Bonnie's educated intelligence when she tells him that noodles were invented in China (93).

The only significant difference from the plot line of Disney's *Beauty and the Beast* is in the way the magic is handled. Baker has retained the enchantress who punishes the arrogant, greedy boy by turning him into a Beast. But all the rest of the Beast's magical effects are virtual reality programs created by the latest computer technology that money can buy. This innovation is pure disaster for the novel.

Beauty: A Novel

1996. Wilson, Susan. **Beauty: A Novel.** New York: Crown.

Portraits fit naturally into "Beauty and Beast." No matter what slant a particular interpretation takes, the story almost always deals with questions of appearance. In this work of contemporary realistic fiction, Beauty is Alix Miller, a 36-year-old painter. Her father is commissioned to paint the portrait of Leland Crompton, a reclusive writer of mystery novels who lives in the woods of New Hampshire. Generations of wealthy Cromptons have had their portraits painted by generations of Millers. But Alexander Miller knows he is not gifted enough as a painter to do the portrait, so he persuades his daughter, Alix, to do it instead.

Leland Crompton suffers from a rare genetic disease called acromegaly, a form of giantism that makes the bones grow out of normal proportion. Because he is frightened of people's reactions to his distorted face, he has hidden himself from the world for a long time. He has good reason for his lack of trust because his own mother hasn't seen him for years because his ugliness distresses her, and years before he loved a young woman who only pretended to love him because he was rich.

Alix, getting to know her subject well enough to paint him, truly comes to love the man he is. She has to leave for a weekend to attend an award dinner for her boyfriend, a selfish, ambitious, handsome news photographer. While she is away, she discovers that her father is dying of cancer. The hard task of nursing him, of helping him die peacefully at home, is made easier by Leland's visits. Her boyfriend, Mark, the equivalent of Cocteau's Avenant and Disney's Gaston, is no help at all. In fact, he leaves her at this most difficult time to further his career. But Leland comes at night, when no one can see him, to sit with Alix's father and let her rest. After her father's death, Alix goes back to Leland's house; he is the refuge and comfort she needs, her dearest friend.

Leland clearly loves Alix, but she cannot persuade him that she loves and wants him exactly as he is. When the portrait is finished he sends her away. Because he has refused to look at the painting, she takes it with her. Months pass, and Alix's phone calls and letter to Leland go unanswered. The housekeeper, to protect him, makes sure he never receives them. Finally, one message gets through, an invitation to a show of Alix's work. Leland comes and is finally willing to look at the portrait of himself. What he sees there persuades him that she sees and loves him truly.

Although Beauty and the Beast do marry and live happily for a time, the story doesn't end there. Alix dies in childbirth, leaving a daughter who will love Leland simply because he is her father, and whom Leland will always love. The change Beauty has made in the Beast is permanent.

This moving, competently written novel is absolutely straightforward, except for the conceit that it is written by Leland Crompton under his pen name of Harris Bellefleur. The rose of the traditional story is there in a necklace Leland gives Alix and a windchime she gives him. The mirror is the portrait, its function not to show Beauty her family but to show the Beast himself. The seasons play a role: Alix and Leland meet in winter, he comes back to her in winter, they marry in the spring, and their child is born during a snowstorm at the end of winter. The symbols are easy to read; no interpretation is required of the reader. The "Author's Note" at the beginning, signed "Harris Bellefleur," tells the reader what to make of the story:

> I know that the legend of
>
> Beauty and the Beast is possible.
>
> Like the fairy tale, this true story has a
>
> lovely heroine and an ugly hero.
>
> Unlike the fairy tale, it isn't Beauty
>
> who needs to discover the man inside
>
> the Beast, but the Beast himself.
>
> Being a true story, there are no physical
>
> transmutations, only intellectual ones;
>
> the only magic mirror that of the soul in love.

Rose Daughter

1997. McKinley, Robin. **Rose Daughter**. New York: Greenwillow.

In the "Author's Note" at the end of her novel, McKinley explains how she came to write a second version of "Beauty and the Beast" almost 20 years after the first one was published. She had married the British writer Peter Dickinson and moved to England, and when she began this book she had finally sold her cottage in Maine, knowing that part of her life was behind her. She writes: "I don't know why the story came to me in the first place, but I know that what fuelled the whirlwind of getting it down on paper was my grief for my lilac-covered cottage and for a way of life I had loved, even if I loved my new life better" (306). McKinley's grief at giving up her cottage and her life there must have been very like Beauty's grief at leaving her family, even though she had much to make her happy at the Beast's palace.

Rose Daughter is very different from McKinley's *Beauty* in every respect but the skill and beauty of the writing. It is an uncommonly difficult book to summarize, and to explain its interpretation of "Beauty and the Beast" would take a book in itself. It makes me want to throw up my hands and say, "Read it yourselves, and then we'll talk about it." Every word counts and not a sentence is wasted. Each image and event seems to have a meaningful place in the story as a whole, but exactly what that place is is far from obvious. The themes are developed with a subtlety that gives the reader no direct answers, and even after a second reading I cannot be certain about some of the connections I've made.

There is more magic in this book than in *Beauty.* Sorcerers and greenwitches are a common part of daily life. The Beast himself was a sorcerer/philosopher before he was transformed. He was turned into a Beast not by a curse but by accident because he came too close to the secrets of the universe that must remain beyond human understanding. He condemned himself to solitude and gave up philosophy, which had filled his heart. He grows roses in a glass house, roses that *are* his heart, but both the roses and his heart are dying. Beauty is a gardener, and when the family moves to the country she discovers roses, the flowers of love that usually only a sorcerer can grow. But they grow for her at the cottage that was mysteriously left to Beauty and her two sisters by an unknown old woman. The Beast needs Beauty to tend to his roses. Roses are everywhere in this book. One of the many threads weaving through the story is the folksong that goes: "And from her heart grew a red, red rose,/and from his heart a briar." Another thread is a recurring dream of Beauty's, which she first had as a very small child. She dreams that she is walking down a long corridor toward something frightful, a monster that will eat her. Over the years the dream changes. She begins to pity the monster, and instead of wanting to run from it starts to move toward it, seeking it out.

Beauty is the shy one in her family. Her sister Jeweltongue is the most learned, and her sister Lionheart has the most physical courage. Beauty is the peacemaker and negotiator because she dislikes confrontation so much. (In the country, Jeweltongue discovers her skill as a dressmaker, and Lionheart learns to train and care for the horses she once rode so recklessly.) When her family is ruined financially, a friendly salamander gives Beauty a magic gift, a small serenity that she can hold in her cupped hands when she needs it. She needs it to look at the Beast's face at their first meeting, but at the end of the book, in the greatest confrontation of all, she does not cup her hands but clenches them into fists, one holding a scrap of her beloved Beast's shirt, the other an embroidered heart her sister made for her so that she might carry her family's love with her to the Beast's palace. Holding both the old love and the new, she runs toward the hostile magic forces that threaten them all and commands them to go: "*There is nothing for you here!*" (297). The sphinxes, manticores, chimeras, and harpies turn into "baffled hedgehogs and bewildered toads, confused spiders, flustered crickets, bumbling bees, disoriented ladybirds and muddled grass-snakes, and hosts of other ordinary and innocent creatures" (297), creatures she herself had introduced into the Beast's lifeless garden.

Only in *Rose Daughter*, of all the versions of "Beauty and the Beast" that I have read, is Beauty given a choice by the Beast between having him be returned to his human form and keeping him as he is. The first choice would bring with it a grand public life of wealth and influence. The second would allow them to live quietly together in Rose Cottage among her family and friends. Beauty must choose for herself and the Beast, and she chooses the Beast and life in the country, which is what *she* really wants. Both for her and for him, his Beast form is not an enchantment that needs to be broken. What Beauty had to change for the Beast was his self-imposed isolation. She cultivated his human heart as she brought the roses of love back to life in his glass house.

"Rusina, Not Quite in Love"

1998. Timpanelli, Gioia. **"Rusina, Not Quite in Love."** In *Sometimes the Soul: Two Novellas of Sicily,* by Gioia Timpanelli. New York: W. W. Norton, 101–84.

Because it is definitely too long to be a short story, this novella is included here with the novels. It is set in a village in Sicily, in an unspecified time that is vaguely nineteenth century. Full of lovely word pictures and snippets of vivid characterization, the story never quite comes together. The plot has threads with loose ends and links that seem to belong together but aren't actually joined. The gaps are perhaps deliberate, either mimicking blind motifs in a traditional tale or to give the story elements of unresolved mystery.

The Beast is one of the merchant's creditors, and he sends a divinely handsome young man to ask the merchant to call on him. He proposes that as payment for his debt the merchant send his daughter Beauty to keep the Beast's old aunt and uncle company. The merchant takes one of the Beast's roses, but nothing follows from the theft. Beauty, Rusina, lives happily with the uncle and aunt, glad to be free of her nasty sisters. She develops a talent for botanical drawing. The Beast is called the Master Gardener and is not at all frightening. His concern is with flowers and the rare plants of forest and meadow; the uncle and aunt, a very odd pair who speak almost entirely in riddles and nonsense, do the regular farming of the estate, with help from Rusina and the neighbors. The Master Gardener is seldom at home, and in the winter lives in a separate, dark little house, an ancient dwelling with only one room and a hole in the roof for the smoke to go out. Here Rusina nurses the Master Gardener through an illness when she returns from her visit to her dying father.

Rusina does a good deal of reflecting on the nature of beauty and love. She knows that she is learning to see things in a new way, and she admires the Master Gardener for his work and for what he teaches her. But, although she is beginning to think of love, she cannot love him because he is so ugly. At the masked ball given by the village each year, Rusina dances with the beautiful young man who was the messenger at the beginning of the story. Is he the Master Gardener? We never find out. The next day Rusina says yes to the Master Gardener when he asks her again to marry him. Whether he then actually becomes beautiful or whether

Rusina now sees him as beautiful through the eyes of love is unclear. The text is carefully ambiguous.

Beast

2000. Napoli, Donna Jo. **Beast**. New York: Atheneum Books for Young Readers.

As the author explains in her note at the end of the book, this young adult novel is based on Charles Lamb's *Beauty and the Beast, or A Rough Outside with a Gentle Heart: A Poetical Version of an Ancient Tale*, published in 1811. Napoli uses Lamb's Persian setting and the name Prince Orasmyn for the Beast and emulates his tone of "propriety and civility" (256). Like the Disney film, this is entirely the Beast's story. It is told by Orasmyn. At the age of 17, he thinks of himself as a man, a gardener, and a scholar prince. He's actually a self-absorbed, pretentious adolescent who glories in heroic tales of battle but can't stand the sight of blood. Roses are his favorite flower, and pride is his besetting sin. On the Feast of Sacrifices he makes a mistake by knowingly allowing a less-than-perfect camel to be sacrificed. His intentions are good, but a malicious fairy uses the chink in his self-conscious perfection to put a curse on him. The curse is that his father will kill him in the next 24 hours. Orasmyn and his father make a plan that will save him, but the fairy somehow modifies the curse. Orasmyn is turned into a lion. He outlives the day, but the fairy gloats: "Only a woman's love can undo the curse. And no woman will ever love you" (2000, 52). She means love him as if he were a man, desire him.

As a lion, Orasmyn makes his way first to India, so that he will at least be able to live in lion country, and then to France, because he heard from visitors to his father's court that the French love roses and French women smell of roses. Perhaps in France he can find a woman who will lift the curse. He finds a conveniently abandoned castle, complete with library, takes it over, and makes beautiful gardens with his paws and mouth. One day a man comes into his rose garden, picks some flowers, and Orasmyn has his chance. Communicating with the man by writing in the dirt with his claws, the lion terrifies him into promising to send his daughter to the castle three weeks from now.

In the time before she comes, Orasmyn laboriously prepares for her comfort. Everything that in other versions of the story is supplied by magic, the lion must acquire the hard way. He plants a vegetable garden with stolen seeds and steals staples like flour and sugar and candles from villagers. He even tames a fox kit as a pet for her. He expects a little girl who might grow to love him, but the daughter, Belle, is a grown woman, brave and capable. She cooks and cleans and gardens and does the shopping, riding the lion to town and trading valuables left in the castle for supplies, and reads to him in the evenings. Orasmyn doesn't explain his situation to her; he has an intuition that he mustn't.

After a time, of course, Belle asks to visit her father, overstays her time, and Orasmyn almost dies of despair; he will not eat or drink. Belle returns at last. She explains that she came back because she missed him, because he makes her happy, and because he needs her:

> All pride flames and turns into ash. The world comes alive in colours that never before existed. I need you, Belle. Oh, how I need you.
>
> "You let me help you; you let me know you." Belle whispers now. "You let me love you." (255)

The spell is finally broken.

In his lion form, Orasmyn has the instincts, needs, physical powers, and physical limitations of the animal. The demands of his new body contradict all his learned fastidiousness. Almost the first thing he does in lion form is mate with two female lions. He has to kill, and he feeds on bloody meat. His body is strong, but he is in constant danger. Survival is an ongoing struggle very different from the heroic battles he used to read about. To hang on to his human mind and heart he prays, following the daily Muslim rituals as well as a lion body will let him. The religion that was once largely a matter of correct forms to him becomes a lifeline. As a beast he learns to be a good man.

I found this book less satisfactory than some of Napoli's earlier fairy tale novels, but the problems are ones of style rather than imaginative content. The italicized Farsi and Arabic words with their accompanying definitions are intrusive, distancing, and often trivial:

> The smell of *sib*—apple—permeates the breath of the rich Persian merchant to my left. He must have chewed the dry fruit on his journey here, for our mid-day meal had no apple. I smell *syah-dane*—fennel—on the breath of the Indian man to my right. (12)

Strings of simple declarative sentences, far too may of them beginning with "I," are plodding and without cadence. The prose strikes me as pedestrian and lacking in nuance, even before Orasmyn becomes a lion. But the novelty of Napoli's invention is strong enough to please most readers.

Short Stories

This list begins with Angela Carter's two versions of "Beauty and the Beast" and ends with Francesca Lia Block's "Beast." It includes parodies, moral tales, fantasy, and science fiction. Only four of the stories were written or published for young adult readers, and one of those, Donoghue's story, demands that readers be at least in the late teens.

1979. Carter, Angela. **"The Courtship of Mr. Lyon."** In *The Bloody Chamber, and Other Stories*. London: Victor Gollancz, 41–51. [Penguin, 1981].

It is a temptation to tell Carter's stories entirely in quotations, because her prose is so delicately nuanced that a paraphrase can't begin to represent them accurately.

"The Courtship of Mr. Lyon" is set in England in a time of automobiles and telephones. The Beast's palace is a small, perfect, Palladian country house. There are only four characters: Beauty; her father; the Beast, whose name is Mr. Lyon; and a King Charles spaniel who is Mr. Lyon's companion. Beauty's father is ruined; the suggestion is that he has ruined himself (48). On his way back from his lawyer, his car breaks down in a snow storm and he finds shelter, food, and a telephone in Mr. Lyon's house. The spaniel is the only living creature he sees. On his way out, he stops to pick the last, miraculous white rose on a snow-covered bush for his daughter. At that the lion-like Beast appears with a great roar. The price for the stolen rose is that Beauty's father bring her to dinner.

During the evening Beauty and her father spend with the Beast, the suggestion is made that the Beast's lawyers could help straighten out her father's business affairs, and perhaps Beauty would like to stay with Mr. Lyon while her father is occupied in London. She is reluctant, but the implication is clear: "her visit to the Beast must be, on some magically reciprocal scale, the price of her father's good fortune. Do not think she had no will of her own; only, she was possessed by a sense of obligation to an unusual degree, and besides, she would gladly have gone to the ends of the earth for her father, whom she loved dearly"(45).

Beauty stays for part of the winter, and then a telephone call comes from London. Her father is rich again, and she is to join him. The Beast asks her to come back to him from London, but there is no time limit set. Beauty was born after her father lost his money, so she enters a life new to her: clothes, restaurants, parties, with her father as her proud escort. She sends the Beast roses, but puts off going back, until she is almost spoiled by the shallow dissipation of her father's world: "Her face was acquiring, instead of beauty, a lacquer of the invincible prettiness that characterizes certain pampered, exquisite, expensive cats" (49). Finally the spaniel comes for her, bedraggled and exhausted from the long journey, and Beauty goes back. She finds the Beast dying in a small, shabby attic room, and cries that if he will have her, she will never leave him. At the touch of her tears, the Beast becomes a man, who still has "a distant, heroic resemblance to the handsomest of all beasts" (51).

This version is subtle, almost subdued, elliptical. The tone of the story is cultivated, the atmosphere slightly overbred. The magic is there, but unobtrusive, only a little incongruous rather than magnificent: roast beef sandwiches and eggs benedict, a diamond or sapphire collar around the spaniel's neck. Beauty doesn't offer herself for her father's life, only for his success in business, and she isn't required to stay forever, only for a visit. This changes the nature of her obligation to return to the Beast. She promises to do so, but only because he will miss her, not because it is part of the bargain. Beauty seems to belong in the Beast's quietly civilized world to begin with, although she is frightened by him. The change in Beauty that is emphasized is a negative rather than a positive one. She becomes less than herself, corrupted, during her time in London. Her union with the Beast is a gentle homecoming. Beauty's choice seems at first to be the old one between her father and the Beast, highlighted because she has no sisters or brothers. It is really a choice between the very different ways these two men see her.

1979. Carter, Angela. "The Tiger's Bride." In *The Bloody Chamber, and Other Stories*. London: Victor Gollancz, 51–67. [Penguin, 1981].

"The Tiger's Bride" is very different from "The Courtship of Mr. Lyon," fierce and bizarre, the emphasis on the animal nature of the Beast. Beauty and her father are Russian. They are traveling in Italy, and her father gambles away everything, including herself, to a strange, masked Beast. The Beast asks merely to see her naked, not that she stay forever. When she refuses, the Beast demands that she must then see *him* naked, instead. Unmasked, a tiger's terrible beauty and "the annihilating vehemence of his eyes" (64) breaks something open in her. Still reluctantly, painfully, she strips herself of her clothing, not to pay the price her father had set on her but to reciprocate the Beast's revelation. When she returns to the palace, Beauty looks in the magic mirror but at first sees her father's face rather than her own. Her father is smiling, not at her but with gratification. The Beast has paid up promptly and his good fortunes are restored. Then the image in the mirror changes and she sees her own face, which she scarcely recognizes. Although she is free now to leave, the vision of the Beast's wild magnificence has changed the way she sees both her father and herself. She strips herself naked again, wraps herself in the fur cloak which is the Beast's parting gift to her, and goes to the Beast's room, with its "reek of fur and piss" and "gnawed and bloody bones" (66). There the Beast with a loving, abrasive tongue strips off the remaining layers of the social skin in which Beauty had been imprisoned. The Beast does not become a handsome prince; rather, Beauty becomes a Beast. And the diamond earrings the Beast had given her when she first came, made of his tears turned into stone as enchantments, freeze the natural movement of the world, turn into water again, and trickle down her beautiful fur.

1983. Lee, Tanith. "Beauty." In *Red as Blood, or, Tales from the Sisters Grimmer*. New York: Daw Books, 149–86.

Tanith Lee's stories, like Carter's and Cocteau's, are intended for an adult audience. She writes them as science fiction rather than the fantasy that seems a natural extension of folktales. Because Lee's story is science fiction and therefore depends on rational explanation of extrapolated technology rather than magic, I find it ultimately unsatisfying. However, the very fact that everything must be explained and justified means that Lee's reading of the tale, what she makes of it, is entirely clear. There is no room for interpretation by the reader; Lee tells you what her story means.

Mercator (the word is Latin for "merchant") Levin and his three daughters live on an Earth that is entirely prosperous since a benevolent alien species came to help out some 200 years before. The price for this help, not initially specified, is that occasionally a human family is asked to send a son or daughter to live with an alien resident on Earth. The choice of which child is to go is left to the family. The request is made by the sending of an unusual rose, and it is a request that somehow can never be refused, although appeals are possible. The young men and women who go to live with an alien are allowed to visit their families whenever they like, but they come less and less often as time goes by and are marked by a deep sadness that seems to indicate their suffering in exile. The aliens when they go among humans are always completely masked; it is assumed that their appearance is too dreadful to be contemplated.

Mercator Levin receives one of the alien roses, ironically at the end of a journey from which his daughter Estar asked him to bring her back a real rose. Of the three daughters, she is the obvious one to go, and she volunteers. One of her sisters is a brilliant musician, the other a poet and pregnant with her first child, whereas Estar is an unhappy young woman who can't find a place for herself in the world. Her name, we are told, means "psyche," a link to the "Cupid and Psyche" folktale.

So Estar goes, and we eventually get all the answers to the mysteries. The aliens are "a perfect people, both of the body and the brain, and spiritually more nearly perfect than any other they encountered" (182). The only problem is that they can no longer reproduce themselves: their very perfection seems to have signaled genetically the end of the line. Therefore they developed the means to implant their embryos secretly in the wombs of women of other species who are in the process of miscarrying and who will never know that the child they so happily bore after all was not their own. The alien child develops in the womb the physical appearance of the host species. Further, these children are only given to families who can bear the emotional loss when the child is eventually taken away. The rose that signaled the recall was never sent until the child "had reached a level of prolonged yearning, blindly and intuitively begging to be rescued from its unfitted human situation" (184).

The aliens' physical appearance, although definitely alien, is, of course, magnificent. They look like marvelous felines, upright, powerful, completely desirable once the shock of strangeness is overcome and the attraction admitted. (Lions seem to be the Beast of choice for authors who describe their Beasts.) The "devouring sadness" on the faces of the children who return to their human families to visit is not for themselves, but for the humans, who will never know the freedom and beauty of their new lives. Estar and her destined lover live happily ever after, each finding in the other a compelling, if alien, beauty. And that's it. It almost seems like an unhappy child's fantasy that she must have been adopted, and that her real parents would have been richer and kinder than the ones she somehow got stuck with. There is no snow storm, no mirror, no treasures sent home, no tabu. There is no need for them. Of the characteristic elements, only the rose remains, and it, too, has a scientific explanation. My pleasure in this tale comes from watching for the variations and for the small phrases that tie the story to earlier versions of "Beauty and the Beast." One can't live it the way one can live Cocteau's or McKinley's tales. Estar is a very distant hero, and the reader is never invited into the story.

1989. Bear, Greg. **"Sleepside Story."** In *The Year's Best Fantasy and Horror,* edited by Ellen Datlow and Terri Windling. New York: St. Martin's Press, 525–55.

Terri Windling introduces this story as "an excellent example of urban fantasy" and "the best fantasy novella of the year" (525). It is an extraordinarily interesting and well-crafted exploration of a young man's transition to selfhood, and proof that the gender of the protagonist is not an essential element of a folk-tale. Bear has carefully and thoroughly reversed the gender of every character in "Beauty and the Beast," and yet the story is recognizably the same tale and carries the same meaning. The setting is a modern urban dystopia with mythic overtones.

Beauty is a 19-year-old boy named Oliver Jones. His father is dead and he lives with his mother and siblings. The two other boys are self-centered thugs, his sister an ineffectual whiner, and the twins just babies. Oliver's father left him in charge when he died, and he knows he is the only one who will help and look after his mother. The rose is a piece of sheet music, which his mother steals for him from the Beast, Belle Parkhurst, the madam of the most famous brothel in the city. Oliver has to go to Belle's house in exchange for his mother's freedom. He takes the Night Metro across town, and on the route from Sleepside, where his family lives, to Sunside, where Belle lives, the train passes a station called Chaste River. It is a winter journey full of danger, and the train driver has the head of a bull and wears a pair of long, silver shears at his belt.

Belle Parkhurst is a small, beautifully dressed, imposing woman. Oliver is revolted by her because she is a whore, a woman who deals in sex. He thinks she brought him here because "she wanted young boy flesh" (533), although they only have supper together and talk. As the days and nights pass, he holds onto his anger and disgust all the more tightly because he begins to be aware of his own deep and unspoken desires. One evening Belle tells him that she will die soon, and that she plans to leave the brothel to him because he's kind, he cares, and he's "never had a woman, not all the way" (536). And she tells him about the curse that was laid on her by her second pimp when she was just a young girl. The curse is that she will be the greatest whore that ever was. The pimp gave her most of his magic, but he didn't give her a way out. She doesn't mind dying, but she doesn't want to die a whore, and to save her from that she needs someone who loves her for no reason. Oliver doesn't want to inherit the brothel. He can see that he hurts Belle by his silence and disdain, and he is touched by her unhappiness; he has even come to admit that he wants her, but still he resists, protesting that he's not even a man yet and that he can't love her because he doesn't know what love is.

Oliver goes home, with Belle's permission, because his mother is sick. He's definitely needed there. The place is a shambles and his mother is wasting away from pining for him. But although his mother tries to keep him there, Oliver is worried that Belle may be dying. Like Avenant and Beauty's brother in the Cocteau film, his brothers have taken the key she gave him and the limousine that brought him home to make a raid on Belle's house. So he makes the journey again on the Night Metro. This time the driver with the bull's head attacks him with the silver shears. But Oliver grabs the threatening shears, kicks the driver in the crotch, and escapes. At Belle's house, he finds he has to pay money to get in because he no longer has the key, just like a customer. He finds Belle dying in a small, bare attic room very different from the lush, rose-carved opulence of the rest of the house. She is suspended above her narrow bed by a web of transparent threads, cords that tie her to every man she has serviced, every customer who came to her house. Oliver cuts them with the silver shears, fighting to free her before she dies. The ghost of the pimp who cursed her appears to persuade Oliver that she isn't worth it, that she was a whore from the day she was born. But Oliver continues to hack away, cuts the last two cords, tells her he doesn't want anything from her, he just wants her to be all right, and kisses her lightly. Then he falls asleep beside her on the bed.

When he wakes up the next morning Belle has become a young woman again, with no memory of what has happened. His brothers are found dead in a room full of money, dressed as pimps—again an echo of Cocteau. Oliver moves out from home and Belle, who changes her name to Lorelei, lives with him. His mother is grudging at first but finally accepts her. "In time, they were married. And they lived—Well enough. They lived" (555).

The imagery in this story is both powerful and subtle. For example, the journey on the Night Metro is the mythic journey from the unawakened state of childhood (Sleepside), across a border dividing parts of the city (a threshold), past Chaste River, to the consciousness of awakened sexuality (Sunside) and maturity. The driver with the bull's head, not all human, not all animal, carries the shears of Atropos, the third of the Greek Fates, who cuts the thread of life. When Oliver grabs the shears and kicks him in the genitals, he seizes control of his own fate. Belle's new name, Lorelei, is the name of the siren who sang on a rock in the river Rhine and lured sailors and fishermen to their destruction. These are just examples; the story rewards a thorough analysis of its images and of the way Bear has developed his theme.

1992. Brooke, William J. **"A Beauty in the Beast."** In *Untold Tales*, by William J. Brooke. New York: HarperCollins, 51–95.

In this cleverly inventive story, both serious and funny, twist follows twist to surprise the reader. It begins with Beauty and the Beast at dinner. This night, and for the next two, instead of asking her to marry him as usual, the Beast tells a moral tale. The lesson of each is that "you must judge something in its entirety, not by any of its parts," and that "appearances are deceptive" (61–62). Beauty is deliberately obtuse, and angry enough to tell a story of her own. It's the story of herself and how she came to be there. For the first time the reader learns that Beauty is hideously ugly, the Beast the handsome one. It is her own ugliness that she cannot accept, her own face that she refuses to look at in the mirror the Beast offers her, even though she came to the castle hoping that the Beast "was a man to whom she could offer something, who would appreciate her as no other had" (69).

"Why were you called the Beast?" she asks him (71). In response, he tells the fourth story. He was once poor and plain. A sorcerer whom he accidentally offended cursed him with extraordinary beauty and the power to fulfill his every wish. The curse will only be lifted when a woman marries him in spite of his handsome face and wealth, not because of it. The invisible servants that wait on him are all the people who came to him feigning love or affection but wanting only their own gain. Beauty, he hopes, will be the woman who frees him. And then comes the next twist in the story. When Beauty realizes that he wants her because she can save him, not for herself, she runs away home, to the place where she is known and seen as herself. But after a week she suddenly notices that none of her family ever really looks at her. Here, she is the invisible servant, and being invisible, having no identity, is worse than being hideous. That night, she sees that the magical rose from the Beast's garden, which has been blooming in her bedroom all this time, is dying. She rushes back to the castle, makes the dying Beast ask her to marry him, and answers "Maybe" (93). The Beast recovers, and Beauty tells him one last story, to get him to admit that her face is very ugly. Then she agrees to stay with him, keep house for him, and have dinner with him every night, but not to marry him. With healthy common sense, she prefers that he keep his magic powers and physical perfection.

1995. Lee, Tanith. **"The Beast."** In *Ruby Slippers, Golden Tears,* edited by Ellen Datlow and Terri Windling. New York: William Morrow, 15–32.

Although Lee's "Beauty" seems to me calculated and technical, it still has the sense of otherness and self-discovery leading to growth and fulfillment that is an essential part of "Beauty and the Beast." "The Beast" has instead a cold decadence that verges on sadism. Although it has a vaguely futuristic setting, it is more horror story than science fiction and has a link to "Bluebeard."

A father who has learned that he is dying of cancer arranges to marry his extraordinarily beautiful daughter to a very rich and powerful man who is a collector of rare and beautiful objects. The father has seen a rose, a pendant made of amber, hung on a necklace of golden briars, in the man's collection, and he knows his daughter is the only woman in the world who could wear it properly. The man, whose name is Vessavion (neither father nor daughter is named), is as blondly, coldly beautiful as the daughter. They look to be superbly matched, and when the father arranges a meeting they fall in love with each other. The wedding takes place at Christmas, and for three months they live in a private world of intense passion. He tells her that she is himself, that if she ever leaves him he will die. But then one day a fleck of blood on Vessavion's cheek arouses doubts in Beauty. She begins to search the house for his secret. In a locked room she discovers that he collects not only beautiful artifacts but also beautiful body parts. When he sees an ugly person who has one incongruously beautiful feature—hair, eyes, teeth, nose, breasts, hand—he kills that person and takes the beautiful feature for his collection. His explanation of his hunger to possess human perfection is pitiful, but Beauty leaves him and returns to her dead father's house for a week. Then she goes back and finds him on their bed, thin, aged, ugly, and quite dead. "She had loved him and she had betrayed him, she had killed him as no other had the power to do. And here he lay to rot on the bed of love. And he had the face of a beast" (32).

Lee has turned "Beauty and the Beast" on its head in a number of ways. Beauty's discoveries are of fatal weakness and lead to death rather than a richer life. She and Vessavion cannot offer each other the opportunity to grow and change.

1995. Vande Velde, Vivian. **"Beast and Beauty."** In *Tales from the Brothers Grimm and the Sisters Weird.* San Diego: Harcourt Brace, 109–28.

This collection of stories by Vande Velde seems to be aimed at children and teens. As the title hints, they are parodies, written with quite a light hand. Like

Disney's film, this version of "Beauty and the Beast" is really the Beast's story, but the reversal is deliberate, part of the parody: "Once upon a time, in a land where even parents had magic, a mother got so upset with her son's bad temper, sloppy clothes, messy room, and disgusting table manners that she said: 'If you're going to act like a Beast, you might as well look like one, too' " (109). So the mother turns her son into a Beast, to stay that way until a good and beautiful woman agrees to marry him. She loves him, but enough is enough.

The Beast goes off to live by himself in the family's *other* castle, and the usual story follows, told from this particular Beast's point of view. Beauty is much later in returning to the Beast from her visit home than she promised because once she got home she got sick and thought she was dying. It took her some time to realize that she was missing the Beast. The story is pleasant, but like all parody it depends on the reader's knowing the original tale.

1996. Fisher, David. **"Beauty v. Beast: Application to Abrogate, Nullify, Rescind, Withdraw, Annul, and/or Otherwise Revoke an Existing Prenuptial Agreement between the Petitioner, Beauty, and the Respondent, Beast."** In *Legally Correct Fairy Tales*, by David Fisher. New York: Warner Books, 77–87.

Beauty has divorced the Beast. O. King Cole, counsel for the petitioner, argues that the couple's four children, the decline in value of the Beast's assets, and the high rate of inflation entitle Beauty to more than the small percentage of his total assets agreed to before their marriage. Cole cites two earlier decisions, *Queen v. Rumpelstiltskin* and *Kingdom v. Old Lady Who Lives in a Shoe*, as precedents.

1996. Walker, Barbara G. **"Ugly and the Beast."** In *Feminist Fairy Tales*. New York: HarperCollins, 49–54.

Barbara Walker states in her introduction that she wrote these stories to turn around the misogynist messages of traditional folktales that beauty is a girl's only asset. On page 52 she also explains the changes she has made to "Beauty and the Beast." The merchant is a thorough businessman and steals the Beast's roses made of real gold because he wants to sell them to recoup his fortunes. His eldest daughter is named Ugly because she is ugly, but she is also kind and good and cheerful. His other six daughters and seven sons love her and appreciate all her good qualities, but when she volunteers to go to the Beast in her father's stead because she is the only one who will not make an advantageous marriage, they agree. The Beast and Ugly grow fond of each other, and Ugly is relieved to learn that the Beast is not an enchanted prince, but really truly what he appears to be. If he were a handsome prince, she could never hope to keep him. They marry, of course, and the story ends thus: "They loved each other truly, because they were free of the narcissism that often mars the relationships of beautiful people; and so they lived happily ever after" (54).

1997. Cashorali, Peter. **"Beauty and the Beast."** In *Fairy Tales: Traditional Stories Retold for Gay Men*, by Peter Cashorali. New York: HarperSanFrancisco, 21–34.

Buddy, also called Beauty, has a father who is interested in nothing but business and two older brothers who are mean brutes. The Beast's palace is a penthouse condo, the stolen rose is an orchid, and the Beast is a "huge someone . . . wearing nothing except a costume made of leather straps and steel rings" (24). He's into rough sex (but nothing cruel) and trains Beauty every night to please him. During the days, Beauty gets interested in reading and learns all sorts of useful skills, including orchid keeping and body building. When he sees his father's face in a bowl of consommé, he goes home for three days with the Beast's permission. At home, he helps his father get his business back from the selfish brothers. In revenge, the brothers put a sleeping potion in his champagne so that he'll outstay his deadline. Fortunately the Beast is still waiting for him, and Beauty realizes for the first time that the Beast is a very handsome man. It was Beauty who had been under a spell, the Beast tells him, and now he is free to stay or go. Beauty wants to stay, with the condition that on that night after dinner the Beast will be Beauty, and Beauty gets to be the Beast.

This story, rather flippant in tone as most of Cashorali's are, has one true fairy tale line in it. Beauty is exploring the penthouse, which is much larger than he expected: "[I]n fact, if there had been even one more room, it would have been endless" (27).

1997. Donoghue, Emma. **"The Tale of the Rose."** In *Kissing the Witch*, by Emma Donoghue. New York: HarperCollins, 27–40.

Although Donoghue's *Kissing the Witch* is published for readers aged 12 to 17, the insights, twists, and writing of these reworkings of folktales are most suited for the upper half of that age range and will speak strongly to adults as well. "The Tale of the Rose" is told by Beauty herself. All the elements of the traditional tale are there, including the inscription Beauty reads in the first book she opens in the Beast's palace. The only substantive change seems to be the local tale about the Beast's castle: "The young queen had been exiled, imprisoned, devoured (here the stories diverged) by a hooded beast who could be seen at sunset walking the battlements" (32). The Beast is veiled when Beauty first meets it, and she never sees its face. But when Beauty returns from her overlong stay at home to find the Beast dying in the garden, she unmasks it and discovers a woman who chose to wear a mask because none of her suitors could see her true face, who she really was. (Only at that point did I realize that Donoghue had used no words that would give the Beast a gender.) Beauty stays with her, "And as the years flowed by, some villagers told travellers of a beast and a beauty who lived in the castle and could be seen walking on the battlements, and others told of two beauties, and others told of two beasts" (40). This superb ending could be read as the different responses of the world to a lesbian relationship.

1999. Mayer, Gloria Gilbert, and Thomas Mayer. **"Beauty and the Beast."** In *Goldilocks on Management: 27 Revisionist Fairy Tales for Serious Managers,* by Gloria Gilbert Meyer and Thomas Meyer. New York: American Management Association, 171–77.

In this humorously modernized version of the tale, the Beast makes the merchant sign a contract to send Beauty to him, but her agreement to return to the Beast is only verbal. The only magic is the conversion of the ugly millionaire to a "Fabio look-alike" once Beauty kisses him. The basic lesson: "Honoring both written and unwritten contracts is its own reward" (174). The bottom line: "In both fairy tales and real life, effective leaders will always do their best to keep commitments and live by their word—whether that word appears in a written document or is sealed by a handshake" (177).

1999. Wheeler, Wendy. **"Skin So Green and Fine."** In *Silver Birch, Blood Moon*, edited by Ellen Datlow and Terry Windling. New York: Avon, 258–88.

This story has all the traditional elements of "Beauty and the Beast," but it takes place in the modern world on an island named Hispaniola. Bonita marries a rich man who has saved her father's bakery business. He is a peculiar husband for her, because she comes from a Catholic Hispanic family and he is one of the black French-speaking Haitians on the island who practice vodoun. Not only that, he looks like a snake and lives mysteriously without visible servants on his large sugar plantation. Although Bonita's new situation is completely strange to her, she finds her husband, Michél Aspic, very kind. Above all, he is willing to wait until she herself wants to come to his bed. The morning after their marriage is finally consummated, all his people return to the plantation. By his consideration for her he has atoned for his sin of pride, an obsession with his own ugliness that kept him from serving his people as the *hougan*, voudon priest, he was raised to be.

2000. Block, Francesca Lia. **"Beast."** In *The Rose and the Beast: Fairy Tales Retold*, by Francesca Lia Block. New York: Joanna Cotler Books, 169–98.

A number of reworkings of "Beauty and the Beast" give the story an Oedipal interpretation: Beauty has to learn to separate herself from her father to love the Beast. Block begins by focusing on the father's excessive attachment to Beauty. He picks the Beast's rose precisely because it is forbidden, because it is so like his favorite daughter. The transgression is the real gift to Beauty; it frees her from her father and brings her a Beast to go to. With the Beast, Beauty grows strong and brave and wild. His devotion is never a burden to her. They understand each other intuitively until Beauty declares her love for him. Then the Beast changes, becomes merely human, and their relationship becomes more ordinary, less than perfect.

Feature Films

Two enormously influential films have been made of "Beauty and the Beast." As different from each other as they could possibly be, Cocteau's *La belle et la bête* and Disney's *Beauty and the Beast* taken together make a most convincing demonstration of the porosity and resilience of folktales. Both are pure fantasy. The third film in this section is realistic fiction and considerably less notable.

La belle et la bête

1946. **La belle et la bête.** Written and directed by Jean Cocteau. Paris. Distributed by Lopert Pictures Corp. (1947, USA, subtitled). DVD Criterion Pictures Corp., 1998.

> Children believe what we tell them, they have complete faith in us. They believe that a rose plucked from a garden can bring drama to a family. They believe that the hands of a human Beast will smoke when he slays a victim, and that this Beast will be ashamed when confronted by a young girl. They believe a thousand other simple things. I ask of you a little of this childlike simplicity, and to bring us luck, let me speak four truly magic words, childhood's "open Sesame": "Once upon a time."
>
> Jean Cocteau

With these words, which appear on the screen at the very beginning of the film, Cocteau acknowledges that folktales are taken as children's stories but addresses himself and his film to the adults who will be his audience. The film is very close to de Beaumont's story, although events and details have necessarily been added.

Beauty's father has lost his wealth and is involved in a court case to try to get some of it back. He seems weak, is quick to hope and even quicker to despair, and has no control over his children. Beauty is beautiful, loving, and dutiful. She does all the work for the family in their reduced circumstances. When her father comes back from the Beast's palace and tells his children what has happened, that he must go back to be killed within three days unless one of his daughters will agree to die in his place, Beauty immediately says she will go. She insists that she must, because her request for the rose has brought this disaster on her father.

Beauty has two sisters who are thoroughly nasty creatures: vain, proud, quarrelsome. Her brother Ludovic is a ne'er-do-well, a self-proclaimed rotter, and proud of it. Cocteau has added a character, Avenant, a friend of Ludovic's who is in love with Beauty and wants to marry her. Avenant is very handsome, but as idle and useless as Ludovic, and he's violent as well. He shoots an arrow that almost kills the family dog, slaps one of the nasty sisters, grabs Beauty when she refuses to marry him and tries to kiss her by force, and presses her to leave this life that is unworthy of her (not that he has anything better to offer). Beauty loves Avenant but won't marry him because she will not leave her father.

At home, Beauty is meek and devoted. Her only decisive act is to sneak out of the house at night to go to the Beast in her father's place. At the Beast's palace, where the Beast tells her "there is no master here but you . . . everything here is at your command," she learns to speak for herself. When the Beast comes to her door at night, his hands smoking with the blood of a fresh kill, she orders him to get out of her room and to clean himself. At the end, when he is dying, she commands him to live. Beauty has an abstract understanding of the Beast's situation to begin with. When, during their first evening together, the Beast tells Beauty, "My heart is good, but I am a monster," she answers "There are men whose ugliness is all within." And when he goes on to say, "Besides being ugly, I have little wit," she answers, "You have wit enough to know yourself." But some time later, when Beauty strokes the Beast's head in affection and he protests, "you stroke me as though I were an animal," she answers, "but you are an animal." By the end, however, she has learned to see him truly. She claims him for herself, calling him not La Bête but Ma bête. And when she finds him dying she tells him, "I am the monster. You must live."

The Beast is a tragic figure of great power. As in de Beaumont's story, he became a Beast through no fault of his own. His parents didn't believe in magic, so the fairies punished them through him. He is very dignified and courtly and cannot bear to have Beauty kneel to him. But he is also a Beast. When he and Beauty are walking in the garden and a deer breaks cover, he shakes with the Beast's need to give chase and kill. Beauty's presence controls him then, but only just. He tells Beauty she must NEVER look into his eyes; her gaze burns him. He suffers because of his Beast nature because he is ashamed of it. But his suffering has brought him wisdom and, as Beauty says, he knows himself. As Cocteau portrays him, the Beast, rather than Beauty, attracts the viewers' sympathy. He is still a Beast, with a Beast's uncontrollable need to kill for fresh blood, but his struggle with his beastliness is profound. The aura of tragic suffering that surrounds him, his complex blend of animal vitality and perception with a human heart, make Beauty look very flat and uninteresting.

Cocteau elaborates on the Beast's magic but leaves it a mystery. In his palace, candles light themselves as someone approaches, the arms of the candelabra move, the eyes of statues open, their heads turn—quietly, slowly, memorably. The Beast's power resides in five things, his five secrets: his rose, his mirror, his horse, his key, and his glove. The key and the glove are Cocteau's invention, as is the Beast's gift of all these things to Beauty when she goes home to comfort her father. If Beauty doesn't come back, he will die, not only of grief but because he has given her everything that matters. There is an added complication, which is very important at the end. The magic key unlocks the door of the pavilion of the goddess Diana in his garden. In this pavilion are all his earthly treasures, the ones not given by magic. When Beauty goes home to comfort her father, she tells Avenant and Ludovic about the key, the pavilion, and the treasure. Avenant and Ludovic decide to go and kill the Beast to free Beauty and to steal his treasure. They take the horse the Beast has sent to bring Beauty back to get to the Beast's palace, while her sisters keep Beauty at home with false tears. But Beauty gets back by using the magic glove and arrives at the same time Avenant and Ludovic do. While she looks for the Beast, the two men approach the pavilion of Diana.

SIENA COLLEGE LIBRARY

They don't trust the magic key, so they decide to break in through the skylight. As they do so, the statue of Diana in the pavilion begins to move, lifts her bow, and shoots Avenant. He falls to the ground, and his body begins to change into that of a Beast. Meanwhile, Beauty has found her Beast dying in the garden. She weeps, and commands him to live. At the very moment that Avenant falls and becomes a beast, the Beast rises from the ground and resumes his proper form as the prince.

Cocteau's *Beauty and the Beast* is a story of dualities. These are most strongly implied visually and seldom put into words. There is constant play of light and shadow. Characters move out of darkness into light and back into darkness. When the Beast sends Beauty home, he tells her, "My night is your day. You'll be there this morning." The Beast is elegantly, sumptuously dressed in black, but his dark clothing sparkles with jewels, and his hideous head is framed by a delicate white collar that stands up like a fan behind it and catches the light. Contrasting scenes are juxtaposed. The action switches back and forth between the petty meanness of Beauty's home, all childish quarrels and dissatisfaction, and the passionate intensity and courtliness of the Beast's palace. The father first sees the Beast in his garden across the carcass of a freshly killed deer lying at the Beast's feet. When Beauty first sees the Beast, in his garden, she faints and falls at his feet, like the deer, and the camera points out the parallel. Mirrors, reflections, and the shadows people cast come up over and over again throughout the film.

Perhaps the most intriguing duality is created by the fact that the Beast, Avenant, and the prince whom the Beast turns into at the end are played by the same actor, Jean Marais. Once you know this, you can't help thinking about it all the way through the film. But for someone who is seeing the film for the first time, it becomes obvious only at the end, when the Beast is transformed into Prince Ardent. The link between Avenant, the beastly man, and the Beast with a human heart and sensibilities is a comment on beastliness and humanity. It has been suggested by some viewers that Avenant's fate is a question of succession. The Beast cannot be restored to his proper form until another takes his place; as Avenant falls, the prince rises. It seems to me, however, that both beasts die in the form that conceals their inner nature, and both are reborn in a form that reveals what they truly are. Marina Warner suggests a different reading of the ending: "So *La Belle et la bête* traces a promise to male lovers that they will not always be rejected, that human lovers, however profligate, can be saved, and it withdraws at the last moment any autonomy in love from Beauty herself" (296–97). In effect, Beauty gets the lover she rejected (Avenant) and loses the one she chose for herself (the Beast). Zipes, in *Fairy Tale as Myth*, takes a similar view, calling the Avenant/Prince Ardent doubling "a cruel joke on Beauty" (44).

Whatever meaning one makes of it, this version of Beauty and the Beast does not moralize. It is preoccupied with meaning rather than education. (Beauty's bookishness has vanished. In fact, there isn't a book in the whole film.) In Cocteau's version, "The deception of appearances becomes not a homily but an existential recognition" (Hearne 1989, 89). Instead of teaching a lesson about the way things should be, the film recognizes "personal dualities of light and dark, reality and fantasy, animal and spiritual, male and female, alienation and reconciliation" (Hearne 1989, 89) as part of the way things are, and explores these aspects of existence.

Beauty and the Beast

1991. **Beauty and the Beast.** Directed by Gary Trousdale and Kirk Wise. Written by Roger Allers and Linda Woolverton. Walt Disney Productions.

The Disney *Beauty and the Beast* is ostensibly for children, but teenagers and adults love it, too. Not all adults, however. Terri Windling, although she enjoyed the film, finds it disturbing:

> Perhaps because it has not been billed as a new story inspired by the old fairy tale—rather, it has been presented to us as if it *were* the old fairy tale, and such is the power of the Disney name that audiences around the world will perceive this as a truth. Yet it's not the old tale. Too many fundamentals have been changed for the film to make that claim—and changed in glib or sloppy ways that lessen the story's classic themes (2000).

Betsy Hearne is bothered by "the violation of profound elements" (Hearne 1997, 145), and so am I. The traces in the film of earlier versions of the story are interesting. (See chapters 9 and 10 of Thomas's book for an account of how the movie was made.) Gaston is surely a form of Cocteau's Avenant, physically attractive but a rotten character, human beastliness compared to the natural bestiality of an animal. The all-singing, all-dancing houseware and furniture are a charming invention for which I think McKinley's novel must have been the inspiration. They have nothing to do with the development of the theme, no significance other than their entertainment value, but they make the movie memorable. I don't dislike this movie because it's cute, or simply because it's Disney, or because it takes liberties with the story of "Beauty and the Beast." All reworkings take liberties, and many make new meanings. I do dislike the particular meanings Disney makes.

First, this story is about the Beast's need to change, not Beauty's. Belle is already perfect: lovely, independent, bookish, and kind. But the Beast has a lot to learn. He was changed into a Beast because he was rude and hard-hearted to a poor old woman who came begging for shelter at his door one cold and stormy night, offering a perfect red rose as recompense. She was, of course, an enchantress in disguise, and turned him into a Beast. Before leaving him, she gave him the perfect red rose and told him that it would measure the limited time he had in which to mend his ways. If he had not learned to love another person and earn that person's love in return before his twenty-first year, the rose would drop its petals and when the last petal fell he would remain a Beast forever. Beauty comes to his castle looking for her father, who had gone off to peddle his absurd inventions and had been attacked by wolves near the Beast's castle. He took refuge there, and the Beast threw him into the dungeon for trespassing. When Beauty arrives to rescue him she volunteers to take her father's place. The Beast hadn't made much progress in the years that passed before Beauty came. The film makes it clear that he must still learn to control his temper and to be polite before he will be able to love someone and have her love him back. There is nothing noble about the Beast, no true animal nature for the human in him to come to terms with, no wisdom through suffering, no self-awareness, no complexity. He is simply a bad-tempered, over-sized adolescent who lacks a proper upbringing. Even the rose is about him, rather than about Belle and her father, and motivates nothing in the plot. It is fair enough to make it the Beast's story—it is very hard not to let the Beast dominate in any case, because he is naturally the most interesting character—but this Beast is completely uninteresting except for his shape, which admittedly is magnificently powerful and beastly.

Second, this story has been reduced to adolescent romance. Belle isn't bookish in de Beaumont's and McKinley's sense. It is delightful that she is a reader, and fairy tales are wonderful reading, but Belle's favorite part of any book is the bit where the heroine meets the prince in disguise. All she can learn from that is that some day her prince will come.

Third, the men in Belle's life do not give her a decent choice. Her father is a good-tempered, eccentric little boy whom she mothers. He doesn't even make it home from the Beast's castle to give her the chance to take his place. Beauty has to go out looking for him and rescue him. The Beast is a rude teenager given to temper tantrums, whom she tames and mothers. Gaston is a stupid brute, the village bully who wants Beauty because she isn't interested in him and who destroys what she loves to possess her by violence. That is the full Disney spectrum of male types, the men Beauty has to choose from. The handsome prince is no more real in this version than in any other. He is simply an abstraction with a pretty face. Besides, he doesn't count because Belle has to choose before the prince appears. She comes to love the Beast because, after she has shaken him up, he is "dear and so unsure." For a Disney heroine, to love is to nurture. She never gets an independent, grown-up man. Feminists have rightly criticized Disney fairy tale productions for their passive princesses. Men ought to take exception to the characterization of the male characters, too.

In this "Beauty and the Beast," Belle doesn't need to learn perception, to see others truly, and to find herself. She already has courage, independence, spirit, and integrity, and there is nothing in the Beast for her to see until she puts it there. In the film, after the Beast has learned table manners and is gently feeding the birds, Belle sings: "There's something sweet and almost kind/But he was mean and he was coarse and unrefined/And now he's dear, and so unsure./I wonder why I didn't see it there before. . . . There's something in him that I simply didn't see." The song gets it wrong. Belle didn't see it because it *wasn't* there before. The songwriter has followed the classic "Beauty and the Beast" line—that Belle has to learn to value what lies beneath the Beast's appearance—but in this film it no longer applies. The Beast's inner being is a good deal less attractive than his furry exterior until Belle takes him in hand.

The Disney *Beauty and the Beast* was advertised and reviewed as a feminist fairy tale, a radical departure from earlier Disney films. But actually, Beauty is just a feisty North American version of Madame de Beaumont's Beauty and a throwback to the Victorian angel in the house, "whose task it is to tame and gentle male lust and animal instinct" (Warner, 294).

Beauty

1998. **Beauty**. Directed by Jerry London. Los Angeles: Citadel Entertainment and Grand Productions.

This made-for-television, feature-length film is based on the novel by Susan Wilson published in 1996. It was first aired on October 25, 1998. Like the book it's based on, it is realistic fiction, with no element of fantasy. Alix Miller is an art teacher who is invited to New Hampshire to paint the portrait of a strange recluse. Her subject, Leland Crompton, suffers from acromegaly, a rare disease that causes abnormal overgrowth of the bones and therefore distorts the face, so he hides from the world that might find him frightening. Actually, it is Leland who is frightened and afraid to trust the love he comes to feel for Alix because he was hurt before by a woman he loved.

Unlike the book, the film ends happily. Leland comes to the city to see a show of Alix's paintings. He finally looks at her portrait of him, which shows him skating, free and full of joy. The two of them walk out of the gallery together, into the world of people, and kiss each other in front of a springing fountain in the public square.

Musical

The Broadway musical version of Disney's animated *Beauty and the Beast* opened in New York at the end of April 1994. It was the first Disney Broadway musical and, when it opened, the most expensive show in Broadway history. The reviewers mostly had mixed reactions. The musical follows the film very closely, with some additional musical numbers, but the physical limitations of human actors and of stage sets make it impossible to create the magical effects of the film's animation.

Poetry

These eight poems are very different, but all of them are very serious in tone, and each one challenges the reader.

[no date]. Alsop, Jaimes. **"Beauty and the Beast."** Endicott Studio, "Coffee House" page, http://www.endicott-studio.com/cofbeuty.html.

This poem is in two parts, the first spoken by the Beast to Beauty, the second by Beauty to the Beast.

1943. Heath-Stubbs, John. **"Beauty and the Beast."** In *Beauty and the Beast*. London: Routledge, 16–18. Also in Hearne, Betsy. 1989. *Beauty and the Beast: Visions and Revisions of an Old Tale*. Chicago: University of Chicago Press, 76–78.

First Beauty and then the Beast speak, alternating twice, in the Beast's garden. Both speak of what they are and how they are changing. Betsy Hearne gives a good close reading of this poem (Hearne 1989, 76–79).

1977. Broumas, Olga. "Beauty and the Beast." In *Beginning with O*. New Haven: Yale University Press, 55–56.

This difficult poem about a woman's discovery of her lesbian sexuality is not well served by a prose summary. With that warning, I give the following flat reading of it. The speaker has experienced sex as pain for years, expecting always that pain pushed far enough would finally become pleasure. The pleasure she discovered in loving a woman was a complete surprise to her.

1979. Lochhead, Liz. "Beauty & The." In *The Grimm Sisters*, by Liz Lochhead. Toronto: Coach House Press (Manuscript Editions), [n.p.].

Beauty merely endures the sexual animality of the Beast at first, "the whole wham bam menagerie," but the poet/narrator promises her that she will change to match him.

1988. Lewis, Bill. "The Beast." Endicott Studio, "Coffee House" page, http://www.endicott-studio.com/cofbeast.html.

The Beast sits alone, wounded by Beauty's loveliness, both hoping and fearing that she will come back to him, comforting himself with fairy tales and recordings of Frank Sinatra and Julie London.

1989. Yolen, Jane. "Beauty and the Beast: An Anniversary." In *The Faery Flag: Stories and Poems of Fantasy and the Supernatural*. New York: Orchard Books, 101–2. Also in *The Year's Best Fantasy and Horror: Third Annual Collection*. 1990. Edited by Ellen Datlow and Terri Windling. New York: St. Martin's, 412.

Beauty is speaking, many years after she and the Beast were married. Her father has died and her sisters almost never write any more. She and the Beast are growing old. She says she has no regrets, but she sometimes wonders what it might have been like to have children.

Yolen's poem set to music is recorded by British folksinger June Tabor on her CD *Against the Streams*.

1990. Strauss, Gwen. "The Beast." In *Trail of Stones*. New York: Alfred A. Knopf, 30–32.

The Beast is speaking after Beauty has left and winter has come to his garden. Beauty sends him quick notes and chocolates, but she keeps postponing her return to the Beast. In his pain and loneliness he becomes more beast-like. He realizes she will never come back, but keeps hoping. The facing illustration by Anthony Browne shows an unshaven man seated at a table. One hand covers his face in a gesture of despair. The other, clenched in a fist on the table, looks as hairy as a beast's paw.

1999. Duffy, Carol Ann. **"Mrs. Beast."** In *The Year's Best Fantasy and Horror: 12th Annual Collection,* edited by Ellen Datlow and Terri Windling. New York: St. Martin's Griffin, 252–54.

The woman who married the Beast is a tough lady who chose her man freely, from a position of independence. She picked one who loves her more than she loves him, who serves her well in every way, whom she dominates. Handsome princes, she warns, bring women grief and pain. Duffy's poem is a lament for all the women, from Eve to Rapunzel to Bessie Smith to Dianna, Princess of Wales, who lose too much because of love.

Television Programs

1987–1990. **Beauty and the Beast**. Produced by Ron Koslow for CBS.

This series of weekly hour-long programs ran in North America and in Great Britain. The setting is contemporary New York City. Beauty is a rich Manhattan woman named Catherine. At the beginning of the series she is raped and left for dead. The Beast is Vincent, a horribly deformed misfit who lives underground. Warner describes him as follows:

> A roaring, rampaging half-lion, half-human creature, he reigns over the subway system of New York as a defender of women and beggars, an urban Robin Hood who was born from an immaculate virgin and the seed of two fathers, the double lord of the underworld, one a good magus, the other a wicked wizard. (312)

Vincent takes Catherine in and looks after her in his underworld until she is well again and returns to her job as an assistant district attorney. By that time Vincent and Catherine have fallen in love with each other, and they join forces against the evil in the city. Vincent's underground community of marginalized people is a more humane place than Catherine's New York. Catherine is attracted to Vincent's world and grows to meet his expectations of her. In one episode, Catherine kisses Vincent to call him back from death in a struggle against his own dark side, a resurrection marked by the classic "Beauty and the Beast" images of blooming roses and fireworks. After this first kiss their sexual union may be assumed, although it is never made explicit, because she becomes pregnant by Vincent. Catherine is murdered after the baby is born, and Vincent fights the forces of evil to reclaim his son. Bacchilega sums up her lengthy analysis of this television series by concluding that, "The magic of the TV 'Beauty and the Beast' simply re-produces Beauty's collusion with the patriarchal world of father and Beast, and glamorizes her self-denial" (86–87). Zipes finds that "despite the 'feminist' touch-up of Beauty in this TV series, the basic plot of submission/domination is merely reformed to make the contemporary beautiful working woman less aware of her bonds" (Zipes 1994, 45).

Internet Resources

An annotated version of "Beauty and the Beast" with links to the notes is available in the "SurLaLune Fairy Tale Pages" by Heidi Anne Heiner at http://members.aol.com/surlalune/frytales/banbeast/index.htm. The site also has pages about the history of the tale, illustrations, similar tales across cultures, modern interpretations, and a bibliography.

Another useful site to check is "The Endicott Studio of the Mythic Arts" at http://www.endicott-studio.com. The Endicott Studio was founded by Terri Windling in 1987, and this Web site is a monthly online journal that premiered in 1997. Several of the poems listed in this chapter are found at this site's "Coffee House." Terri Windling's very thoughtful essay on the Disney film and "the question of where precisely should one draw the line between use and abuse of fairy tales in creating art for modern audiences" is at http://www.endicott-studio.com/forbewty.html.

Classroom Extensions

The following suggestions may be adapted for use with other tales in this book.

Beast in the Attic

In both Angela Carter's story "The Courtship of Mr. Lyon" (1979) and Greg Bear's story "Sleepside Story" (1989), Beauty finds the Beast dying in a small, bare attic room of the palace. What meaning can you make from that room in each story?

Five Stable Elements

Betsy Hearne identifies five stable elements that form the core of the tale and make it recognizable as "Beauty and the Beast," no matter what changes a particular reteller has introduced: the seasonal cycle, the movement from city to country to the Beast's palace, the rose, the Beast's garden, and magic. Look for these elements in one of the novels, films, or short stories listed in this chapter. Explore the significance and function of each element in the story chosen. For longer reworkings the work could be done in groups, one group per element, and the group findings reported to the whole class. Or each group could look for all five elements, with one member responsible for each element and the other members contributing insights and ideas to the discussion.

Initiation

The first chapter of *New Tales for Old* makes the argument that all folktales are initiation stories. Look at Greg Bear's "Sleepside Story" and Emma Donoghue's "The Tale of the Rose" (or any other version of the tale). What do they say about initiation? Do they have something to say that has meaning for your own life?

King Kong

Anthony Browne's picture book *King Kong* has a quotation from "Beauty and the Beast" as an epigraph on the page following the title page. Is *King Kong* a version of "Beauty and the Beast?" What makes you think so?

Pictures and Text

Most writers of "Beauty and the Beast" don't describe the Beast in any detail. The Beast's actual appearance is left to the imagination of the reader. Readers can give the Beast a face that fits the meaning they make of the story. However, illustrators of picture books and filmmakers can't help showing what the Beast looks like. Look at the Beast in Nancy Willard's and Mercer Meyer's picture book versions of the tale, and in the Cocteau and Disney films. What do these images of the Beast say about him? How do they change the story? Would you rather be left to imagine the Beast for yourself? Why or why not?

Polar Opposites

The phrase "Beauty and the Beast" is used frequently in newspaper headlines, magazine advertisements, and everyday conversation to describe two individuals or things that are the opposite of each other in appearance or character. What meaning does the phrase carry in these situations? How might someone who knows something of the history of the story and several versions of it respond to that phrase?

Strauss and Browne

Gwen Strauss's Poem "The Beast" is accompanied by Anthony Browne's picture of a man in despair. Read the poem and the picture together as if they were a single piece.

Filling the Gaps

Gioia Timpanelli's "Rusina, Not Quite in Love" has a number of gaps in it that readers may choose to fill. There are elements in the story whose meaning is never clearly stated. Explain, for example, the small dark house, the beautiful young man, or the Master Gardener's aunt and uncle. Is it significant that Rusina describes her father as brave, hopeful, a teller of stories? Why? How do the recurring images of the rose, a memorable element from earlier versions of this tale, fit together to make meaning in this story?

The Tale Type

Maria Tatar's *The Classic Fairy Tales* groups the canonical version by Madame de Beaumont with seven very different but related tales, including Straparola's "Pig King," Grimm's "Frog Prince," and Carter's "The Tiger's Bride." Compare one or more of these other stories to Madame de Beaumont's "Beauty and the Beast," looking for the fundamental similarities and for the differences that reflect the teller's culture and give rise to different, and even contradictory, interpretations of the tale type as a whole.

Endnotes

1.   The spelling of Madame Le Prince de Beaumont's name varies. It also occurs as Leprince de Beaumont and as LePrince de Beaumont.

References

Anderson, Graham. 2000. *Fairy Tale in the Ancient World*. London: Routledge.

Bacchilega, Cristina. 1997. *Postmodern Fairy Tales: Gender and Narrative Strategies*. Philadelphia: University of Pennsylvania Press.

Bettelheim, Bruno. 1975. *Uses of Enchantment: The Meaning and Importance of Fairy Tales*. New York: Vintage Books.

Brewer, Derek. 1980. *Symbolic Stories: Traditional Narratives of the Family Drama in English Literature*. Cambridge: D. S. Brewer.

Bryant, Sylvia. 1989. "Re-Constructing Oedipus Through 'Beauty and the Beast'." *Criticism* 31(4): 439–53.

Clute, John, and John Grant, eds. 1997. *The Encyclopedia of Fantasy*. London: Orbit.

de Beaumont, Madame Le Prince. 1980. "Beauty and the Beast." In *The Classic Fairy Tales,* compiled by Iona Opie and Peter Opie. Paperback edition. New York: Oxford University Press, 182–95.

Gad, Irene. 1991. " 'Beauty and the Beast' and 'The Wonderful Sheep': The Couple in Fairy Tales: When Father's Daughter Meets Mother's Son." In *Psyche's Stories: Modern Jungian Interpretations of Fairy Tales*, edited by Murray Stein and Lionel Corbett. Willamette, IL: Chiron Publications, 27–48.

Guroian, Vigen. 1998. *Tending the Heart of Virtue: How Classic Stories Awaken a Child's Moral Imagination*. New York: Oxford University Press.

Hearne, Betsy. 1989. *Beauty and the Beast: Visions and Revisions of an Old Tale*. Chicago: University of Chicago Press.

———. 1997. "Disney Revisited, Or, Jiminy Cricket, It's Musty Down Here." *Horn Book* (March/April): 137–46.

Leavy, Barbara Fass. 1994. *In Search of the Swan Maiden: A Narrative on Folklore and Gender*. New York: New York University Press.

Opie, Iona, and Peter Opie. 1980. *The Classic Fairy Tales*. Paperback edition. New York: Oxford University Press. [1974. Oxford University Press].

Tatar, Maria. 1987. *The Hard Facts of the Grimms' Fairy Tales*. Princeton: Princeton University Press.

————. 1992. *Off with their Heads!: Fairy Tales and the Culture of Childhood*. Princeton: Princeton University Press.

Tatar, Maria, ed. 1999. *The Classic Fairy Tales*. New York: W. W. Norton.

Thomas, Bob. 1991. *Disney's Art of Animation: From Mickey Mouse to Beauty and the Beast*. New York: Welcome Enterprises.

Thompson, Stith. 1961. *The Types of the Folktale: A Classification and Bibliography. Antti Aarne's Verzeichnis der Märchentypen,* translated and enlarged by Stith Thompson. 2d revision. FF Communications, no. 184. Helsinki: Suomalainen Tiedeakatemia.

Warner, Marina. 1994. *From the Beast to the Blonde: On Fairy Tales and Their Tellers*. London: Chatto & Windus.

Windling, Terri. 2000, October 24."Beauty and the Beast." The Endicott Studio. http://www.endicott-studio.com/forbewty.html.

Zipes, Jack. 1989. *Beauties, Beasts and Enchantments: Classic French Fairy Tales*. New York: New American Library.

————. 1994. *Fairy Tale as Myth/Myth as Fairy Tale*. Lexington: University of Kentucky Press.

————. 1999. *When Dreams Came True: Classical Fairy Tales and Their Tradition*. New York: Routledge.

Zipes, Jack, ed. 2000. *The Oxford Companion to Fairy Tales*. Oxford: Oxford University Press.

CHAPTER 2

JACK AND HIS STORIES

When thinking about folktales in conjunction with the name Jack, almost all of us immediately conjure up the image of a young boy, often lazy but always respectful of his mother, who climbs a beanstalk and has numerous encounters with the giant. If it is not that Jack who comes to mind, then it might be the one who defeats giants in this realm instead, or perhaps the one that is the hero of the Jack tales in the United States, who outwits the devil along with giants and other "worthy" opponents.

Needless to say, there are plenty of "Jacks" in the body of folklore, both in the new world and the old. The name Jack has a long history of being used as a nickname for the given name John, and as early as the thirteenth century was used to denote a member of the "common folk." Since the beginning of the fifteenth century in English mystery plays, Jack has been illustrated as "Everyman-as-survivor" (Clute and Grant, 510). Herbert Halbert acknowledged "Jack" as a type of trickster-hero, not the admirable prince of fairy tales but a quick-witted, not always too scrupulous, clever lad (186). By the eighteenth century Jack had become the John Doe of oral tradition in England, as demonstrated by the numerous nursery rhymes that use Jack as the male character, including "Jack and Jill," "Jack Sprat," and "Jack Horner." Jack was also a favored name for numerous heroes in the Scottish traveler's tales. "Jack's popularity grew throughout England and Ireland at the same time that Britain was colonizing the world. Immigrants from Britain and Ireland brought Jack to the imperial colonies, including the Caribbean where Jack is the most popular human character among Black Bahamian tellers" (Lindahl, xvi).

In this chapter we examine the two most prevalent of the Jack stories: "Jack and the Beanstalk" and "Jack the Giant Killer." Although we often differentiate between these two tales, these two stories are both identified as the same tale type, AT 328: The Boy Steals the Giant's Treasure. The tales both originate in Great Britain and are extremely popular in North America. Jack is the generic name for a folk hero who is clever and often gains his ends immorally and often through luck rather than hard labor and virtue. It is the character of Jack, rather than the individual tales, that is the major focus of this chapter.

"Jack and the Beanstalk" relates the tale of a foolish young boy's trade of a cow for a handful of beans.

When Jack returns home from the market, his distraught mother tosses the beans out of the window. During the night, the beans grow into a huge beanstalk that Jack immediately climbs. At the top of the beanstalk Jack meets the wife of a giant, who protects him from her flesh-eating spouse. Jack repays her kindness by taking one of the giant's treasures. Jack repeats this adventure three times, but on the final return journey he is followed by the giant. Upon reaching the ground, Jack immediately chops the beanstalk down, the giant tumbles to his death, and Jack and his mother live with riches for the rest of their days.

In "Jack the Giant-Killer," Jack kills a number of giants and is aptly rewarded. Many versions of this tale make use of the same motifs as "The Valiant Tailor" (Type 1640). The entry in *Funk & Wagnall's Standard Dictionary of Folklore, Mythology, and Legend* states that "basically it is the same story as 'Jack and the Beanstalk,' belonging to the stupid-ogre group of tales" (Leach 1949, 535).

"Jack and the Beantree" is virtually the same tale as well. "The general European versions do not have the beanstalk episode. . . . The Scotch and Irish forms of this tale do not have the beanstalk, and usually have a clever girl who steals the giant's wonderful possessions" (Halbert 1943, 190).

Tale Type: AT 328

The Boy Steals the Giant's Treasure. Jack and the Beanstalk. The horse, the light, etc. Finally the giant is killed. Sometimes joined with Type 327. Cf. also Types 531, 1525.

I. *Expeditions to the Giant.* (a) The hero sets out to steal from a giant to get revenge for former ill-treatment, or (b) to help a friendly king, or (c) as a task suggested by jealous rivals, or (d) he ascends to sky on magic beanstalk and finds the giant's house.

II. *Giant robbed.* (a) By threatening the giant with an approach of an overwhelming army and locking him up to protect him, or (b) putting too much salt in the giant's food, so that he goes outside to get water, or (c) fishing through chimney (d) he steals from the giant a light, a horse, a violin, etc. (e) He tricks the giant into giving him magic objects; e.g., a cap of knowledge, an invincible sword, a cloak of invisibility, and seven-league boots.

III. *The Giant captured.* (a) The giant is beguiled into a cage and taken to court. (b) The giant is tricked into killing himself. (Thompson 1961, 119–20)

Motifs:

G610. Theft from ogre.

G610.1 Stealing from ogre for revenge.

G610.2 Stealing from ogre to help a friendly king.

G610.3 Stealing from ogre as a task.

H1151. Theft as a task.

H911. Tasks assigned at suggestion of jealous rivals.

F54.2. Plant grows to sky.

K335.0.1. Owner frightened from goods by report of approaching enemy.

K337. Oversalting food of giant so that he must go outside for water.

K316.1. Theft from giant by fishing through chimney.

D833. Magic object acquired by tricking giant. Giant persuaded to give the object to the hero.

D1162. Magic light.

H1151.9. Task: stealing troll's golden horse.

D1233. Magic violin.

D1300.2. Cap gives magic wisdom.

D1400.1.4.1. Magic sword conquers enemy.

D1361.12. Magic cloak of invisibility.

D1521.1. Seven-league boots. Boots with miraculous speed.

G520. Ogre deceived into self-injury.

G514.1. Ogre trapped in box (cage).

H1172. Task: bringing an ogre to court.

A History of "Jack the Giant Killer" and "Jack and the Beanstalk"

In contrast with other tales discussed in this book, Jack's stories have a long recorded oral history in both parts of the Western world.

Jack in the Oral Tradition

Jack has been part of the folklore landscape of the English-language-speaking world as far back as one can research. However, this Jack was a character often off limits to women and children because of the scatological and obscene references within the tales. Only when editors decided to market the tale to children were these "undesirable" elements eliminated from the printed tales (Lindhahl, xiv).

In Europe

Iona and Peter Opie suggest connections between some of the tricks in "Jack the Giant Killer" and prototypes in Northern mythology: "His possession of a cloak of invisibility, cap of knowledge, shoes of swiftness, and sword of sharpness, all second-hand articles which he seems to have acquired from Tom Thumb or from Northern mythology" (59). They also maintain that there is no early mention of either "Jack the Giant Killer" or "Jack and the Beanstalk" in British oral tradition. The story of "Jack the Giant Killer" appears to be a united string of anecdotes first published in the early eighteenth century in two parts. Knowledge of Jack and his feats became well known in that century, demonstrated in the first chapter of Henry Fielding's *Joseph Andrews* (1742), when Fielding writes of "John the Great, who, by his brave and heroic actions against men of large and athletic bodies, obtained the glorious appellation of the giantkiller" (1974, 61). Henry Fielding "asserts that the story of the giant-killer—which he had heard as a child—was "finely calculated to sow the seeds of virtue in youth" (Lindahl, xv). In his notes to his collection of tales, Joseph Jacobs (1898) also points to earlier literary references to "Jack the Giant Killer' in Joseph Fielding's *Joseph Andrews* and to Perseus's "Invisible Helmet" from Greek mythology. The verse, "Fee-fi-fo-fum, I smell the bloud of an Englishman" has an older history as well; it occurs in *King Lear* (Shakespeare, ca. 1605). This formula, Jacobs maintains, is common to all English stories about ogres and giants (243). When Perrault's "Le Petit Poucet" was translated into English in 1724 as a chapbook, it included the famous bloodthirsty refrain of the giant of the Jack tales. This refrain was not part of the original French text (Warner, 313). Giants were definitely on the scene, but there was no "real" sign yet of the most famous giant fighter!

In North America

Joseph Sobol addresses Jack's adaptability in taking on the "protective coloration" from the various cultures in which he is found. Jack, Sobol reminds us, is "a universal type; yet, because of his broadness of definition he lends himself to localization, so that people in widely divergent settings could feel . . . that 'Jack was a boy, just like we were' " (1992, 15). The Jack tales from the Appalachian Mountain region demonstrate this best: "The Jack tales, perhaps better than any other collection of oral narratives, exemplify the universality of motifs and characters endemic to specific folk literature, while simultaneously maintaining a particular individuality contingent upon the localized cultural traditions and customs of different world folk cultures" (1997, 245).

Appalachian Jack's roots are in the British Isles and Germany. Jack (or Hans) has become a symbol of "the male principle in any of its lowly or earthy expressions" (Sobol, 16). Herbert Halbert, in his appendix to Richard Chases' collection *Jack Tales*, states that:

> It is not hard to interpret the very direct symbolism in the heroes people use in their tales and legends. We realize a little uncomfortably that in these tales as told in the Southern mountains

"Jack" is an ordinary poor boy who achieves success only in one of two ways: either by his wits, or by sheer luck—and the latter method predominates . . . Here we have an almost mocking contradiction of what has been called "the American fairy tale"—that honesty and hard work are the means to success. (186, 187)

Jack in Print

The literary history of "Jack and the Beanstalk" is traced back to the first appearance in print as a skit, "Story of Jack Spriggins and the Enchanted Bean," which was published in the tract *Round about Our Coal-Fire or Christmas Entertainments* in London by J. Roberts (1734) (211). The next publication of this story was more than 70 years later, in 1807, when it appeared twice: *The History of Mother Twaddle and the Marvelous Achievements of Her Son Jack* by B.A.T. and *The History of Jack and the Bean-Stalk, Printed from the Original Manuscript, Never Before Published* by Benjamin Tabart. Opie and Opie state that these two stories came from separate sources and that Tabart's tale is the source of all subsequent retellings, including that by Joseph Jacobs (1974, 212). Maria Tatar examines the "refinements" made to "The History of Jack and the Beanstalk" by George Cruickshank and other early retellers of tales. She states that Cruickshank felt there were elements in the tale that were not suitable for children and, in his version,

> rambled on about the evils of "idleness and ignorance " and introduced a fairy who tells a reformed Jack: "I have long wished to employ you in a difficult and important matter, but I could not trust you whilst you were so careless and idly disposed; but now, that you have this day shaken off that slothful habit, and have determined to be active, diligent, and trustworthy, I no longer hesitate." (1992, 18)

Tatar refers also to Benjamin Tabart's "moral" revisions to his version of the tale by having Jack "rightfully" regain his father's possessions that were previously stolen by the giant. In this tale, also, Jack becomes a reformed character "who is at the outset 'indolent, careless, and extravagant' " and is transformed "into a son who is both 'dutiful and obedient' " (1992, 198). Many of the elements in the 1807 version of "Jack and the Beanstalk," edited by the rationalist philosopher William Godwin, however, were ignored in subsequent retellings. These elements included the fairy who tells Jack about his father when Jack promises to do everything she tells him to do. According to this fairy, Jack's father, once rich, kind, and generous, was treated badly by the giant, who stole all his riches. The giant then murdered Jack's father and spared his mother's life as long as she never told anyone what had happened. The fairy had been Jack's father's guardian, but because of a transgression of fairy law, all her powers had been denied. (Why Jack's father would have to suffer for this transgression is not mentioned.) Her power had been restored on the day that Jack went to sell the cow, and it was her influence that set everything in motion. "Any damage he does to the Giant will be justified, for all his wealth was really Jack's" (Brewer 1980, 46). Marina Warner states that the Godwin-Tabart variant has the giant's wife telling Jack about the social wrongs that were committed against his family (321).

Joseph Jacobs published his versions of the two stories in 1898. In his notes to "Jack and the Beanstalk," Jacobs states that he first heard this version in Australia around 1860 and points out the differences between his version and that printed in a chapbook by E. S. Hartland, entitled *English Folk and Fairy Tales* (Camelot Series). The object of the meeting with the fairy "was to prevent the tale becoming an encouragement to theft! I have had greater confidence in my young friends, and have deleted the fairy who did not exist in the tale as told to me" (238). Jacobs's commentary on "Jack the Giant Killer" shows the previous literary roots of this tale. "From two chap-books at the British Museum (London, 1805, Paisley, 1814?). I have taken some hints from 'Felix Summerly's' (Sir Henry Cole's) version, 1845. From the latter part, I have removed the incident of the Giant dragging the lady along by her hair" (242). Jacobs points out various "problems" with the chapbook version, which he labels "a curious jumble" (242). The first part of the tale, involving the fleabite blows and the slit pouch, parallels that of the Brothers Grimms's "The Valiant Tailor" and "The Thankful Dead" episode, where Jack is helped by the soul of the person he helped bury, "is found as early as the *Cento novelle antiche*; and Straparola, xi, 2" (243). Warner comments that the early versions of the Jack stories at times strike "a chivalric, Arthurian note straight from medieval romance, as Jack performs acts of knight errantry, rescuing damsels and dispatching one ogre after another" (314).

John Newbery's *A Little Pretty Pocket Book*, published in 1744, included two letters to the reader from Jack the Giant-Killer. Newbery had reformed Jack considerably from his chapbook days and now had him championing "the importance of reading and obedience for children who wish to become happy and successful adults, rather than the virtues of robbing and killing giants" (O'Malley, 22). In the earlier chapbooks, Jack was recognized as a remarkable figure for his subversive trickster qualities and not for his obedience, kindness, or devotion to literacy, as Newbery portrayed him.

Laura Kready provides an early chronology of tales in England in *A Study of Fairy Tales* (1916). Among the chapbooks published by William Dicey and Cluer Dicey (1700–1800) is "The Pleasant and Delightful History of Jack and the Giants."

> Of Jack the Giant-Killer, in Skinner's Folk-Lore, David Masson has said: Our Jack the Giant-Killer is clearly the last modern transmutation of the old British legend, told in Geoffrey of Monmouth, of Corineus the Trojan, the companion of the Trojan Brutus when he first settled in Britain; which Corineus, being a very strong man, and particularly good-humored, is satisfied with being King of Cornwall, and killing out all the aboriginal giants there, leaving to Brutus all the rest of the island, and only stipulating that, whenever there is a particularly difficult giant in any part of Brutus' dominions, he shall be sent for to finish the fellow (Kready, 186).

Differences Between the European Jack and His North American Cousin

There has been more dialogue among folklorists and critics about the differences between the two Jack traditions than about the perceived meaning of the tales. Martha Wolfenstein claims that "in the English tale Jack uses the beanstalk to obtain presents for his mother; the American emphasis is more on masculine exhibition" (112). The gun and knife stolen by the American Jack represent symbols of masculine prowess rather than magical sources of wealth taken by the European Jack, but the third item, the coverlet from the giant's bed that is adorned with bells, is the equivalent of the harp. "Both may stand for the strange sounds which the child hears in the night and which he takes as signs of his father's sexual prowess" (Wolfenstein, 112).

> The protagonists of the European Jack tales are often characterized by naiveté and a general lack of intelligence, but the North American Jack is a self-reliant and cunning trickster figure. . . . The American Jack tales also maintain a certain disparity from their European cousins through the incorporation of traditions and customs endemic to the Appalachian region. Instead of stealing the giant's gold or the mythical hen that lays golden eggs in the European version, the Appalachian Jack steals the giant's rifle and knife, which is indicative of the importance of these "real" objects to the American storytellers. (Leeming, 245)

The Jack Tales, collected by Richard Chase and published in 1943, were the creation of a single family in North Carolina (Lindahl, xvii). Chase recognized the differences between the two types of Jacks, claiming that the American Jack was a "true American hero." "Our Appalachian giant-killer had acquired the easygoing, unpretentious rural American manners that make him so different from his English cousin, the cocksure, dashing young hero of the 'fairy tale'; Jack is the unassuming representative of a very large portion of the American people" (Lindahl, xxiii).

It is the American Jack's homelessness, isolation, and self-reliance that set him apart from his British counterpart. Two other important differences between the two Jacks are the use of magic and the identity of the donor. In the British variants, the magical elements aid the hero; in the American tales, the magic is used against the hero. The donor, or the character who aids Jack in his quest, is usually a magical being who rewards Jack for his kindness with a magic gift to help defeat the evil giant. In the American variants, however, the donor is usually a rich, landed man who, although not providing any magical aid, does provide Jack with food, money, weapons, and clothing (Lindahl, xxviii). The major difference, however, is that "the British tale celebrates the lower classes, the American tales celebrate Jack" (Lindahl, xxx).

Overview of Critical Interpretations of Jack's Tales

1894: The entry on "Jack and the Beanstalk" by E. Cobham Brewer in the *First Hypertext Edition of The Dictionary of Phrase and Fable*, states: "A nursery tale of German invention. The giant is All-Father, whose three treasures are (1) a harp—i.e. the wind; (2) bags full of treasures—i.e. the rain; and (3) the red hen which laid golden eggs—that is, the genial sun. Man avails himself of these treasures and becomes rich." In the entry for "Jack the Giant-Killer," Brewer refers to Yonge's interpretation that the tale is based on the Scandinavian tale of Thor and Loki, and to Masson, who maintains it to be "a nursery version of the feats of Corineus in Geoffrey of Monmouth's marvellous history," but maintains that neither interpretation is correct. He then states: "Military success depends (1) on an *invisible coat*, or secrecy, not letting the foe know your plans; (2) a *cap of wisdom*, or wise counsel; (3) *shoes of swiftness*, or attacking the foe before he is prepared; and (4) a *resistless sword*, or dauntless courage" (Brewer).

1948: Humphrey Humphreys discusses the symbolism and the actuality of the giant beanstalk in the tale of "Jack and the Beanstalk." Alan Dundes reprinted this article in 1965 to demonstrate the possible fallacies made by non-folklorists when analyzing folklore. The beanstalk, Dundes asserts, is not represented in the majority of the versions of this tale other than in Great Britain and North America.

1951: William Desmonde's article was also reprinted by Dundes in 1965. Desmonde, a Freudian psychoanalyst, offered his interpretation of "Jack and the Beanstalk" based on what Dundes asserts is probably a version of the tale from a children's anthology rather than the oral tradition and on "common assertions" that have may have no basis: "how does one demonstrate what Desmonde calls the 'fact' that beans are a common symbol for testicles?" (Desmonde 1965, 287).

1955: Martha Wolfenstein discusses differences between the British and the American versions of "Jack and the Beanstalk," concluding that "the English version, with its emphasis on giving and getting, its golden treasures and magical sources of supply, as well as the theme of a boy making things up to a mother whom he has made to suffer, has many more prephallic components than the American one" (113).

1972: Maureen Duffy contends that the giant symbolizes a fierce old father, a cannibal who devours his children so they will not supplant him. Jack must conquer the giant to displace him and destroy the giant's sexual monopoly (102).

1974: Julius Heuscher uses the example of "Jack and the Beanstalk" to demonstrate how gold can become more and more spiritual:

> Jack acquires a sack full of gold pieces but soon they are spent; a little longer are the benefits derived from the hen which lays the golden eggs; but Jack's ultimate victory over the giant occurs when he is able to bring down to earth the golden harp. The gold pieces represent the crude metal as having only a material value. In the beautifully shaped golden eggs, the metal alludes to the formative forces of life. However, both the full aliveness and the permanence of its value is established only when the gold is transformed into a musical instrument yielding marvelous tunes which can be repeated and varied forever. (242)

1976: Bruno Bettelheim focuses on the magic bean seeds and their miraculous growth. He states that children understand this growth as "a symbol of the miraculous power and of the satisfactions Jack's sexual development can bring about: the phallic phase is replacing the oral one; the beanstalk has replaced [the cow] Milky White" (190). Jack's adventures with the ogre are manifestations of Jack's struggles to overcome the phallic stage to mature and become an independent human being (190). The bag of gold symbolizes the resources Jack and his mother need, but these are not renewable resources and therefore Jack needs to obtain the hen that symbolizes the satisfaction of all physical needs. The aesthetic needs, art and beauty, are symbolized by the harp.

> As Jack gains full humanity by striving for and gaining what the harp represents, he is also forcefully made aware—through the ogre's nearly catching him—that if he continues to rely on magic solutions, he will end up destroyed . . . But in cutting down the beanstalk Jack not only frees himself from a view of the father as a destructive and devouring ogre; he also thus relinquishes his belief in the magic power of the phallus as the means for gaining him all the good things in life. (191–92)

Bettelheim also fastens on the failure of Jack's mother to help him develop his masculinity. She ridicules him for his foolish trade, not realizing or recognizing his transformation from child to adolescent. "This story teaches . . . that the parents' error is basically the lack of an appropriate and sensitive response to the various problems involved in a child's maturing personally, socially, and sexually" (193). Bettelheim decries the changes made in this tale to "provide moral justification" for Jack's deeds. These changes, Bettelheim maintains, rob the story of its deeper psychological meaning and destroy its poetic beauty. "The original . . . is the odyssey of a boy striving to gain independence from a mother who thinks little of him, and on his own achieving greatness" (1976, 193n).

1976: Francis Lee Utley, in the introduction to Max Luthi's book *Once Upon a Time: On the Nature of Fairy Tales*, states that Luthi insisted on the importance of national style in folk and fairy tales. The British and American versions of "Jack and the Beanstalk" are used to demonstrate this point. His mother beats him because of his foolish bargain while her substitute in the clouds, the ogre's wife, helps Jack win the three magic objects. "The English bag of gold, hen who lays the golden eggs, and singing harp becomes a rifle, a skinnin' knife, and a coverlet with bells. What would a Kentucky hillbilly be without his gun?" (Luthi 1976, 14–15)

1977: Michael Hearn discusses early attempts to censor "Jack the Giant Killer" in his introduction to the story in *Classics of Children's Literature*. In 1856, Samuel Griswold Goodrich protested these tales of horror, commonly put into the hands of youth, as if for the express purpose of reconciling them to vice and crime (Hearn, iv). Hearn also points to the bowdlerizing of the tales by Joseph Jacobs and Andrew Lang to make them conform to public opinion. Hearn continues to state that "little has changed since the eighteenth century. Children will read what they will, whether it be 'Jack the Giant Killer,' the violent modern Japanese comic book, or the American daily newspaper" (ix).

1977: Stith Thompson suggests that the reason for the theft of the giant's treasures is the primary difference in the various versions of the tale. Sometimes Jack is on a mission to help a friendly king or on a quest for a king on the recommendation of jealous rivals (38). Traditionally, to aid in his escape, the hero of the tale bluffs owning magic objects such as the cap of knowledge, an invincible sword, a cloak of invisibility, and seven-league boots from the giant (38).

1980: Derek Brewer asserts that "Jack and the Beanstalk" is a story about growing up, a story about a mother, a father, and a child. Selling the cow may represent the need of the child to leave the cozy maternal home; Jack's hiding places in the ogre's home represent the kitchen of the mother figure. Like Bettelheim, Brewer believes that the magic beans represent developing sexuality. The beanstalk is a phallic symbol "symbolic of the protagonist's developing sense of his own growing masculine power, his need to challenge and defeat the father. Chopping down the beanstalk then symbolizes a certain self-destructive, regressive urge" (49). On the other hand, the story may revolve around class distinctions: The wealthy (gold and hen) and cultured (harp) giant resides above the poverty stricken boy and his mother. This in fact may legitimize Jack's thefts. "As this form of the story seems to have evolved in the second half of the eighteenth century we may reasonably think of the virulence of class antagonism of the time, most evident in the French Revolution but noticeable in England also" (50). Brewer also addresses Godwin's 1807 revision of "Jack and the Beanstalk," stating that Godwin's literary rationalization "attempts to create a liberalistic imitation of the morality of the normal everyday world, whereas the story is concerned with psychic confrontations of a different kind, though the story's imagery is selected from the everyday world before being placed in fantasizing juxtapositions" (46).

1981: Bruno Bettelheim restates his theories on "Jack and the Beanstalk" as he discusses the role of the stopping of the life-giving milk and the fear of being weaned. It is the mother figure in the sky who helps Jack on his journey to independence and maturity, but by the end of the tale his own mother realizes his development.

> As the ogre pursues Jack down the beanstalk, he cries for his mother to cut it down. But she knows that doing this for Jack will not free him from seeking magic solutions to life's real problems. . . . So she hands him the ax with which he chops off the beanstalk, depriving himself of any further reliance on magic solutions to life's real problems at the dame time as he frees himself of those anxious fantasies of being devoured or otherwise destroyed which are the inescapable consequence of relying on others to provide one with what one needs for oneself. (1981, 18)

1984: Robert Darnton comments on the four false propositions in Bruno Bettelheim's interpretations of folktales: (1) that the tales are usually intended for children, (2) that the tales always must have a happy ending, (3) that they are "timeless," and (4) that the familiar North American version can be applied to any society. An example is: "I mean to take issue with the anachronistic and reductionistic use of Freudian ideas . . . Jack and the Beanstalk (an oedipal fantasy, although there is some confusion as to who is castrated, the father or the son, when Jack chops down the beanstalk)" (266, n.5). Darnton maintains that this Jack is obviously British and that the French giant killer belongs to another species. (43)

1984: Max Luthi considers the "fee fo fum" refrain to be connected to the awakening from the magical sleep of the trance. "From the aesthetic point of view it operates in the fairytale like a phase expected by the listener who indeed, in the times when fairytales were told among adults, was always an expert on the genre" (1984, 47).

1987: Nina Mikkelsen asserts that the American version of "Jack and the Beanstalk" ("Jack and the Beantree") is a tale of sexual initiation demonstrating the early stage of the child's sexual awakening. She contends that the Freudian implication assigned by Bettelheim cannot be ignored in this version either. The mother, through the use of ridicule, suppresses her son's aspirations to male sexuality. It is only through ascending to the giant's house that Jack obtains self-confidence and masculine power through the treasures he liberates from the giant (50).

1987: Maria Tatar refers to the plot of "Jack the Giant Killer" as stable but with ample room for variation. She states that because skillful storytellers can take the same tale and give it individual interpretation and color, the tone of the tale may change, as may the nature of the hero. She quotes Robert Darnton when comparing different national versions of this single tale type, concurring that one can register the changes from "English fantasy to French cunning and Italian burlesque" (1987, 103).

1989: Joyce Thomas looks at giants in her exploration of the stories of Jack. "All the Titans, the giants, trolls and ogres, are essentially the same character type, their respective nomenclature, like that of the Wee Folk, being culturally derived rather than used to distinguish crucial differences among them" (76). She introduces the Titans and Cronus from Greek mythology and the Norse myth of Ymir and discusses how their individual attributes and stories have become attributes of the more recent giants. In Cronus, for example, "one sees a violent, bloody, cannibalistic foe done in by another's deceptive cunning and his own appetites—here, appetites of cannibalism and violence" (77). The giant has come to represent the "dumb jock" of fairy tales: His massive size, in direct opposition to his feeble brain, is constantly contested with the small stature but colossal cunning of the human protagonists. "Many of the demarcations made between child protagonist and adult foe come into play, though now one can more easily identify with the adolescent hero because of his proven mental abilities" (79). In "Jack and the Beanstalk" Jack must face an ogre who, like Cronus and Polyphemus, is bloodthirsty and extremely dangerous. The ogre's "famous chant echoes independently of the tale, appearing in other tales as well; the versified statement perfectly conveys the essence of his nature and appetite" (80). The giant, Thomas claims, is the incarnation of excess, "ranging from brute strength and size to gluttony, cannibalism and the avaricious, pointless acquisition of material possessions" (82). Because the protagonist and the giant are of the same gender, Thomas suggests that the giant is the human's dark shadow, symbolizing irrational, instinctual, or life-denying forces that attack the hero. "In defeating his foe, the hero wins over his own 'giant' tendencies: the temptation to yield to brute strength and aggression, to unrestrained appetites in force, food or sexual activity which would negate his humanity" (83). His treasures, too, show a negative aspect of the giant. He hoards gold that he does not need or spend and he locks away artistic creations such as the harp from mankind. This gigantic hoarding and his size and stereotypical character represent an exaggerated portrayal of every antagonist's role (84).

1990: Alison Lurie states that "Jack the Giant Killer" teaches a lesson about how to deal with the "big, stupid, mean and ugly people" one will meet in life, and that this is a more useful lesson than any taught by video games. "Jack doesn't zap the giant with a laser gun, because in real life when you meet a bully or an armed mugger or a boss who wants to push you around you probably won't have a laser gun. What Jack does is to defeat the giant by using his intelligence and powers of invention" (25).

1991: Samuel Fohr discusses the spiritual symbolism in both stories of Jack's adventures. The pickax, which Jack uses to dispense one of the giants, is a symbol of the Divine Spirit; the fact that Jack forcefully places this ax in the giant's head denotes the growth of the Divine Spirit (71). The central focus in "Jack and the Beanstalk" is the turning from external interests to inner spiritual interests, as symbolized by the planting of the magic beans and the climbing of the resulting beanstalk. The gold exemplifies the sun, the goose (or hen) that lays the golden eggs represents the Spiritual Sun that is never depleted, and the harp is a symbol of creation. "Once one has 'climbed' the Divine Spirit and reached the Spiritual Sun, one no longer needs the 'ladder' and thus it can be 'cut down' or given up. In the end the spiritual journey takes us completely beyond the cosmos, World Spirit and all, to the realm of happiness 'ever after' " (74).

1992: Joseph Sobol identifies Jack with the culture hero or shaman figure of mythology as he moves "freely between natural and spiritual worlds, subduing evil, restoring harmony, and bring[s] back blessings to the community" (4).

1992: Maria Tatar points to the splitting of the father figure, in "Jack and the Beanstalk," into two separate beings: the dead father and the cannibalistic ogre. "This splitting, so customary in tales where events are orchestrated by women, is virtually unheard of in male-centered tales and puts 'Jack and the Beanstalk' in a class by itself when it comes to popular stories" (199). Tatar maintains that it is difficult not to recognize the double presence of incestuous desire (mother) and cannibalism (father) in the tale. "All this might seem far fetched were it not for the fact that incest and cannibalism are habitually linked to a precultural phase marked by the inability to differentiate. . . . Both Freud and Fenichel remarked on the connection between cannibalism and incest, which seemed to them, as cultural taboos, (not always explicitly) related" (1992, 199). This story of Jack, therefore, relates to the pre-oedipal dread of being devoured. Jack never transfers the heterosexual attachment to his mother to another female but manages to remain at home as a devoted son (199).

1997: Margery Hourihan considers "Jack and the Beanstalk" a typical example of a hero narrative. She states that because the tale is told from the hero's point of view, the reader is required "to approve, or at least condone, criminal and extremely selfish behaviour on the part of the hero" (39). Hourihan refers to the 1807 version of the tale by Talbert: "Jack not only steals the giant's possessions, he manipulates and deceives the giant's kindly wife, who several times saves his life, and finally he abandons her, perhaps to her death, when he cuts down the beanstalk" (40). She disagrees with Bettelheim's interpretation of the cutting down of the beanstalk as an act of freedom from his father. She maintains that although the tale certainly celebrates the emergence of youth over unjust authority, "the story also endorses both the highly questionable means by which Jack acquires the ogre's wealth and his exploitation of the ogre's wife. The ogre does, in part, represent fears which must be confronted, but the overarching significance of this tale is the celebration of Jack's entry into the patriarchy, his joyous achievement of dominance" (152).

1997: David Leeming's entry on "Jack and the Beanstalk" states that this is an important tale not only because of its widespread popularity but because of the many common motifs that it incorporates: the apparently foolish bargain, the giant plant that leads to another world, the outwitting of an enemy by hiding, and the theft of magic objects by the hero (243).

1998: Marina Warner explores the role of the ogre in fairy tales in general and in the Jack tales in particular. This is a male hero's tale in which the ogre's appetite tests the hero's strength and cunning in survival. When the boy gains control of the ogre's magic, he becomes rich and powerful. Thus, these tales are predominantly about social betterment rather than psychosexual anxieties (311). Warner differentiates between the two Jack tales: The beanstalk climber is a simpleton and a wastrel who makes good in spite of himself; the giant killer is filled with dark humor and his tale is much darker and full of viscerally explicit imagery (316). "The clodhopping character of fairy tale ogres and giants, their mighty tyranny and equally mighty fall clearly reflect wishful thinking about authority figures from fathers to kings" (319). Warner states that the popularity of these tales engages with the historical conditions at the time the stories were told.

1999: Ann Beneduce, in her notes to her picture book version of the tale, states that Jack's story is based on King Corineus of Cornwall. Geoffrey of Monmouth wrote about Corineus's courage and cleverness in ridding the countryside of giants. The oral accounts of Corineus's exploits evolved into an entire series of giant killer tales, of which "Jack and the Beanstalk" is the most popular and by far the most interesting variant of "Jack and the Giant-Killer" (32).

1999: Matt Kane, in his exploration of connections between "Jack and the Beanstalk" and lunar and solar significance, states that there is a secret within the tale, passed on for more than 10,000 years. This secret is the one that aids Jack in reaching the summer solstice. In his analysis of Jacobs's version, Kane expounds on the cow as a perfect metaphor for the moon. The bean's crescent shape is also reminiscent of the shape of the moon in one of its phases as well as representing the hopes of new beginnings at the New Year (162). The number of beans, five, is also significant because it represents, among other things, the number of days the sun seems to stand still during a solstice. To further convince his readers of the connections, Kane turns to the version of the tale edited by Mary Jane Goodwin, including the story of Jack's father, whose death is the death of the sun that brightens the upper world; the ogre represents the new moon that brought about the death through a solar eclipse (169). Other analogies drawn by Kane include the oven in which Jack hides as the lunar eclipse, the ogre exhibiting all the traits of a bear, the hen that lays the golden eggs representing the full moon and her eggs the gibbous moons that precede and follow her in the month, and the harp as a symbol of the moon.

1999: Brian Szumsky considers "Jack and the Beanstalk" a discourse on cultural and political socialization that is tied up in ideological and historical circumstance (11). He analyzes the two major nineteenth-century versions, the literary and overtly moral tale transcribed by Tabart and Godwin and Jacobs's ostensibly oral and secular version, in great detail. Jacobs's purpose was to create a hero who is not as lazy or dull as the other Jacks, one who is cunning and "an entrepreneur who takes a level-headed risk when he makes the deal, but one that is not without a measure of recourse due to the bean-man's verbal promise of refund if not satisfied" (18). Szumsky states that both transmitters edited their materials to make them culturally sanctioned tales and that, in Jacobs's version, the taking of the giant's treasures is legitimized in the context of a capitalistic-colonial mindset. "The colonial impulse implicit in the overthrow of the giant (both in Tabart and Jacobs) is legitimized in an implied moral binary of 'good-bad,' and pragmatized through a typically colonial construction of an 'us-them' dichotomy" (19).

> As a capitalist, then, Jack overcomes his disadvantage (size, power) through manipulation and opportunism (physical and verbal disguises). He destroys the giant not directly through physical power or prowess like David and Goliath, but by his greater wit or cunning. Significantly, he displays may of the same behaviors as the giant in the original transgressions—his misrepresentation of himself, his subsequent act of murder, and his co-opting of property. (1999, 26)

2000: Graham Anderson, in his discussion on ancient antecedents for fairy tales, comments that in the fragmentary beginning of the Sumerian text of *Bilgames* there is a description of the goddess Inanna's father's ship being caught up in a storm, which is similar to the first chapbook edition of "Jack and the Beanstalk." He states that this detail in Jack's story is often dismissed as a clumsy moralizing of the story to validate Jack's taking of the giant's treasures but that, in fact, the storm depriving Jack's father of his treasures and his life may be a very old part of the tale (187).

2000: Ruth Bottigheimer discusses the three groups of the "Jack and the Giant Killer" cycle of adventures: Jack defeating his foes physically using familiar tools of hunters (horn), farmers (spade), and miners (pick); outwitting the Welsh giants and then joining the Knights of the Round Table; and the constant attacks on giants in defense of country and king. "When Jack tales were rewritten for refined sensibilities later in the 18th and 19th centuries, the crudity of their gory killings disappeared, King Arthur faded away, Jack became an earthy Everyboy, and the Giant a geographically localized unlocalizable married oaf, reachable only by the magic bean that grew endlessly heavenward" (267). Thus the tale incorporated contemporary fairy tale elements of social rise through magical enrichment.

In her entry on "Fractured Fairy Tales," Bottigheimer (2000, 172) discusses the changes made to the Jack tales (see Table 2.1).

Table 2.1. Jack: Then and Now

Chapbooks (Jack the Giant Killer)	Modern (Jack and the Beanstalk)
Plucky hero kills a series of (usually cannibalistic) giants	Only one giant on the horizon
Enriches himself with their treasures	Jack's thievery is piecemeal: first the gold, then his hen, and finally his magical harp
Gorily detailed deaths: decapitations, disembowelments, transfixations	Arranged accident by falling down the beanstalk

Reworkings of Jack in Novel Form

Why, quoth Jack, I desire nothing but the old rusty Sword, Coat and Slippers, which are at your Bed's-head. Quoth the Giant thou shalt have them, and prithee keep them for my Sake, for they are Things of excellent Use. The coat will keep you invisible, the Cap will furnish you with Knowledge, the Sword cut in sunder whatever you strike, the Shoes are of extraordinary Swiftness; they may be Serviceable to you, and therefore take them with all my Heart. (Opie and Opie 1974, 71)

There are three reworkings in novel form of the Jack tales. The earliest one (two novels brought together in one volume) focuses on "Jack and the Giant Killer" and the other two on "Jack and the Beanstalk."

Jack of Kinrowan

1995. de Lint, Charles. **Jack of Kinrowan.** New York: TOR. [*Jack the Giant-Killer*, 1987; *Drink Down the Moon*, 1990, originally published by Ace Books].

"We'll be like that little tailor in the fairy tale—remember? 'Seven with one blow.' No! I'll be the valiant tailor. And you . . . you'll be Jack the Giant Killer" (de Lint, 60).

Jack the Giant-Killer, the first novel, was the 1988 Casper winner. This Canadian Science Fiction/Fantasy Award, now known as the Aurora Award, is awarded for the best work in Canada published in English in a given year.

In this urban fantasy, de Lint introduces an ordinary Jack, a young woman named Jacqueline Rowan, who lives in Canada's capital city. "De Lint's Ottawa is a magical place where ordinary people become heroes" (Ketterer, 119). Until her encounter with the fairy world, Jacky Rowan lived in the easily recognizable city but soon became familiar, perhaps too familiar, with the otherworldly aspects of the area. For those acquainted with Ottawa in the 1990s, many of the settings will be familiar. For fans of other de Lint stories, other Ottawa "landmarks," such as Tamson House, also will be easily spotted. "That is an old magic place—a doorway to the Otherworlds of the spirits who were here before we came" (de Lint, 38).

De Lint draws substantially on his knowledge of folklore, informing the reader about the role of a Jack. She was "the Jack, after all. She killed a giant, didn't she?" (134). This novel pays homage to the idea that Jack had come to mean "Everyman" in England as well as to the idea that Jack represents the trickster-hero in the traditional tales. "She's a Rowan and a Jack—haven't you said so yourself? What she doesn't win through pluck, she wins through luck. That was always the way with Jacks even in the old days" (149). "The Jacks were always pucks. They were the fools and the tricksters of Faerie, and knowing that, she knew Kerevan's true name was Jack as well" (209). Kerevan tells Jacky, "I'm a Jack, too, though my Jack days are gone now. Jack Gooseberry was the name then, and wasn't I the wild one?" (215). But at the same time, "I didn't trust you. . . . [I]t was too convenient—a Jack out of nowhere, willing to help, Kate Crackernuts at her side" (215). And Jacky's friend Kate Hazel is indeed by her side throughout her adventures. "Hazel—that's the Crackernut you know. A wise tree—not so lucky as the Rowan, to be sure, but sometimes clever thinking will take you farther than ever luck could. It's more dependable too" (76).

Jacky is a reluctant hero, thrown into her adventure after witnessing a terrifying spectacle of nine Harley Davidsons circling a young boy and moving in for the kill. She realizes several things simultaneously: There is a watcher in one of the houses, silent and hidden; the boy is not a boy at all but "a little man no taller than a child, with a tuft of white hair at his chin, and more spilling out from his red cap" (10); and the riders are not men at all, but empty shadows. When the bikes leave, the little man is damaged. Jacky runs to the house of the watcher, but it is now empty and deserted. The little man has disappeared as well, leaving behind his little red cap. It is the cap of knowledge given to Jack the Giant-Killer in the old tales. "It is because of the cap that you finally do *see*. We're around you all the time, Jacky Rowan. Though in a few years, it'll be only the Unseelie Court that walks the twilight shades of your world. Wear that cap long enough and you won't need it to *see* any more" (31). A second hob, Dunrobin Finn, stitches a spell into her jacket and her shoes, and like her namesake, the spell allows her to be invisible (24). With these weapons in hand and the aid of Kate, the watcher, or the wizard of Kinrowan, Arkan Garty, who greatly resembles another famous trickster, "good old Reynard," and Eilian Dunlogan, the swan man, Jacky challenges the giants in their keep and frees the Laird's daughter, who has been kept captive there. At the end of the novel, Jacky is given charge of the castle of the Kinrowan and its trust. "With the help of her best friend Kate (Crackernuts) Hazel and a swanlike prince, she demonstrates that force and violence are not necessary to overcome brutality if one has faith in the imagination" (Zipes 1994, 152).

The second novel, *Drink Down the Moon*, focuses on a different group in the fairy world. The first novel is acknowledged: "Last autumn there had been a struggle between the two Courts, a struggle the Seelie faerie won. The Wild Hunt had been freed from centuries of bondage, the Gruagagh of Kinrowan had given his Tower to a Jack, and the Unseelie Court was cast to the winds—many of them slain" (233). The musician Johnny Faw meets the half-sisters Jenna and Jemi Pook and, with the help of Jacky, Kate, and Finn from the first novel, brings about an uneasy resolution between the Unseelie and the Seelie Court once again. Charles de Lint made wide use of a variety of other elements and motifs of folklore as well. Some of the most prevalent are "The Wild Hunt" and the world of the Faerie as well as numerous literary references and references to popular culture.

Similarities Between the Novels and Folklore Sources

Katherine M. Briggs summarized the traditional tale "Jack the Giant-Killer" as a two-part story. Jack's adventure begins with the killing of the giant who was terrorizing the area around Cornwall. De Lint incorporates the battle between Jack and the Giant Galligantua, who lives in an enchanted castle and has captured the Duke's daughter and transformed her into a white hind. "The magistrates proclaimed that the Giant's treasure should be given as a reward to anyone who killed the giant. . . . Jack . . . dug a great pit outside the Giant's cave, covered it over with sticks and earth, and blew a loud blast on his horn" (329). Jacky in *Jack of Kinrowan* also destroys the giant with a horn, but this particular horn belonged to the Wild Hunt. The horn plays a significant role in de Lint's tale of power and personal achievement; Jacky must discover the location of the horn as well as control its power. "The sound of it was loud and fierce. At that first blast, the Court drew back from her—even the giants. She blew it again and again until its sound was all that filled the cavern—a wild, exulting sound that thrilled the blood in her veins, making it roar in her ears. She could feel its power fill her. The Hunt was coming. The Wild Hunt. And she was its mistress now" (de Lint, 208). The traditional Jack finds a verse on the castle gate directing him to blow the trumpet because it would cause the downfall of the giant. He blows the trumpet, and when he cuts off the giant's head, the transformed animals all regain their original form. Jack is rewarded with marriage to a Duke's daughter and given a large estate by the king (Briggs, 331).

In his review of *Jack of Kinrowan*, Gahan Wilson states that de Lint does "a thorough job of researching the actual legends of the world of Faerie and, what's more—and what is very rare, indeed—go[ing] out of his way to give open-handed credit to those scholars and researchers who spent so much time gathering all that useful information" (12). Kate is surprised at Arkan's knowledge of cars: "And they didn't have them when people were putting together fairy tales, either. Andrew Lang hadn't been much of a hot rodder and Perrault wasn't known for his skill in the Grand Prix" (de Lint, 119). De Lint also remains true to several of the "conventions" in the world of fairy tales: "It's always the youngest son—not the eldest or the middle, but the third, the youngest son, that wins through in the end. It's in all the stories" (de Lint, 132).

Related Tales

Three traditional folktales that are intertwined with the story of Jack in two of de Lint's novels are "Kate Crackernuts," "The Valiant Tailor," and "The Giant Who Has No Heart in His Body." Other folktales that are alluded to are "Elves and the Shoemaker" and "The Seven Swans."

"Kate Crackernuts"

"Kate Crackernuts" has not been designated as a tale type. The motif that most firmly identifies it is L145.1: Ugly sister helps pretty one. The two stories classified with this motif are "Tattercoats" and "Kate Crackernuts." The entry in *The Storyteller's Sourcebook* reads:

> Kate Crackernuts. Queen sends stepdaughter to hen wife. To eat nothing before coming. Third time she obeys and sheep's head jumps from pot onto her shoulders. Her stepsister Kate takes Ann in search of aid. Kate guards sleeping prince and follows when he rides out to fairy ball. She takes nuts from bushes and rolls them to fairy babies who drop silver wand which she realizes will cure her sister. On the second night she likewise gets magic bird to cure prince. She and sister wed prince and his brother. (MacDonald, 324)

In the novel *Kate Crackernuts*, by K. M. Briggs (Greenwillow, 1979), the author reworks the traditional tale into the drama of the seventeenth-century witch wars between the Scots and the English. "A wicked step-mother hires a witch to give her stepdaughter the head of a sheep . . . a psychological drama; the intensity of the rite of passage undergone by the protagonists can easily be understood as translating the fantasy elements into adolescent psychosis" (Clute and Grant, 140).

"The Valiant Tailor"

"The Valiant Tailor," Tale Type 1640, is described as "Seven with one stroke. While fleeing defeats the enemy. Kills wild-boar. Also incidents belonging to the stupid ogre and the clever man." Briggs entitles this tale "John Glaick, the Brave Tailor." John kills the giants through cunning and is rewarded with a royal bride. In time, this reluctant "Jack" is called by his father-in-law to quell an uprising and through perverse luck manages to frighten the enemy away. His giant-killing skills are never called upon again, and he lives "a long, happy, and good life as king" (Briggs, 342).

"The Giant Who Has No Heart in His Body"

Also known as "The Ogre's Heart in the Egg," this is Tale Type 302. Sometimes the ogre's heart in the egg stands alone from the rest of the tale. "The hero follows instructions, finds the ogre's soul hidden away, and kills the ogre by destroying the external soul" (1977, 93). De Lint refers to this tale in the second part of *Jack of Kinrowan* and gives the reader some help in identifying this particular tale. Jacky discovers that there are more than 260 versions of this tale. "Most of the versions she found were similar to the Scandinavian story. . . . In that one, the giant's heart was hidden far away from the giant's castle" (de Lint, 317). Two variants are also specified: "Kostchi the Deathless" from Russia and the Italian version from Calvino's collection of folktales, "The Body Without Soul" (de Lint, 317). See the Appendix for other reworkings of this tale.

Jackie and the Giant

1998. Jones, Linda. **Jackie and the Giant.** A Faerie Tale Romance. Wayne, PA: Dorchester Publishing.

In this historical romance, Jackie, a thief, is almost caught by the giant in her first attempt to break into the Cloudmont Estate to steal a Faberge egg on display in his bedroom. She takes instead a gold mouth harp that has been carelessly left on the display case. The giant of a man has a good sense of smell and is puzzled by the bouquet of lavender-scented water in his room. In her second attempt, Jackie falls down the vine that she had climbed to the second floor balcony and is apprehended. For some reason, the giant decides not to prosecute but instead brings her into his home, where she becomes close to his son. When Kevin, the son, makes a trade with a neighbor boy for magic beans, Jackie reassures him that they are indeed magic but instead of producing a beanstalk, they are good for three wishes. With the help of the magic beans, Kevin, his father, and Jackie become a family and "live happily ever after."

This is a quick read that ingeniously incorporates the elements of the tale. Other tales in the series retell "Bluebeard," "Cinderella," "Goldilocks," and "Little Red Riding Hood."

Crazy Jack

1999. Napoli, Donna Jo. **Crazy Jack**. New York: Delacorte.

Napoli begins her tale with Jack as a young boy, secure and happy on the family farm with his parents and with his close friend Flora living nearby, during the sixteenth century in England. Unfortunately for Jack and his family, Jack's father makes a wager and looses the fields. This causes great discontent in the family, and when Jack talks to his father about the pot of gold at the end of the rainbow, his father vows to retrieve it. Jack witnesses his father's ascent onto the cliffs and out of sight.

Having established the reason behind Jack's resulting crazy behavior, the story advances seven years and begins to incorporate the major elements from the traditional tale. Jack is forced to sell the cow and trades it for beans the colors of the rainbow. These beans have a history: They have been housed in the pockets of clothing that once belonged to Jack's father. It is the memory of his father that propels Jack into planting the beans at the foot of the cliff and climbing it when it grows. "In fleshing out the tale, Napoli gives individual humanity to the archetypal hero: Jack is driven up the cliff by the force of his love for both his father and Flora" (Adams, 81). Napoli also fleshes out the woman who lives with the giant. She left her husband only for the gifts the giant gave her and, because she has no loyalty to the giant, she is eager to aid Jack. She provides intriguing nuggets of information about Jack's father during Jack's three visits to the castle as well as encouraging him to take the hen, the pot of gold, and the lyre. These magic items become quite ordinary when they are brought down the beanstalk: The hen lays ordinary eggs but still on command; the gold becomes stones in the pot but they are perfect building material, and the pot provides a never-ending supply of them; and the lyre must be played to produce the beautiful tunes. The reader never finds out much about the giant himself.

Although the townspeople have labeled him crazy, Jack is very aware of what is happening most of the time. Although financially secure after his second trip up the beanstalk, Jack knows that Flora is about to marry another man because of his behavior. He reflects on his father's early comment about needs. "We needed three things: food on the table and a roof over our heads and each other. It's the third thing he forgot, the most important one" (Napoli, 113). It is this comprehension that spurs Jack's third climb. He takes with him an ax, thinking that he could kill the giant, but leaves it at the base of the beanstalk when he realizes that he cannot. This journey is treacherous, but the woman finds him again. Before he can help her get away, the giant returns. The novel follows the traditional denouement here, but following the pattern established by Napoli, upon impact with the ground the giant transforms into an ordinary male human body, mangled beyond recognition.

Jack returns home and, freed from his obsession with his father, is no longer considered crazy. He and Flora have all three things they need now!

This is a Jack who is easy to identify with and care about. Flora, too, is a sympathetic figure. And the giant? We are left to our own devices on that subject.

Short Stories

Only recently have these two tales been widely adopted (adapted) by writers of short stories.

1985. O'Driscoll, Elizabeth. **"Jack's Mother and the Beanstalk."** In *Rapunzel's Revenge*: *Fairytales for Feminists*. Dublin: Attic Press, 17–19.

When Jack returns home with the beans, it is his mother who climbs up the beanstalk the next morning. After a confrontation with the giant (which she wins), she realizes that he is a former client of hers when she was an investment consultant. He had run away with her money as well, so she figures out his net worth and her percentage of his assets. She also takes his hen and golden harp. She quickly descends the beanstalk and "womanfully" chops it down, then directs Jack to chop it into firewood as a further investment for their future.

1993. Kress, Nancy. **"Stalking Beans."** In *Snow White, Blood Red*, edited by Ellen Datlow and Terri Windling. New York: William Morrow, 90–104.

In this tale, Jack is older and married but certainly no wiser than his traditional counterpart. The story examines Jack's relationship with his wife and his mistress (the giant's wife) and his own failings. There is no happy ever after in this reworking of the tale. For more mature readers.

1994. Garner, James Finn. **"Jack and the Beanstalk."** In *Politically Correct Bedtime Stories*. New York: Macmillan, 67–71.

Jack trades the exploited cow for some magic beans that his mother throws out the window. When the beanstalk appears, Jack quickly climbs it and immediately makes off with one of the giant's treasures. However, the beanstalk has been uprooted before he could make his downward journey, so Jack remains in the giant's sky communing with the dozen or so other beanstalk climbers who have arrived through the ages. Tongue-in-cheek and ironic in tone.

1994. Hood, Daniel. **"The Wealth of Kingdoms (An Inflationary Tale)."** In *The Year's Best Fantasy and Horror, 7th Annual Collection*, edited by Ellen Datlow and Terri Windling. New York: St. Martin's Press, 365–68. First published in *Science Fiction Age* (November 1993).

Daniel Hood is the art director for an international financial affairs company. In this tale he offers a tongue-in-cheek parody of the microeconomic and macroeconomic issues arising from Jack's ascent into wealth through the golden eggs. This "oral presentation" also mentions the firm Grimm & Grimm, Never-Never Land, Oz, Wonderland, Charming Government, The Ministers of Straw, Wood and Brick, Rumpelstiltskin, Queen Snow White, Hansel and Gretel, Princess Cinderella, and Prime Minister Riding Hood.

1995. Galloway, Priscilla. **"Blood and Bone."** In *Truly Grim Tales*. Toronto: Lester, 16–35.

> One of the most ingenious of the stories is a retelling of "Jack and the Beanstalk" from the point of view of the ogre's wife. The tale gives a plausible explanation for why the ogress protects Jack from her husband, and the meaning behind the ogre's well-known chant of "Fee, fi, fo, fum." The tales are quite sophisticated . . . and their cleverness and the rather sardonic, even foreboding, tone may give older readers a new view of folktales. (*Horn Book* 1996, 78)

A chilling ending to this tale resonates long after it is finished.

1995. Vande Velde, Vivian. **"Jack."** In *Tales from the Brothers Grimm and the Sisters Weird*. San Diego: Harcourt Brace, 53–70.

Jack's journey into town to sell the cow ends with him drinking the proceeds of the sale in the pub. When he is tossed out into the street, he assumes that he has arrived at the land of the sky people (after all, he was lying flat on his back and looking up at the stars!). Effie feels sorry for him and tries to help. Jack has decided that she is a lady giant and cooperates with her as far as he can stumble. She is late coming home and a tad afraid of her father (who Jack has now decided is an ogre). From his hiding place in the kiln oven, Jack sees the treasure and decides to take it for himself. However, when he arrives home he finds that his adventure and his treasure just might be the result of too much beer. A parody of the traditional tale.

1996. Walker, Barbara G. **"Jill and the Beanroot."** In *Feminist Fairy Tales*. San Francisco: HarperSanFrancisco, 63–70.

"In this new story, Jill climbs down into darkness and conquers her own fears for the sake of her mother. White, red, and black, the colors of her beans, are also the traditional colors of the triple Goddess as Virgin, Mother and Crone" (63). This time the beans make a ladder into the Earth, which Jill descends. She meets a dwarf who gives her a tour of the area, including the gem garden. Jill steals one of the talking gems and manages to climb back home and chop down the beanstalk (closing the entry into the underworld). After having the gem cut, she lives happily and healthily with her mother. The gem never talks again, but it does listen.

1997. Jacobs, A. J. **"Jack and the Beanstalk."** In *Fractured Fairy Tales*. (As featured on Jay Ward's *The Adventures of Rocky and Bullwinkle and Friends*.) New York: Bantam, 163–68.

Jack becomes a baseball hero by using magic beans to aid the team to victory. During the final game of the season, when the Boston Beans play the Giants, Jack miscalculates and climbs the beanstalk while the Giants punt and win the series. Unfortunately, at the top of the beanstalk Jack meets another giant with a much different game on his agenda.

1998. Richerson, Carrie. **"Juanito, the Magic Beans, and the Giant."** *Realms of Fantasy* 4 (4) (April): 54–60, 83.

The setting of the traditional tale has been shifted to the Festival of Tlaxochi-maco and the time of Cortes. When Juanito and the narrator of the tale escape into the land of the giants, they find an ally who shares his treasures with them: "He brought out a magical quetzal bird, which laid eggs of solid gold . . . his magical pipes of bone. . . [and] his magical purse, full of gold coins" (1998, 60). It is in the realm of the giants that the oppressed people gather strength and strategy to descend the beanstalk and become victorious. A "historical" and "cultural" reworking of the traditional tale.

1999. Lindskold, Jane. **"The Beanstalk Incident."** In *Twice Upon a Time,* edited by Denise Little. New York: Daw Books, 67–93.

This is a courtroom drama about the reputation of a newly arrived aristocrat, Sir John Aurelion. The plaintiff, Mistress Cloudcroft, tells her story about the thefts and the death of her husband so eloquently that the judge has no option but to unmask Sir John as plain Jack. It is Jack's bad luck that his case is heard by a judge who loves a well-told story. Lindskold makes numerous allusions to other familiar folktale characters, including the Frog King and Reynard the Fox.

1999. Mayer, Gloria Gilbert, and Thomas Mayer. **"Jack and the Beanstalk."** In *Goldilocks on Management: 27 Revisionist Fairy Tales for Serious Managers.* New York: American Management Association, 15–20.

This is a truncated reworking of the traditional tale. By means of a beanstalk, Jack, a disadvantaged child, manages to obtain a goose that lays golden eggs. Unfortunately for Jack, due to a dispute over the property rights in the goose, the beanstalk is axed and Jack loses access to a newly established market. However, the initial transaction provides Jack and his mother with a substantial annuity.

Basic lesson: "Innovative solutions result from 'outside the box' thinking" (16). Bottom line: "The 'beanstalk effect' thrives only in the fertile environment of personal security arising from managerial tolerance" (19).

1999. Scarborough, Elizabeth Ann. **"Mrs. Myrtle Montegrande vs. The Vegetable Stalker/Slayer."** In *Twice Upon a Time,* edited by Denise Little. New York: Daw Books, 289–309.

Mrs. Jackson, the defendant's mother, takes the stand as a character witness to answer questions put to her by the counsel for the defense, a cat dressed in high leather boots. There are numerous charges against young Jack, who believes he was not stealing but taking back items that were illegally taken from his father in the first place. And how did he know this? Ms. Mab Golightly had informed him of this state of affairs when he first ascended the beanstalk. It is the court's decision that Ms. Golightly misled the young lad and, although he is found guilty of one count of giantslaughter, he is given a lighter sentence.

1999. Waggoner, Tim. **"The Castle and Jack."** In *Twice Upon a Time,* edited by Denise Little. New York: Daw Books, 198–203.

Imagine the fate of the poor castle as it awaits the return of its giant owner. It is particularly anxious because it knows that it made a major mistake when it did not detect the intrusion of the beanstalk and the tiny thief into the giant's realm. After realizing that its master will never return, the castle awaits its time to punish the thief. Decades pass and then Jack discovers the law of gravity. "What goes up . . ." (203).

2000. Cadnum, Michael. **"Mrs. Big: 'Jack and the Beanstalk' Retold."** In *A Wolf at the Door and Other Retold Fairy Tales,* edited by Ellen Datlow and Terri Windling, New York: Simon & Schuster Books for Young Readers, 35–43.

The giant's wife relates how she and her husband end up living in the clouds as the result of a trade with a peddler. Her husband is a gentle giant, struggling to create a poem that will satisfy the poetic background of his wife. On the fateful day of Jack's visit, the giant, enraged by possible danger to his wife, chases Jack to the beanstalk and falls to his death. The narrator does not plan to harm Jack or seek revenge on him, but watch out for that same peddler who sold Jack the magic beans.

Films and Stage Plays

1952. **Jack and the Beanstalk**. Directed by Jean Yarbrough and starring Bud Abbott and Lou Costello.

Costello plays Jack, an adult problem "child." "In the story of 'Jack and the Beanstalk,' which a child reads to him, Jack acts the part of the giant killer and imagines the power and social acceptance that he cannot achieve in reality. In the end, play and fantasy give way to the real world of adult authority" (Haase, 266).

1982. **The Faerie Tale Theatre: Jack and the Beanstalk**. Directed by Lamont Johnson and staring Dennis Christopher, Elliot Gould, and Jean Stapleton.

Dennis Christopher is Jack, the idealistic hero who trades his cow for the magic beans and has numerous encounters with the giant (Elliott Gould) and the giant's wife (Jean Stapleton) that are not quite the traditional fare. Suspense and comedy follow this Jack on his adventures.

1987. Sondheim, Stephen, and James Lapine. **Into the Woods.**

Although Jack is not the only fairy tale character in the musical comedy *Into the Woods,* he does play a major role. In the woods Jack, along with Cinderella, Snow White, Little Red Riding Hood, Rapunzel, and Sleeping Beauty, get their hearts' desire but with ominous effect.

The play begins with a plot among the baker, his wife, and the witch to break the spell of barrenness that had been cast upon the baker. The witch explains that the spell can be broken if they, in three days' time, secure the four ingredients she needs for a potion: "the cow as white as milk, the cape as red as blood, the hair as yellow as corn, and the slipper as pure as gold" (Flatow 2001). The baker decides to do this on his own, but before he sets off, he takes with him six beans that were in his father's jacket pocket. When he meets Jack, the fateful deal is made and all follows its due course (sort of). The second half of the play explores the subsequent intertwined lives under the threat of the giant's wife, who comes down a second beanstalk to avenge her husband's death and to offer the audience a chance to consider another point of view.

This musical is directed "at the point of Jane Yolen's *Briar Rose* when the heroine is about to plunge deeply into a transformative investigation of her family's past (and to fall in love)" (Clute and Grant, 503). The Broadway play won three Tony awards, including best music and lyrics, and five Drama Desk Awards. It also won the New York Drama Critics Circle for Best Musical of 1988.

The book of the same name, adapted and illustrated by Hudson Talbott (New York: Crown, 1988), was made after the fact from the Broadway musical. It weaves characters from several classic fairy tales into a parable about the joys and sorrows of adulthood. Information on the musical and its various tours can be found at stonehillmusical.homestead.com/itwinfo.html.

Poetry

These two tales have not seemed to attract much attention from poets.

1982. Hay, Sara Henderson. **"Story Hour."** In *Story Hour*. Fayetteville: University of Arkansas Press, 1.

Hay opens her collection of fairy tale poetry by bringing the reader's attention to the fact that we celebrate Jack's victory over the giant although it is Jack who is the thief and murderer. She connects the modern audience to that of the Brothers Grimm: "a round-eyed listener, with no foolish questions" (1).

1989. Roston, Ruth. **"Secretly."** In *The Year's Best Fantasy, 2nd Annual Collection,* edited by Ellen Datlow and Terri Windling. New York: St. Martin's Press, 87–88. First published in *Pandora* 19 (Spring 1988).

The poem focuses on Roston's fascination with giants and their reaction to the gutsy tailor and the boy with the slingshot. Most of the references are to "Jack and the Beanstalk."

Picture Books

Picture book reworkings have been widely available since Raymond Briggs first played with the tale in 1970.

1970. Briggs, Raymond. **Jim and the Beanstalk.** Illustrated by the author. New York: Coward, McCann & Geoghegan.

Jim discovers a beanstalk outside the window, climbs it, and knocks on the castle door hoping to get some cornflakes for breakfast. An elderly giant invites Jim inside and assures Jim that he will be perfectly safe because the giant no longer has any teeth to eat juicy little boys. The giant tells Jim about an earlier visit by a boy named Jack, who stole some of his father's treasures and his happiness as well. Jim decides to help the elderly giant to see better (by fetching a pair of glasses that have been made especially for the giant in the world below), to eat better (by fetching newly made false teeth), and to look better (by fetching a red wig). The giant feels so much better that he thinks he might be interested in eating fried boy again. Jim quickly descends the beanstalk and chops it down. The giant drops down a huge gold coin and a thank you note.

1986. Haley, Gail E. Jack and the Bean Tree. Illustrated by the author. New York: Crown.

Gail Haley's Appalachian version of "Jack and the Beanstalk" begins with a magic bean that is swallowed by the narrator. "All the colors of the bean went into my head, rooted, and turned into a Story Bean Tree. It's been growing there ever since. Every bean on that tree has a story inside." Haley's story follows the traditional format but has been retold with an oral "mountain" voice. The items taken by Jack are a magic tablecloth, the dancing hen that also lays golden eggs, and a harp. Although Jack does not feel any remorse for killing the giant, he does spare a few thoughts for the giant's wife. "He felt right sorry for Matilda and wondered how she was getting' on up in skyland—but that, children, is a story for another night."

1992. Scieszka, Jon. The Stinky Cheese Man and Other Fairly Stupid Tales. Illustrated by Lane Smith. New York: Viking.

Jack is the narrator of these nine intertwined and outrageously retold tales.

1993. Muir, Frank. Jack and the Beanstalk. Illustrated by Graham Philpot. London: Conran Octopus.

Frank Muir's Jack has a detailed history. His father was bespelled by a witch in a cooking accident. Jack was the school bully but too short to really be effective. Instead he used his bean shooter to great advantage. When Jack runs out of ammunition he willingly sells the cow for a chest full of beans. He climbs the beanstalk and meets the witch and the giant. Jack bites the giant on the nose and escapes down the beanstalk with the witch. As the giant lands on his head, all of the witch's spells are undone and she also disappears. The giant regains his shape as Jack's father and Jack is in tears because, whereas he could get away with anything with his mother, having his father around is another story. He plants another bean and quickly climbs out of sight, never to be seen again. However, years later, the first astronauts tell about a strange sighting and a number of small dents in their space ship that look as if they had been created by a bean shooter. A far-fetched reworking of the tale!

1995. DeSpain, Pleasant. Strongheart Jack & the Beanstalk. Illustrations by Joe Shlichta. Little Rock, AR: August House.

In his introduction, Despain explains the source of his version of the tale, which "includes the 'heart' of the tale, often omitted, involving the cruel history of the giant and Jack's family prior to the time the story begins." This Jack is a lazy Jack who has to be threatened by his mother to do anything at all. But when the beanstalk grows, Jack has no qualms about climbing it instantly. His mother gives him a silver sword to take with him, one that has been inscribed to his father, Sir Jerold. He is accompanied by Octavia, the village cat, who knows the history of Jack's family and how to get him past the obstacles at the top of the stalk. These obstacles include a warrior tribe of cacti, a riddling tortoise, and fierce guard dogs. Jack meets Elinor who, along with her younger brother, is kept captive by the giant. All of the action takes place on this one visit to the castle. Jack finds not only a fortune but a bride.

Although published under the "Little Folk" imprint, DeSpain's picture book can be used with students in junior high school. The illustrations have a dark and timeless tone that is appealing to older readers.

1999. Beneduce, Ann Keay. Jack and the Beanstalk. Illustrated by Gennady Spirin. New York: Philomel.

In this tale that is very close to an early variant, Beneduce establishes Jack's curious nature in the first paragraph, which also provides the motivation for Jack's repeated visits to the giant's home. This reworking includes the fairy and her telling of the family history once Jack arrives at the top of the beanstalk. It was her magic that caused the beans to grow so that Jack could avenge his father. The author's note informs the reader that this version is based primarily on an 1881 version that incorporates the idea of duty as the motivation for Jack's actions rather than greed. This Jack is also very clever, considering that at the beginning of the story his mother considers him too young to get a job. After his first adventure, which gains him his father's lost fortune, Jack disguises himself as a blacksmith's apprentice and then a tinker's helper.

The illustrations firmly set the tale in Elizabethan England. Spirin "takes full advantage of history to explore fanciful costuming, ornate border designs, and architectural motifs in the intricate watercolor imaginings of his fairy-tale countryside" (Del Negro 1999).

1999. Walker, Richard, and Niamh Sharkey. Jack and the Beanstalk. New York: Barefoot Books.

In this marriage between the energetic "oral" text and the eclectic and fantastic illustrations, Walker and Sharkey have produced a reworking that shouts a frolicking tale. This Jack manages to take the three items from the giant on the same evening, with additional help from his mother at the bottom of the stalk. He uses a rope as a catapult to toss the giant into space, where he may still be today.

2000. Osborne, Mary Pope. **Kate and the Beanstalk.** Illustrated by Giselle Potter. New York: Atheneum Books for Young Readers.

Kate is entrusted with the selling of the cow so she and her mother can survive, but she trades it without thought for magic beans. Like Jack, Kate climbs the magic beanstalk and finds a castle in the clouds. She meets an older woman, who explains that the castle's former owner was a noble knight who was killed by a giant who left the nobleman's young wife and child homeless. The woman asks Kate to recover the three treasures and give them to the rightful owners. Kate agrees and continues to the castle, where she meets a giantess who hires her to work in the kitchen. When the giant arrives, Kate hides and watches him and the hen that lays a golden egg. The giant falls asleep after his meal, and Kate immediately takes the hen, descends the beanstalk, and hides the hen to give to the widow and child when she finds them. She then disguises herself, climbs up the beanstalk, and is hired by the giantess again. This time, Kate removes a bag of money and hides it along with the hen. She disguises herself again and repeats her adventure, but this time the harp calls out to the giant, who gives chase. When Kate chops down the beanstalk and the giant is killed, her mother recognizes him as the foe who defeated her husband. Kate realizes that the treasures she has rescued are her own family property and that the peddler and the old lady are in fact a fairy who was testing Kate to see if she was worthy of her inheritance. Kate and her mother are taken up to the castle, hire the giantess as cook, and live a happy and contented life.

The illustrations are whimsical and dark enough to satisfy young adult readers.

Graphic Novels

There is only one version in comic book format at this point in time, but what a find! Caldecott-award winning illustrator David Macaulay illustrates this tale for his first foray into the world of comics.

2000. Macaulay. David. **"Jack and His Mom and the Beanstalk."** In *Little Lit: Folklore & Fairy Tale Funnies,* edited by Art Spiegelman and Françoise Mouly. New York: Joanna Cotler, 50–53.

Set in contemporary times, in this story Jack plants the magic beanstalk himself and climbs it to discover a castle, a "sizable" woman, and the truth behind the wicked giant's wealth. When this giant falls, he crushes Jack's house. He and his mother reclaim their inheritance just in time for lunch. Lucky for Jack and his mother, the sizable lady made fresh beanstalk! A fun version, if not exactly innovative.

Internet Resources

The 1898 version of "Jack the Giant Killer," by Joseph Jacobs, complete with illustrations and a brief commentary, can be found at http://www.gandolf.com under "Cornish Giants."

1997. **"The Jack and the Beanstalk and Jack the Giant-Killer Project, University of Southern Mississippi,"** http://www-dept.usm.edu/~engdept /jack/jackhome.html.

This is a text and image archive containing several English-language versions of the tales representing some of the more common varieties of the tale during the eighteenth, nineteenth, and early twentieth centuries. It follows the same format as the "Cinderella Project" and the "Little Red Riding Hood Project" but does contain three unusual items for educators: an uncut, 16-page penny book, a journey up the beanstalk that explains how books were made in the early nineteenth century, and an 1860s board game based on "Jack and the Beanstalk."

1999. **"The Jack and the Beanstalk Main Page, " SurLaLune Fairy Tale Pages,** http://members.aol.com/servsystem/frytales/jack/index.htm.

Web site author Heidi Anne Heiner provides the articles "The History of Jack and the Beanstalk," "The Annotated Jack and the Beanstalk," "Tales Similar to Jack and the Beanstalk," "Jack and the Beanstalk Themes in the Arts," "Jack and the Beanstalk Illustrations," "Jack and the Beanstalk Annotations," and a bibliography. A very useful site.

Classroom Extensions

The following suggestions may be adapted for use with other tales.

"Fee Fo Fum"

In her note, "About the Story" in her picture book, Beneduce comments that "Shakespeare, who would have read Geoffrey's account, has a character refer to the tale in *King Lear* (3.4). By Shakespeare's day it was well known throughout England, Scotland and Ireland." Why did Shakespeare use this allusion? Discuss.

Mary Shelley and Jack

Marina Warner, in *No Go the Bogeyman*, discusses William Godwin's version of the tale. She also discusses Godwin's daughter Mary, who later became Mary Shelley, the creator of Frankenstein. Do you think that Godwin's preoccupation with his vision of the ogre and the downfall of cruel giants and tyranny overthrown has a parallel in his daughter's famous work? Discuss.

Novel Study: *Jack of Kinrowan*

Darkness and Light

Jack of Kinrowan (de Lint 1995) focuses on the battle between good and evil in the world of fairy. This battle is heightened further by the fact that it is taking place in the New World.

The time of darkness has come to our world—to Faerie. They moved here from the crowded moors and highlands to their old homeland when the mortals came to the open land. But the Host followed too and here, here the Unseelie Court grows stronger than ever before. Would you know why? Because your kind will always believe in evil before it believes in good. There are so many of you in this land, so many feeding the darkness . . . the time for the Seelie Court can almost be measured in days now. (de Lint, 182–83)

What other novels can you think of that deal with the battle between the dark and the light in such a manner? What are the Seelie and UnSeelie Court? Several of Charles de Lint's other novels also deal with the immigration of the Old World Faeries and the resulting interaction with the Native Spirit World. What do you conclude from these works?

Fairy Tale Collections

"Jacky had never been one for fairy tale collections when she was young, but since the events of last summer, she'd taken to collecting them with a vengeance" (de Lint, 316). What fairy tales would help in the battle between light and darkness? What fairy lore would be helpful to know? De Lint addresses the well-known aversion to iron by stating that "Faerie that dwell in the city have become acclimatized to the sting of iron over the years—though they give up something in exchange for that immunity. Their life spans are shortened and they are no longer as hardy" (113). Some valuable advice includes: "Running water slows them—they can't cross it easily. And if they're chasing you, turn your coat inside out and you'll lose them for a time" (113). When Jemi offers Johnny a drink in the fairy world, she assures him: "Don't worry. It's just some beer that Jenna brews. It won't keep you for a hundred years or anything—that's just in the stories" (281). Is it?

Images of Giants

Charles de Lint uses many references to folklore and mythology in his re-working of the Jack tales. Discuss the following quote about the giant:

Gyre the Elder, greasy-haired, with a nose almost as big as the rest of his face. A hunch back that rose up behind his head. Hands, each the size of a kitchen tabletop. Chin and nose festooned with warts, some almost four inches long. If she had been at home and run across this creature in a picture book, she would have laughed. As it was, her legs gave way and she fell to her knees on the hard rock ground. (de Lint, 168–69)

What are the most frequent descriptors used when referring to giants? Are they used consistently? How do these descriptors form our perceptions of these folklore characters?

Jack the Trickster

What contemporary trickster can be compared to the traditional Jack? What is the trickster's role in our society? Has its role changed in the last few centuries? Discuss.

Popular Culture References in *Jack of Kinrowan*

Charles de Lint refers to various aspects of popular culture when telling his story of Jack. The movies referred to include *The Last Gangster,* with Edward G. Robinson (13) and *Ghostbusters,* with Bill Murray (205). De Lint uses the phrase "Beam Me Up Scotty" from *Star Trek* and refers to author Stephen King (55) and recording artists Alice Cooper (102), the Eurythmics (254), Kate Bush (471), and Ian Tamblyn (473). Do these, and other popular culture references, add anything to the understanding of the story he is telling?

Recommended Folklore Books

The following titles and authors were recommended by de Lint as part of his story:

Ronald Douglas, *Scottish Lore and Folklore* (1982)

Alan Garner, *The Guizer* (1975)

Katharine Briggs, *The Folklore of the Cotswolds* (1974)

E. Estyn Evans, *Irish Folk Ways* (1957)

Robert Graves, *The White Goddess* (1948)

Ernest Baughman, *Type and Motif: Index of the Folktales of England and North America* (1966)

Gwyn Jones, *Scandinavian Legends and Folktales* (1974)

books by Stith Thompson, Jane Yolen, and William Mayne

Beatrice de Regniers, *The Giant Book* (1966)

Peter Asbjørnsen and E. Moe Jorgen, *East of the Sun and West of the Moon and Other Tales* (1963)

Also mentioned are Oscar Wilde, William Dunthorn, and Rudyard Kipling's *Pook of Puxill.*

Would knowledge of these works help the reader in understanding de Lint's story? Does the reader need to be well versed in folklore to understand and appreciate de Lint's "Jack" stories? Why or why not?

"Wild Hunt"

The first book of *Jack of Kinrowan* focuses in part on the aspect of the Wild Hunt. These ghostly hunters who ride through the sky on stormy evenings are known in nearly all parts of the world. They are supposedly ghosts of the restless dead, and their appearance presages evil for the community in which they appear. Research the Wild Hunt and compare de Lint's modern riders to the traditional ones. A young adult novel that focuses on these riders is Jane Yolen's *The Wild Hunt* (Illustrated by Francisco Mora; published by Harcourt & Brace, 1995).

References

Adams, Lauren. 2000. Review of *Crazy Jack. Horn Book* 77(1) (January/February): 80–81.

Anderson, Graham. 2000. *Fairytale in the Ancient World*. New York: Routledge.

Beneduce, Ann Keay. 1999. *Jack and the Beanstalk*. Illustrated by Gennady Spirin. New York: Philomel.

Bettelheim, Bruno. 1976. *The Uses of Enchantment: The Meaning and Importance of Fairy Tales*. New York: Alfred A. Knopf.

———. 1981. "Fairy Tales as a Way of Knowing." In *Fairy Tales as Ways of Knowing: Essays on Märchen in Psychology, Society and Literature*, edited by Michael M. Metzger and Katharina Mommsen. Bern: Peter Lang, 11–20.

Bottigheimer, Ruth. 2000. "Jack Tales." In *The Oxford Companion to Fairy Tales: The Western Fairy Tale Tradition from Medieval to Modern*, edited by Jack Zipes. Oxford: Oxford University Press, 266–68.

Brewer, Derek. 1980. *Symbolic Stories: Traditional Narratives of the Family Drama in English Literature*. Totowa, NJ: Rowman & Littlefield.

Brewer, E. Cobham. [1894]. *First Hypertext Edition of The Dictionary of Phase and Fable*, http://www.bibliomania.com/Reference/PhaseAndFable/data/671.html#Jack.

Briggs, Katharine M. 1970–1971. *A Dictionary of British Folk-Tales in the English Language*. 4 vols. London: Routledge & Kegan Paul.

Chase, Richard, ed. 1943. *The Jack Tales*. Boston: Houghton Mifflin.

Clute, John, and John Grant, eds. 1997. *The Encyclopedia of Fantasy*. London: Orbit.

Darnton, Robert. 1984. *The Great Cat Massacre and Other Episodes in French Cultural History*. New York: Basic Books.

Del Negro, Janice M. 1999, December 1. "The Big Picture." *The Bulletin of the Center for Children's Books*, www.lis.uiuc.edu/puboff/bccb/1299big.html.

Desmonde, William H. 1965. "Jack and the Beanstalk." In *The Study of Folklore*, edited by Alan Dundes. Englewood Cliffs, NJ: Prentice-Hall, 1965, 107–9. [1951. Reprinted from *American Imago* 8: 287–88].

Duffy, Maureen. 1972. *The Erotic World of Fairy.* New York: Avon.

Flatow, Sheryl. 2001. "Synopsis of *Into the Woods,*" stonehillmusical.homestead
.com/itwinfo.html.

Fohr, Samuel Denis. 1991. *Cinderella's Gold Slipper: Spiritual Symbolism in the Grimms' Tales.* Wheaton, IL: Quest Books.

Haase, Donald. 2000. "Jack and the Beanstalk: The Film Version." In *The Oxford Companion to Fairy Tales: The Western Fairy Tale Tradition from Medieval to Modern,* edited by Jack Zipes. Oxford: Oxford University Press, 266.

Halbert, Herbert. 1943. "Appendix." In *The Jack Tales,* edited by Richard Chase. Boston: Houghton Mifflin, 183–200.

Hearn, Michael Patrick. 1977. "Preface." In *Classics of Children's Literature, 1621–1932. A Collection of 117 Titles Reprinted in Photo-Facsimile in 73 Volumes.* Selected and arranged by Alison Lurie and Justin G. Schiller. New York: Garland, iii–ix.

Heuscher, Julius E. 1974. *A Psychiatric Study of Myths and Fairy Tales: Their Origin, Meaning and Usefulness.* 2d edition. Springfield: Charles C. Thomas.

Horn Book. 1996. Review of *Truly Grimm Tales* 72(1) (January–February): 78.

Hourihan, Margery. 1997. *Deconstructing the Hero: Literary Theory and Children's Literature.* London: Routledge.

Humphreys, Humphrey. 1965. "Jack and the Beanstalk." In *The Study of Folklore,* edited by Alan Dundes. Englewood Cliffs, NJ: Prentice-Hall, 103–6. [1948. Reprinted from *Antiquity* 22: 36–38].

Jacobs, Joseph. 1898. *English Fairy Tales.* New York: Schocken Books. 1967. [Reprinted by Dover].

Kane, Matt. 1999. *Heavens Unearthed in Nursery Rhymes and Fairy Tales.* Altoona, PA: Golden Eggs Books.

Ketterer, David. 1992. *Canadian Science Fiction and Fantasy.* Bloomington: Indiana University Press.

Kready, Laura F. 1916. *A Study of Fairy Tales.* Boston: Houghton Mifflin.

Leach, Maria, ed. 1949. *Funk & Wagnalls Standard Dictionary of Folklore, Mythology, and Legend.* New York: Funk & Wagnalls.

Leeming, David Adams, ed. 1997. *Storytelling Encyclopedia: Historical, Cultural, and Multiethnic Approaches to Oral Traditions Around the World.* Phoenix: Oryx Press.

Lindahl, Carl. 1994. "Introduction. Jacks: The Name, The Tales, The American Traditions." In *Jack in Two Worlds: Contemporary North American Tales and Their Tellers,* edited by William Bernard McCarthy. Publications of the American Folklore Society. New series. Chapel Hill: University of North Carolina Press, xiii–xxxiv.

Lurie, Alison. 1990. *Don't Tell the Grown-Ups: Why Kids Love the Books They Do*. New York: Avon.

Luthi, Max. 1976. *Once upon a Time: On the Nature of Fairy Tales*. Bloomington: Indiana University Press.

———. 1984. *The Fairytale as Art Form and Portrait of Man*. Bloomington: Indiana University.

MacDonald, Margaret Read. 1982. *The Storyteller's Sourcebook: A Subject, Title, and Motif Index to Folklore Collections for Children*. Detroit: Gale.

Mikkelsen, Nina. 1987. "Richard Chase's *Jack Tales*: A Trickster in the New World." In *Touchstones: Reflections on the Best in Children's Literature, Volume 2*, edited by Perry Nodelman. West Lafayette, IN: Children's Literature Association, 40–55.

Nicolaisen, W. F. H. 1978. "English Jack and American Jack." *Midwestern Journal of Language and Folklore* IV (Spring): 27–36.

O'Malley, Andrew. 2000. "The Coach and Six: Chapbook Residue in Late Eighteenth-Century Children's Literature." *The Lion and the Unicorn* 24(1): 18–44.

Opie, Iona, and Peter Opie. 1974. *The Classic Fairy Tales*. New York: Oxford University Press.

Sobol, Joseph Daniel. 1992. "Introduction: The Jack Tales Coming From Afar." In *Southern Jack Tales*, by Donald Davis. Little Rock, AR: August House, 11–23.

Szumsky, Brian E. 1999. "The House that Jack Built: Empire and Ideology in Nineteenth Century British Versions of "Jack and the Beanstalk." *Marvels & Tales* 13(1): 11–30.

Tatar, Maria. 1987. *The Hard Facts of the Grimms' Fairy Tales*. Princeton, NJ: Princeton University Press.

———. 1992. *Off With Their Heads! Fairytales and the Culture of Childhood*. Princeton, NJ: Princeton University Press.

Thomas, Joyce. 1989. *Inside the Wolf's Belly: Aspects of the Fairy Tale*. Sheffield, England: Sheffield Academic Press.

Thompson, Stith. 1961. *The Types of the Folktale: A Classification and Bibliography. Antti Aarne's Verzeichnis der Märchentypen*, translated and enlarged by Stith Thompson. 2d revision. FF Communications, no. 184. Helsinki: Suomalainen Tiedeakatemia.

———. 1977. *The Folktale*. Berkeley: University of California Press.

Warner, Marina. 1998. *No Go the Bogeyman: Scaring, Lulling and Making Mock*. London: Chatto & Windus.

Wilson, Gahan. 1999. "Everything Old Is New Again: The Return of the Lord (Dunsany)." *Realms of Fantasy* (December): 10–16.

Wolfenstein, Martha. 1965. "Jack and the Beanstalk: An American Version." In *The Study of Folklore,* edited by Alan Dundes. Englewood Cliffs, NJ: Prentice-Hall, 110–13. [1955. Reprinted from *Childhood in Contemporary Cultures,* edited by Margaret Mead and Martha Wolfenstein. Chiacgo: University of Chicago Press].

Zipes, Jack. 1994. *Fairy Tale as Myth, Myth as Fairy Tale,* The Thomas D. Clark Lectures: 1993. Lexington: The University Press of Kentucky.

CHAPTER **3**

TWO BALLADS:
TAM LIN AND
THOMAS THE RHYMER

She rambled through memory as you would wander from room to room in an old house you once lived in, filling it with stories: This happened here, and this here. Maybe they did, and maybe you only wished they had; wishes blur so easily into truth. (McKillip 1996, 65)

Evelyn Wells defines the traditional ballad as "a song that tells a story in simple verse and to a simple tune. It is the product of no one time or person . . . . [I]ts medium is word of mouth rather than print" (5). Like a folktale, each successive singer makes the song (and story) his or her own, and there is no authoritative version. The Scottish ballads have long made their mark on published retellings as many writers, notably Robert Burns and Sir Walter Scott, have not only drawn inspiration from them but have aided in their preservation (Lyle 1994, 9). Terri Windling, in her discussion on fairy ballads, states: " 'Tam Lin' has captured the imagination of more fantasy authors and artists than any other single ballad, perhaps because of its sensual theme and unusual hero: an independent, courageous stubborn young woman, pregnant with her woodland lover's child, determined to save him from the Faery Queen and the unearthly Faery Court" (Windling 1994). Because of the many connections between these two Scottish border ballads, this chapter focuses on both. An interesting component is a look at the number of full-length novel interpretations of Tam Lin in comparison to the novels based on any of the other folktales discussed in this book. It is also intriguing to compare the relatively small number of poetic or short story reworkings of the ballads with these other folktales.

87

"Tam Lin"

The story of "Tam Lin" supposedly took place at Carterhaugh, just outside the town of Selkirk, Scotland, where the Ettrick and Yarrow Rivers meet. Carterhaugh refers to the flat land next to the river belonging to a family named Carter or where the local carters used to meet. The word "haugh" means a piece of flat land next to a river. The following synopsis is based on Robert Burns's version of the ballad, published in 1792.

❧ ───

Young Janet has been warned, along with all the other young ladies in the area, not to go into the woods of Carterhaugh. It is rumored that a forfeit would have to be paid to an elfin man who patrols the area. This forfeit could be their rings, cloaks or maidenhead. Headstrong and adventuresome, Janet pays the warning no heed and picks some roses at the well within the woods. A young man appears and questions her about her actions, both picking the roses and appearing in the woods without permission. Janet informs the young man that the property belongs to her and that she has to answer to no one. During the course of the afternoon, Janet and the young man do much more than talk. When Janet's father discovers that she is pregnant, he demands the name of the child's father and makes plans to marry her off. She refuses to name anyone but returns to Carterhaugh to confront her lover. When she plucks the roses at the well, the elfin knight stands before her and demands to know what she is planning to do about their child. Janet, too, has some demands. She wishes to know more about her lover's history. Tam Lin explains how, when one day riding on his grandfather's land (his grandfather is the earl of Roxburgh), he fell from his horse and was caught by the queen of the fairies, who took him "in yon green hill to dwell." It has been a pleasant stay, but Tam Lin now fears that it is his turn to be the sacrifice, the teind to Hell, the fairy folk pay every seven years. This payment is to be made this very night on All Hallows' Eve. When Janet asks Tam Lin if she can help him, he tells her how she must make her way to Miles Cross at the midnight hour to watch the fairy ride. Janet is to pull him down off his horse and hold him fast and fear him not regardless of what happens next. Tam Lin tells Janet that he will be recognizable on his milk-white horse because his right hand will be gloved while his left hand will be bare, and that his hair will be down and his hat up.

Janet agrees to help Tam Lin and makes her way through the darkness of night and forest to the crossing in time to see the fairy procession make its way from their world through hers. She pulls Tam Lin off the horse and holds him through his many transformations: an esk (lizard), adder, bear, lion, hot iron bar, and burning gleed, which she quickly throws into the well. Tam Lin emerges in his human form and she wraps her green cloak over the naked young man and leads him home. Before they get clear away, however, the queen of the fairies shouts curses on both Janet and Tam Lin, stating that if she had known Tam Lin would escape with the help of a mortal lover she would have taken out his two gray eyes and replaced them with wood. But Janet has won and Tam Lin is free to marry her and help raise their child.

In Sir Walter Scott's rendition of "Tam Lin," the queen speaks of the image of a heart of stone to replace his heart of flesh rather than of eyes of wood.

"Thomas the Rhymer"

Just outside the town of Melrose in Scotland, under the shade of the Eildon Hills, stands a monument commemorating the location of the infamous Eildon Tree from this ballad. In the town of Earlston (Ercildoune), a tower still stands that is said to have belonged to Thomas the Rhymer. It is from this house that he left this world again to go to his fairy queen when summoned by her message of a white stag and a white hind walking through the streets of the town and past his tower. Thomas is said to have left his home and friends and returned to the Eildon tree, where he vanished forever. These locations and that of Carterhaugh are said to be within a 25-mile radius of each other.

🍂 _____

While resting on Huntlie bank, Thomas sees a fair lady by the Eildon tree. She is wearing green silk and her horse's mane sports 59 bells. He comments on her beauty, stating that she must be the queen of heaven. No, she answers, but I am the queen of elfland and have come to see you. She dares him to kiss her, warning him that if he does so he will belong to her and will serve her for seven years. A small price to pay for such a kiss, thinks Thomas, and he kisses her soundly. The fairy queen and Thomas mount her milk-white horse and go swiftly to a wide desert where the living land has been left far behind. Here she shows Thomas three "ferlies" (miracles): three roads or passages. The first is a narrow road, beset with thorns and briers. This is the path of righteousness that few look for. The second road is twisted, a path of wickedness, which the queen explains some call the road to heaven, and the third road is bonny. It is filled with beauty and leads to the land of the fairy. Thomas chooses this road and the queen tells him that while he resides within her boundaries, he is not to speak or he will forfeit his chance to return to his own time. He agrees and they resume their ride through large bodies of water. Upon arrival, the fairy queen offers Thomas an apple and a tongue that can never lie once he can resume speaking. Thomas cannot refuse her gifts, and for seven years he is not heard from again.

_____

Thomas of Ercildoune, or Thomas the Rhymer, was well known in Scottish history for his prophesies, which he recorded in rhyme, as did Nostradamus centuries later.

Categories

Margaret Read MacDonald and Katherine M. Briggs discuss the ballad "Tam Lin" in view of tale type numbers. However, both ballads are better known through the numbers assigned to them by Francis James Child in his collection of English and Scottish ballads.

Tale Type Numbers and Motifs

The entry in Margaret Read MacDonald's *Storyteller's Sourcebook* (135) for the motif F324 lists the following.

Motifs:

Youth abducted by fairy. See also Type 312D.

F324.3.1: Tamlane. Tamlane rides wider shins around church and finds himself in elfland. Betrothed grabs him when riding with Queen of Elfland on Halloween. She holds him through successive transformations (D757) and restores him.

Katharine M. Briggs states that the ballad of Tam Lin is a variant of Type 425 with the following motifs:

Motifs:

F320: Fairies carry people away to fairy land

C515: Tabu of plucking flowers

F.301.1.1.2: Girl summoning fairy lover by plucking flowers

D.610: Repeated transformation

D.757: Disenchantment by holding enchanted persons during successive transformations

Briggs contends that:

> This ballad is a compendium of Scottish fairy beliefs. The carrying away of anyone who is unconscious of fairy ground, the transformations of mortals to fairies when they are kidnapped, the teind to Hell, the disenchantment through various transformations, finally confirmed by the putting on of a mortal garment, are all worth noting. Scott gives the same tale a literary form in "Alice Brand." (1970, 502)

Child Ballad Numbers

English and Scottish Popular Ballads (1976), originally published by Francis James Child at the end of the nineteenth century, is a five-volume collection that includes every traditional English and Scottish ballad that Child was able to find in manuscripts, in earlier collections, and through the efforts of folklore scholars. Child identified 305 groups of ballads, some of which have over a hundred variants. Each numbered "Child Ballad" is accompanied by an essay that places it within a broader cultural and historical context and the variants in full text. Child's definition of a ballad included the following criteria: It tells a story, the emphasis is on action and dialogue rather than characterization or description, and it has an anonymous or folk origin. An introductory essay by Dani Zweig, complete with references and further links, can be found on the Internet as "Early Child Ballads." "Tam Lin" is known as Child Ballad Number 39 and "Thomas the Rhymer" as Child Ballad Number 36.

Natascha Wurzbach and Simone Salz compiled a motif index of the Child Ballads. They define the motif as having a certain degree of importance within human experience and therefore signally something out of the ordinary (Wurzbach and Salz, 2). Following are their motifs for "Tam Lin."

Motifs:

Love against family's wishes

Longing (for lover)

Meeting (of lovers in greenwood; secret)

Pregnancy (as indication of secret love)

Abortion (prevented)

Abduction (by otherworldly being [elf-queen])

Captivity (of man; at hands of otherworldly being)

Devil, pact with

Magic (bewitchment [of man by otherworldly being])

Magic (spell, breaking of [by unconditional fulfillment of wishes] / help rescue [of bewitched man]) (Wurzbach and Salz, 90)

Their motifs for "Thomas the Rhymer" are not as numerous. They include the following.

Motifs:

Greenwood (as scene of encounter with otherworldly being)

Otherworldly being, encounter with (elf-queen)

Abduction (by otherworldly being)

Fairyland (mortal's journey into) (Wurzbach and Salz, 89)

A History of the Ballads "Tam Lin" and "Thomas the Rhymer"

The Scottish ballads are not extremely old, dating only from the Middle Ages. "What *can* be extremely old about them is their content, since narratives and motifs pass from one genre to another" (Lyle 1994, 9). Some of the earliest references to fairy monarchy in Lowland Scotland are found in the romance of *Thomas of Ercildoun*, where a fairy queen is described as meeting the hero and conducting him to the elfin realm. This work, however, is almost certainly of English origin, although it would appear to have a Scottish tradition behind it (Spence, 142). Emily Lyle makes reference to Thomas, stating that "the earliest references in the ballads to historical characters or events are to the late thirteenth century, the time of the earliest poet named in Scots, Thomas of Ercildoune called the Rhymer, who lived in the reign of Alexander III and is the protagonist of 'Thomas the Rhymer' " (1994, 9). Essentially, however, early evidence of these ballads is almost impossible to locate. Lyle refers to her search for "Tam Lin," stating that "many songs were printed on broadsides or in little pamphlets called chapbooks, and I turned over thousands and thousands on the look-out for a version of 'Tam Lin' without ever finding one" (1994, 10). But then, she continues, she was given a copy of an eighteenth-century chapbook that contained a version of that ballad. Lyle points out that one of the strongest elements in Scottish ballads is the supernatural that is sometimes experienced directly as meetings between mortals and supernatural folk (1994, 13). This is certainly the case in the two ballads under discussion.

The earliest variant of "Tam Lin" included in Child's collection was from *The Scots Musical Museum*, edited by James Johnston and published in 1792. Robert Burns combined a border version that localized the action near Selkirk with Ayrshire traditions known only to him (Lyle 1994, 275). Child collected "Thomas the Rhymer" from Sir Walter Scott's *Minstrelsy*, published in 1802. Another early version was transmitted by Mrs. Brown to Alexander Fraser Tytler in April 1880 and printed by Jamison in his preface to "True Thomas and the Queen of Elfland." The version by Scott was obtained from a woman who resided not far from Ercildoune and was revised with help from Mrs. Brown's manuscript.

Overview of Critical Interpretations of the Two Ballads

Although the interpretations often refer to both ballads, we have separated this discussion to facilitate easier access for those interested in only one of them. However, there is much overlapping of commentary in several of the publications below.

Tam Lin

1932: An overview of fairy folklore is presented in the introduction to "Tam Lin" in Scott's *Minstrelsy of the Scottish Border*. Elements that are evident in the various versions of the ballad include the color green for fairy clothing, the ringing of bells on the bridles of the fairy horses, the time span of seven years, and the teind to hell (a sacrifice or tithe). Carterhaugh is identified as a plain at the conflux of the Ettrick and Yarrow Rivers in Selkirkshire (II, 377). Robert Burns called the central figure Tam Lin, whereas Scott referred to him as Tamlane.

1950: Evelyn Wells discusses the fairy world as portrayed in these two ballads. She states that the fairy folk usually visit our world on a temporary errand to court a mortal, as in "Tam Lin"; to secure a teind to hell as in "Thomas the Rhymer"; or to kidnap a mortal nurse for a fairy child (139).

1956: Albert Friedman asserts that few ballads embrace as much ancient folklore as does "Tam Lin": the tabu grounds of Carterhaugh, the symbolism of the rose as a flower protected by the fairy folk, the teind to hell, transformations, and the redemption through immersion in water. It is not revenge that drives the fairy queen's lament about her failure to replace Tam Lin's eyes with that of wood but rather her failure to take security precautions by letting him return to the mortal world with the secrets of the land of fairy (41).

1959: Bertrand Bronson maintains that "the evidence of a singing and dancing tradition of whatever sort, connected with Tam Lin, or Tamlene, or Thomalyn, or Thom of Lyn, or Thomlin, is frequent enough from the middle of the sixteenth century, but we are in darkness as to the nature of what was sung or danced about him" (327).

1959: Lowry Wimberley examines the variations of the ballad in reference to elements of traditional folk beliefs and connections to tales outside of Scotland. He acknowledges the purely Scottish background of "Tam Lin" but points to the transformation sequence and its parallels to the Cretan fairy tale discussed in the introduction to the Child's Ballads by Helen Child Sargent and George Lyman Kittredge, the story of Thetis and Peleus, according to Apollodorus, and the tale of Menelaus and Proteus in the "Odyssey" (338). He feels that a significant feature in the rescue attempt is the fact that Tam Lin is entirely helpless and can do nothing to save himself other than give Janet explicit directions. Janet is the one who has to do it all, including covering him with her green kirtle (or mantle). This covering or clothing him in human garments may offer complete immunity to the fairy spells (390). Here, the sacrifice of eyes and heart is thought to be a common contract between mortal and elf in the case of broken faith (391). Other elements of folklore discussed include that of naming (the use of name magic in the transformation and rescue), the enchanted wood (where Janet meets Tam Lin and eventually saves him), sacred wells, the symbolism of roses and the color green, and Halloween.

Wimberley also employs the ballads of "Tam Lin" and "Thomas the Rhymer" to discuss the physical attributes of the fairy: they are not diminutive at all, they can disappear at will, but "with the exception of Thomas Rhymer and the fairy leman in *Tam Lin* there is no reference in our ballads to the colour of the elfmen. Tam is called an 'elfin grey' . . . True Thomas . . . wears a green costume during his sojourn in the fairy realm" (176).

1965: Willa Muir explores the belief in fairies and the affiliation between those beliefs and early Christianity. Because of their belief in the strong, dark powers of the other world, the people of the border regions were anxious to be christened, to have protection against those powers. If the rite of baptism was done carelessly, however, the protection was not accorded, as in the case of young Tam Lin, who "was snatched away in spite of him having been christened, because his step-mother had been careless" (127). Another strong belief was that of the boundary line between this world and that of faerie, which opened up during specific times of the year. The most ominous crack in time fell between the end of summer and the beginning of winter, the time when the souls of the dead returned to the land of the living: Halloween (128).

Muir looks closely at the ballad of "Tam Lin." It begins, she reminds us, cheerfully enough, with reference to the high regard that Tam Lin has in the world of faerie. Perhaps this is why he has the power to visit the greenwood at his will; the greenwood acts as an annex to the archaic world, which was still haunted by the aura of ancient fertility cults. "Seduction usually happens when a ballad heroine visits the greenwood, and invariably results in pregnancy" (129). Janet is at first presented as a passive victim, although she demonstrates a great deal of spirit and courage as well. Muir feels that the passivity of the heroine is but a convention and that Scott, boggling at the tale, produced coy alternatives that do not ring true to the Scottish countryside (129). Although the ballad does not tell us how Janet discovers Tam Lin's name, she does so and uses it with authority when she returns to the woods, heavy with his child. He fears she is about to pick a herb to cause an abortion; she fears he was not christened. To allay her fears, Tam Lin tells her of his history. In southern versions he is the grandson of the Earl of Roxburgh; in northern versions he is the eldest son of Lord Forbes. Muir feels it is more than a pat coincidence that this meeting occurs on the eve of Halloween, the only chance that Janet will have to rescue him from the land of fairy (131). In Scotland, Muir tells us, November is known as the "Black Month," the darkest time of the year, and thus presents Janet with a severe trial of nerves to traverse the woods during that time (131). The ballad evokes ancient, high magic, the magic of transformations blended with the immersion in water. Most of the versions finish the ballad with the queen's lament, but two of the northern versions follow with a commendation on the spirit of the heroine. These variants and endings have a Norse flavor to them, with their frank appreciation of will and courage. These two variants also did not warn the heroine from the woods in the first part (134). No longer a light and pleasant tale, it is "more like a Hallowe'en hair-raiser than a playful wooing" (138).

According to Muir, France is the origin of much of the imagery in this ballad. The silver bells on the fairy queen's horses reflect Louis XI's 1461 entry into Paris with silver bells on the horses of all the nobles (138). The transformation magic was also known all over France and, until the time of Mary Queen of Scots, France and Scotland were bound together quite intimately, sharing their tales and songs (138). "It is more than likely that gay Tam Lin, the transformation magic, and the existence of Elfland were 'all in the air' as popular pre-Reformation traditions long before Burns was born" (138). Burns took these themes and merged them into an eerie ballad that is therefore not known elsewhere (138). Other elements of an older tradition include the noble background of both Janet (in southern versions) and Margaret (in the northern ones) so they would be "exemplars for ordinary people in a hierarchal society" (139). Muir asserts that Calvinist reformers, recognizing the strength of the ancient beliefs and traditions, knew that to gain supremacy they would have to control the ballad world. This world was considered their enemy, and as early as 1533 censorship attacks were made on "fond books, rhimes and other lewd treatises" and attempts were made to re-write them with "positive" images. The old ballads, however, continued to survive with their pre-Reformation traditions until they were written down in the eighteenth and nineteenth centuries (139). Janet's anxiety about christening and Tam Lin's explanation about his being "ill sained" demonstrate an archaic link to the time of the ancient gods rather than to that of Christianity, which was a later Presbyterian infiltration into the tale (141).

The figure of Tam Lin himself is still a puzzle. The older forms of his name (Tom a Lin; Thom o Lin) present Lin as a place name that appears as a locality in many other ballads as well as the De Danann gods in Ireland who came from Loch Linn (140). Muir feels that the ballad itself is from the Norse tradition because it is Norse in spirit: "Tam Lin and Janet were none the worse for their peculiar experiences because they and the strength of spirit, will and courage that belonged to the Norse world" (141).

1969: E. B. Lyle compares "Tam Lin" to other traditional tales of recovery from the fairy troop, such as the Scandinavian tale "*Helga pattr proissonar*" to further understand the traditional beliefs held in that ballad. Janet's action of taking holy water in her hand and casting a compass around was associated with recovery from the fairies. The white horse is also traditional, as is its position in the fairy troop (179). Lyle points out that the fairy queen's wish that she had taken out Tam Lin's eyes relates to a belief that fairies blind those who had acquired the power to see them (182). The classical legend of "Peleus and Thetis" is also discussed in comparison to the ballad. Peleus imprisons Thetis in his arms while she shape-shifts in an attempt to escape, but Janet keeps Tam Lin safe by holding him while he is transformed into various shapes against his will (183). These shapes differ in the variants, but Lyle suggests that there are three basic forms: a snake, a fierce animal, and either hot metal or fire (184):

> The ballad's eclectic use of material indicates that the ballad-maker, while thoroughly familiar with tradition, was free from an uncritical belief in the factual truth of the narrative, which is not to say that many of those who sang the ballad did not consider it to be a record of events. Certainly, the traditional tale on which it is based would have been told "for true." (185)

1970: Katherine Briggs considered "Tam Lin" one of the most important of all the supernatural ballads because of the many fairy beliefs it embodies, including the fairy ride with all its trappings, Halloween as a time of fairy power and of death, shape-shifting spells, the Fairy Queen, and the fairy teind to hell (449).

1970: E. B. Lyle continues the examination of the ballad by comparing the openings of the variants of "Tam Lin." She contends that the popular opening of the ballad was borrowed from other ballads, and that this "new" opening allows the freedom to omit the greenwood incident with its account of the rape (1970a, 42).

1970: In another article, Lyle provides a correlation between the teind to hell and the folk belief in changelings. The fairy folk carried away unbaptised babies so they could be sacrificed as the teind instead of one of their own (1970b, 178). Only in the ballads of "Tam Lin" and "Thomas the Rhymer" is there any mention of this feudal practice in regard to the land of the fairy. "It is possible that both . . . drew on a tale where the payment to hell and the return to earth were already linked, but in the absence of other evidence for the story, it is perhaps more likely that the two narratives are directly linked" (1970b, 180). Lyle also discusses the traditional function of Hallowmas (November 1) as one of the ancient quarter days in Scotland and one of the two dates (the other being Beltane) when the half-yearly rents were due. Perhaps the teinds of the fairy folk were rendered at the same time as those to their human counterparts (1970b, 180). The narrative of "Tam Lin" unites two separate beliefs: that a mortal who has been taken by the fairy folk can be recovered when they ride at Halloween and that the fairy folk pay mortals as a tribute to the devil (1970b, 181). "Comparison with the *Thomas of Ercildoune* stanza suggests that the two beliefs may have come together with the custom of making payments at Hallowmass, and that, if Tam Lin had not been rescued at Halloween, he would have been in imminent danger of being paid to the devil the next day" (1970b, 181).

1971:   Katharine M. Briggs identifies the type of fairy involved in these two ballads as "Heroic." These fairies are of human stature or sometimes beyond it and live in an underground fairyland that is removed a little from the common world. Here time passes at a different rate and "they revel, dance, hunt and sing like humans, only upon a grander scale" (14). Briggs states that the "Fairy Queen who took True Thomas away with her was as large as a mortal woman, and the Fairy Court who held Tamlane prisoner was obviously the same" (20). She continues her discussion by stating that Thomas the Rhymer was the go-between who arranged the human pipers for the fairy revels and that Halloween was one of two dates on which the human world and the fairy world touch (20): "The belief that the fairies were fallen angels not bad enough for hell is mixed with the idea of the lost Heroic Races, for we see in Tamlane that every seven years, the fairies must pay a tribute to Hell" (21).

1971:   Lyle discusses the variants of the ballad of "Tam Lin" and elements of traditional folklore that Robert Burns apparently amalgamated into his retelling of the ballad.

1971:   John Niles considers the geographic centers of the ballad. The events in the first part modulate between two opposite and hostile centers: Carterhaugh, usurped by Tam Lin, a place of woods and flowers, forbidden and threatening in a specifically sexual way, and Janet's father's castle, a fortified place of stone (339). "The processes of generation—sex, pregnancy and birth—are alien to the barren walls of her home" (340). The critical events take place at a third, transitional location at a transitional point of time, All Hallows' Eve.

   Niles also suggests that Tam Lin's first concern about the unborn child is selfish. He is concerned primarily to preserve his own flesh and blood. But this selfish concern forces him to reconsider Janet as a human being rather than a sexual object. "Faced with the possible destruction of his child, Tam Lin addresses Janet no longer as an aggressor but as one with a common concern, and thus he takes his first, grudging step back toward humanity" (341). At Miles Cross, the roles are reversed. Now Tam Lin is the passive actor who must be "ravished" back into human form by his aggressor, Janet. Niles points to the hunting images here and the parallels between the original hunt in which Tam Lin fell to the power of the fairy queen and the hunt or fairy ride Janet interrupts. Tam Lin is no tame prey, however, as all of the transformations he undergoes are "the horrors which people the dreams of children and which still linger behind the daylight world of adults" (342). The shapes all connote danger and, to many people, extreme repugnance. "The erotic connotations of the embrace are reinforced by the persistence of the element of *heat* or *warmth* in the sequence of transformations" (343). Niles stresses the life-assertive aspects of the ballad, the fact that it is a testament to the enduring power of human love and the celebration of the power of that love to break down, transcend, or undermine walls. "On one side is Tam Lin, a young man being 'kept' by the Queen of Fairies. On the other side is Janet, a young woman being 'kept' by parental restraints. Release for both is made possible when Janet determines to act in defiance of all prohibitions: act, whatever the cost" (345).

1972: David Buchan briefly discusses the "Tam Lin" variant collected from James Nichol, a "well-read and intelligent man, a disciple of Tom Paine," whose text retains many of the old oral elements but also reflects the inroads made by literacy upon the unconscious mind of the folk (227).

1972: Maureen Duffy makes a brief comparison between "Tam Lin" and Andersen's "Snow Queen": Both Kay and Tam Lin are rescued by a human who loves them (308).

1972: Walter Haden compares "Tam Lin" to other folktales such as the "Swan Maiden" type that incorporates "Beauty and the Beast." He asserts that "Tam Lin" is concerned with a love great enough to overcome not only the natural obstacles such as parental opposition but also the considerable impediment of Tam's otherworldly nature (46). He also explores the forms of transformation Tam Lin undergoes in Janet's arms and compares them to those in "Peleus and Thetis," among other tales. Haden also considers the motif of abduction under the apple tree and makes connections from "Tam Lin" to Mallory's *Morte D'Arthur*, the ballad "King Orfeo," and "Thomas the Rhymer." He concludes his article by stating that:

> No stronger theme could be desired for a ballad than that of "Tam Lin": love strong enough to conquer not only the natural but the supernatural as well. Nor has the story's preoccupation with the occult and the supernatural diminished interest in the ballad's bizarre rituals of mutation and metamorphosis. . . . I[I]t is the ballad's relationship to the great universal themes and motifs of other durable literature—from classical legend to nursery nonsense rhyme—that have kept "Tam Lin" alive and well for so long." (49)

1976: In Child, correlations are made between the transformation scene in "Tam Lin" and an ancient Cretan fairy tale. The tale concentrates on a young musician who had been taken by the nereids into their world for the sake of his music. When he falls in love with one of them, he turns to the wise woman of the village for help. She advises him to seize his beloved by her hair just before cock-crow and hold on, without fear, regardless of the shapes she may assume, until the cock crows. He held tightly as she changed into a dog, snake, camel and fire, and eventually "won" his bride in her true and beautiful form. Unfortunately she never spoke, and after a year and the birth of their child, the musician went for advice again. The wise woman told him to threaten the woman that he would throw their child into a hot oven if she would not speak. His wife cried out, "let go of my child, dog," and taking the baby, disappeared for all time (67). The editors also point out that "The Tayl of the young Tamlene" is mentioned as being told by shepherds in *Vedderburn's Complaint of Scotland* (1549), and there are no variants outside of Scotland (66).

1978: Caroline Geer discusses some of the qualities of the land of fairy, including the fact that it is outside the realm of our recognized time, it has a parallel social structure to that of humans, it is a land of wealth, there are warnings against eating food there, there is generous rewarding of those who come to the fairies' aid, and there is swift punishment for breaking of tabus. The two worlds seem to exist simultaneously but not in the same context of time or space.

1978: John Niles begins his discussion of "Tam Lin" with a look at the history of its publication and contends that the Burns variant, the most well-known version, is not traditional but literary. He points out several subtle word changes from an earlier variant known to Burns and how they transform the meaning of the text, but it is not until the story enters the realm of the supernatural that Burns's changes and additions become more frequent. Niles explains these changes and additions as a result of Burns's fascination with the supernatural: "Tam Lin's metamorphosis into a bear and a lion (A32) and into a burning gleed (A34)—in Burns's holograph, burning *lead*—seem to be the result of a desire on Burns's part to magnify terror" (51). The changes made by Burns include (154–55):

> Additions or omissions of words or syllables *metri causa*
>
> Adoption of a fairly consistent Scots dialect
>
> Improvement of story line
>
> Highlighting of the romantic element
>
> Development of the actor's emotions
>
> Changes of fact
>
> A fascination with atmosphere

Niles states that by changing a simple word, Burns converted Janet from a potential murderess of a newborn child into a young woman seeking to abort an unwelcome child. Child, influenced by Burns's text, altered the other versions accordingly (158n.10). Niles claims that the popularity of Burns's version lies in the fact that it is well written and that Burns did little that is different from what many good folk singers do, taking what he liked from tradition and combining it with what he liked of his own.

1981: Alchemy is the focus of Julian Wasserman's article on "Tam Lin." He regards the various transformations that Tam Lin undergoes in the light of the alchemical process from the gold in Janet's hair to the esk, which was thought to ignite fire, and therefore frequently placed at the beginning of alchemical symbols. He states that the order in which the transformations are presented in the A version implies a refinement typical of both the popular and esoteric branches of alchemy (31). The meaning of the "double rose" can also be found in alchemy: "The double rose, the combined red and white rose adopted by Henry VII after the Wars of the Roses, became an important alchemical emblem which frequently symbolized the resolution of the dualism or tension between matter and spirit as symbolized by the colors red and white respectively" (32).

1985: Lauren Lepow compares the tale of "Tam Lin" to *Jane Eyre*. She begins by detailing the common elements in all the variants of the ballad: a maiden encounters an "elfin" knight, she is impregnated by him, she discovers that he had been a mortal man before his abduction by the Fairy Queen, he is in immediate danger of being the teind to hell, and Janet can save him by holding him fast as he is transformed into numerous terrifying beasts. The ballad, she concludes, is like "Beauty and the Beast" concerning redemption, through love, from enchantment (111). She then articulates the similarities between Jane (also known as Janet, but only to Rochester at moments of special intimacy) and Janet. Both are strong-willed and independent, both are the chief actor in their respective stories (112). They are fully human and earthy but both have an aura of the supernatural around them. Janet wears green, the traditional color of fairy garb, and has power (natural love) strong enough to overcome the Fairy Queen. Jane is also associated with the fairy world through the color green and her apparently other-worldly appearance and power (114). Other parallels include the following:

1. Tam Lin and Rochester are both enthralled by evil powers and can be redeemed only by the power of love (115).

2. Bertha Mason Rochester and the Fairy Queen are present, threatening forces, who gain their power from the fall, physically and metaphorically, of the male actors (115).

3. The fate forecast for the heroes is similar: Tam Lin will be paid as teind to hell, and Rochester's hell is created for him by Bertha (115).

4. Both males must undergo multiple transformations. Evil powers change them into a number of non-human forms; the power of love ultimately changes them into their true shape. Tam Lin's redemption occurs overnight, whereas Rochester's transformation is a lengthy process, and "his changes of form are both less literal and more meaningful" than those of Tam Lin (118).

Lepow states that it cannot be proven that Bronte knew "Tam Lin," but the parallels demonstrate strong circumstantial evidence that the ballad had permeated her consciousness by the time she wrote *Jane Eyre* (121).

1991:   David Buchan, in his review of ballads of otherworld beings, refers to three taleroles (the interactive function served by a character in a narrative) for the supernatural ballads: Bespeller, Bespelled, and Unspeller. The Bespeller is the Otherworld being who casts a spell on the mortal, the Bespelled is the mortal, and the Unspeller is the character responsible for the lifting of the spell (1991a, 142). "Tam Lin" and "Thomas the Rhymer" are two of the nine ballads Buchan discusses. Within the nine ballads, these two are part of the subgroup that end happily and romantically. Buchan assures the reader that even if you are "taken" by the fairy world you may well, given certain conditions, return to this life, but if you have dealings with creatures from a water-Otherworld, your relationship will end disastrously (1991a, 145). "As well as telling a good story, they convey cultural knowledge through an exposition within narrative of the Otherworld and the Otherworld beings: their nature, characteristics, and practices" (1991a, 148).

1991:   Buchan discusses taleroles in ballads and their function to convey useful cultural knowledge. The supernatural ballads transmit information about the dangers in human relations and in relationships between humans and those of the Otherworld. More specifically, "Tam Lin" offers specific knowledge of the transformation ritual in escaping the Otherworld; "Thomas the Rhymer" demonstrates how to gain freedom by dutifully performing the required service (1991b, 75).

1991:   Jean Freedman suggests that this ballad may be part of the woman's genre, sung by women and articulating women's sentiments about an unwed pregnancy, abortion, and premarital sexual relations. She considers "Tam Lin" an inversion ballad in that it presents a world that is the reverse of the patriarchal, Calvinist society of the time: "In the real world that the creator of 'Tam Lin' inhabited, a pregnant spinster would have faced shame, clerical punishment, and the expectation of the poverty and marginality due to a single mother. . . . 'Tam Lin' presents a world in which women hold both material and spiritual power, a world where men are fairly helpless creatures who look on while powerful females— Janet and the Queen of Elfinland—perform the action" (10).

1993:   Sandra Marie Guy analyzes "Tam Lin" and "Thomas the Rhymer" along with two other ballads in her thesis on fairy abductions and rescues. She is specifically interested in the function of the fairy actions as literary devices and the folklore presented in the abductions and rescues (1). These literary devices include:

   ❖ *Composition of subject matter.* The focus of "Thomas the Rhymer" is not the rescue of Thomas, as the ballad considers only the meeting and the abduction of Thomas by the queen. The larger part of all the variants describes the journey rather than Thomas's capture. "Tam Lin," on the other hand, focuses on the rescue of the hero from the Otherworld. All action that takes place in "Tam Lin" may be traced back to the fairy presence (11).

❖ *Setting.* "Thomas the Rhymer" presents a primary example of the supernatural realm functioning as setting. The journey presents a "vivid and frequently horrific description of the area through which the two traveled" (13). The setting of "Tam Lin" has less to do with the physical surroundings than with the inhabitants of the fairy court itself. It is the fairy ride that is brought to life here. Darkness reflects directly on the fairy queen's motivations; the blacks and browns of the horses mirroring her malevolence and cruelty (1993, 15).

❖ *Character and its development.* The role of the Faery Queen in "Thomas the Rhymer" is as a warning device and guide. She warns Thomas that if he kisses her, he must become her lover. But once he does kiss her, no further mention of her role of lover is made. She then becomes a guide for the journey. The role of the Fairy Queen in "Tam Lin" is only indicated by her threats as Janet rescues her lover. There is no indication that the Queen is the cause of Tam Lin's transformations during the rescue (18). There is only brief character development of Thomas himself; the only attribute that is apparent is his willingness to disregard the Faery Queen's warning. The remaining narrative is primarily concerned with the description of his journey to the Otherworld (61).

The abductions and rescues, according to Guy, reflect the medieval audience's interest in the fairy realm. Motivation for the abduction finds its roots in medieval popular culture, and the "fairy mistress" theme is very prevalent in "Thomas the Rhymer." It is not so prominent in "Tam Lin"; in the concluding stanzas of the ballad, the Faery Queen refers to Tam Lin as a knight of her court rather than as a lover (22). Other traditional motivations for the abduction motif include the role of music, the presence of the teind to hell, hunting, fairy "Moving Days," and trespass on sacred groves (25). The appearance of a body of water in these two ballads reflects a traditional location of Fairyland across an expanse of water (31).

Guy clarifies the "Moving Days" as the pagan transitions of the year: November 1, Samain, is the festival of the dead at the beginning of winter, and May 1, Beltaine, is the rebirth of Spring. The fairy ride was thought to take place on midnight of these two evenings as the fairy court was moved from one location to another, journeying through the mortal realm on the way (36). Guy also explores the meaning of the apple tree, or in the case of Thomas, the Eildon tree. Eildon, as she points out, is not a species of tree but rather is defined as the Scottish variation of eld, meaning old or aged. "Because of the oral nature of the ballads, the assumption that the tree was of a certain species depends entirely on the transcription's capital letters in Child's collection; otherwise, the tree from which Thomas was abducted is simply an old tree, venerable in its representation of nature and its mystical components" (39). Traditional tabus of customs in fairyland are also discussed. These include tabus against eating, drinking, and speaking.

Guy next focuses on the rescues from fairyland. Thomas is more restored than rescued, giving the impression of the Fairy Queen as a benevolent character. He fulfills his bargain with her and not only gains his release but is bestowed with additional gifts of clothing in elven colors and fabrics. The Fairy Queen is not at all benevolent in regard to Tam Lin. Guy maintains that the folklore has been grossly misinterpreted or carelessly confused in the latter ballad (52). She discusses in detail

❖ The reference to Samhain or Halloween evening. Guy believes the evidence points to Beltaine instead (52).

❖ The transformations into wild animals, which may be attributed to the remains of a primitive, nature-worshiping philosophy, but the transformations into a naked man and iron cannot, because they do not represent anything of which mortals would be frightened. The well-known aversion of fairies to iron would seem to prevent any such transformation from taking place (53): "The most that one can assume concerning the fairies' use of iron in Tam Lin is that the creators of the ballad mistakenly placed the fairy fear of iron in the character of the mortal Janet" (54).

❖ Janet's final instructions in the rescue are grouped into three categories: covering Tam Lin with her green mantle/kirtle, dipping him in milk and water, and uttering the name of Tam Lin. The power of naming and the bathing in water and milk has considerable background in folk belief. However, the sprinkling of holy water instead of the ritual bathing may be the result of the ballad's development and travel throughout Scotland (56). Guy also queries the specification of the color green. In "Thomas the Rhymer, " the Faery Queen was wearing the green, whereas in this ballad it seems to be a protection *against* fairies (57).

Guy concludes this examination by stating that:

> The ballad's presentation of the sheer amount of folk tradition, however confused, is where its complexity lies; nearly every action or speech by the characters alludes to some fairy belief, from Janet's disturbance of nature to initially call Tam Lin to her use of the power of naming as the final action in her lover's rescue (58).

1993: Lewis Spence discusses the history of some of the elements found in these two ballads. He states that the Fairy Queen came to be regarded as a kind of sorceress capable of foretelling the future and of guiding people to fame and fortune in Elizabethan times (142). He also discusses the fairy ride in "Tam Lin," where

> the Fairy Queen is followed by three separate courts in her night-riding, the "head court" being clad in robes of green. This head court, judging from one version of the ballad, was composed of knights and ladies, while another mentions that it was made up of footmen, grooms and squires, maidens and knights, the black, the brown and white steeds which the several courts bestrode being in keeping with the rank or station of their riders. (144)

Spence also claims that one of the most notable illustrations of shape-shifting in fairy lore is found in this ballad (144).

1993: Polly Stewart examines the treatment of women characters in selected Child Ballads to point out the cultural lessons that these texts may be imparting to and about women. She does not consider "Thomas the Rhymer" in the study because the plot is entirely driven by supernatural elements (56). Stewart devises a four-part paradigm in analyzing success and failure on the cultural and personal level: personal and cultural failure, personal failure and cultural success, personal success and cultural failure, and personal and cultural success. "Tam Lin" is included in the final category comprising women who gain what they want and who also meet cultural expectations for success (65). The lessons for women from all these ballads are not very positive:

> That a man will take from a woman what he can and will punish her for being his victim; that a woman's needs are not a primary consideration either for her family or for men outside her family; that, for a woman, stepping outside the house is a dangerous act; that a woman's resources for protecting her interests are slim indeed. By horrible example, a woman learns how not to get killed. (66)

1994: Emily Lyle notes that Burns combined a border version of "Tam Lin" that localized the event near Selkirk with Ayrshire folk traditions known only to him (275).

1995: Robert Georges and Michael Jones discuss "Tam Lin" in their introductory textbook on folkloristics. They concur with Albert Friedman that "Tam Lin now knows the secrets of the fairy world, to the chagrin of the queen of fairies, who regrets not having torn out his 'two grey eyes' and replaced them with wooden ones as a security precaution" (60).

1995: In his exploration of metaphor and meaning in folksongs, Barre Toelken refers to Flemming Andersen's contention that some gestures and actions are virtually always followed by anticipated plot details. Andersen "suggests that the pulling of a flower is almost always a prelude to sexual assault and relates the action to magic, probably in view of the immediate appearance of the aggressive male, as in 'Tam Lin' " (128). However, Toelken feels that it may have another meaning entirely:

> Tam Lin erroneously accuses Janet of pulling a rose in order to abort her pregnancy with his child. As an earlier audience would have recognized immediately, however, the rose in English folklore was associated not with abortion but with female genitalia and active sexually. The ballad drama of "Tam Lin" focuses not on abortion but on a pregnant Janet's vigorous actions in recovering her lover from the fairy world, an assertion of life, not death, quite constant with the traditional associations of the rose. Some irony is produced when the audience apprehends the heroine's actions before her lover does. (92)

Toelken concentrates on the earthbound aspects of the ballad rather than on any aspects of the rescue and transformations. Other elements of this ballad include the horse, because most folksong references to water and wells include an equine character, and Tam Lin's horse is indeed standing by the well; the color green, which indicates bad luck in England; and the symbolic meaning of the combing of hair, which is related to an indication of readiness for marriage or a willingness to be courted or approached. Andersen, according to Toelken, declares that the action of sewing or combing hair, usually followed by a romantic encounter, can be understood as a meaningful, recognizable expression of a lady's secret (unvocalized) longing for a lover as well as a figurative prologue to romantic action.

1997: Martha Hixon's dissertation focuses on awakening and transformations in the three folktales "Sleeping Beauty," "Snow White," and "The Frog Prince," along with the ballad "Tam Lin." She examines the history of these four tales from their literary beginnings to contemporary reworkings, considering the variations and constants in the tellings and seeking to discover the source of the resonance of the core motifs that give them their continual allure for literary and visual retellers (12). She states that although ballads are different in form and purpose from the folktales, some ballads have characteristics in common with them: "Magic, generally transformations and enchantment, and supernatural beings such as fairies and witches infuse the narratives of these ballads and contribute to the action of the plot as in traditional fairy tales" (183). "Tam Lin" is usually categorized as a supernatural ballad, but the narrative concerns social issues encountered in this world as much as it does the land of faerie (185). The basis of narrative in this ballad is that illegitimate pregnancy and the heroine's defiance of socially accepted sexual behavior are rewarded rather than punished. "Nearly all the versions begin with an introductory warning that established the topic of this ballad—loss of virginity—and the intended audience—young, unmarried girls"(187). Hixon speculates that given such a theme, the listener would expect a cautionary narrative about the dangers of flirting and premarital relations, but whether this message is actually behind the telling depends on the teller, the audience, and the culture and time period of the telling itself (187).

Hixon speculates that Janet's impetuous and self-determined character causes her to reject the male authority of her father and Tam Lin. She has violated conventional accepted behavior by inviting a sexual liaison, refusing to marry to give her child a father, and considering an abortion. Her situation provides the catalyst for Tam Lin's disenchantment, and her reasons for holding onto him are as much born out of practicality as they are out of love (192). Thus, the tale is as much a story about a woman's social conflict as it is about supernatural events. It features a strong female character, focuses on a distinct female problem, and is told primarily from Janet's point of view (193). Janet's attitude and actions are condoned as, after a huge battle, she wins the conflicts with the fairy queen as well as with society and marries the man of her choice. "That it is the female who saves the man in this story both makes the tale an interesting inversion of the traditional hero motif and establishes a particular relevancy for modern readers" (194).

1997: Bob Johnson of the band Steeleye Span discusses why "Tam Lin" is an important part of the band's music. " 'Tam Linn' is another 'gigantically' deep ballad, another alchemical text about transformation and holding on through the many changes to achieve the 'gold' at the end. (Notice the maiden wears 'gold' in her hair as a symbol of purity and 'wholeness' of the self" (Roseman).

1997: Evelyn Perry analyzes the ballad to describe "current devaluations of folk literature" to suit child audiences (32). Janet's claims on Carterhaugh are just as determined by the rules of her culture and, although she goes against the authority of the warning, she is doing so to preserve order and control. "For this, and for Janet's reaction to the arrogance of Tam Lin, we continue to support her character" (36). Tam Lin gains our sympathy when he describes his fate if he remains in the Otherworld.

> The tale of Tam Lin holds within its frame a series of transgressions made on both sides: On one, Janet's visit

to Carterhaugh, extramarital sex and pregnancy. On the other, Tam's visit to the mortal world, and a disruption of the tithe system. And on both sides, outlawed love. The transgressions made against the rules of the natural, mortal world, the Good, keep the unnatural, immortal world, the Evil with all its dangers, at bay. Keeping evil at bay ensures the survival of the Good and keeps intact its system of rules. Nevertheless, protecting the authority and control of Good through transgressions, quite symmetrically, requires a transgression of the rules of Evil. Janet must wait for Tam Lin at Miles Cross, pull him from his horse (much as the Fairy Queen did) and withstand certain tortures before he is fully restored to the mortal world. (37)

1997: Kimberly White takes a different stand in her study on "Tam Lin." She feels that Janet was raped and that Tam Lin's subsequent rescue is not done out of love but for economic and social reasons. Although the ballad is centuries old, the attitudes and choices are similar to those faced by women in contemporary society (4). White contends that Robert Burns and Sir Walter Scott both altered the ballad considerably, changing the tone and influencing subsequent interpretations of it (7). She also looks to other tales of transformation and reviews the published criticism on three aspects of the ballad: the supernatural elements, the Burns version in comparison to traditional versions, and the textual analysis of the ballad. White charges that when the sexual assault is acknowledged, the meaning of the ballad changes considerably. It can be "interpreted as the story of a young woman, the victim of rape and circumstance, who must strike a bargain with her assailant so that both their needs are met: she gains a father for her illegitimate child and he escapes imprisonment and possible death" (23).

"Thomas the Rhymer"

n.d.: George Eyre-Todd considers Thomas's "Sir Tristrem" to be the earliest authentic Scottish poem. However, it is Thomas's adventure in the fairy world that has made his fame. "The narrative of his intercourse with the elfin queen, whether composed by himself or not, is extant to the present day, and forms one of the most characteristic of the Border Ballads" (13).

1875: In his introduction to Thomas's writings, James Murray discusses the importance of Erceldoune during the twelfth and thirteenth centuries, the power of Thomas's prophecies, and the ballad that records Thomas's adventures in the land of the fairy folk. According to the popular belief of the late nineteenth century, Thomas is expected to revisit this world once again when he is called.

1932: The introduction to Scott's chapter "Thomas the Rhymer" concentrates on the historical background of the central figure. He was a celebrated prophet and poet with the surname of Lermont or Learmont (IV, 79). The Eildon Tree no longer exists, but the spot where Thomas delivered his prophecies is now marked by a large stone called the Eildon Tree Stone (IV, 83). *Brewer's Dictionary of Phrase and Fable* supports this identification: "thirteenth century border poet and seer; also called Thomas Learmont; reputed author of a number of poems, including one, on Tristram (which Scott believed to be genuine); fabled to have predicted the death of Alexander III of Scotland, the Battle of Bannockburn, and the accession of James VI to the English throne" (*Brewer's*, 946)

1950: Evelyn Wells associates the term "rhymer" with a courtly poet and Thomas the Rhymer, in particular, a sort of Scottish Merlin, whose historical identity has been blended with that of the singer who told of his romance with the fairy queen and the acquiring of his power of prophesy. Thomas does not die a mortal death; years after his return to the mortal world he disappears forever into the fairy world (76).

1956: Albert Friedman introduces "Thomas the Rhymer" with reference to Scottish legend about the thirteenth-century poet Thomas of Ercildoune who, after spending seven years in elfland, eventually became as famous a seer as Merlin (39).

1959: Bertrand Bronson states that "one may justly suspect the non-singing Sir Walter Scott of inventing Thomas the Rhymer's biting rejection of the Elfland Queen's gift of 'the tongue that can never lee'. . . [since] . . . Thomas' insistence here on the crippling effects of truth-telling may be obvious enough to the reader, but it is too subtle for the musical phrase. The irony of the interchange is lost in the singing and the hearer is baffled by the long explanation" (xi).

1959: Lowry Wimberley concludes that "Thomas the Rhymer" provides a "Cosmo graphical compromise between Christianity and pre-Christianity, especially when the fairy queen gives Thomas the power to see the roads to heaven, hell, and fairyland" (116). The correlation between the tabu of speech in fairy land and the power of the name is also made.

1966: C. E. Nelson looks to the published history of the seven versions of the ballad. Before the eighteenth century there was no mention of the ballad or any trace of the story of the journey independent of a series of prophecies (139). Textual and narrative analysis proclaim that four of these versions can be traced to Mrs. Brown's manuscript, which was sent to her nephew, a friend of Sir Walter Scott, in 1800. The remaining versions can be traced to the common geographical point, the ancient village of Erceldoune. Nelson concludes that Mrs. Brown heard an earlier version, modified the text, and originated a second-generation ballad that was stronger than the first and became the recognized variant in subsequent collections (148).

1970: E. B. Lyle compares a variant of the ballad with *Thomas of Erceldoune.* Lyle's hypothesis is that "the internal inconsistencies and oddities in the narrative of *Thomas of Erceldoune* are compatible with the theory that *Thomas of Erceldoune* was based on an early form of *Thomas the Rhymer*" (1970b, 26).

1971: Angus Wilson, in his introduction to Peter Haining's collection of Scottish fantasy and horror stories , praises the choice of "Thomas the Rhymer" as the first selection in the anthology because it is representative of "the first great Scots historian of the fairy realm, Thomas the Rhymer. We have no doubt from the beginning of the sinister nature of the beguiling other world of Scotland" (Haining 1971, 12). In the editorial introduction, Thomas is credited with having written the first piece of poetry known to exist in the English language. The editorial note also comments on the fact that Sir Walter Scott owned a valley not far from Thomas's Earlston known as "Rhymer's Glen," and according to one biographer, "spent many of his happiest times in this place with its associations with the shadowy past" (19).

1972: David Buchan explores the corpus of Mrs. Brown's ballads in detail. He discusses the ballad world of distanced settings and aristocratic characters along with the localizing aspects that made the ballad relevant to the folk. "For his seven years service to the Queen of Elfland, Thomas receives, as any laird's retainer might, a coat and shoes, though in his case they are 'of even cloth' and 'of velvet cloth' " (79). A key element in the construction of the ballad is the triad of tabus against physical contact with the fairy folk, against the eating of fairy food, and against speech with the fairy folk (117). Thomas breaks the first tabu, which places him in the Queen's power; she then prevents him from breaking the second. He restrains himself from breaking the third because failure to comply would put him in the power of not only the Queen but the entire fairy host (117). A series of topographical motifs constitutes another pattern in the ballad. Thomas lies on the grassy bank that in Celtic and Lowlands Scots folklore symbolizes the entrance to the fairy world; he visits the Otherworld garden, where the fruit may not be eaten; he views the three roads that lead to Heaven, Hell and Elfland; and he crosses the Otherworld water-barrier (118). Buchan illustrates the connections between the tabus and the typographical motifs and the ballad and other "journey to the Otherworld" tale types.

1972: Maureen Duffy states that the moments of tabu-breaking are all moments of lowered resistance: falling asleep, sickness, being out alone and at night. Sometimes the danger is unconscious but deliberately courted. True Thomas falls asleep on Huntlie Brink, a name that suggests a fairy hill. She claims "Thomas the Rhymer" as a literary influence for "La Belle Dame Sans Merci": "The ballad is one of the finest in English. Scott's additions can only fall sadly short but they contain one or two interesting parallels for Keats's poem" (283). The pale kings and princes are from Part II, which foretells the fate of various Scottish kings; Part III supplies the time of year, autumn, when Thomas is finally called away; the fairy song; the warrior of the lake; and Tristrem on his sick bed with Isolde's hand to nurse him (284).

1973:   Fenton Wyness claims that Thomas is reminiscent of Merlin in his mysterious history and powers. He discusses the historical evidence, the thirteenth-century romance of Sir Tristrem, and the prophecies accredited to Thomas. However, many of the "frets" attributed to him were pronouncements made long after his time. "From the 14th century onwards, the fabrication and circulation of 'frets'—in the name of Thomas the Rhymer—was accepted as being an effective way of striking fear into one's enemies—indeed the same basis as the witches' spell and wartime propaganda" (62).

1975:   The focus of Kathryn Herron's research is the motif of the Otherworld visit in "Thomas the Rhymer." "It is through his prophecies that Thomas the Rhymer has been remembered in history, but ironically it is through the romances and later ballads that his prophecies have been able to sustain any importance and interest" (30). She compares the ballad with the myth of Orpheus and the legend of Taliesin: All three main characters are recognized as the first poets of their people and are associated with the myth of Aeneas and his journey to the Otherworld. Herron also draws comparisons between the ballad and the story of Christianity. "Since Thomas is not allowed to eat the fruits, the Fairy Queen has provided him with bread and wine, the symbols of the body and blood of Christ. It is a communion that has already transpired between the lady and Thomas under the Eildon Tree" (45). Both Christ (God made man living on Earth) and Thomas (a man living among immortals) leave the place they are visiting, only to return some other day. Christ has left his actions and sayings in the New Testament, whereas Thomas achieved immortality through his poetic prophecies. Both were endowed with words of wisdom and both act as guides to the soul after death (46).

Herron also discusses similar tales encompassing the Otherworld motif from Norse mythology, Ireland, and literature. For example, Keats uses the same theme of the fairy lady appearing to a human and taking him to the land of the fairies in "La Belle Dame Sans Merci," and Coleridge relates a similar voyage to a place where supernatural people are met, the hero's learning experience , and the telling of the story by the hero after his return in *Rime of the Ancient Mariner* (62). Herron concludes that "Thomas the Rhymer" retains both conventions of the religious influence of the visit to heaven and hell and the lady of the Otherworld as a derivation from either mythology or folklore (71).

1989: Bob Stewart and John Mathews explore the Eildon Hills of "Thomas the Rhymer" along with other actual places in legendary Britain. In their introduction they correlate the Eildon Hills with Sherwood Forest and Thomas the Rhymer with Robin Hood, Wayland Smith, and Robert Kirk. The strongest connection is between Thomas and Merlin. "Merlin derives from very detailed and enduring traditions that connect the land, prophesy, and, to a smaller degree, the cosmology and magical psychology of the bards and druids ... the prophetic traditions (of which Merlin, Thomas the Rhymer and others are a part) deal with power routed through an individual for purposes of magical transformation, wisdom and enlightment" (37). The ballad relates the initiation of Thomas, who had to see, understand and, after asking the right questions, remain silent for seven years (53).

1990: Paul Edwards probes the theme of ambiguous seductions in Keats's "La Belle Dame Sans Merci," Spenser's *The Faerie Queene,* and "Thomas the Rhymer." In his discussion Edwards concedes that there is confusion with Christian mythology and ethics in all three tales. "Like the creator of 'Thomas the Rhymer' the monkish recorders of old tales found themselves poised uneasily between the moral codes of their Christianity, and a pagan past, fairly recent, to which their culture was still deeply, if ambiguously, devoted. My argument is that a similar tension was experienced by the poets of the romantic period" (203).

1992: Robert Stewart considers "Tam Lin" and "Thomas the Rhymer" to be two powerful and important initiatory visions. According to Stewart, the stages found in "Thomas the Rhymer" are 1) sleeping under a sacred tree, the hawthorn; 2) meeting the Faery Queen; 3) traveling with her into the Underworld; 4) wading through rivers of blood (sometimes blood and tears); 5) the absence of the sun and moon, but the sound of the roaring sea; 6) a vision of a garden and an apple tree; 7) a warning concerning the fruit; 8) the fruit being transformed into bread and wine; 9) a vision of three roads: wickedness, righteousness, and elfland; 10) service in Elfland, with gifts of a green coat and shoes and the tongue that cannot lie; and 11) the return to the human world (57). Stewart explores these stages individually and concludes that: "Thomas understands the true nature of his adventure, and offers to pluck the fruit as a gift to the Queen of Elfland. It is this act of simple sacrifice and direction that enables Thomas to continue his journey unchallenged, and furthermore, it is his offering of the fruit that transforms both him and the Queen" (131).

1993: Lewis Spence refers to the belief that mortals must not consume fairy food: "In the ballad of *Thomas the Rhymer* the Fairy Queen proffers the hero an apple from a tree in a green garden that they reach at the end of their journey, but he refuses the same. But in the romance that treats of his adventures, she warns him not to touch the elfin fruit" (164).

1994: Emily Lyle refers to the historical background of the ballad, pointing out that Thomas of Ercildoune, called the Rhymer, lived in the reign of Alexander III and is the protagonist of a fourteenth-century romance-prophesy called *Thomas of Ercildoune*. The ballads as we know them were not known to exist before the eighteenth century (10). Ercildoune is the old word for Earlston, and Scott uses it, according to Lyle, because of the connection to the historical rhymer whose legendary sojourn to fairy land and prophecies had been known since the fourteenth century (275).

1997: Suzanne Gilbert examines the connection between James Hogg's "Kilmeny" and "Thomas the Rhymer." She feels that the connection is not as significant in the theme of supernatural abduction as in the visionary experience and its transmission in the community through legends, ballads, and poetry. Hogg noted that the events in "Kilmeny" are all founded on popular traditions. "So is also the romantic story of Kilmeny's disappearance and revisiting her friends, after being seven years in Fairyland. The tradition bears some resemblance to the old ballads of Tam Lean and Thomas of Erceldon; and it is not improbable that all three may have drawn their origin from the same ancient romance" (45). Gilbert points out that during Hogg's lifetime Thomas was still a traditional hero and an icon of Scottish culture (53 n. 9).

Reworkings of the Ballads in Novel Form

⟨𝒪⟩f the English fantasists, Tolkien seemed to have been most influenced by traditional ballads. His essay "On Fairy-Stories" makes use of a quotation from one of the most haunting fairy ballads, that of Thomas the Rhymer or True Thomas (Child no. 37). The passage, which Tolkien cites to illustrate his conception of the enchanted world of Faerie, is the Queen of Elfland's description of the three great roads to Heaven, Hell, and Fairyland. The first is the "path of Righteousness," narrow, thorny, and little used. The second is the "path of Wickedness," broad and lily strewn. The third is neither good nor wicked, merely Other. (Attebery, 17)

Terri Windling (1994) agrees with this sentiment, commenting that, "The best place to find magical balladry is in the Border Country between England and Scotland. From that lovely, much-disputed land, with its complex and brutal history, come some of the best-known and most evocative songs including 'Tam Lin' and 'Thomas the Rhymer'." As a narrative, these ballads contain many of the most important beliefs about fairies, such as the sinister Faery Queen, the transformations, the teind to hell, and the amoral hedonism of the fairy folk, which have become staples of modern fantasy (Clute and Grant, 921).

The story of "Tam Lin" is part of John Myers Myers's novel *Silverlock*. This novel, first published in 1949, was republished by Ace in 1996. Chapter XX, "Meetings at Miles Cross," tells the story of a very pregnant Janet attempting to gain the freedom of her baby's father from the fairy queen. The chapter follows the traditional pattern of the ballad very closely and allows the narrator, once Janet and Tamlane disappear from sight, to meet with the queen herself and continue his adventures. *Silverlock*

> is a story of high adventure and fantastic transformations—written throughout in a slangy, mid-twentieth-century American style, a style redolent of cracker-barrels, Tall Tales, and the tradition of so called South-Western humour. It also contains an underlying streak of brutality which is not untypical of those rude influences. . . . Shandon [Silverlock] soon finds that he has been stranded in a land of myths, legends, and famous fictional characters. (Pringle, 38)

Thomas's story, blended with that of Tam Lin, is a crucial element in Sheri Tepper's novel *Beauty*, discussed in Chapter 8 of *New Tales for Old*.

The majority of reworkings are based on "Tam Lin," but these frequently incorporate elements of "Thomas the Rhymer" as well. This section looks first at the novels based primarily on "Tam Lin" before turning to novels focusing on "Thomas the Rhymer."

The Queen of Spells

1973. Ipcar, Dahlov. **The Queen of Spells**. New York: Viking.

This first-person narrative, published as a young adult novel, tells the tale of young Janet Carter and her relationship with the "horse thief" Tom Linn. C. W. Sullivan, in his article about reworkings of the ballad in contemporary young adult novels, states that the novel follows the plot of the ballad almost point for point, with the additional material of Janet's everyday life fleshing out the story (145). "Set in the late 1800s and various activities from herding cows to plucking chickens, provide the realistic background which allows the reader to orient himself or herself against which are set in the non-realistic aspects of the Green World" (Sullivan, 145). Janet's narrative takes place during her teen years, from the time she is 11 years old (1876) until her rescue of Tom and her return to the family home in 1884 in rural America. Ipcar provides a version of the ballad for her readers at the end of the novel.

Janet is the third of seven daughters of a respected farmer. She is independent and enjoys her freedom and her explorations at the old Linn place. She meets Tom at the old homestead, and over the span of several years becomes very close to him; in fact, she becomes pregnant with his child when she is 18. She refuses to name the father, and when her father decides to assign the blame, she claims that no one is to blame but herself and that her lover will come back. Her father gives her until the end of the month (October) for this to happen. When

Janet approaches Tom and he explains what she must do to save him from the Queen of Spells, Janet does not believe him and refuses, at first, to take part in the quest. However, she soon sets out to beat the fairy troop to Miles Cross. Janet and her horse are separated in the river when she tries to cross with the fairy troop. She is rescued by two men and a bear in a boat and taken to a gypsy encampment, where she meets Billy Blin and a gypsy woman who takes her in and feeds her herbal tea and allows her to rest inside the wagon. Janet sees "swags of paper roses . . . draped across the ceiling" (Ipcar, 103) and a chart of the stars: shapes of the constellations. "She recognizes the Great Bear and Little Bear, the two lions, and the serpent" (Ipcar, 103–4). There is also a large circus poster: "A fierce snarling lion leapt through a ring of fire, [and a] . . . snake charmer stood wound about by a gigantic hissing snake" (Ipcar, 104).

Billy accompanies her to Miles Cross but takes her new horse, a wedding gift from Tom, and his mount, and disappears, leaving her alone. "She heard a great rushing wind through the branches above her, and then a strange unearthly sound—weird wailing and the jingling of many bells. . . . Bright lights twinkled and shone through the darkness" (Ipcar, 108). Janet watches as a circus parade passes before her: wagons pulled by grey horses followed by a succession of knights. The first, the knight of stars, is on a black steed; the second, the knight of hearts, on a brown one; and the third, the knight of roses, on a white horse. Janet pulls Tom off the white horse as the cry rises: "Tom Linn's awa'!" (Ipcar, 109). Janet and Tom are run down by the Black Riders, and when Janet awakens she is in a circus wagon without Tom. She searches through the circus grounds, meeting, among others, the snake charmer, Madame Draco. Janet volunteers to play a tune on the magic flute:

> Janet stared, paralyzed with horror, her heart suddenly pounding, as a giant serpent reared up before her, uncoiling out of the basket. Coil after coil cascaded out, twisting and looping across the floor. She dropped the flute and turned to flee, but the snake's powerful coils swung looping around her legs and body . . . memory of Tom's words. . . . As the snake turned to make another pass, Janet seized it by the neck just below the head. . . . The cold hard snake was like an iron bar in her hands—a bar that began to grow thinner and thinner, and straighter, and more rigid. . . . Janet opened her eyes. It was the iron bar of a cage that she grasped so tightly. . . . The bar had been ice cold, but now it was growing hot. It was burning her hands, and she wanted to let it drop. (Ipcar, 117)

The bar transforms into a flaming hoop of fire, and Janet finds herself facing two lions, one of which charges her, digging its claws into her shoulder. She soon realizes that "it was no lion, but a great shaggy bear that held her tightly in his great paws, and they were dancing, revolving awkwardly to a gay waltz tune" (Ipcar, 118). Janet does not panic, secure that Tom will not harm her, but she feels as if she's being crushed by the bear. "Oh, Tom! You said you wouldn't hurt me or our child!" (Ipcar, 119). Janet immediately finds herself back with the gypsy woman in the wagon having her cards read. During this reading, the final battle for Tom's mortal life is staged between Janet and the gypsy woman, the Queen of Spells. Janet is shown two final cards. The first is the black spotted two, which changed instantly into a pair of china doll's eyes, "wobbling there grotesquely, bobbing and rocking until they settled staring wildly askew. . . . If I had thought that Tom Linn would look at another woman, I would have plucked out his two gray eyes and put in eyes of wood!" (Ipcar, 125). The second card is the ace of hearts: "If I had thought Tom Linn could ever love another woman, I would have torn the heart from his breast and put in a heart of stone" (Ipcar, 125). When Tom is transformed from rose petals into burning coals, Janet flings them into the elephant's tub of water and Tom emerges whole and mortal. They are given a wedding ring and blessing from Billy and cross the river on their horses "from one world into the other" to find that Janet's father has died before they return. They receive Janet's mother's blessing and settle down to await the birth of their child.

Ipcar deals with the change in setting by having Tom, the grandson of the Earl of Roxburgh, be the companion of the Faery Queen for 300 years. Because he was only nine when he first entered the Queen's world, she sent him back to Earth to become a grown man. Because so much time has passed in the mortal world, the Queen arranges a new place in the world for him to return to (Ipcar, 83). Traditional elements that are woven into this retelling include Halloween, roses (on wallpaper, their scent, rose bushes), Miles Cross, the place in the "forbidden woods," the white horse, transformations, and the teind to hell. Other elements that play a large role in the novel are ballads, promises, tarot cards, and Christianity. Martha Hixon examines Ipcar's treatment of premarital pregnancy, first of Janet's sister and then of Janet herself, in her explorations of the transformation motif. Ipcar's novel implies that teenage pregnancy and shotgun weddings were a common reality of rural life in the nineteenth century: "This note of realism remains true both to the narrative content of the ballad and to the overall cultural content: a girl who allows herself to get pregnant out of wedlock has traditionally been viewed as a rebellious deifier of authority and a girl to be rejected" (Hixon, 198).

The Perilous Gard

1974. Pope, Elizabeth Marie. **The Perilous Gard**. New York: Houghton Mifflin. Reprinted by Puffin in 1992.

This 1974 Newbery Honor Book is set in mid-sixteenth-century England when Queen Mary was on the throne and Elizabeth soon to succeed her. The protagonist, Kate Sutton, lady-in-waiting to Elizabeth, is sent away to the remote castle Elvenwood Hall as a result of a misunderstanding. In addition to this banishment, Kate is not allowed to go any farther than the nearest village, a mile from the Hall. However, on her first visit to the village she discovers that she is not welcome there, either.

Elvenwood Hall, or the Perilous Gard as it is also known, has been the scene of tragedy and of mysterious otherworldly events. Its owner, Geoffrey Heron, sees her safely there and departs, promising to return some time after All Saints' Day.

Kate is left in the care of the castle servants, who tell her the story of Geoffrey's missing daughter and his young brother Christopher, who caused the disappearance. Kate is also acquainted with the Harper, Randal, whom she first met when he was singing a stanza from "Thomas the Rhymer" on her trip through the woods to Elvenwood. Geoffrey took him in one harvest time years ago when he became ill with the fever: "[F]ever nearly killed him, and he never got his wits back properly afterwards" (21). He is constantly "looking for the way in again. . . . [T]here's one way in through the stone of the tower, and another way in over the wall by the well, and another way in by the oak leaf, with never a bough" (23).

A holy well on the castle grounds is the setting for most of the action in the novel. Kate sees pilgrims visit the site as well as Christopher who, over time, tells her about Cecily, Geoffrey's daughter, and her disappearance into that well. Eventually, Kate goes into the well, the world of the Fairy Folk, to bring back Christopher, who has been taken by the Queen of the Fairies, and to rescue young Cecily. Kate is a spirited heroine, and the relationship between her and Christopher is vibrant and real. The lessons gained through her knowledge of the ballad "Tam Lin" aid Kate in her rescue attempt. The former identity of the Harper remains an intriguing question. This is an appealing reworking of both ballads, recommended for readers age 12 and above.

Fire and Hemlock

1985. Jones, Diana Wynne. **Fire and Hemlock**. London: Methuen. Reprinted in 2000.

> For four years she had seemed always to have had this book, with no idea where it came from. Now she knew it had arrived when she was 12. . . . [The] first two ballads were "Thomas the Rhymer" and "Tam Lin." Of course, when she was 12, she had not known that Tam was simply a North Country form of the name Tom. (303)

Jones presents a complex retelling of the two ballads in which Polly, a contemporary young woman of 19, battles the Fairy Queen for the soul of her friend Thomas Lynn. The novel is divided into five parts, with the first three devoted to flashbacks recounting a second set of memories from the time Polly was 10 and first met Thomas to the age of 15, when she unwittingly made a bargain with the fairy folk. A photograph hanging in her bedroom, entitled *Fire and Hemlock*, and an old book of supernatural stories that both seem to have altered substantially work as catalysts for Polly's recovery of these earlier memories. She now remembers that Halloween in the past when she accidentally attended a funeral, met the musician Thomas Lynn, and helped him in choosing six pictures, which were his legacy and of which *Fire and Hemlock* was one. A washed-out Thomas befriended the young girl and together they concocted a fantasy adventure about themselves as heroes-in-training. Over the following five years, Polly and Thomas extended their fantasy adventures through letters and postcards, parcels of books, and occasional encounters. During this time they also discovered that the events in their supernatural adventures have the unnerving tendency to come to life.

> Despite the similarities of names, it was not "Tam Lin" but "Thomas the Rhymer" whom Tom Lynn most resembled. He had been turned out too, with a gift. And Laurel had been furious with him at the time . . . so the gift had been given with a twist. Anything he made up would prove to be true, and then come back and hit him. . . . She had become connected to the gift because she had helped Mr. Lynn make up Tan Coul. . . . [The] gift had been intended to be conveyed through the pictures Tom had been allowed to take—shoddy, second rate pictures—Polly had mixed the pictures up. (307)

In the fourth section of the book, Polly, armed with her newly regained memories, tracks Thomas down and discovers why and how their relationship abruptly ceased and why her old memories have been replaced with others. She arrives in the nick of time to help Thomas fight his final battle with the Fairy Queen. The final section of the book focuses on Polly and Thomas as they reexamine their relationship in light of their involvement with the forces of the faerie world.

Beneath the folklore elements of the story, there is a strong portrait of an intelligent, imaginative, flirtatious, and insecure young girl growing up. Jones has a remarkable ability to grasp the basic elements of the myths and ballads, twist them sharply, then fit them without undue stress into patterns of her own making. The *Horn Book* review states: "Rich in literary allusions and musical references, this complicated but powerful novel succeeds in part because Polly's fantastical memories and actions are firmly grounded in her ordinary friendships, school activities and family relationships" (*Horn Book*, 58).

Seventeen of the twenty-six chapters begin with segments from "Tam Lin," and the remaining nine chapters are headed with segments from "Thomas the Rhymer." C. W. Sullivan states that

> One of Jones' subtlest and perhaps, most effective changes, was to make the events of the "Tam Lin" ballad cyclical instead of singular; that is, the story of the man captured by the Elf Queen and the woman who loves and wants to rescue him becomes a recurring pattern, a series of seductions and attempted rescues (some successful and some not) down through the ages. (146)

Because this story is but one in a cycle of stories, Sullivan explains, the "changes" made by Jones to the ballads in the telling of her story are not changes at all. Rather, they are the differences between the repetition of this cycle and that of earlier ones (146). Therefore it is not crucial that pregnancy be an issue in this novel or that Thomas does not disappear from this world but only from Polly's sphere of awareness as the result of a spell cast by the Fairy Queen's present consort. Polly holds her Thomas emotionally as Janet held her Thomas physically.

Jones also fills the novel with as much music as she can to "replicate" the musical environment of the traditional ballads: Each of the five sections of the novel is labeled as if it is a musical movement. Tom is a cellist, first with the British Philharmonic and then with his own group, The Dumas Quartet, and several of the other key players in the novel are involved, or have been involved, with musical instruments (147).

Evelyn Perry points out that Polly consciously reads both ballads and considers how they inform her reality: "This allows the tales to exist in the original without offending potential audiences. The way in which these tales are the root of this novel, describe folk literature as the root of all literature—thus re-establishing its importance and vitality" (42).

Tam Lin

1991. Dean, Pamela. **Tam Lin**. The Fairy Tale Series. New York: TOR.

The ballad "Tam Lin" is transplanted to a college in Minnesota in the early 1970s in Pamela Dean's reworking of the story. Aimed at an adult audience, the book nevertheless is accessible and appropriate for mature young adult readers. The detailed and authentic world of college life establishes a firm foundation for the adventures of student Janet Carter and her newfound (but hardly young) group of friends. *VOYA* reviewer Carolyn Shute states that, "modern-day Janet, like her ancient counterpart in the Scottish ballad, moves from adolescent passions and uncertainties to maturity, resolution and strength in braving the wrath of the Faerie Queen to rescue her own true love" (*VOYA*, 238). Dean includes a full-text version of "Tam Lin," Child A at the end of the novel as well as some of her thoughts about the story. Dean says she had been fascinated by the story since she first heard it sung by Fairport Convention. "I like the fact that the girl got to rescue the boy, the way she went straight to Carter Hall the moment somebody told her not to, the fact that she was the one who plucked the rose, the shape-shifting, the ominous and ambiguous ending that gives the Faery Queen the last word" (Dean, 459). The themes of the ballad, with the fear of pregnancy and college angst, dictated the setting of her retelling.

The novel begins with Janet Carter as a new student at Blackstock College, where her father has been an English professor for 22 years. Although her family live in town, Janet moves into the student residence, where she makes new friends and, with them, meets fellow students Nick Tooley, Thomas Lane, and classic professors Melinda Wolfe and Medeous. The novel explores her relationships through the beginning of her fourth year in college, when she fights her battle to save her lover and unborn child. After a single sexual episode with Thomas at Chester Hall, Janet becomes pregnant. When Janet contemplates an herbal abortion, Thomas replies: "Look, I'm in a mess so terrible that I can't even begin to describe it, and if you would have the goodness to stay pregnant until after Hallowe'en, you would help me more than I can say. . . . It's only four days away" (Dean, 429). Thomas finally confides his fears and background to a mystified Janet.

If you were in the habit of vanishing under a hill into a realm where time stood still, then, supposing you wanted to live in the world again . . . you might very well decide to got to college to catch up on what the world had been doing. Adolescents are awkward, they know nothing, nobody is surprised at any ignorance they display, Mingle with college students and nobody would notice you twice. (Dean, 431–32)

And as in the traditional ballad:

She had me from the minute I fell off that horse. And every seven years, the Queen of Faerie pays a tithe to Hell. It's seven of her years, not of ours, it depends on what she does and where she goes, but she's been teaching at Blackstock for seven years, and this year is the time. She doesn't pay with one of her own, she pays with one of us. . . . They have all these theories on how one escapes. But the only method anybody had ever seen actually work was to have a pregnant woman come and drag the intended victim off his horse on Hallowe'en and hang onto him for dear life while he turned into everything under the sun. (Dean, 435–36)

For readers already familiar with the ballad, Dean has offered plenty of foreshadowing and preparation for Janet's final confrontation with the Faery Queen. The annual Halloween ride has not gone unnoticed; Janet accidentally witnessed a ride during her first year at the college:

The first riders came, sedately walking, down the broad path to the bridge. The horses were as black as coal. Their manes and tails were braided and strung with beads and ribbons that did not sparkle, but glowed, with a light that showed the riders but cast no shadow. The riders were strung with beads and ribbons, too, covered with flowing clothes of no familiar pattern. Their faces were pale and solemn. Their yellow hair blew behind them, though they went slowly and there was little wind. These were the first three, who may have been men or women. The fourth was a woman in artful tatters of red and green. . . . She had red hair, not like Janet's or Melinda Wolfe's, but like black wood with a red grain in it. . . . The three riders and the woman on the black horses passed by, stirring up the gravel, and swung onto the highway. Behind them were smaller horses, brown, homely-looking ones. . . . They, too, were alight with beads and ribbons. On them were men and women exceedingly beautiful, but looking, after the four who had just passed, as homely as the horses. . . . She did see Melinda Wolfe, in a dress that looked sometimes green and sometimes gray, and knew her by her red hair and the tilt of her head. . . . They went by, too; and behind them on white

horses came people Janet knew. . . . Kit Lane, like a dark copy of
Thomas. (Dean, 201–2)

On Halloween, during her fourth year at college, Janet pulls Thomas off the
horse and is confronted with a lion, a snake, a dove, a swan, and finally a burning
brand that she rolls into the water. And, like her namesake in the traditional ballad, Janet is rewarded with saving Thomas's life and, indirectly, the life of their
unborn child.

Dean has included additional elements in her impressive reworking of the
novel, including the present from the college ghost, who tosses books out of the
window. It is the titles and content of these books that help Janet in her rescue of
Thomas. "All the other books are either connected with Classics, or else they're
about women who get pregnant out of wedlock and suffer for it" (Dean, 388). It is
the book of ballads and the stories of "Tam Lin" and "Thomas the Rhymer" that
help Janet face Professor Medeous, the Faery Queen. The ghost is Victoria
Thompson, another former student who killed herself because of a pregnancy
and an unfaithful lover. This student, with allusions to the traditional ballad, was
Margaret Roxburgh.

Fred Lerner contends that "these books make demands on the reader, and
many of today's readers may be unprepared to meet those demands. . . . [Dean's]
Tam Lin will have more to offer readers acquainted with the works of Shakespeare and his contemporaries" (162). The film *Shakespeare in Love* includes several of the historical actors introduced in Dean's novel. Martha Hixon, however,
feels that Dean diluted the immediacy of the ballad story with the original material included in the novel, which for many fantasy readers detracted from the
enjoyment of the story. The focus is not, as readers may expect, on the supernatural elements of the story but on the situations encountered by most college students in learning how to interact with others. Hixon explains that Dean ties into
one of the major plot elements of the ballad, that Janet chooses her own actions,
including participating in premarital sexual relationships and how Dean's choice
of setting is very significant for her focus. College life in the 1970s provides the
cultural context in which contraceptives and abortions are first fairly accessible
to young unmarried women and acceptable sexual behavior for young adults was
in a state of flux (Hixon, 200). Evelyn Perry, on the other hand, deems Dean's
novel, with "her modernization and expansion, [to] coexist with the beauty and
symmetry contained in the original. While her narrative departs from the original
greatly, to include current studies in literature and the life of a modern college
student, she does not leave out any aspect of the original ballad. This is a retelling
that truly adds to and enhances the tale of *Tam Lin* without distilling it" (46).

A Winter Rose

1996. McKillip, Patricia A. **Winter Rose**. New York: Ace.

Rois Melior is the narrator of this reworking of "Tam Lin." which takes place
during the Middle Ages. Rois lives near a village: "a scattering of houses, the stolid
inn, a sagging tavern, an apothecary, the smithy, a stable, a baker, a weaver, a

chandlery, the mill, and a swath of green in the middle of it" (7). Rois, her sister Laurel, and her father Mathu are fascinated by the mysterious return of Corbet Lynn to his neglected home at Lynn Hall. "They said later that he rode into the village on a horse the color of buttermilk, but I saw him walk out of the wood" (1). Rois hears the stories and the rumors of curses and murder and watches as her sister Laurel becomes infatuated with Corbet at the expense of her fiancé Perrin. She also watches the struggle Corbet faces as he attempts to reestablish his home:

> Corbet built his walls and his stable, roofed his rooms, spoke of clearing fields and finding water, but he lived among us as if each action might make him more human, as if each wish, spoken, might make itself true. But it was little more that his father had done, sitting in Anis' house, watching, pretending that he belonged in that safe world, among those laughing squabbling children, that the opening door would not lead him back to the cold and empty shadow world that claimed him. (96)

Rois becomes Corbet's unwitting ally in his quest to free himself from the family curses and the seemingly inevitable return to the other world and its queen. As an herbalist, Rois wanders freely through the woods during all types of weather and at all times of day or night. On one of these journeys she stops by the well covered with roses, witnesses the fairy ride, and is given a gift by one of the riders. This gift is her own mother's wedding ring. Her mother died of some strange wasting disease, not eating but staring out the window and waiting, for who knew what or whom. When Laurel follows in her mother's footsteps, sitting at the window and wasting away, Rois knows that she must act immediately. But where to find the disappearing Corbet Lynn?

As do Jones and Dean, McKillip employs a cyclical pattern to embrace "Tam Lin" in her story. But in this case, the pattern revolves around three generations of the Lynn family. Nial Lynn, Corbet's grandfather, was universally hated, a man who abused his son and caused his young wife to flee; Tearle Lynn, Corbet's father, was rumored to have killed his father and, cursed for his action, vanishes from the village. It is during one of Corbet's absences from Lynn Hall that an un-aged Tearle returns to die. His body is kept in the icehouse all winter, but when Rois goes to see it that spring, the body has changed. The young face it had worn has aged as it might have done naturally; he is no longer spellbound (255). But his final death and the fairy queen's imprisonment and control of Corbet and Laurel cause Rois to challenge the queen:

> She was the death of the year, and she harvested in the dead of winter. She was transforming my world around me, reaching out to those I loved, changing them to suit her season. She had my mother, she had Corbet; she would take Laurel, she would take me in the end, because I would follow my heart. But neither of us knew what could or couldn't do within her wood. (219)

Rois's ultimate battle takes place at Lynn Hall during her shadow wedding to Corbet. She knows she must hold fast and argue for his return to the mortal world. During the ceremony, Corbet is transformed into her mother, his fierce grandfather Nial, roses and their thorns, fire, and a Corbet who tells her he has never loved her at all but has always loved Laurel. But through it all, Rois refuses to let go until the end, when she will give him freedom: "Freedom. From me, from this house, from her wood. I will hold you fast until you stand free of us all. And then I will leave you" (243). He continues to change, and Rois continues to hold fast as he transforms from ivy to human and to ivy again and again until Rois awakens in her own bed at home. She has won. "I did not know who I had rescued from the wood: Laurel, or Corbet, or all of us, or if, in the end, I had only rescued myself" (248).

Although this novel is directed at an adult readership, it is totally accessible to young adult readers. Unlike Dean's contemporary retelling or Ipcar's young adult novel, this book makes no reference to the pregnancy that figures so largely in the traditional ballad.

Thomas the Rhymer

1990. Kushner, Ellen. **Thomas the Rhymer**. New York: TOR. Winner of the 1991 World Fantasy Award, the 1991 Mythopoeic Award and designated as a 1991 "Book for the Teen Age" by the New York Public Library.

This novel, written in four parts, or voices, relates the story of a young man who arrives mysteriously one day and just as mysteriously disappears for seven years, returning a much-changed man. Meg and Gavin are an older couple living near Eildon Hills, and it is Gavin who introduces the reader to Thomas and the neighbor Elspeth. At the onset of the novel, Thomas is already known as the gifted harper, Thomas the Rhymer. Thomas takes the reins of the story next, following the outline of the ballad to tell his tale. When Thomas returns, Meg takes up the tale, focusing on his successful wooing of Elspeth. It is Elspeth's voice that completes Thomas's story. "It is a singer's story, powerful when read aloud and equally moving when read to oneself" (Lerner 1992, 162). The writing is musical, flowing along the page in rhythms that recreate the ballad world.

Ellen Kushner aptly demonstrates her background knowledge of the Child ballads, using excerpts from various ones, including "Tam Lin," to introduce the different sections of the novel. The character Elspeth explains this: "And the queen, Tam Lin's queen, was Thomas' queen as well. But I was no Fair Janet, I knew" (232). The ballad "The Trees Grow High" inspired the last third of this novel, and the middle section, which was set in the Land of Faerie, makes use of the ballad "The Famous Flower of Serving Men," which is the story of a woman whose husband is murdered by thieves hired by the woman's own mother. She disguises herself as a man to join the king's court, and her husband returns to earth as a dove, shedding blood red tears through the forest. This is the context of the riddle Thomas is set to solve by the Faery Queen's own court. There are also allusions to a wide variety of folktales within the body of the story.

Thomas's tale begins with a flash of movement on the hill as he sits by the Eildon Tree. It is a lady on a fine horse whose mane and bridle are strung with silver bells. She is wearing a green dress, and although he does not know who she is, she knows him well. For the price of a kiss, which he willingly gives, and more, Thomas must follow the lady for seven years. He rides with her and crosses the water past the boundary of Middle-Earth. When he reaches for a peach, the queen reminds him: "But first, you had better learn to control your appetites. Your forefather Adam also thought it would be a fine thing to eat of the fruit of the Tree—I see he merely set the mode for mortals, and taught you nothing to profit from his example" (71). Thomas is made to choose among the three roads. The first is "the rough sort of path a woodman makes to mark his trail . . . twisted down, dark and treacherous and the briars looked fierce" (73). It represents Paradise for the dead. The second path is a proper road and well maintained, but it has "that over-tended look, like one of the king's deer-hunting parks, where there may be no stones left for a horse to stumble on, and people ride mostly to show off their new clothes" (73). The third path, the one Thomas chooses, is no road at all but a wide sweep of valley and hillside covered in mist. His covenant with the lady is that he remain with her for a full seven years (earth time) and that during that time he speak to no one but herself while she is alone. He may, of course, sing his ballads to anyone he wishes. After the seven years pass, too quickly although they are filled with as much frustration as joy, the queen gives Thomas a parting gift: "From seven years of silence, your tongue had been bred to truth, and great truth. Take the fruit now, and eat it, and know the tongue that cannot lie" (166).

Thomas's tongue never lies, but it takes some doing to be comfortable being someone who never lies and only tells the truth whether you want to hear it or not. "Every question seemed to take him unawares; and if he wasn't careful, he'd answer them all, from 'Where did I put my knitting?' to 'Will it rain, do you think?' He was right, too" (187). Elspeth promises that she will never berate him for telling the truth, but "it was like the story of the seal-woman's husband where he promises never to strike her, but of course, he does—well, not *just* like, for Thomas never turned into a seal and vanished; but the same because it is impossible to adhere to grandiose vows under mundane circumstances" (206). After 21 years of marriage, two white deer walk fearlessly into town, and Elspeth knows that Thomas is about to return to his Faery Queen. His death releases him from a great illness, but is it really death?

> A beautiful woman held Thomas in her arms. His face was drawn in pain, his thin hands convulsed. He looked dark and shriveled, shrouded with her long golden hair, his harrowed face pressed to her green mantle. The woman looked up at me, and smiled. Then she laid him down, gently, on the bed. Or so it seemed. I saw the crook of her arm, and the folds of her green mantle encompassing a man's form. Then they were gone. For a moment, the smell of apple blossoms hung in the air. (246)

Terri Windling reports in "The Music of Faery" on Ellen Kushner and Jane Yolen traveling the Scottish borders together. Yolen was doing research for her picture book version of "Tam Lin" and Kushner was doing research for *Thomas the Rhymer*. Kushner told Windling that

> I knew Thomas was my story. He holds the mythic power of King Arthur in the hearts of poets: the artist who is literally seduced by his muse, comes closer to her than any human should do to the source of his art, and is profoundly changed. He can never be at home in this world again, and yet he must continue to live in it ... I don't think I've written the definitive Thomas; I've just written my Thomas, the Thomas who addressed issues that were upon me in those years. Twenty years from now, I might like to do him again. (Windling 1994)

See Chapter 1 to see how Robin McKinley has done this with "her" story! Among her many other accomplishments, Kushner, along with folk singer Jane Tabor, has performed a musical version of the novel in London. Terri Windling, in her entry in *The Oxford Companion to Fairy Tales*, comments that Kushner's novel "entertains and enchants as we follow the harper 'into the woods'—but Kushner is also exploring a theme relevant to all creative artists: the story of a man who follows his muse to the point of danger—and beyond" (Windling 2000, 283).

The Rhymer and the Ravens

1995. Forrest, Jodie. **The Rhymer and the Ravens: The Book of Fate.** Chapel Hill, NC: Seven Paws Press.

In the ninth century, the bard Thomas Sigryggson, the son of a Norse earl and a Welsh bondswoman, escapes the wraith of a wronged husband by sailing with his half-brother to Wales. Thomas is sickened by the battles of the Norse berserkers led by his brother and deserts the raiding party. He falls asleep under a tree and awakens to find himself watched by a beautiful woman, Moira, who seduces him and takes him to the land of faerie. The journey takes him to a crossroads, where a three-faced statue of Hecate stands guarding a road to a quiet green meadow, which is wide and well packed; a road that is choked with thorns and briers and angles quickly out of sight; and a steep road that labors up a hill to end on a cliff. His journey is filled with new people as well: Aubrey, the pooka; Caraid, the human seer; and Rhys, the King of Faery and Moira's husband. Thomas is charged with returning to Earth to go to Asgard, the home of the Norse gods, to steal the two ravens, Thought and Memory, from Odin. These are to be used as a bargaining chip between the old gods and the new religion that is entering the area. The constant warring between these two factions is threatening the world of the fairy folk. Thomas is given several gifts to aid him in his quest: true speech and prophesy, a flute, a harp, and mistletoe as a bribe for Loki.

Thomas has lost seven years by the time he returns to his world, which has been invaded by Danes. Various meetings and journeys later, Thomas meets with Loki, who unlocks the door to the ravens' hall for him. Thought and Memory willingly go with Thomas as Asgard begins to self-destruct after Loki uses the mistletoe to kill Balder the Good. The destruction is also influencing the land of faerie; Moira's plan did not see fruitation. Thomas meets with Moira but only to say farewell. She does not tell him about their unborn child. The book ends there, but the story is continued in *The Elves' Prophesy: The Book of Being* (Seven Paws, 1996) and *The Bridge: The Book of Necessity* (Seven Paws, 1998).

Short Stories

" 'Tam Lin' and brave Janet seem to hold a special fascination for modern women, both those who write and those who read fantasy and juvenile fiction" (Hixon, 202). In the past few years, writers of short stories have become equally partial to retelling the ballads "Tam Lin" and "Thomas the Rhymer."

"Tam Lin"

1986. Vinge, Joan D. **"Tam Lin."** In *Imaginary Lands,* conceived and edited by Robin McKinley. New York: Greenwillow, 181–212.

Jennet's story begins on a perfect Midsummer's Day festival that she is told by her father not to attend. But in the end she goes, carrying with her his warning not to go near Carter Hall, "a ruin on land she has inherited from her mother. It had burned down a hundred years ago. For years she had heard tales that it was haunted; the tales had haunted her, until she had stolen away to see it for herself" (187). Vinge's version is complicated by the fact that Jennet's mother made her own way into the fairy world just after Jennet was born. Jennet finds Tam Lin and willingly pays his forfeit for being in the woods. Her romance, like Janet's in the ballad, leaves her pregnant and ready to rescue her lover from the Faery Queen. But when she does, something seems to be wrong:

> His face was as fair as she remembered, and yet a light had gone out of it; faint lines furrowed between his brows. In the cold blue moonlight she could not tell if he looked any more human. . . . She had freed his soul, and her own. If there was no longer magic in his touch, it was not more than she should have expected. With every choice, something was lost forever. (212)

1990. Munro, Alice. **"Hold Me Fast, Don't Let Me Pass."** In *Friend of My Youth*. Toronto: McClelland & Stewart, 74–105.

The story begins with a journal entry describing Walter Scott's courthouse and the environment around it. Hazel, the journal writer, is a middle-aged Canadian widow who is on a pilgrimage to reclaim the wartime memories of her husband while visiting his cousin in Scotland. Hazel had heard the stories about the young girl he had met there and his adventures. She meets Dudley Brown, who tells Hazel that the elderly cousin is still alive, as is the young girl, who is now the middle-aged owner of the hotel. Hazel is taken to meet her husband's cousin, who claims she never met the husband but does recite a poem. "A rigmarole about fairies, some boy captured by fairies, then a girl called Fair Jennet falling in love with him" (95). There are parallels to the ballad and to the contemporary world of the Scottish village, including Dudley Brown. Although not an actual reworking of the ballad, the story incorporates the major elements in a contemplative look at happiness.

1997. Edghill, Rosemary. **"The Phaerie Bride."** In *Elf Magic,* edited by Martin H. Greenberg. New York: DAW, 39–64.

Jonet's situation is reminiscent of Cinderella's: She is not allowed to attend the ball at which her stepmother and stepsisters are hoping to find husbands. The prince is looking for a mortal wife as a willing sacrifice to pay the teind to hell. The stepmother realizes this and delivers her detested stepdaughter as a bride. Before the fated moment, Jonet and her prince fall in love, and he leaves on the morning after the wedding to sacrifice himself. She follows him for four months, meeting supernatural helpers, and discovers that she is pregnant. She faces a trial at which she must correctly identify her bespelled husband. She saves him, their unborn child, and herself and returns as the rightful owner to Carterhall to find her stepmother gone. The major elements of the ballad are amalgamated with folklore and biblical motifs to create this tale of star-crossed lovers.

"Thomas the Rhymer"

1996. Walker, Barbara G. **"Thomas Rhymer."** In *Feminist Fairy Tales.* New York: HarperSanFrancisco, 55–62.

Walker introduces her story by stating that it is almost a straight retelling from the ballad: "Like Orpheus and the worshipers of Mnemosyne before them, Celtic poets believed that true inspiration lay in this Goddess's underworld Cauldron ... various guises of Cerridwen, Mab, Brigit, or the Morrigan. She appeared in Arthurian legend as Morgan le Fay.... Her priests served a seven-year apprenticeship" (55).

Unlike the traditional Thomas, however, this one has no talent for poetry before his sojourn with the fairy queen. He follows her to her land, not for the sake of a kiss but because she has drugged him with claret. He is not riding with her but running beside her horse, his hand clutching the stirrup. The three roads are differentiated by light. The first was "illuminated by a white light. The second was bathed in a red glare. The third was dark" (59). While in the land of fairy, Thomas is taught all manner of secrets of loving and to make the kind of poetry that would keep listeners spellbound. He is also taught to play the harp. Once he returns to his own time, he becomes a renowned bard who lived happily ever after.

This "straight retelling" seemingly has taken some liberty to make the fairy queen seem even more powerful. But when you are the queen of fairy, is that not power enough?

1997. Glassco, Bruce. **"True Thomas."** In *Black Swan, White Raven,* edited by Ellen Datlow and Terri Windling. New York: Avon, 256–76.

This story was inspired not only by the ballad but also by an article by Carl Sagan describing a thirteenth-century girl's description of how she was taken to a "city up in the clouds" by the fairies. Thomas begins his tale in Erceldoune after his return from the land of the fairy. He is known, and feared, in this thirteenth-century village, for knowing the correct answers to all questions: "The truth is often easier to find than it is to tell"(262). Thomas thinks back to the fairy that he caught in the Eildon Tree when he was 17. He was attacked by fairies and taken to a room where, although he knew that he should not eat the food or drink the wine, "a sweet cloudy liquid was poured in my mouth as I lay bound, until I choked and swallowed" (264). The alien queen and Thomas converse until they decide to journey to the land of faerie itself. He continues his lessons and gains immense understanding about the universe and remains with the queen for seven years, until she is to die and be eaten by the next queen, who will then have all her memories and language. When Thomas returns, he finds that 150 years have passed and no one he knows remains, but he knows that "the organs the Queen put in me are working perfectly, that I am free of disease, that barring accidents or murder I will live for many decades more on this good green world. I reach for my mead and sip it, and I taste the memories of distant bees, a very long way from Home" (276).

1997. McCrumb, Sharyn. **"John Knox in Paradise."** In *Foggy Mountain Breakdown*. New York: Ballantine Books, 37–47.

The narrator is a young Scot visiting America. He is conversing with a young woman who is rather enigmatic and confusing. She keeps referring to the stories and places of Celtic myth and legend as if they are still vibrant and alive. Somehow she ends up with him on the return flight to Scotland. He is determined to show her the tourist spots; she is equally determined to seek out the visionary places of the old ballads and tales. In frustration, he asks himself: "I wonder what Thomas would have shown the Queen of Elfland if they would have stayed in this world? I suppose they'd have skipped John Knox's house" (40). Later, as the woman relates it all to the Tennessee kinfolk back home, the young man becomes even more perturbed: "She finds history in the strangest places, and misses it entirely when it's really there" (41). After their first kiss, the woman becomes the guide and takes him to Earlston, feeds him an apple, and captures his heart. They stay seven days later than they had planned but eventually she returns to America. When he receives a Christmas card from her depicting two deer on the front, he knows he's going to follow her. Light in tone, this story connects the old tales and the old country with the descendants in the new world.

Poetry and Song Lyrics

"We should never forget that the ballad is a sung genre with a whole musical dimension that is not caught by the printed text; to gain full appreciation, every opportunity should be taken of listening to live or recorded performances" (Lyle 1994, 12). The two stories began in poetic form, and several of the reworkings have been attempts to have their words "sing" in other formats as well. A contemporary poetic retelling, but not a reworking, by Kevin Crossley-Holland is in his anthology, *British Folk Tales: New Versions* (New York: Orchard, 1987, 270–82).

1979. Lochhead, Liz. **"Tam Lin."** In *The Grimm Sisters*. Toronto: Coach House Press, [n.p.].

The conversation directed at "Janet" begins by decrying the magic Janet experienced in her meeting with Tam Lin. The poem uses phrases and elements from the ballad to produce a sardonic look at the narrator's friend's relationship with her lover and her pregnancy. "Tell me what about you?/How do you think Tam Lin will take all the changes you go through?"

There are also numerous recordings of both ballads available on CDs that tell the tales in a more traditional way.

"Tam Lin" can be found on the following recordings: Fairport Convention, *Leige and Lief*; *The Best of Sandy Denny*; Steeleye Span, *Tonight's the Night Live*; Pyewackett, *The Man in the Moon Drinks Claret*; The Mrs. Ackroyd Band, *Guns and Roses*; Pete Morton, *Frivolous Love*; Broadside Electric, *Amplificatea*; and Frankie Armstrong/Brian Pearson/Blowzabella/Jon Gillespie, *Tam Lin*. "Thomas the Rhymer" can be heard on Steeleye Span, *Now We are Six*; and Robin Williamson, *Five Celtic Tales of Enchantment*.

Picture Books

Two traditional retellings of "Tam Lin" in picture book format were published in the early 1990s. Jane Yolen's *Tam Lin*, published in 1990 (San Diego: Harcourt Brace Jovanovich) and illustrated by Charles Mikolaycak, is filled with the colors of the Scottish countryside. Yolen states that:

> I have actually been to the area where the ballad takes place. Carterhaugh is now a working farm with a great home not open to the public. But an enterprising American can stand on a far hill and with a good pair of field glasses see a wee bit of it. . . . Of course ballads rely on compression and end rhymes to get across the story. I had to flesh out, even add things. But I hope I kept that air of mystery, trembling moist in the air, that sense of foreboding, adventure and, in the end, resolution. (144–45)

Susan Cooper's *Tam Lin*, illustrated by Warwick Hutton (New York: Macmillan, 1991) is based on a different version of the ballad than the Yolen tale. Cooper's heroine is Margaret, and the prose is less poetic than Yolen's. Both authors completely ignore the fact of the young girl's pregnancy. Evelyn Perry feels that, although Yolen has taken care to include many essential elements in her tale, the symmetrical elements of Tam's transgressions and the audience's concern for the welfare of Tam, Jennet, and their child are lost: "Thus we are left with the hero's journey, paled in scope and severity. . . . Without the sexuality of the original ballad, the socio-literary relevance of *Tam Lin* is disastrously undermined, and the balanced beauty of the tale is gone" (40). Martha Hixon also feels that Jane Yolen "reinterprets the meaning . . . shifting it from signifying the loss of virginity to representing the act of claiming her birthright. . . . The act still represents entry into adulthood; loss of virginity is a woman's right of passage, and claiming the birthright is a man's" (194). Cooper's version focuses on the romantic love interest and retains a subliminal hint at the ballad meaning of "picking roses" (196).

Two other picture books have taken the tale and reworked it to make it their own. *Wild Robin,* by Susan Jeffers (E. P. Dutton, 1976) retells the story from *Little Prudy's Fairy Book* by Sophie May (Lee & Shepard, 1893), which was loosely based on "Tam Lin." This retelling is about a little boy and his sister Janet, who rescues him from an elf, and it is aimed at a much younger audience than young adults.

1991. Muller, Robin. **The Nightwood.** Toronto: Doubleday Canada.

Using yet another version of "Tam Lin," Muller tells the story of Elaine, who attends a fairy ball at a nearby enchanted forest called Nightwood. She plucks the rose that summons the fairy knight, who is about to be sacrificed as a teind to hell. Elaine, like Janet and Margaret, saves her loved one (he is never a lover in these picture book versions) through the many transformations he undergoes through the agency of the Elfin Queen. Reviewer Terri Lyons writes: "The story literally pulsates with suspense and foreboding, but, as will every good folktale, all is right with the world in the end. . . . [T]he paintings are extremely detailed and busy . . . full of wonderful nasty creatures . . . better suited to individual perusal by older children" (89).

Graphic Novels

Charles Vess has included both ballads in his ongoing comic book series as well as in his collected works in the graphic novel *Ballads.* Both the comic books and the graphic novels contain articles about the ballads and contemporary society, discography notes, and information about the musicians who have recorded the ballads. The character Tam Lin also appears in the graphic novels (and the comic book series) *The Books of Magic* (DC Comics), created by Neil Gaiman. Tam Lin retains his identity from the ballads but is only a small part of this complex collection of stories.

1997. Vess, Charles. **"Tam-Lin."** In *Ballads.* Abingdon, VA: Greenman Press, 47–61. Reprinted from the comic book *The Book of Ballads and Sagas,* no. 4.

Written and illustrated by Charles Vess, the story of "Tam Lin" is more of an illustrated story, with full-page illustrations facing a page of text enveloped in a frame of a woman and her hair, than a comic book, with several small panels per page. Vess concentrates on Tam Lin's thoughts as the tale is told, first as a monologue and then as dialogues between Tam Lin and the Piper and Tam Lin and Janet. This is no longer Janet's tale, and the Faery Queen plays no role at all. The introduction to the graphic novel by Paul Chadwick states that: "The playscript/ facing page illustration was a move to simplify execution to beat a deadline. But it brought forth something special in the artist, a heightened attention to decoration and design" (5).

1997. McCrumb, Sharyn. **Thomas the Rhymer.** Illustrated by Charles Vess. In *Ballads.* Abingdon, VA: Greenman Press, 28–37. Reprinted from the comic book *The Book of Ballads and Sagas,* no. 1.

Following closely the traditional Child Ballad, McCrumb extends the story by use of dialogue and a stronger and more involved ending to the tale. The time in the Land of Faerie is dealt with in just a few panels, but the time after Thomas's return demonstrates his wisdom and the slow passing of time until indeed, Thomas and the Faery Queen are reunited for ever. The black-and-white illustrations aptly recreate the time of magic, the travels to the land of fairy, and the time spent waiting for Thomas's return. The illustrations are dynamic and filled with movement and magic.

Internet Resources

There is a great deal of interest on the Internet in ballads and folklore in general. Besides the Early Child Ballad site mentioned previously in this chapter, there is a Tam Lin Web ring which, among other things, includes discussions on Thomas the Rhymer, modern retellings and recordings of the ballads, and analysis and artwork relating to the traditional ballads themselves.

Because several of these sites are useful for a fuller understanding of the ballads and the contemporary fascination with their meanings, I discuss them here in detail. Information on the Internet is, by its very nature, transitory or only semi-permanent, and I apologize in advance if this information can no longer be located.

1997. Kitaguchi, Abigail. **"The Tam Lin Pages,"** http://www.tam-lin.org.

Among the plethora of information on "Tam Lin," Kitaguchi has included information on exploring the ballad, comparing minor and major variations among versions, and interpreting the symbols from the ballad. The "Tam Lin" resources pages include a listing of related books and recordings of the tale. This site also includes comparisons between "Tam Lin" and "Beauty and the Beast" and other ballads such as "Thomas the Rhymer." The interpretations of the symbols, based on Kitagichi's own understanding, include discussions of plucking a rose, getting the child's name (or that of the father), Halloween, Faerie Horse, transformation, the green mantle, and the Queen of the Faeries. In the pages comparing "Tam Lin" to "Thomas the Rhymer," Kitaguchi includes the text of "Thomas the Rhymer" and states that similarities include the interest of a mortal man for the Queen of Faeries, the setting and means of the "abduction," the time period of seven years, the teind to hell, and the relationship between the Queen and both Tam Lin and Thomas. This latter point, of course, also offers the greatest contrast between the two ballads. Thomas poses no threat to the Queen and in fact receives a gift and a promise for his service when he is released back into the world from whence he came. Tam Lin, a probable sacrifice, needs rescue and returns to the mortal world through trial and tribulation on the part of his human lover.

The most valuable aspect of this Web site is the resource pages. Kitaguchi amalgamates versions in print "books containing versions of the ballad and/or other information, linked to web sites where appropriate"; "Tam Lin"-related Web sites, including the "Tam Lin" Web ring; movies based on "Tam Lin"; stories based on or inspired by "Tam Lin," including almost all the novels, short stories, picture books, and graphic novels discussed in this chapter as well as several on-line short story versions; and "Tam Lin" in music, with information on the group name and the album on which the version can be found. "Tam Lin and Scotland" includes maps and photographs of places connected with the ballad. Kitaguchi includes a dictionary of words and phrases used in Child 39A. An extremely valuable resource is "The Big Storyline Table," which analyzes specific elements from the ballad and, at the time of writing, the 27 different versions including the Child variants and those sung by contemporary recording artists such as Steeleye Span, Frankie Armstrong, and Fairport Convention.

"Ballads and Broadsides: 'Tam Lin'," http://www.legends.dm.net/ballads /tamlin.html.

A brief introduction to the ballad, including references to Jane Yolen's picture book and the novels referred to in this chapter, prefaces this list of annotated links to Web sites about "Tam Lin." Several of the links are no longer viable, but there are worthwhile links to a Web site on Child's ballads and various articles and illustrations of interest.

"Ballads and Broadsides: 'Thomas the Rhymer'," http://www.legends.dm .net/ballads/thomas.html.

This page links primarily to the "Faerie Lore and Literature" page, which includes the ballad, complete with notes, a link to the fourteenth-century romance attributed to Thomas, and a history of the tale. There is also a link to an essay on Ellen Kushner's *Thomas the Rhymer*.

Classroom Extensions

The following suggestions may be supplemented by the myriad of information available on the Internet, as discussed above.

The Heroic Ideal

Diana Wynne Jones explains the myriad of influences underpinning her *Fire and Hemlock*. One of these is a desire to have a real female hero, one with whom all girls could identify. This is the reason behind the name "Polly"; the Greek word "poly" means "more than one; many or much" (Jones, 134). Polly's picture, called *Fire and Hemlock*, is very peculiar; sometimes there seem to be many people in it and sometimes not (135). The female hero behaves throughout like a woman and not like a pseudo-man. But Jones's major influences were four underlying principal myths and legends:

❖ For the emotive aspect of the story, the ballads of "Tam Lin" and "Thomas the Rhymer," the foray into the supernatural world of the imagination to save your loved one.

❖ For the shape of the story, *The Odyssey:* "the way it had largely to be told in flashback. Homer's *Odyssey* starts in what we have to call present-day Ithaca, and when Odysseus himself finally appears, at least half of *his* story is in flashbacks" (1989, 135). Jones states that this aspect gave her Polly, the female narrator, Tom's recent divorce from Laurel and her way of bending the truth, and the tie-in with the teind to hell. "Put this together with the gift of true-speaking the Queen gives Thomas the Rhymer, and you have Laurel's gift to Tom: that everything he imagines will come true" (135).

❖ The organizational underpinning of the narrative was T. S. Eliot's *Four Quarters:* "This, on a purely technical level, gave me a story divided into four parts and featuring a string quartet" (138). It also gave her the setting and atmosphere for the funeral and the vases.

❖ For the kernel of the story, the myth of Psyche and Cupid. "Tom in fact has Cupid's attributes, although few people seem to notice. . . . Who is mostly blind and goes to work with a bow?" (139). Jones states that this was an important aspect for the book because "people do lose sight of their ideals quite often in adolescence and young adulthood; they tend to see life as far too complex and then come up with the idea that things are only real and valid if they are unpleasant or boring" (139).

Reread the novel to see if you can find traces of these (and other) influences on this multilayered novel.

Literary Allusions

Pamela Dean's novel *Tam Lin* is filled with allusions to the writings of William Shakespeare, particularly *Hamlet;* Chaucer; Keats's "La Belle Dame Sans Merci"; and Christopher Fry's play *The Lady's Not for Burning*. Find these allusions and the originals and discuss the possible reasons for their inclusion in the story line.

Orpheus and "Thomas the Rhymer"

Kathryn Herron compares the legend of Orpheus and the story of "Thomas the Rhymer." The differences are minute. Both are poets. Orpheus plays the lyre and Thomas plays the harp. Orpheus, motivated by spiritual love, descends into Hades to fetch his wife. Thomas, obliged by physical love, accompanies the Faery Queen into the Otherworld. There are numerous other close similarities between the two characters. Both appear at the court of the King and Queen of the Otherworld, both return to Earth alone, both are known as prophets after their return, and both are shown to be Christ-like after the journey (Herron, 30).

Make your own comparison between these two stories. Are they as closely aligned as Herron suggests?

A Parcel of Books

In her novel *Fire and Hemlock*, Diana Wynne Jones includes references to a number of books that Thomas sends to young Polly, hoping that they will provide some answers and direction for her. These books were of great importance to Jones herself when she was a child and provide a sound basis for the development of an understanding of fantasy. The parcel includes Anna Sewell's *Black Beauty*, a collection of Sherlock Holmes stories, Stowe's *Uncle Tom's Cabin*, tales of King Arthur, Dumas's *The Three Musketeers*, Tolkien's *Lord of the Rings*, Kipling's *Kim*, *The War of the Worlds* by H. G. Wells, *The Man Who Was Thursday* by Chesterton, Lewis's *Philandra*, G. K. Chesterton's *The Napoleon of Notting Hill*, John Buchan's *The Thirty-nine Steps*, Philippa Pearce's *Tom's Midnight Garden*, James Kinsley's *The Oxford Book of Ballads*, and a book of fairy tales. Jones comments to her readers about fairy tales through her protagonist: "[O]nly thin, weak thinkers despise fairy stories. Each one has a true, strange fact hidden in it, you know, which you can find if you look" (1989, 144). In which way would any of these books help someone in a battle with the Fairy Queen? How did they help Polly?

Roses

All of the novels retelling the story of "Tam Lin" utilize the image of roses. What is the significance of roses in the traditional ballad? How and why are roses significant in the retellings? What do roses symbolize in Western culture today? What did they signify in the past? In the language of flowers, the color of the roses is also very significant. Does this seem to be the case in the contemporary tales?

Shakespeare and Thomas

There is evidence that William Shakespeare was familiar with the prophecies of Thomas the Rhymer. "In a certain play, which it is traditionally unlucky to name [Macbeth], a clear adaptation of one of Thomas's verses is found. The original reads:

> *Feddarate Castle sall ne'er be ta'en*
>
> *Till Fyvie wood to the siege is gaen.*
>
> (Stewart, 127)

How did Shakespeare adapt these lines, and how did he use them in the action of his play? Thomas's prophesy came true in a later century when William of Orange made battering rams out of Fyvie wood and entered the previously unconquered Castle of Feddarate (127).

Triads

Jones writes about her female characters and their arrangement in triads. Discuss the following:

> All the female characters are arranged in threes, with Polly always at the centre. There are Nina (who is silly), Polly (who is learning the whole time), and Fiona (who is sensible); there are Granny, Polly, and Ivy, old, young and middle-aged respectively. The first threesome may not strike people as significant, but taken along with the second, I hope it begins to suggest the Three-Formed Goddess, *diva triforma*. Towards the end of the book, Granny takes on the role of Fate and Wisdom quite overtly, shearing fish and explaining the riddle of the ballad of *Tam Lin*. Laurel is of course an aspect of this goddess. Consequently, the most important threesome is Laurel, Polly, Ivy. Ivy is the mundane parasitical version of Laurel, evergreen and clinging—Laurel as the Lorelei in Suburbia, if you like. And Polly—make no mistake—is intended to be an aspect of Laurel too—Laurel as Venus and the Fairy Queen. But she is the aspect that appears not in *Tam Lin* but in *Thomas the Rhymer*, the good and beloved Queen that Thomas first mistakes for the Virgin Mary and then submits to. The adventures Polly and Tom have together fairly carefully echo this second ballad. (Jones, 137)

Tristrem and Isolde

"It was for the casting the romance [already known] into Scottish verse that credit is given to the Rhymer; and his composition soon became known throughout Europe as the best version of the famous tale" (Eyre-Todd, 16). What is this famous tale, and is the Rhymer still given credit for the best version? What about Wagner's opera?

Using Ballads in the Classroom

The activities related to ballads that you can do are limited only by your own imagination and creativity. Some possibilities are providing a story for a ballad fragment; writing a ballad on a contemporary topic; and rewriting a traditional ballad to reflect current events. Topics that were of immense interest to the ancient ballad singers and writers include crime, historical events, the supernatural, disasters and accidents, romantic tragedy, domestic tragedy, outlaws and pirates, and love and sentiment. How do these compare with the subjects of ballads written today?

References

Attebery, Brian. 1980. *The Fantasy Tradition in American Literature.* Bloomington: Indiana University Press.

Brewer's Dictionary of Phrase and Fable. 1981. Edited by Ivor Evans. New York: Harper & Row.

Briggs, Katharine M. 1970. *A Dictionary of British Folk-Tales in the English Language. Part A: Folk Narratives, Volume 2.* London: Routledge & Kegan Paul.

———. 1971. *The Personnel of Fairyland: A Short Account of the Fairy People of Great Britain for those who tell Stories to Children.* Detroit: Singing Tree Press.

Bronson, Bertrand Harris. 1959. *The Traditional Tunes of the Child Ballads: With Their Texts, according to the Extant Records of Great Britain and America. Volume I. Ballads 1 to 53.* Princeton: Princeton University Press.

Buchan, David. 1972. *The Ballad and the Folk.* London: Routledge & Kegan Paul.

———. 1991a. "Ballads of Otherworld Beings." In *The Good People: New Folklore Essays,* edited by Peter Narvaez. New York: Garland, 142–54.

———. 1991b. "Talerole Analysis and Child's Supernatural Ballads." In *The Ballad and Oral Literature,* edited by Joseph Harris. Harvard English Studies 17. Cambridge, MA: Harvard University Press, 60–77.

Child, Francis James. 1976. *English and Scottish Popular Ballads, Volume I,* edited by Helen Child Sargent and George Lyman Kittredge. New York: Gordon Press.

Clute, John, and John Grant, eds. 1997. *The Encyclopedia of Fantasy.* London: Orbit.

Duffy, Maureen. 1972. *The Erotic World of Fairy.* New York: Avon.

Edwards, Paul. 1990. "Ambiguous Seductions: 'La Belle Dame Sans Merci,' 'The Faerie Queen,' and 'Thomas the Rhymer'." *Durham University Journal* 51(2): 199–203.

Eyre-Todd. George, ed. n.d. *Early Scottish Poetry.* London: Sands and Co.

Freedman, Jean. 1991. "With Child: Illegitimate Pregnancy in Scottish Traditional Ballads." *Folklore Forum* 24: 3–18.

Friedman, Albert B. 1956. *The Viking Book of Folk Ballads of the English-Speaking World.* New York: Viking.

Geer, Caroline. 1978. "Land of Faery: The Disappearing Myth." *Mythlore* 5(2): (Autumn): 3–5.

Georges, Robert A., and Michael Owen Jones. 1995. *Folkloristics: An Introduction.* Bloomington: Indiana University Press.

Gilbert, Suzanne. 1997. "Hogg's 'Kilemeny' and the Ballad of Supernatural Abductions." *Studies in Hogg and His World* 8: 42–55.

Guy, Sandra Marie. 1993, May 14."With Fairy Forth Y-nome . . ."(SO 1.169): A Study of the Fairy Abductions and Rescues in 'Thomas the Rhymer,' 'Tam Lin,' 'Sir Orfeo,' and 'Sir Laundal'." Master's thesis, Lehigh University.

Haden, Walter D. 1972. "The Scottish 'Tam Lin' in the Light of Other Folk Literature." *Tennessee Folklore Society Bulletin* 38: 42–50.

Haining, Peter, ed. 1971. *The Clans of Darkness: Scottish Stories of Fantasy and Horror.* New York: Taplinger.

Herron, Kathryn E. 1975. "The Motif of the Otherworld Visit of Thomas the Rhymer." Master's thesis, University of Rhode Island.

Hixon, Martha Pittman. 1997. "Awakenings and Transformations Re-visioning the Tales of 'Sleeping Beauty,' 'Snow White,' 'The Frog Prince,' and 'Tam Lin'." Ph.D. dissertation, University of Southwestern Louisiana.

Horn Book. 1985. Review of *Fire and Hemlock* (January/February): 58.

Jones, Diana Wynne. 1989. "The Heroic Ideal—A Personal Odyssey." *Lion and the Unicorn* 13(1): 129–40.

Lepow, Lauren. 1985. " 'They That Wad Their True-Love Win': 'Tam Lin' and 'Jane Eyre'." *Massachusetts Studies in English* 10(2): 110–26.

Lerner, Fred. 1992. "Tell the Old Stories Again." *VOYA* (August): 159, 162.

Lyle, E. B. 1969. "The Ballad 'Tam Lin' and Traditional Tales of Recovery from the Fairy Troop." *Studies in Scottish Literature* 6: 175–85.

———. 1970a. "The Opening of 'Tam Lin'." *Journal of American Folklore* 83: 33–43.

———. 1970b. "The Relationship Between Thomas the Rhymer and Thomas of Erceldoune." *Leeds Studies in English* 4: 23–30.

———. 1970c. "The Teind to Hell in 'Tam Lin'." *Folklore* 81: 177–81.

———. 1971. "The Burns Text of 'Tam Lin'." *Scottish Studies* 15: 53–65.

Lyle, Emily. 1994. *Scottish Ballads.* Edinburgh: Canongate Press.

Lyons, Terri L. 1994. "A Scottish Folktale Re-painted." *CCL* 73: 88–89.

MacDonald, Margaret Read. 1982. *Storyteller's Sourcebook: A Subject, Title, and Motif Index to Folklore Collections for Children* . Detroit: Gale.

McKillip, Patricia A. 1996. *Winter Rose.* New York: Ace.

Muir, Willa. 1965. *Living with Ballads.* New York: Oxford University Press.

Murray, James A. H., ed. 1991. *The Romance and Prophecies of Thomas of Erceldoune.* London: Facsimile Reprint, Felinfach Llanerch. [Originally published in 1875].

Nelson, C. E. 1966. "The Origin and Tradition of the Ballad of 'Thomas the Rhymer': A Survey." In *New Voices in American Studies,* edited by Ray Browne, Donald Winkelman, and Allen Hayman. Lafayette, IN.: Purdue University Studies, 138–50.

Niles, John D. 1971. "Tam Lin: Form and Meaning in a Traditional Ballad." *Modern Language Quarterly* 38: 336–47.

——. 1978. "A Traditional Ballad and Its Mask: Tam Lin." In *Ballads and Ballad Research: Selected Papers of the International Conference on Nordic and Anglo-American Ballad Research,* edited by Patricia Conroy. Seattle: University of Washington, 147–58.

Perry, Evelyn M. 1997. "The Ever-Vigilant Hero: Reevaluating the Tale of Tam Lin." *Children's Folklore Review* 19(2): 31–49.

Pringle, David. 1988. *Modern Fantasy: The Hundred Best Novels: An English Language Selection, 1946–1987.* New York: Peter Bedrick.

Roseman, Ken. 1997. "Ballad Musings: An Interview with Bob Johnson from the English Folk-Rock Band Steeleye Span." *The Book of Ballads and Sagas,* no. 4. Abingdon, VA: Greenman Press.

Scott, Sir Walter. 1932. *Minstrelsy of the Scottish Border. Vol. II* and *Vol. IV.* Edinburgh: Oliver and Boyd.

Spence, Lewis. 1993. "The Fairy Life." In *A Fairy Tale Reader: A Collection of Story, Lore and Vision,* edited by John Matthews and Caitlin Matthews. London: Aquarian Press, 142–67. [Reprinted from *Fairy Traditions in Britain,* Rider, 1943].

Stewart, Polly. 1993. "Wishful Willful Wily Women: Lessons for Female Success in the Child Ballads." In *Feminist Messages: Coding in Women's Folk Culture,* edited by Joan Newlon Radner. Urbana: University of Illinois Press, 54–73.

Stewart, R. J. 1992. *Earth Light: The Ancient Path to Transformation Rediscovering the Wisdom of Celtic and Faery Lore.* Shaftesbury Dorset: Element.

Stewart, R. J., and John Mathews. 1989. *Legendary Britain: An Illustrated Journey.* London: Blandford.

Sullivan, C. W. 1986. "Traditional Ballads and Modern Children's Fantasy: Some Comments of Structure and Intent." *Children's Literature Association Quarterly* 11(3) (Fall): 145–47.

Toelken, Barre. 1995. *Morning Dew and Roses: Nuance, Metaphor and Meaning in Folksongs.* Urbana: University of Illinois Press.

VOYA. 1991. Review of *Tam Lin* by Pamela Dean. 14(4) (October): 238.

Wasserman, Julian. 1981. "Alchemy and Transformation in the Ballad 'Tam Lin.' " *Mississippi Folklore Register* 15(1): 27–34.

Wells, Evelyn Kendrick. 1950. *The Ballad Tree.* New York: Ronald Press.

White, Kimberly Ann Kennedy. 1997, August. " 'And he never once asked her leave': A Reinterpretation of the Scottish Ballad 'Tam Lin'." Master's thesis, Interdisciplinary Program, University of Oregon.

Wimberley, Lowry C. 1959. *Folklore in the English and Scottish Ballads*. New York: Frederick Ungar. [Reprint of 1928 edition]. [Chapter on "The Ballad Fairy" reprinted In *A Fairy Tale Reader: A Collection of Story, Lore and Vision*, edited by John Matthews and Caitlin Matthews. London: Aquarian Press, 1959, 196–218].

Windling, Terri. 1994. "The Music of Faery." *Realms of Fantasy* 2 (December). Available online at www.endicott-studio.com/forcbmof.html.

———. 2000. "Thomas the Rhymer." In *The Oxford Companion to Fairy Tales: The Western Fairy Tale Tradition from Medieval to Modern*, edited by Jack Zipes. Oxford: Oxford University Press, 283–84.

Wurzbach, Natascha, and Simone M. Salz. 1995. *Motif Index of the Child Corpus: The English and Scottish Popular Ballad*. Berlin: Walter de Gruyter.

Wyness, Fenton. 1973. *More Spots from the Leopard*. Aberdeen: Impulse.

Yolen, Jane. 1991. "The Route to Story." *New Advocate* 4(3) (Summer): 143–49.

Zweig, Dani. 1997, May. "Early Child Ballads." http://www.pbm.com/~lindahl /ballads/early-child.

CHAPTER **4**

Andersen and Three Tales

This chapter begins with an introduction to Hans Christian Andersen. Following that are sections on three of his tales: "The Snow Queen," "The Emperor's New Clothes," and "The Princess on the Pea." These three are bundled together in this chapter because we don't have enough material on them to devote a chapter to each. There are no summaries of critical interpretations for "The Emperor's New Clothes" and "The Princess on the Pea" because we haven't found any extensive enough to mention. The two other Andersen tales included in this book, "The Little Mermaid" and "The Wild Swans," appear in separate chapters.

Hans Christian Andersen, 1805–1875

Hans Christian Andersen is by far the most famous writer of literary fairy tales. "Beauty and the Beast" is more widely known than any of the Andersen tales, has inspired more retellings and reworkings, and has received more analytical attention, but Madame de Villeneuve, who wrote the tale, and Madame de Beaumont, who retold it in its canonical version, are hardly household names. Hans Christian Andersen, on the other hand, is as synonymous with fairy tales as the Brothers Grimm. His stories are included as a matter of course in fairy tale collections. The common assumption is that his fairy tales are the same kind of story as those of the Grimms and Perrault: folktales from the oral tradition retold by a particularly gifted writer. In fact, only a very small number of Andersen's 156 tales are folktales retold. The rest, including some of the most famous, like "The Little Mermaid" and the "Snow Queen," are his own inventions. Nor are they all fairy tales in the narrow sense of wonder tales. "The Ugly Duckling," for example, is really a fable. Andersen stories mix the folktale forms of the wonder tale, folk tale, local legend, and fable with the literary elements of satire and irony in a way so uniquely his own that they have become a genre in themselves.

Andersen's Story

Andersen's writings contain a good deal of Andersen the writer. His own experiences of life and his personality were such strong forces in shaping his tales that discussions of the stories almost inevitably draw on the story of his life. There are a number of biographies and biographical sketches of Andersen available in English. The definitive work is Elias Bredsdorff's *Hans Christian Andersen: The Story of His Life and Work*. More readily available in North American libraries is the volume on Andersen in Twaynes's World Author Series, *Hans Christian Andersen*, by Bo Grønbech. A short and very readable piece on Andersen by Rumer Godden appeared in *Horn Book Magazine* in 1990. There is, of course, an entry on Andersen in the *Oxford Companion to Fairy Tales*, edited by Jack Zipes. All of these accounts have the same substance, although the length of the treatment varies, because Andersen's life was well documented. He was famous as a writer in his own lifetime, not only in Denmark but also in Europe, England, and North America. His letters were preserved, and he wrote two autobiographical pieces, *The True Story of My Life* (1847) and *The Fairy Tale of My Life* (1855).

Andersen was born into poverty in Odense on the Danish island of Funen in 1805, the son of a shoemaker and a washerwoman. His father read him *The Arabian Nights*, La Fontaine, and the plays of the Danish Romantic writer Ludvig Holberg. His grandmother told him stories and took him with her to the old people's asylum, where she worked as a gardener. There he spent time in the spinning room and listened to the old women tell folktales and legends (Grønbech, 17). Like a folktale hero himself, Andersen left home at the age of 14 to find his fortune in Copenhagen. He tried his luck as a dancer and as a singer, living on the edge of starvation in the most miserable lodgings for three years, always writing, until he found a patron who offered to send him to school for a proper education. School was torture to him. He was several years older than his classmates, already very tall and awkward, dreadfully conscious of his poverty. But he persevered through six years and passed his university entrance examination, the equivalent of an undergraduate degree today. His first poems were published in the next year, 1829.

Hans Christian Andersen had an enormous confidence in his own literary gifts and enormous ambition. He insisted from the beginning that he would be a swan, although at first he seemed very much like the ugly duckling of his story. His genius allowed him to cross the class barriers of nineteenth-century Europe. He met the royal families of several kingdoms, was a guest in a number of noble houses, and called the greatest writers of the time his friends. But emotionally he never grew into swan-like confidence. Something of the self-doubts of the ugly duckling remained always with him, and he was often unhappy. To be rich in talent and noble in spirit is not the same as having your place in the world assured by birth. Perhaps it was due to his lack of social confidence that when he fell in love, as he did three times, he loved hopelessly, and never married. "The Steadfast Tin Soldier" and "The Little Mermaid" reflect his perhaps self-pitying understanding of these passages in his life. Against them, however, can be set "The Swineherd," a cuttingly funny story that is not at all touching, in which the prince-turned-pigkeeper takes revenge on the shallow princess who scorned him.

Andersen's ambition was to become famous as a *digter*, a serious author of high art. He first wrote poetry and plays, then novels and travel books, all of which were translated into other languages, and he had established his reputation as a writer in Denmark and abroad before he published his first little book of four fairy tales, *eventyr*, which included "The Princess on the Pea" and "The Tinderbox," in 1835. Other collections followed, eventually 25 in all, and proved to be his most successful work. He called the first ones "Fairy Tales Told for Children," *Eventyr Fortalte for Børn*, and said that he wrote them as a digression from what he considered his more important work. But they were as much appreciated by adults as by children, and he began to acknowledge his adult audience. From 1843 on the phrase "told for children" was dropped from the titles of the collections of his tales. In the same year he wrote to a friend:

> The first ones I wrote were, as you know, mostly old ones I had heard as a child and that I usually retold and recreated in my own fashion; those that were my very own, such as the "The Little Mermaid," "The Storks," "The Daisy," and so on, received, however, the greatest approval and that has given me inspiration! Now I tell stories of my own accord, seize an idea for the adults—and then tell it for the children while still keeping in mind the fact that mother and father are often listening too, and they must have a little something for thought. (Grønbech, 92)

Content and Style of Andersen's Tales

Bengt Holbek has identified seven of Andersen's stories as retellings from Danish oral tradition: "The Tinderbox," "The Travelling-Companion," "The Wild Swans," "Little Claus and Big Claus," "The Swineherd," "All That Father Does Is Right," and "Simple Simon." Andersen said that "The Princess on the Pea" was a story he heard as a child, and "The Emperor's New Clothes" is based on a Spanish folktale he read. These are only nine out of 156 stories. The rest are Andersen's own inventions, although some of them have folktale motifs in them.

The stories can be divided into two classes: "[O]ne is told with a twinkling humour, is fast-moving, sometimes whimsical and even a little malicious at times; the other is more serious and slower" (Holbek, 172). All of them have an acuteness of characterization, and many of them contain descriptive passages and independent episodes only loosely tied to the plot. In these ways they are unlike folktales. They do sound as though they are being told aloud, however. Listen to the opening of "The Snow Queen":

> Now we are about to begin and you must attend! And when we get to the very end of the story, you will know more than you do now about a very wicked hobgoblin. He was one of the worst kind; in fact he was a real demon. (*Tales of Andersen and Grimm*, 613)

Andersen often told stories to children, and he loved to read his work aloud at every opportunity. The narrator's voice is always present in his tales, introducing, commenting, explaining, implying. This active presence of the teller makes possible the irony so characteristic of Andersen (but completely absent in traditional folktales) that delights older readers.

Andersen's fairy tales comment on human life much more directly than folktales from the oral tradition do. In his introduction to *Tales of Grimm and Andersen,* W. H. Auden writes of the Andersen tales: "Compared with the Grimm tales, they have the virtues and the defects of a conscious literary art. To begin with, they tend to be parables rather than myths" (xviii). He illustrates this statement with the passage from "The Snow Queen" in which Kay is trying to make the "Ice Puzzles of Reason" spell the word "Eternity":

> Such a passage could never occur in a folk tale. Firstly, because the human situation with which it is concerned is an historical one created by Descartes, Newton, and their successors, and secondly, because no folk tale would analyze its own symbols and explain that the game with the ice-splinters was the game of reason. Further, the promised reward, "the whole world and a new pair of skates" has not only a surprise and subtlety of which the folk tale is incapable, but, also a uniqueness by which one can identify its author. (xviii-xix)

The one thing we expect from a fairy tale is a happy ending, yet many of Andersen's tales end unhappily, or so it seems. My undergraduate students are shocked when they get to the end of "The Little Mermaid" or "The Little Match Girl" and wonder whether they aren't too sad for children. Ursula Le Guin, writing about Andersen's "The Shadow," says, "I hated it when I was a kid. I hated all the Andersen stories with unhappy endings. That didn't stop me from reading them, and rereading them. Or from remembering them . . ." (61). Celia Catlett Anderson tells a similar story about "The Pine Tree":

> When we read this tale to our son, then eight years old, he had tears in his eyes and commented that it was the saddest story he had ever heard. Initially, I judged this as a negative reaction, a rejection of the story, but I was wrong. He returned to the story again and again. Like the small boy who rips the golden star from the tree's branch and pins it to his chest, our son took something shining from the story and, for all I know, wears it to this day. (123)

In Andersen's tales, death does not usually mean defeat. For the little mermaid it is not death but victory over death. For the little match girl it is the loving arms of her grandmother in heaven, which are just as real as the cold and hunger she leaves behind. While the pine tree burns to ashes it remembers, and so is given again, the beauty of the world that it missed while living. Andersen was a nineteenth-century Danish Christian. He was very possibly influenced by Pietism, a life movement in the folk community in Scandinavia that tempered the rather sterile dogmatism and formalism of nineteenth-century Lutheranism. One stream of Pietist thought is a romanticism about death, holding that life is a road to heaven for the faithful. But Pietism also held that even the alienated, even the estranged, are visited by the eternal. Another religious influence on Andersen may have been N. F. S. Grundtvig, preacher, poet, hymn writer, educational reformer, historian, and an enormous cultural force in Denmark during Andersen's life. For Grundtvig, "Faith was liberated from being an achievement. Instead, it became identical with a child's confidence and trust" (Thaning, 126). Grundtvig preached "not to call upon sinners to repent and do penance, but to awaken the child to rejoice in God's fatherly feeling for him" (Thaning, 125). Certainly we know from his letters that Andersen had a childlike and vivid sense of God's fatherly responsibility for him; like Grundtvig, he saw the beauty and goodness of God's creation in the smallest details of the living world around him.

Andersen's tales have enough of his own religious views in them to make today's readers nervous. In places, they are sentimental—but so are the works of Charles Dickens and George MacDonald and Lewis Caroll, and the Grimm versions of German folktales. Sentimentality, especially on the subject of children, is characteristic of nineteenth-century literature.

Auden, noting that Andersen's style is unique, wrote:

> It is rarely possible, therefore, to retell an Andersen story in other words than his; after the tough and cheerful adventures of the folk tales, one may be irritated with the Sensitive-Plantishness and rather namby-pamby Christianity of some of Andersen's heroes, but one puts up with them for the sake of the wit and sharpness of his social observations and the interest of his minor characters. (xix)

Andersen stories have been retold, however, in other words than his. They are necessarily far more widely known in translation than in the original, and they have often been freely retold, that is to say, adapted.

Andersen's Tales in Other Words

Danish is not a world language. Therefore, most people know Andersen's fairy tales in translation. The *World Edition* of 1900, which included 43 of the tales, was published in 12 countries. According to Erik Dal's count in 1955, "the number of languages in which one at least of his fairy tales is to be found, is about 80" (137). In 1981, Spink put the number at over 100: "It is said that, of the world's literature, only the Bible has a larger circulation" (62). Viggo Pedersen, taking into account shortened and adapted translations, estimates that, "In the case of the most popular tales of them all, such as 'The Ugly Duckling' there are certainly several hundred versions, and the numbers may well run into four figures" (1997, 101).

Unfortunately, Andersen's Danish is fiendishly difficult to translate because he mixes formal and colloquial Danish with extraordinary subtlety, and his prose is both carefully precise and fluidly idiomatic. Most Andersen scholars agree that to appreciate his fairy tales fully one has to read them as they were written, in Danish. Even in good translations, important shades of meaning and tone are inevitably lost.[1] However, for most readers there is no alternative to translations.

There is no such necessity for what Grønbech calls "approximate versions," retellings that change the original stories to make them more acceptable to the tastes of the editors or their anticipated audience. Such changes are very common in versions published for children. According to Viggo Pedersen, most modern English translations of Andersen's tales are shortened versions: "[H]appy endings are introduced . . . and social satire and person-centered sentimentality tend to be left out, together with 'literary' romantic features like descriptions of scenery." Interestingly, the shortened versions are more like a folktale than Andersen's original story was (1997, 102). Other common changes include elaboration with explanatory additions, making the language more childish to suit children, toning down violence, removing anything that suggests sexuality, and adding explicit morals where Andersen leaves them to be inferred (Grønbech, 140).

Notions of what can be understood by children and what is acceptable to readers of all ages change over time. A nineteenth-century English version of "The Princess on the Pea" changed the title to "The Princess and the Bean" to accommodate Victorian sensibilities. Although this particular alteration seems ridiculous now, we don't have to look very far to find similar changes made in the name of decency in our own time. In his article "HC and PC," W. Glyn Jones describes the changes made in 1992 by American editors to his new translation of 11 Andersen tales. Andersen's conversational, oral style was made more formal and literary. "Graphic" description and "disrespectful" phrases were removed, as were any words and phrases that had the slightest religious or sexual connotations. For example, in "The Emperor's New Clothes," "Heaven preserve us" became "O my goodness," and in "The Little Mermaid" every instance of the word "breast" was removed. Possible racial sensitivities led to cutting the adjective "white" in "The Little Mermaid" and "Thumbelina," the word "Chinese" wherever possible in "The Nightingale," and "Egyptian" as the language the stork speaks in "The Ugly Duckling." The lesson to be learned from all this is that one version of an Andersen tale is not as good as another if it's Andersen you want.

Reception of Andersen's Tales

Popular and beloved though the Andersen tales are, they have always had their critics. In 1835 a reviewer of the very first collection worried about its effect on children. The story of the princess on the pea, for example, appeared to this reviewer "not only to be indelicate but also indefensible, for the child will imbibe the false impression that ladies of high rank must be terribly thin skinned" (Grønbech 1980, 90). Roger Sale, writing in 1978, finds them far too personal and too pretty. Further, he dislikes the satire, the pointed morals, and the literary adornment:

> Of all the major reputations among authors of children's litera-
> ture, Andersen's is much the hardest to understand or justify. Yet
> for precisely these reasons he is useful here, as a way to mark the
> transition from fairy tales to later children's literature, because
> what is wrong with his work is, almost without exception, what is
> wrong with all inferior children's literature and what mars even
> some of the masterpieces. (64)

Still, new versions in picture books, in collections of selected Andersen tales, and in collections of fairy tales by different authors are published every year. The explanations given for this continued popularity are very different and largely based on the content or meaning of the tales. Jack Zipes, for example, takes his usual reductive materialist approach:

> It is striking, as I have already stressed, when one compares
> Andersen to other fairy-tale writers of his time, how he con-
> stantly appeals to God and the Protestant ethic to justify and
> sanction the actions and results of his tales. Ironically, to have a
> soul in Andersen's tales one must sell one's soul either to the aris-
> tocracy or to the bourgeoisie. In either case it was the middle-
> class moral and social code that guaranteed the success of his
> protagonists, guaranteed his own social success, and ultimately
> has guaranteed the successful reception of his tales to the
> present. (96)

Zipes has written so much on fairy tales that his ideological analysis is likely to dominate discussion on the subject. There is danger that he will be taken too seriously and be allowed to run away with the picnic basket. To put his approach into perspective, however, one has only to consider his reading of "The Princess on the Pea" in the chapter from which the preceding quotation is taken: " 'The Princess and the Pea' is a simple story about the essence of true nobility. A *real* prince can only marry a genuine princess with the right sensitivity" (94). It's hard to believe, but Zipes has either chosen to ignore or entirely missed Andersen's irony, just as the first reviewer did in 1835. Nor is Zipes's reading the only possible interpretation of Andersen's politics. Pedersen (1995) has found revolutionary sentiments in Andersen's tales, Peter Brask notes that "the fairy tales are full of derision and biting satire toward the bourgeois world" (18), and Niels Ingwersen looks at Andersen as a subversive writer who depicts his middle-class and patri-cian audience as his antagonist.

Ursula Le Guin and Celia Anderson, in the passages quoted previously in this chapter, remark on the way Andersen tales stay with their readers. John Cech suggests that they work that way because Andersen connects with secrets in his readers, "emotional realms" ranging from "the deepest yearnings to the most petty jealousies and vanities" that we all have in common and find so difficult to tell. Volker Klotz notes the same immediacy of connection to fundamental hu-man experiences in the tales as a reason for their broad appeal, and adds to that the immediacy of Andersen's narrative style. As the story's teller, Andersen places himself both in the story and in the audience, bridging the gap between the momentary here-and-now of the telling and the distant there-and-then of the narrated events (Klotz, 246).

Andersen's fairy tales, taken as a body of work, are as layered and textured as life itself. For that reason, I particularly like Grønbech's overall reading of the tales:

> The fairy tales emphasize the gospel of an open mind and imme-diate emotion; they speak the case for the small, overlooked crea-tures, and they let it be understood that existence is richer and greater than our limiting notions of good and evil, so rich as never to be exhausted. . . . [They] are one great rejection of any uniformalization of life and any conformalization of people. . . . The fairy tales say that if you live intensely with your immediate surroundings they will come to life for you, and then the great mechanism [of an impersonal physical universe] loses all inter-est. (130–31)

Grønbech suggests that Andersen's stories challenge the reader, and in their challenge lies the reason for their longevity: "The fairy-tales are not a harmless and innocent reading. If you know how to read, they leave your soul disturbed" (131).

"The Snow Queen"

"The Snow Queen" is the longest of Andersen's fairy tales, really a novella, made up of seven loosely connected parts. The quest for the lost boy that ties the parts of the story together, and the animal and magical human helpers Gerda meets on her way, are recognizable folk motifs. But the story is not based on any particular folktale, and the richness of detail in the settings, and the importance of those settings to the story, are very literary indeed. "The Snow Queen" is one of Andersen's most characteristic, and most successful, fairy tales. The following synopsis is rather lengthy, but I have tried to include in it most of the significant details that the critical interpretations summarized in this chapter refer to.

&.

First Story, Which Deals with a Mirror and Its Fragments

A very wicked demon made a distorting mirror that reflected everything lovely and good as ugly and horrid. The demon's pupils took the mirror all over the world, and finally tried to carry it up to heaven to mock the angels. But the mirror fell to the earth and broke into innumerable pieces. These pieces did even more harm than the mirror, for they spread everywhere, and people who got a sliver of it in their eyes saw everything as twisted, while those who got a sliver in their hearts had their hearts turn to lumps of ice.

🐾 ——

Second Story: About a Little Boy and a Little Girl

Two children named Gerda and Kay lived in attic rooms of two adjoining houses. Their parents had made a little garden on the roof with rose bushes and other flowers, and Gerda and Kay often sat in the garden and played together like brother and sister. In the winter their grandmother told them stories about the Snow Queen. One summer day Kay got a grain of the mirror glass in his eye and another sliver in his heart. Then he began to despise the roses for their imperfections and to mock Gerda and the grandmother. One winter day, when he was playing with the other boys in the town square, he hitched his sled to the sleigh of the Snow Queen, who drove away with him, far into the north.

🐾 ——

Third Story: The Garden of the Woman Learned in Magic

Nobody knew where Kay had disappeared to, and everyone thought he was dead. But when spring came the sunshine and the swallows convinced Gerda that he must still be alive, and she set out to look for him. She accidentally wound up floating down the river in a boat and came to a beautiful garden that belonged to an old woman who knew magic. In the garden bloomed flowers from every season, all at the same time, but the old woman made the roses vanish into the ground so that they wouldn't remind Gerda of Kay, because she wanted to keep Gerda with her for company. But after some time had passed Gerda noticed a rose painted on the old woman's hat. Then she remembered Kay, and cried, and her tears falling on the ground brought the roses back up. They were able to tell her for certain that Kay was not dead, for they had not seen him underground. Gerda asked the other flowers in the garden for help, but each had only its own story to tell. So Gerda ran barefoot out of the garden to look for Kay, and found that it was late autumn.

🐾 ——

Fourth Story: The Prince and the Princess

A little later, Gerda asked a sociable crow whether he had seen Kay. The crow thought perhaps Kay was the boy who had passed the test set by the princess of that land, and so had married her and was now the prince. With the help of his sweetheart the crow sneaked Gerda into the palace and up to the bedroom where the prince and princess slept, and Gerda thought for a moment that she had found Kay. But the prince was someone else. However, the prince and princess were sympathetic and sent Gerda on her way in a golden carriage, with plenty of beautiful warm clothing and dainty provisions.

🐚 ───

Fifth Story: The Little Robber Girl

In a dark wood robbers attacked the carriage and killed the postilions, the coachman, and the footmen. The old robber woman wanted to kill Gerda and eat her, but her little daughter stopped her because she wanted Gerda herself as a pet. The little robber girl was wild and rough and a little cruel, but when Gerda learned from the pigeons that they had seen Kay with the Snow Queen, she sent Gerda off on the back of her pet reindeer, north to Lapland.

🐚 ───

Sixth Story: The Lapp Woman and the Finn Woman

In Lapland Gerda and the reindeer stopped at a poor little hut and told the old woman who lived there their stories. The Lapp woman told them they had much farther to go and sent them on to the Finn woman with a letter written on a dried codfish. They traveled on under the northern lights to the Finn woman, who warmed them and fed them. She had magic so powerful that she could tie all the winds of the world up with a piece of twine. The reindeer asked for magical help for Gerda, but the Finn woman answered that she could not give Gerda greater power than that she already had because of her innocent heart. Then she sent Gerda, barefoot and without mittens, on the reindeer to the Snow Queen's estate. There the reindeer had to leave her. The Snow Queen's guard, enormous living snowflakes, attacked Gerda at once, but Gerda said the Lord's Prayer, and her frozen breath turned into angels, who broke the snowflakes into pieces with their spears and touched Gerda's hands and feet so that she hardly felt the cold.

🐚 ───

Seventh Story: What Happened in the Snow Queen's Palace and Afterwards

In the middle of the Snow Queen's palace was a frozen lake that the Snow Queen called The Mirror of Reason. Its surface was broken into thousands of identical pieces that fit together perfectly. Here Kay, almost black with cold, had been making patterns and words out of bits of flat ice, which were called the Ice Puzzles of Reason. The Snow Queen had promised him that if he could make the ice pieces spell the word Eternity, he would be his own master, and she would give him the whole world and a new pair of skates. But he never could manage to make the word, and when Gerda found him he was sitting so still that he seemed frozen to death. Gerda embraced him and cried hot tears that melted the ice in his heart and the bit of mirror that had frozen it. And she sang him a hymn she had been taught at home about roses and the Christ Child. Then Kay began to weep, and when his tears had washed the glass splinter out of his eye he recognized Gerda and held her tight. They were so happy that the ice pieces danced for joy, and when they came to rest they spelled the word Eternity. So Kay was free, and Gerda kissed him until he was warm and well. Then they went home, stopping to visit the Finn woman and the Lapp woman and meeting the robber girl on their way. Everywhere they went they found spring. When they reached their home they went up to the grand-mother's room, where everything was still the same. But as they went through the door they realized that they had grown up. They sat under the roses, holding hands, still children at heart, and the grandmother read to them from her Bible: "Without ye become as little children ye cannot enter into the Kingdom of Heaven."

A History of "The Snow Queen"

According to Naomi Lewis, *Snedronningen*, "The Snow Queen," was first published on December 21, 1844, in a small paperbound edition. It was also included in a collection of Andersen's tales, *Nye Eventyr, Anden Samling*, in 1845.[2] It was completed in less than three weeks. Andersen wrote to a friend that the story "took hold of my mind in such a way that it came dancing out over the paper" (Lewis).

We know from Andersen's second autobiography, *The Fairy Tale of My Life*, published in 1855, that two of the elements in the story, Gerda and Kay's rose garden and the Snow Queen herself, come directly from memories of his childhood. The garden was based on one his mother had made on the roof of their house, in a chest filled with earth placed in the gutter where their house joined the next one. The Snow Queen's abduction of Kay was inspired by something his father had told him. On a winter's day his father had pointed to a shape made by the frost on the window pane that looked like a woman with outstretched arms, and said jokingly, "She is come to fetch me." When his father died the next year, Hans Christian's mother said that the ice maiden had fetched him. In the story, Kay first sees the Snow Queen through a frost-covered window, and is frightened. The next winter, the Snow Queen steals him away.

By 1844 Andersen had stopped calling his fairy tales children's stories. Nevertheless, "The Snow Queen," like his other well-known tales, most often turns up in English translation in illustrated versions for children. It has also frequently been adapted as a children's play. (The first such adaptation was made by L. Loveman and published in London in 1913.) This may in part be the case because the two main characters in the story, Gerda and Kay, are definitely children. Andersen frequently uses the adjective "little" with their names (little Gerda, little Kay). Although they discover that they have grown up when they reach home again at the end, their love for each other throughout the story has nothing to do with romance and everything to do with innocence. In the fourth story, when Gerda thinks the boy who married the princess might be Kay, she is not at all jealous or disconcerted, only happy to have found him safe. It is the innocence of Gerda's love for Kay that makes others help her and gives her power to defeat the Snow Queen.

In the reworkings for older readers described in this chapter, Gerda and Kay are made into adults, or at least adolescents, and this change has a radical effect on the story. The innocent love of friendship becomes the possessive love of desire. Frequently, this change makes Kay hopelessly weak or a complete rotter, and

Gerda a victim who needs to learn to see the world differently. It is as if she, not Kay, has the distorting splinter of glass in her eye, and once she gets rid of it she leaves Kay behind and takes up with the little robber girl or the Snow Queen.

The three novels discussed below follow the structure of Andersen's "The Snow Queen" quite closely. The short stories are made up of pieces, as if Andersen's tale had been broken into fragments that the authors have rearranged like one of Kay's clever ice puzzles in the palace of the Snow Queen. The only film version of "The Snow Queen" that I've come across is a feature-length Finnish film with German subtitles. I haven't seen it myself, but have heard that it is a darkly Jungian interpretation with an emphasis on sexuality.

Critical Interpretations

1967:   Christine E. Fell identifies the rose and the snowflake as symbols of life and death, good and evil in "The Snow Queen." White is the color of snow, "the cold, sterile colour of the Queen," and represents the evil of spritual death (84). Red is the color of love, of blood, and of roses. Roses are the symbol of life and are associated with Christ in the hymn that Gerda sings to Kay. Kay rejected the imperfection of living roses for the perfect beauty of snowflakes. The opposition of the snowflake and the rose "deliberately touches off all the overtones of snow/winter/death and of spring/Easter/Resurrection" (84).

1971:   Vivian Robinson's reading of "The Snow Queen," and especially her interpretation of the stages of Gerda's journey, make an interesting contrast with Wolfgang Lederer's reading (see below). Kay is searching for reality, from which he is separated by his evilness. Gerda is a kind of Christ figure reaching out to the lost man. The Snow Queen is beautiful on the outside but has a black heart.

The first stop of Gerda's journey is in the flower garden of the old woman who knows magic. Robinson calls this "the world of hope and consolation" (188). The roses there give love and hope, in contrast to the narcissus, which is as self-centered as Kay has become. The second stop, Gerda's second stage of development, is in the world of the Prince and the Princess, "which symbolizes riches or materialism, power, and artificiality" (190). Here Gerda sees the effects of court authority and, in the appointment of the ravens to a court position, the security of a place within the hierarchy of power. The third stage of the journey takes place in the world of the robbers. Power is the focus of this world, also, but it is the power of brute force, outside the law and therefore outside society, and it is dangerous and ugly. Next Gerda travels through "the world of the very, very poor, the Lapland Woman and the Finland Woman" (192). Here she finds a deep, old wisdom, not Christian but able to recognize that the power of Gerda's loving and innocent heart is greater than any power magic could give her. Finally, the Snow Queen's world of ice "symbolizes emptiness, hollowness, unhappiness, and coldheartedness," a frozen hell (193). Gerda's warmth and tears release Kay, and their joy causes the ice fragments to spell the word "eternity." "Through the impelling drive of love, she gained the knowledge she needed to find the lost child and to solve the ice puzzle" (194). Gerda and Kay return to the garden where their journeys started. Although grown-up now, they are children in their hearts and therefore can enter the kingdom of heaven.

1978: Roger Sale doesn't like most of Andersen's work, but he admires "The Snow Queen" for its "grand, atmospheric writing about nature" (70). He suggests, without enough explanation, that the story is about what the cold Danish winters mean to the people who live through them. The glass splinters in Kay's eye and heart affect him only once winter comes. Then the Snow Queen takes him, because his frozen heart makes him hers. The Snow Queen is a natural force, neither good nor evil. She creates beauty and perfection and is beautiful and perfect herself. Her realm, which includes Denmark in winter, is dazzling, ordered, and, since it is frozen, as unchanging as eternity. However, salvation is not in that frozen perfection but in the less than perfect world of changing seasons that Gerda travels through to bring Kay back. "The story is long because it must be, in order to show the world, when it is not dominated by the Snow Queen, is not paradise but the world, multiple, varied, usually helpful to a distressed girl if it doesn't have to go far out of its way to do so" (71).

1986: Wolfgang Lederer takes a psychoanalytical approach to "The Snow Queen," first reading the story through Andersen's life and then reading the story onto Andersen's life. His interpretations fill a book, *The Kiss of the Snow Queen*, and cannot be completely summarized here. Notably, he sees the effect on Kay of the glass splinters as typical male adolescence, with its two tasks of differentiating from girls and women and finding a positive male identity (27). So Kay is rude to Gerda and the grandmother, goes to play with the bigger boys, and rejects sentiment in favor of science. The Snow Queen herself is death, but Kay does not die completely, because she only kisses him twice. "The death Kay dies . . . is the defensive-protective hibernation of the emotions during adolescence" (30).

The old woman with the flower garden is also death, but "she is the goddess of organic death, just as the Snow Queen is the goddess of crystalline death" (41). In her garden Gerda forgets about Kay; she is in the adolescent girl's flower stage, "the stage of development that follows upon the awakening of puberty," and has withdrawn, "as many girls do after their first brush with sex . . . to the safety of self-absorbed, narcissistic isolation" (43). The old woman wants to keep Gerda with her, but once Gerda remembers Kay she returns to the real world. The two crows in her next adventure may be related to Odin's two ravens, named Thought and Memory. Certainly Gerda has now remembered Kay. In any case, "she is once again in touch with her animal instincts and drives, and they, of course, once again put her on the trail of Kay" (47). The princess, who invites Gerda to stay, is another stage of female adolescent development, "the riddle princess who yearns for but fears womanhood and who therefore sets impossible tasks and obstacles for the men who woo her" (51).

But Gerda moves on and is captured by the little robber girl. The little robber girl, according to Lederer, is "an embodiment of animal spirits and animal life" (56) and also represents another developmental stage, a temporary escape from "eventual heterosexual involvement, but this time by means of a detour into homosexuality" (57). Her reindeer, Ba, represents Gerda's instincts, which carry her to the Lapp woman and the Finn woman, shamanistic wise women who help. But Gerda's instincts are not allowed to take her all the way to Kay: "Though driven (and carried) by animal instincts, she is not to prevail by carnal love; at the critical moment the flesh deserts her, and it is her innocence and religious devotion that carry her through" (62–63).

In the palace of the Snow Queen Gerda finds Kay trying to arrange the ice pieces of the Mirror of Reason so that they make the word "eternity." The Snow Queen "is Reason herself," and "reason is the death of Faith and of childhood" (65). The "eternity" that Kay is trying to put together is immortality achieved through the intellect, through fame (67). The "eternity" that the ice pieces form of their own accord once Kay is released and weeping in Gerda's embrace is "the sexual eternity, or immortality, of the race" (69). Gerda and Kay find when they return home that they are grown up. But here Andersen suddenly stops short of the logical ending of the story. Kay and Gerda do not marry. They sit with the grandmother, holding hands, children still.

In his "Epilogue," Lederer concludes that "The Snow Queen" is a redemption story that shows that men need women in a way that women do not need men:

> If Kay were not rescued, were not redeemed by Gerda, he would continue his frigid intellectual games amid the vacuous light show of the aurora borealis forever—and he would never *come alive*. The most moving passages of the story are those relating to the reunion of Gerda and Kay. Speaking to what we deeply know but do not know we know, they remind us how lonely we are or have been; how if we are men, we need the validation, the confirmation, the redemption by woman; and if we are women, how the redemption of such a lonely man is one of the magic feats, one of the miracles a woman can perform. (183)

1988: Naomi Lewis's "Introduction" to her picture book version of "The Snow Queen," illustrated by Angela Barrett, is only two pages long, but I find it the most attractive and interesting of all the commentaries on the story that I have read. Lewis points out that "of all Andersen's major tales, it is the most free from ill fortune, sorrow, unkind chance. Kay and Gerda make their own luck, good or bad, as they go." The Snow Queen isn't evil: "with her awesome beauty and mystery, she is of a quality that transcends evil. She is the terrible power of winter; she is also, perhaps, *experience*, a magic outside childhood." Lewis classes "The Snow Queen" with the great quest stories of Malory, Tolkien, Le Guin, and older myths. She points out two unusual, perhaps unique, aspects of the story. The first is the "vivid," "haunting" presence of the seasons: "This isn't a matter of description; the seasons move with the plot; they reflect and direct it at every turn." The second is the role of female characters in the story:

> By chance or not—and I think by chance—*The Snow Queen* is the only great classic fairy tale in which every positive character is a girl or woman—Gerda, the grandmother, the witch, the princess (but allow here for the prince and the raven too), the robber girl, the Arctic women, the Snow Queen herself, while the victim to be rescued is a boy. Yet all are such decided individuals that few of us notice this. Which is just as it should be.

1993:   Ellen Brown's sympathies are with the Snow Queen, who is lonely and cold. As a child she felt she ought to admire Gerda and denounce the Snow Queen, but she found the Snow Queen, with her magic, power, strength, and freedom, much more attractive than good, pathetic little Gerda. As an adult, Brown summarizes the message of the story as follows:

> What does this story teach me? That other women are my enemy: I will have to oppose them to gain the love of men. That there is power in being feminine, as long as we are feminine in the ways defined by patriarchy: Gerda's power is in her goodness, her devotion, and her many tears. . . . That girls are expected to be good (and it helps to be beautiful). That mirrors are evil—we shouldn't look too closely at ourselves. That we must decode the Father's language, inscribe the Father's word—*Eternity*—to attain a happy ending. (5)

1995:   Verena Kast, in *Folktales as Therapy*, identifies "The Snow Queen" with the "Animal Bridegroom" tale type. The central motif is the long and dangerous journey a woman must make to free her bridegroom from the curse that prevents him from remembering his love for her or finding his way back to her. Kast reads the basic message of "The Snow Queen" as follows:

> Once we notice what is wrong with things, we can say goodbye to an easy peace of mind; the realm of the demonic can no longer be wished away. At this point we have a choice between playing a cold and theoretical game of understanding—brilliant though it may be—or of going on a 'blood and guts' search for what has been lost. (57)

1998: Novelist A. S. Byatt was one of the women writers invited to explore their favorite fairy tales in *Mirror, Mirror on the Wall*. She links "The Snow Queen" with three folktales that also have images of ice, glass, and mirrors: the Grimms's "Snow White" and "The Glass Coffin" and a Norwegian story of the princess on the glass mountain. She recognizes the standard opposition Andersen has set up "between cold reason and warm-heartedness" (71) and his added Christian message that the eternity of the beautiful snow crystals is false; true eternity is loving innocence embodied in the Christ-child. "Science and ice are bad, kindness is good. It is a frequent but not necessary opposition" (71). She disagrees with Andersen's message:

> Even as a little girl I could not see why the beauty of the snowflakes should be bad, or what was wrong with reason. Graham Greene wrote that every artist has a splinter of ice in his heart, and I think artists recognize the distancing of glass and ice as ambivalent matter, both chilling and life-giving, saving as well as threatening. (72)

In the stories, art and reason, that is to say, the work of the intellect, are separated by ice or glass from a woman's normal life of love, marriage, children, and death. Byatt was already interested as a child in choosing the world of art and ideas, if choice there had to be, and "found an illicit encouragement (which was also a warning of coldness) under the ostensible message of the ice tales" (83).

1998: Deborah Eisenberg also chose "The Snow Queen" for her piece in *Mirror, Mirror on the Wall*. For her, " 'The Snow Queen' seems like a mysterious bell tolling nearby—definitive but inscrutable, full of unearthly meaning" (111). Andersen emphasizes the dichotomy between the Snow Queen's frozen world of cold reason, in which Kay is trapped, and Gerda's living world of changing beauty, where all things help her. "So how can we not understand the story to be a parable about the dangerous illusions of science in contrast to the numinous reality of Christianity?" (111). But there are other possible readings. There is room for "a meditation on the divided self—divided into its male and female, its rational and emotional, its individual and societal aspects—no one of which can survive without its complement" (111). The story could be construed as a criticism of the class structure, in which "Gerda appears as the power of endurance and clarity which is the glorious birthright of the poor" (112). If Kay's time with the Snow Queen is read as "the vigorous apprenticeship of the aesthete," the story may "convey a warning to those who (like Andersen) engage in making art, and a critique of the artistic temperament (like Andersen's)" (112). It could be drawing on Andersen's own experience of depression and mourning "a damaged capacity for love," or be "a joyful tribute to the richness of the world and the potency of compassion," or even "a satirical view of the inaccessible and (as the current cliché has it) 'withholding' male" (112).

Eisenberg's point is that "The Snow Queen" mirrors back one's own preoccupations, and so what she saw in it changed over time. But as a child, she saw in it "a description—even, to some extent, an analysis—of the narcissistic personality, a personality in a trance of self, withering away in its encapsulation, becoming increasingly fragile and depleted as it searches for relief in the very source of its imprisonment" (113). Kay is rescued by Gerda's compassion, and Gerda is the hero of the piece. But the Snow Queen herself is so much more compelling than Gerda:

> Andersen appears to be roaming, overwhelmed and dazzled, through the terrain of his own creation, whose features are so hallucinatory they seem to be disclosed to the reader in flashes of lightning. And part of the tremendous vitality of the story no doubt proceeds from the author's struggle to hide from himself exactly what it is he reveals so stunningly to us, and to the severity with which he repudiates the very impulses which generate the narrative: clearly the Snow Queen's allure is so potent it seems that her author himself is in danger of being lost to her. (117–18)

1998: Vigen Guroian, an Orthodox theologian, recognizes that on one level "The Snow Queen" is a romantic response to eighteenth-century Enlightenment rationalism, but finds that it also tells us where evil comes from and how to love. Evil is explained in the opening story of the mirror, which has echoes in it of the story of the tower of Babel and the story of Lucifer's rebellion against God. "These biblical tales teach that pride, inordinate desire, and egoism interrupt and shatter the harmony and communion of innocent life" (116). Gerda and Kay at the beginning of the story "are like Adam and Eve in the garden of Eden before the Fall, when the first couple walked with God and were in unbroken communion with each other and with creation" (117). The bits of broken mirror in Kay's eye and heart make him disrupt this communion, and Kay becomes mean and cold, self-obsessed, "a little beast" (119). He becomes the Snow Queen's prisoner of his own accord: "He is the prisoner of his own young ego and inordinate self-love that is symbolized ultimately by his self-imprisonment in her ice-castle" (120).

Gerda's quest for Kay is "love on a mission to reclaim the beloved and restore complete communion" (122). Love is the answer and remedy for evil. Gerda's tears and the hymn she recites to Kay, a hymn they sang together as children, melt the ice and bring Kay the tears that wash the sliver of glass out of his eye. The fact that the hymn is from their childhood is important to Guroian: "Andersen seems to have believed that the good memories of childhood possess profound redemptive power and, are capable of opening our hearts to goodness and love for the rest of our lives" (123).

Guroian also sees in "The Snow Queen" a story of "one of the most fundamental forms of division and alienation in human experience—the alienation of man and woman from one another" (124). The sitcoms on prime time television watched by teens and subteens "humorously objectivize the body as a specimen for sexual browsing and fantasy," and "the sexes play out a deadly and demeaning game of lure and pursuit" (124). "The Snow Queen" as a corrective to this view tells us that Gerda is necessary to Kay's humanity, and Kay is necessary to Gerda's completeness: "The wholeness of man and woman depends upon a relationship of complete mutuality" (127). But Guroian disagrees with Lederer's view that either Kay's or Gerda's role is gender-specific.

As Gerda and Kay embrace in the hall of the Snow Queen, the ice pieces of the puzzle Kay had been vainly trying to solve dance for joy and come together to spell the word he couldn't make: "eternity." Guroian concludes, "In Hans Christian Andersen's *The Snow Queen*, goodness and immortality are rightly considered in relation to the communion in love that ought to exist between man and woman" (127).

2000: The entry under "Snow Queen, The" in *The Oxford Companion to Fairy Tales* quotes Andersen's own explanation that the story is about "the victory of the heart over cold intellect." It goes on to add that "it is also a perceptive psychological allegory of male adolescence, depicting an evolution from alienation to sensibility through the power of love."

Reworkings of "The Snow Queen" in Novel Form

These three novels represent a wide range of fictional possibilities. The first is a very long and very serious work of science fiction. The second is a mass-market romance. The third is a respectable young adult novel that adds elements of the *Kalevala*, the Finnish national epic, to Andersen's story.

The Snow Queen (Vinge)

1980. Vinge, Joan D. **The Snow Queen**. New York: Dial Press.

On the planet Tiamat the seasons change very slowly. Winter lasts for 150 years, and during that time a Snow Queen rules, chosen from among the Winter people who live on the northern half of the world. When summer comes and the south becomes too warm, the Summer people move north, a Summer Queen is chosen, and the Snow Queen and her consort are sacrificed to the Lady of the Sea. Tiamat is a tributary world of the Kharemough Hegemony. The Kharemoughis are a civilization of technocrats who use a revolving black hole for faster-than-light travel. During Tiamat's winter the Hegemony keeps a base on Tiamat and supplies the Winters with technology in exchange for "the water of life," an extract from the blood of a sea mammal that can stop the human body from aging for a period of time. At the end of each winter, the Hegemony abandons Tiamat because the passage through the black hole is too dangerous during the planet's summer. They take with them or destroy every piece of technology, with the result that the summer reign is a primitive time and the people of Tiamat never get a chance to build a technological base of their own. Any native of Tiamat who leaves the planet can never go back, because the Hegemony has a secret to protect: the sea mammals, mers, that are killed for the water of life are intelligent beings.

Vinge acknowledges that Andersen's "The Snow Queen" gave her "the seeds of this story" and that Robert Graves's *The White Goddess* provided "the rich earth in which it grew." All seven of the stories that make up Andersen's tale can be found in the 536 pages of Vinge's novel. Varner and Miller have traced the parallels between the Andersen original and Vinge's reworking, and it would take too much space to include them all here. But the most important can be pointed out as examples of Vinge's imaginative use of Andersen's story.

The demon's distorting mirror is the distorted vision of the Hegemony that leads to a deliberate fragmentation of society: the Kharemoughi's own rigid caste system, the enmity between Winters and Summers on Tiamat that focuses on the use of technology, and the artificial isolation of Tiamat to conceal the secret of the mers for the most selfish of reasons.

Vinge's Gerda and Kay are Moon and Sparks, two Summer children who grew up together in a poor fishing village under the care of their grandmother. The glass splinters in Kay's eye and heart are Spark's uncertainty about who he is. His father was an unknown off-worlder and he himself has a curiosity about the machinery that Summers are supposed to despise. That curiosity is partly inherited and partly cultivated by Sparks as a link with the unknown father he wishes he knew. His uncertainty is a weakness that allows the Snow Queen to capture him and make him her consort. Moon (Gerda) is a more dominant figure than Andersen's heroine. She is actually a clone of the Snow Queen, the Queen's very image, intended by the Queen to ensure her a form of immortality when winter ends. She is also a sibyl, a kind of human computer that can tap into a source of ancient knowledge assembled in the golden age of the Old Empire for the good of the whole living world. She becomes the Summer Queen at the end, with a duty to the future far greater than her own need to rescue Sparks. She has to break the pattern into which Tiamat has been frozen by the Hegemony and heal her whole world.

The Snow Queen (Avery)

1996. Avery, Anne. **The Snow Queen**. New York: Love Spell.

This romance novel is set in Boston and Colorado Springs in the 1890s. Hetty Malone (Gerda) and Michael Ryan (Kay) were childhood sweethearts. They plan to marry after Michael finishes medical school and establishes a practice in Colorado Springs. His hope is to find a cure for tuberculosis (TB), the disease that killed his mother when he was a small boy. Two years go by, and Michael still hasn't sent for Hetty. Her mother has just died, so she is free, and she packs up and travels to Colorado Springs to find out what's wrong with Michael and to fix it.

She finds Michael much changed. He's completely absorbed in his private war with death. The sufferers from TB who flood into Colorado Springs because the altitude and climate are their only hope for a cure keep dying. Michael feels responsible for all of them. He hardly sleeps, spending hours looking for the cure or the reason for the disease in his laboratory "where logic and the spirit of scientific inquiry reigned supreme" (148). It is his refuge from the human suffering that he can do nothing about. He is cold with his patients, his compassion "buried under layers of ice" (325). Hetty begins to interfere, providing his patients with the comfort of loving sympathy. She also chips away at Michael's reserve toward her. And in the end she succeeds. When Michael allows himself to cry with a little boy whose mother is dying, the ice melts. He accepts the fact that sometimes death just happens, "it didn't have a reason and no one was responsible" (370). And he finally understands what Hetty has been trying to tell him about love:

> Love wasn't a divisible part of living, to be shut away and hidden from the dark side of existence. It was at the center of it all, the foundation on which everything else was constructed. And if it couldn't always offer an explanation for the evil that life sometimes seemed to throw at people, at least it offered the meaning that made that life worth living. (378)

The Snow Queen isn't personified in this novel, and Avery really uses only the beginning and end of Andersen's story. Hetty's trip to Colorado Springs and her time there have nothing to do with Gerda's journey. But the main theme is clearly recognizable, and the story makes easy and reasonably entertaining reading.

The Snow Queen (Kernaghan)

2000. Kernaghan, Eileen. **The Snow Queen**. Saskatoon, Sask: Thistledown Press.

In this novel for young adults, the little robber girl gets a name of her own, Ritva, and half of the story. The first few chapters alternate between Gerda and Ritva's separate stories. After the robbers capture Gerda, when Ritva decides to go north with Gerda to help her rescue Kay, their stories merge into a single narrative. Kernaghan has made Ritva a Saami shaman-in-training. Her disgusting old mother is a Saami shaman, her father a Finnish soldier turned bandit. The spirits of wind, water, and trees tell her in a dream that she should go with Gerda on her quest, like one of the powerful shaman-heroes of the old tales. She belongs to the wild outdoors.

Gerda, by contrast, is a naïve, practical little person entirely at home in the cozy nineteenth century Danish interiors where Kernaghan places her. She reminds me of Jo and Meg March rolled into one. As a child, before this story begins, she was a tomboy who played all day with her quick-witted, mischievous little friend Kay. Now she is almost 16, enjoys the sedate frivolities of social life in their village, and writes poetry. Kay has become an intellectual "sobersides," who neglects Gerda to dance attendance on his parents' house guest, Lady Aurore, a mysterious and very beautiful woman of great learning. Lady Aurore is, of course, the Snow Queen. Instead of stealing Kay, she invites him to come to Sweden to be her research assistant in writing a book on the secret pattern of the universe.

The Snow Queen is truly a destructive force. The Lapp woman tells Ritva and Gerda about her:

> They say she was one of the wise ones who dwelt in the northern wastes, who lived in solitude with their books and manuscripts, and practised their wizard's arts. . . . She was a powerful wizard, but not powerful enough to control her magic, and in the end it possessed her. Now they call her the Drowner of Heroes and Devourer of Souls. . . . Once, they say, in a fit of spite she ripped the sun and the moon out of the sky and hid them away beneath a mountain. (90–91)

When Ritva and Gerda reach the palace of the Snow Queen, the story is substantially different from Andersen's. The Snow Queen gives them three impossible tasks. After they fulfill them with a mix of magic and ordinary human ingenuity, the Snow Queen breaks her word. Now she demands that Ritva sacrifice her reindeer, Ba, in exchange for Kay. Gerda refuses to permit such a thing, and Ritva turns to magic again, singing everyone in the palace to sleep. They grab Kay and run, and here is the most significant difference. Gerda doesn't hug Kay, or cry over him, or sing to him. Kay doesn't weep, nor does his heart thaw out. Gerda and Ritva take him just as he is. And he stays that way.

The magic in this novel runs side-by-side with historical realism. Ritva finds their way north in a shamanic trance, but she and Gerda travel part of the way with walrus hunters and the rest on foot, every step. Ritva fights an epic duel of magic with the pursuing Snow Queen after they get Kay away, but the three of them are picked up by a ship full of scientists on a geographical expedition to map the coast of Spitzbergen. On board the ship, Kay is more interested in the work of the cartographers than he is in Gerda. And Gerda realizes that her love for Kay is something she has outgrown: "She had been to the farthermost edge of the world, where earth and day end. There was no road, now, that she would be afraid to travel. How could she be content to dream away her life in a southern rose garden?" (157). Instead of marrying Kay, she will go traveling with Ritva.

Short Stories

1991. Greenberg, Joanne. **"With the Snow Queen."** In *With the Snow Queen,* by Joanne Greenberg. New York: Arcade, 3–78.

This very long short story uses Andersen's tale as an extended metaphor. It is set on Earth some time in the future. Time travel has been discovered and is used for "remedial living," to go back in time to undo accidents and crimes. The state carefully controls all aspects of human life for the public good. The many regulations are all reasonable, but joy has been replaced with caution, and choice with acquiescence. This "reasonable" state of affairs is the Snow Queen's ice palace. Sema, the main character, is both Gerda and Kay. As Kay, she feels paralyzed, only half alive, "a woman lacking purpose and identity except as someone's wife and mother" (23). As Gerda, she sets out to rescue herself, traveling back in time so that she can live the last 20 years differently.

She had blamed her parents for pushing her into an early marriage to ensure her safety and security and the state for her later lack of choice. Back in time, she discovers that she had made her own choices then, and that laziness and self-pity had turned her into Kay, frozen her heart. So she puts her second chance to good use. She makes a productive and interesting career for herself as a research agronomist. Reluctantly, and against all the rules for time travelers, she falls deeply in love and makes a life with the man. At the end of her 20 years of grace she has to stage her own death so that her husband and child will not be left with an unexplained disappearance. Unfortunately, she discovers when she gets back to the future that her (second) husband died while looking for her. She is devastated:

> This meant that once again, yet again, she would be only half invested in a present like Kay, the Snow Queen's boy victim, and half looking, like Gerda, for the missing part of herself. The cold she now felt was the Snow Queen's cold: numbness, evasion, forgetting, the covering, equivocating snow. (78)

(Trying to follow how the time travel works in this story is mind-boggling. But if one accepts the fact that no explanation can be offered for how the mechanism, the Luria Belt, actually works, it does all make sense in the end.)

1994. McKillip, Patricia A. **"The Snow Queen."** In *The Year's Best Fantasy and Horror: Seventh Annual Collection,* edited by Ellen Datlow and Terri Windling. New York: St. Martin's Press, 239–53. [1993. *Snow White, Blood Red,* edited by Ellen Datlow and Terri Windling. New York: Avon, 360–87].

The setting is New York City, some time recently. Gerda and Kay are married, but she's afraid he's lost interest in her; she sees "contracts in his eyes, and the names of restaurants, expensive shoes" (242). The Snow Queen is a fabulous socialite named Neva who's into dependent men and kinky sex. She snares Kay at a party, and Gerda walks out into the snow to freeze to death. Without Kay, life is not worth living. The little robber girl, Briony, tries to mug Gerda. But when she realizes how desperate Gerda is, she takes her to an all-night diner for hot chocolate, where she and the waitress talk Gerda into staying alive:

> But if you keep pretending and pretending, one day you'll stumble onto something you care enough to live for, and if you turn yourself into an icicle now because of Kay, you won't be able to change your mind later. The only thing you're seeing in the entire world is Kay. Kay is in both your eyes, Kay is your mind. Which means you're really only seeing one tiny flyspeck of the world, one little puzzle piece. (246)

The words "icicle" and "puzzle piece" in this passage are pointers to the biggest difference between this story and Andersen's: McKillip's Kay and Gerda are both Andersen's Kay—uninteresting, victims of obsession, closed to real life and loving. There's no Andersen's Gerda in the story at all, and that's why the conclusion is unsatisfying: Gerda discovers an interest in growing flowers and gets Kay back, by accident. Briony and Jennifer the waitress are the best part of the story. There are some clever plays on Andersen's text, such as the crossword puzzles for ice puzzles, and a man named Crow. There are also many references to ice and snow and cold. But underneath these surface reflections, this story hasn't much to do with Andersen's "Snow Queen."

1998. McCrumb, Sharyn. **"Gerda's Sense of Snow."** In *Once Upon a Crime*, edited by Ed Gorman and Martin H. Greenberg. New York: Berkeley, 399–416.

The title is a play on the Danish novel *Smilla's Sense of Snow*. In this case, the snow is cocaine, and the Snow Queen is a drug dealer. Poor Kay has been on the skids for a number of years, and Gerda feels she lost her childhood friend long ago. But he disappears altogether one winter, and when spring comes, Gerda decides to look for him. It's not clear where the story starts, but Gerda winds up someplace like Hollywood. All the elements of Andersen's story are here, changed a little where necessary to fit a modern setting with no magic in it. The big shift is the replacement of rationalism and the awesome power of a northern winter with drug addiction.

1999. Link, Kelly. **"Travels with the Snow Queen."** In *The Year's Best Fantasy and Horror: 12 Annual Collection*, edited by Ellen Datlow and Terri Windling. New York: St. Martin's Griffin, 1–13.

Gerda tells the story of her search for Kay in the voice of a disillusioned, resentful young woman whose lover has left her. Most of the key elements of the story are here: the princess, the robber girl, the Lapp woman, the Finn woman, the Snow Queen's sleigh, and Kay's ice puzzle. The garden of the woman skilled in magic is missing. Gerda follows a trail of shards from the broken mirror, her bare and bleeding feet the map of her journey. She doubts whether Kay still loves her, and everyone who helps her tells her he doesn't, that he isn't worth the trouble. This is a notable change from Andersen's original, in which the sunshine and the swallows encourage Gerda to look for Kay. She carries with her a list of apologies, explanations, and accusations she wants to make to Kay; she isn't ready to let go yet.

Between plot episodes Gerda makes cynical comments about the fairy tale of love:

> Ladies. Has it ever occurred to you that fairy tales aren't easy on the feet? . . . No, really, Think about it. Think about the little mermaid who traded in her tail for love, got two legs, two feet, and every step was like walking on knives. And where did it get her? That's a rhetorical question, of course. (2)

Link has added some folktale motifs: Gerda and Kay had a talking cat when they lived together; the helpful princess is Briar Rose; Bae, the reindeer, is really the son of the Lapp woman, bespelled by the Finn woman because he made rude comments about her weight, and he can be changed back by a kiss. A kiss can also break the enchantment on Kay, but once Gerda finds him she decides she doesn't love him any more. So she leaves Kay, unkissed, where he is: "Someday, someone will probably make their way to the Snow Queen's palace, and kiss Kay's cold blue lips. She might even manage a happily ever after for a while" (13). Gerda herself, having learned to stand on her own feet, takes a job traveling for the Snow Queen.

2000. Block, Francesca Lia. "Ice." In *The Rose and the Beast: Fairy Tales Retold*, by Francesca Lia Block. New York: Joanna Cotler Books, 199–229.

Gerda tells this dark, pain-filled story. She is a painter and is so open to the feelings of those she loves that when her mother died of breast cancer Gerda's own hair fell out and she developed a lump in her breast. Kai is a musician who lives in the apartment across from hers. They see each other but don't actually meet until Gerda goes to the club where he has a gig, the Mirror. Kai sings songs about a shard of glass in his eye that he can't cry away because he has no tears. He comes to her after the show and immediately recognizes her as "his other half." They become lovers and plant flowers in their window boxes. Gerda paints him and Kai gives her all of himself except a secret pain that he refuses to talk about, the pain in his songs.

From the very beginning Gerda is afraid that she will lose him. When the Snow Queen comes to the Mirror she is Gerda's fear personified: "My fear so beautiful that I almost desired it—her. She was the porn goddess, ice sex, glistening and shiny and perfection" (216). Kai is lost to Gerda:

> I would have ridden on a reindeer or the back of a bird, I would have gone to the North Pole and I would have woven a blanket out of the threads of my body. I would have ripped out my hair and had implanted a wig of long silver blond strands, cut my body and sewn on whole new parts. I would have flayed my skin to find a more perfect whiteness beneath. . . . These are the things of stories and I couldn't do any of them. All I could do was to go back to my room and pull down the blinds and paint. (218–19)

In the spring, Gerda asks a bird and the roses if they have seen Kai, and they tell her that she should go see the Snow Queen. Gerda finds Kai sleeping at the Snow Queen's feet. In her icy, beautiful presence Gerda cries hot tears on Kai, and when he wakes he kisses her. The story closes with a single, enigmatic sentence standing separate at the end of the text: "Once he and I were children, before this happened" (229).

Poetry

1989. Gilbert, Sandra M. **"The Last Poem About the Snow Queen."** In *The Year's Best Fantasy: Second Annual Collection*, edited by Ellen Datlow and Terri Windling. New York: St. Martin's Press, 365–66.

The poem begins with a quote from Andersen's story: "Then it was that little Gerda walked into the Place, through the great gates, in a biting wind. . . . She saw Kay, and knew him at once; she flung her arms around his neck, held him fast, and cried, 'Kay, little Kay, have I found you at last?' But he sat still, rigid and cold." An unidentified narrator addresses Gerda, presumably at this moment, as if this were the end of the story. Despite all her careful preparation and optimism she has reached her destination barefoot and freezing and finds that Kay has become an inseparable part of the icy cold.

1993. Eiler, April. **"The Snow Queen."** In *The Snow Queen*, by April Eiler. Palo Alto, CA: Line Dance, 9–10.

The voice could be Gerda's or that of any other woman deserted and betrayed by her lover. She found her love in the Snow Queen's palace and led him away. But then he betrayed her, took her shoes and food, and tied her to a tree. No helpers like those in Andersen's fairy tale rescued her. She saved herself where others like her had perished.

"The Emperor's New Clothes"

Tale Type 1620 is *The King's New Clothes*, summarized as "an impostor pretends to make clothes for the king and says that they are visible only to those of legitimate birth. The king and courtiers are all afraid to admit that they cannot see the clothes. Finally a child seeing the naked king reveals the imposture" (Thompson, 461). D. L. Ashliman's collection of folklore and mythology electronic texts, found at http://www.pitt.edu/~dash/type1620.html, includes variants of this tale from Asia, England, and Denmark. This Danish variant, first published in 1837, was based on a Spanish story recorded by Don Juan Manuel (1282–1348) and reworked by Hans Christian Andersen. "The chief idea behind this tale concerns the weakness of people: they are afraid of the opinions of people, afraid to see things as they are, and dare not to be honest to themselves" (Grønbech, 105). According to Freud, however, Andersen's tale is not basically honest because at the dream level it is the naked person himself who discovers his own nakedness and feels defenseless (Pickard).

Short Stories

1995. Dalkey, Kara. **"The Chrysanthemum Robe."** In *The Armless Maiden and Other Tales for Childhood's Survivors,* edited by Terri Windling. New York: TOR, 194–203.

The young Japanese emperor is given a gift by an old established (and not necessarily loyal) family. When he receives the robe and its warning that it can only be seen by those who are wise, he decides to call the bluff, announcing that anyone proclaiming that the emperor is naked would be put to death. His plans become derailed when his child calls out during the procession. This is a heavy price to pay for the gaining of wisdom.

1996. Fisher, David. **"Tailor v. Emperor: Motion for Summary Judgment."** In *Legally Correct Fairy Tales.* New York: Warner, 7–11.

The tailor has taken his case before the court because the emperor refuses to pay for his latest suit of clothing. "Notwithstanding that the rank and file in the Palace did praise and compliment the clothing, the Emperor accepted the word of a minor and has refused to pay the agreed-upon fee" (9). The defense maintains that the Emperor was "subjected to scorn, ridicule, embarrassment, and humiliation" (10). The exhibits of clothing presented before the court do nothing to clarify the case, and the plaintiff's motion for summary judgment is denied.

1996. Walker, Barbara. **"The Empress's New Clothes."** In *Feminist Fairy Tales.* New York: HarperSanFrancisco, 209–16.

All of the characters in Andersen's tale are male, and Walker felt this ignored "centuries of female intimacy with all matters of dress and fabric arts" (209). This tale is about a Chinese empress and her female courtiers and female dressmakers. She is undoubtedly cleverer than her male counterpart, although she too walks around without any clothes on.

1996. Wisenberg, S. L. **"After the Procession."** In *North American Review.* 281(4) (July/August): 13.

This short story reflects the thoughts of the child who denounced the emperor as a fool and became the community's scapegoat when the new order did not live up to expectations.

1997. Cashorali, Peter. **"The Queer Garment."** In *Gay Fairy & Folk Tales: More Traditional Stories Retold for Gay Men.* New York: HarperSanFranciso, 16–24.

There was once an emperor who was very concerned that he appear straight even though no one in his empire was straight. One day two flamboyant designers arrived, discovered that everyone was unhappy, and contrived to make a suit for the emperor of fabric that was "capable of conferring an absolutely straight appearance" (18). Needless to say, an old nearsighted man set everyone "straight." This reworking is an imaginative look at self-deception.

1998. Andersen, Hans Christian. **The Emperor's New Clothes: An All-Star Retelling of the Classic Fairy Tale**. New York: Harcourt & Brace.

This short story, packaged in an illustrated picture book format, features the writing talents of such celebrities as Liam Neeson, Harrison Ford and Melissa Mathison, Angela Lansbury, Dr. Ruth Westheimer, Madonna, Jonathan Taylor Thomas, Dan Aykroyd, Robin Williams Calvin Klein, Rosie O'Donnell, Fran Drescher, Joan Rivers, Steven Spielberg, General H. Norman Schwarzkopf, and John Lithgow. Each of the individual segments, written by the celebrities listed above, has one full-page illustration accompanying it. The illustrators include Quentin Blake, Maurice Sendak, Daniel Adel, David Christiana, Chris Van Allsburg, Berkley Breathed, Kinuko Y. Craft, Steven Kellogg, Tomie dePaola, Michael Paraskevas, Fred Marcellino, Don Wood, Graeme Base, and William Joyce.

A fund-raiser for the Starbright foundation, the story is retold from various viewpoints and narrated by a very curious and clever moth.

1998. Brett, Simon. **"The Emperor's New Clothes."** In *Once Upon a Crime*, edited by Ed Gorman ad Martin H. Greenberg. New York: Berkley Prime Crime, 290–301.

In this sardonic and tongue-in-cheek gangster story featuring "Emp" and his court, the entire kingdom is at risk when Emp becomes born again and insists that all his employees do the same. At risk, that is, until a young man "points out the truth" that the man looks and acts ridiculous, and things get back to normal. Too bad for the young man, however, because Emp was never good at accepting advice!

1999. Kress, Nancy. **"Clad in Gossamer."** In *Silver Birch, Blood Moon*, edited by Ellen Datlow and Terri Windling. New York: Avon, 81–91.

Jasper, the Emperor's less-fortunate brother, explains why, although he knew the tailors were scoundrels, he encouraged their behavior and his brother's belief in magic. After numerous failed attempts at murdering his brother, Jasper tries "embroidery and silk" when consumed with jealousy over his brother's bride (84). Things are never what they seem, as Jasper discovers when he is clad in gossamer.

1999. Mayer, Gloria Gilbert, and Thomas Mayer. **"The Emperor's New Clothes."** In *Goldilocks on Management: 27 Revisionist Fairy Tales for Serious Managers*. New York: American Management Association, 43–50.

This is a fairly straightforward marriage of Andersen's tale with numerous references to popular culture and the world of high fashion. The naïve bystander is not a child, however, but a well-known consumer advocate.

Basic lesson: "Individuals without a vested interest are the only reliable sources of accurate information" (45). Bottom line: "Prudent managers weigh the source of any information received and act with a commitment commensurate with their instinct for its reliability" (49).

1999. What, Leslie. **"The Emperor's New (And Improved) Clothes."** In *Twice Upon a Time,* edited by Denise Little. New York: Daw Books, 228–39.

The two brothers had always been con artists in their native land and so continued the tradition when they visited a eastern European country. This tale moves the setting into contemporary times and incorporates allusions to such popular icons as Leonardo di Caprio and the Green Party. The scheme this time is not to sell the translucent cloth to the emperor but to sell special goggles that make the cloth visible! The story ends up happily ever after . . . well, for almost everyone. Poor elder brother Jusef: He now lives destitute in Newark, a bitter man who endlessly plots his revenge.

Poetry

There is only one entry in this category at the time of this writing, but it is one that may have encouraged writers to consider reworking this tale.

1990. O'Connor, Sinead. **"The Emperor's New Clothes."** On the CD *I Do Not Want What I Haven't Got.* Ensign Records.

O'Connor uses the title as an allusion to the entire story of deception and fear. "Through their own words, they will be exposed. They've got a severe case of the emperor's new clothes."

Picture Books

There have been several reworkings of this story in picture book format that are suitable for young adult audiences even though their target audience may seem to be younger readers.

1989. Calmensen, Stephanie. **The Principal's New Clothes.** Illustrated by Denise Brunkus. New York: Scholastic.

Although the intended audience is younger children, young adults will enjoy the premise of this tale and the illustrations.

1997. Lewis, Naomi, trans. **The Emperor's New Clothes.** Illustrated by Angela Barrett. Cambridge, MA: Candlewick Press.

Although Lewis's translation is attuned to Andersen's original tale, it is the setting that makes this a book worth considering. The emperor in this version lives in 1913, and the illustrations include early automobiles, biplanes, and other technological advances of the early part of the century. The book, like the emperor's home, is populated by a wide variety of canine friends. Each double-page spread has a different feel to it, from the silhouettes (which Andersen also used) to the newspaper format and the vignettes, which include an interesting solution to portraying an emperor wearing his new clothes. A foreword by the author provides a brief history of the story itself.

1999. Lasky, Kathryn. **The Emperor's Old Clothes.** Illustrated by David Catrow. Orlando: Harcourt Brace.

In this continuation of "The Emperor's New Clothes" a simple farmer finds the emperor's old clothes on his way home from the market and decides to put them on. The narrative is satisfying, incorporating the traditional tale with newer versions, but it is the illustrations that shine and make this appropriate for young adult readers.

"The Princess on the Pea"

This very short story, published in Andersen's first collection of fairy tales in 1835, is a folktale in origin. It is classified as tale type AT 704, *Princess on the Pea.* "A princess is recognized by her inability to sleep in a bed which has a pea under its dozen mattresses." It consists of a single motif, H41.1, which is identical with the tale type. Variants have been found in the folk traditions of Sweden and India (Thompson, 240). Andersen's title is sometimes translated as "The Princess and the Pea," although the linking word is "on" in the original Danish.

Novels

At the time of this writing, there was only one novel that reworked Andersen's story.

1999. Levine, Gail Carson. **The Princess Test.** Illustrated by Mark Elliott. The Princess Tales. New York: HarperCollins.

This pretty pink book is the second of Levine's Princess Tales, following her popular *Ella Enchanted.* She has spun Andersen's very short story into a very short novel for a suggested audience aged 7 to 12, but the irony inherent in the original tale and the skill of Levine's pleasantly humorous elaboration could interest older readers.

The princess, Lorelei, is actually the daughter of the village blacksmith. Her extreme physical delicacy makes life difficult for her, and for her parents, from the day of her birth, but she is as sweet and good-natured as she is thin-skinned. Prince Nicholas meets and falls in love with her in the village and arranges to bring her to the palace to take the princess tests devised by the anxious, finicky king and queen to find their son a suitable wife. She beats the assembled competition of princesses-by-birth quite honestly and marries Nicholas with the approval of his parents.

Levine has managed to keep the gentle absurdity of Andersen's story, and the carefully crafted coherence of her inventions gives her novel the tidy charm, the sense of miniaturization, that is one of the pleasures of the original.

Short Stories

Authors have only begun to play with this tale in short story format in the last few years.

1995. Garner, James Finn. **"The Princess and the Pea."** In *Once Upon a More Enlightened Time: More Politically Correct Bedtime Stories*, by James Finn Garner. New York: Macmillan, 21–22.

The prince's only criterion for a bride is "the royal authenticity of a wommon who could share his regal delusions of privilege and persunal worth" (22). The queen, "for her own codependent and Oedipal reasons," doesn't really want him to marry. The princess who comes along in the storm finds the pea when she dismantles her excessive bed to distribute the extra mattresses among the poor and is shocked "that someone would waste food like that" (25). It turns out that she channels and will be a true princess again next Tuesday. That's good enough for the prince. They marry "in accordance with her metaphysical timetable" (27), and live happily "never quite knowing who would turn up at breakfast" (28).

1997. Jacobs, A. J. **"Princess and the Pea."** In *Fractured Fairy Tales*, told by A. J. Jacobs. New York: Bantam Books, 77–80.

The king is looking for an heiress. He lost one years ago, but he'll recognize the right one because she won't be able to sleep on a pea. The court jester, Million Laughs Charlie, tries several times to pass off his friend Clyde in drag as the princess, but Clyde sleeps soundly every time. When Charlie's neighbor turns out to be unable to sleep on a pea, she gets a million gold crickles and her choice of any man in the kingdom. She takes Clyde.

1999. Mayer, Gloria Gilbert, and Thomas Mayer. **"The Princess and the Pea."** In *Goldilocks on Management: 27 Revisionist Fairy Tales for Serious Managers*, by Gloria Gilbert Meyer and Thomas Meyer. New York, American Management Association, 133–39.

A modern-day prince, 37 years old and lonely, has not been able to find the woman who is right for him. Several candidates have looked good, but each proved to have a fatal flaw: a passion for gummi bears, or for watching *Love Boat*, or for reading *True Confessions*. He sends away for a Hammacher Schlemmer "Princess Identification System" that tests a potential spouse's "kinesiological sensitivity" (133)—basically 20 layers of mattresses and one pea "of the specially bred variety Mendel's Pride" (134). The system takes a lot of time and trouble to put together, but it does the job. A young woman who seems perfect for the prince in every respect spends the night, and her suitability is verified by the discomfort the pea causes her.

Basic lesson: "The validation of credentials may require substantial effort—but such effort is worth it" (136). Bottom line: "Although validating credentials can be a detailed and cumbersome task, it is absolutely crucial to any business. Indeed, failure to valuate credentials thoroughly may result in outcomes that are embarrassing, dangerous, and financially devastating" (139).

Picture Books

Picture book versions of this story abound. However, there are only a few that actually rework the tale; these are discussed below.

1982. Stevens, Janet. **The Princess and the Pea**. Adapted from Hans Christian Andersen and illustrated by Janet Stevens. New York: Holiday House.

Stevens puts Andersen's irony into the illustrations. The king and prince are lions, and the queen is a tiger. The princesses inspected by the prince and his mother, who goes with him on his travels, are other kinds of animals, each rejected for failing at something she couldn't possibly do well. The right princess who comes to the palace door in the storm is, of course, a tiger like the queen! A more subtle irony is that the animals look so realistically substantial and furry that the human clothing they wear seems ridiculously constraining. The text is an adaptation of Andersen's.

1993. Campbell, Ann. **Once Upon a Princess and a Pea**. Illustrated by Kathy Osborn Young. New York: Stewart, Tabori & Chang.

Princess Esmerelda runs away to escape marrying King Frobius, who is 53 years old and almost toothless. "Meanwhile, in another kingdom," Prince Hector sets off in his red roadster, supplied with hard peas by his mother, to find a true princess. After three failures, he heads home in a rainstorm and picks up a soaked Esmerelda on the way. Although the queen's doubts about her are strengthened when Esmerelda is found standing in line for breakfast in the kitchen the next morning with the servants, the pea proves her a true princess. Hector and Esmerelda marry, and the pea is put on display in the castle, "which is where it is today, unless someone has moved it."

As this summary shows, Andersen's story has been considerably embellished and adapted. The colorful illustrations have an angular sophistication that puts them well into young adult territory.

Musical

Once Upon a Mattress was first produced in New York in 1959. The music is by Mary Rodgers, the lyrics by Marshall Barer, and the book by Jay Thompson, Marshall Barer, and Dean Fuller. It was staged again on Broadway in 1967 and 1997. The story is considerably expanded, and the cast includes a wizard and the Nightingale of Samarkand.

Graphic Novels

There is only one example of "The Princess and the Pea" in the comic book format.

2000. McClintock, Barbara. **"The Princess and the Pea."** In *Little Lit: Folklore & Fairy Tale Funnies*, edited by Art Spiegelman and Françoise Mouly. New York: RAW Junior, 62–63.

As in Janet Stevens's picture book, the royal family are all felines, while the available princesses belong to other animal species. The young woman in rags who appears at the palace door in a rainstorm is obviously going to fit in because she is a white cat. The dialogue in this very short story is contemporary. The prince calls his parents Mom and Dad, and the queen worries that her son "can't make a commitment." The last line suggests that Princess Leotine's sensitivity will have disadvantages: While telling the prince how happy she is, she also complains about a stone in her shoe.

Internet Resources on Hans Christian Andersen

Using "Hans Christian Andersen" as a search term turns up a number of Web sites. Because Andersen is a Danish national treasure, the Danish Consulate in New York (http://www.denmark.org/home/index.shtml) and the Royal Danish Embassy in Washington (http://www.denmarkemb.org/and2.html) offer a number of links.

A personal site, http://hca.gilead.org.il, set up in the fall of 2000, is rich in information, including an "Annotated Web-o-graphy" page, a complete list of Andersen's fairy tales and stories, a list of the 30 most popular tales, links to the Andersen Homepage of the Danish National Library, and much more.

Classroom Extensions

The following classroom extensions may be adapted for use with any of Andersen's tales or any of the other stories under discussion.

Puzzle Pieces

The short stories listed in the "Snow Queen" section are made up of pieces of Andersen's "The Snow Queen," as if Andersen's tale had been broken into fragments that the authors have rearranged like one of Kay's clever ice puzzles in the palace of the Snow Queen. For any of the short stories, identify the pieces that come from Andersen and map their new arrangement. What kind of story do they tell now? What are its meanings, and how are they different from Andersen's story?

Love and Innocence

Andersen's Gerda and Kay are definitely little children. Their love for each other is the innocent love of friendship rather than the possessive love of desire. In all of the reworkings of "The Snow Queen" given in this chapter, Gerda and Kay are teenagers or adults. Must this necessarily change the nature of their love for each other? If Gerda's love for Kay is the love of desire, how does it change her quest?

The Woman Skilled in Magic

The woman skilled in magic is the piece of Andersen's story most often missing in the reworkings. For example, she isn't there in Kelley Link's "Travels with the Snow Queen." What is her function in Andersen's tale? What happens to the story if she's left out?

Endnotes

1. For readers interested in the problems of translating Andersen into English, the articles by Pedersen (1997) are informative without being too technical. The essay by Erik Dal gives an overview and examples of changes, some of them delightfully dreadful, made by translators and retellers in a number of European languages.

2. The entry for "The Snow Queen" in the *Oxford Companion to Fairy Tales* states that the story was first published in the 1845 collection, *Nye Eventyr, Anden Samling.* The title of the collection is misspelled in the entry as *Evyntyr,* and the collection is wrongly identified as "Hans Christian Andersen's second collection of tales." Andersen had in fact published a collection of fairy tales every year since 1835. I presume this error is based on a mistranslation of the phrase *Anden Samling,* which can mean "another collection" as well as "second collection." Signe Toksvig also gives 1844 as the publication date in her book *The Life of Hans Christian Andersen.*

References

Anderson, Celia Catlett. 1986. "Andersen's Heroes and Heroines: Relinquishing the Reward." In *Triumphs of the Spirit in Children's Literature,* edited by Francelia Butler and Richart Rotert. Hamden, CT: Library Professional Publications, 122–26.

Auden, W. H. 1952. "Introduction." In *Tales of Andersen and Grimm.* Selected by Frederick Jacobi, Jr. New York: The Modern Library, xiii–xxi.

Brask, Peter. 1986. "Andersen's Love." In *The Nordic Mind: Current Trends in Scandinavian Literary Criticism,* edited by Frank Egholm and John Weinstock. Lanham, MD: University Press of America, 17–35.

Bredsdorff, Elias. 1975. *Hans Christian Andersen: The Story of His Life and Work.* London: Phaidon.

Brown, Ellen. 1993. "In Search of Nancy Drew, the Snow Queen, and Room Nineteen: Cruising for Feminine Discourse." *Frontiers: A Journal of Women Studies.* 13(2): 1–25.

Byatt, A. S. 1998. "Ice, Snow, Glass." In *Mirror, Mirror on the Wall: Women Writers Explore Their Favorite Fairy Tales*, edited by Kate Bernheimer. New York: Anchor Books, 64–84.

Cech, Jon. 1985. "Hans Christian Andersen's Fairy Tales and Stories: Secrets, Swans and Shadows." In *Touchstones: Reflections on the Best in Children's Literature, Volume 1*, edited by Perry Nodelman. West Lafayette, IN: Children's Literature Association, 14–23.

Dal, Erik. 1955. "Hans Christian Andersen in Eighty Languages." In *A Book on the Danish Writer Hans Christian Andersen: His Life and Work*. Copenhagen: Det Berlingske Bogtrykkeri, 132–206.

Eisenberg, Deborah. 1998. "In a Trance of Self." In *Mirror, Mirror on the Wall: Women Writers Explore Their Favorite Fairy Tales*, edited by Kate Bernheimer. New York: Anchor Books, 100–120.

Fell, Christine. 1967. "Symbolic and Satiric Aspects of Hans Andersen's Fairy-Tales." *Leeds Studies in English*. 1: 83–91.

Glyn Jones, W. 1992. "HC and PC." *Professional Translator & Interpreter* 3: 18–20.

Grønbech, Bo. 1980. *Hans Christian Andersen*. Twayne World Authors Series 612. Boston: Twayne.

Guroian, Vigen. 1998. *Tending the Heart of Virtue: How Classic Stories Awaken a Child's Moral Imagination*. New York: Oxford University Press.

Holbek, Bengt. 1990. "Hans Christian Andersen's Use of Folktales." In *The Telling of Stories: Approaches to a Traditional Craft: A Symposium*. Odense: Odense University Press, 165–82.

Ingwersen, Niels. 1993. "Being Stuck: The Subversive Andersen and His Audience." In *Studies in German and Scandinavian Literature after 1500*, edited by James A. Parente Jr. Columbia, SC: Camden House, 166–80.

Kast, Verena. 1995. *Folktales as Therapy*. Translated by Douglas Whitcher. New York: Fromm International Publishing.

Klotz, Volker. 1985. *Das europäische Kunstmärchen: Fünfundzwanzig Kapitel seiner Geschichte von der Renaissance bis zur Moderne*. Stuttgart: J. B. Metzler.

Le Guin, Ursula K. 1985. "The Child and the Shadow." In *The Language of the Night: Essays on Fantasy and Science Fiction*. New York: Berkley Books, 59–71.

Lederer, Wolfgang. 1986. *The Kiss of the Snow Queen: Hans Christian Andersen and Man's Redemption by Woman*. Berkeley: University of California Press.

Lewis, Naomi. 1988. "Introduction." In *Hans Christian Andersen's The Snow Queen*. Illustrated by Angela Barrett. New York: Henry Holt.

Pedersen, Viggo Hjørnager. 1990. "A Mermaid Translated: An Analysis of Some English Versions of Hans Christian Andersen's 'Den lille Havfrue'." *Dolphin* 18: 7–20.

———. 1995. "Politics and Religion in the Tales of Hans Christian Andersen." In *Translation: Religion, Ideology, Politics*, edited by Todd Burrell and Sean K. Kelly. Binghamton, NY: Center for Research in Translation, 154–67.

———. 1997. "Description and Criticism: Approaches to the English Translations of Hans Christian Andersen." In *Text Typology and Translation*, edited by Anna Trosberg. Amsterdam: Benjamins, 99–114.

Pickard, P. M. 1961. *I Could a Tale Unfold: Violence, Horror & Sensationalism in Stories for Children.* London: Tavistock.

Robinson, Vivian U. 1971. "Adult Symbolism in the Literary Fairy Tales of the Late Nineteenth Century." Ph.D. dissertation, University of Nebraska, Lincoln.

Sale, Roger. 1978. *Fairy Tales and After: From Snow White to E. B. White.* Cambridge, MA: Harvard University Press.

"Snow Queen, The." 2000. *The Oxford Companion to Fairy Tales*, edited by Jack Zipes. Oxford: Oxford University Press.

Spink, Reginald. 1981. *Hans Christian Andersen: The Man and His Work.* 3d edition. Copenhagen: Høst.

Tales of Andersen and Grimm. 1952. Selected by Frederick Jacobi, Jr. New York: The Modern Library.

Thaning, Kaj. 1972. *N.F.S. Grundtvig.* Translated from the Danish by David Hohnen. Copenhagen: Det Danske Selskab.

Thompson, Stith. 1961. *The Types of the Folktale: A Classification and Bibliography. Antti Aarne's Verzeichnis der Märchentypen*, translated and enlarged by Stith Thompson. 2d revision. FF Communications, no. 184. Helsinki: Suomalainen Tiedeakatemia.

Toksvig, Signe. 1934. *The Life of Hans Christian Andersen.* London, Macmillan.

Varner, Vicci K., and Ricky E. Miller. 1987. "Soil and Seed: Vinge's Use of Andersen and Graves in *The Snow Queen*." *Extrapolation* 28(4): 360–67.

Zipes, Jack. 1999. *When Dreams Came True: Classical Fairy Tales and Their Tradition.* New York: Routledge, 1999.

CHAPTER 5

THE LITTLE MERMAID

Hans Christian Andersen fashioned "The Little Mermaid" from diverse elements, but fundamentally the story is a literary tale that is recognizably his own. The folkloric elements that have been identified are the plot itself, as inspired by de la Motte Fouque's story *Undine*; Paracelsus's doctrine of elementary spirits; the ballad "Agnete and the Mermaid"; and the folktale "The Mute Queen" (for the scene in which the mute mermaid lives in the palace) (Holbek, 166). Andersen also incorporated varied aspects of traditional and literary tales about selkies, nixes, Lorelies, and Melusines. In all of these traditions, a fairy creature can remain on Earth as a bride to a mortal only under certain conditions (Warner 1994, 396).

This chapter looks briefly at some of these influences before concentrating on the critical interpretations of Andersen's most prominent tale and its most well-known adaptation, the Disney film. In actuality, there have not been too many other renderings of this storyline published since Andersen made it his. Although some short story variants were produced in the 1990s, this chapter includes only one reworking in novel form and two poems. Most of the short stories have been reactions to the Disneyfication of Andersen's tale, which is summarized here.

Andersen begins his tale with a description of the underwater world of the Sea King and his subjects. Grandmother, the first character that speaks, tells the Sea King's daughters of the ceremony that they will embark on when they are 15 years old.

❧ ──

The mermaids will have "permission to rise up out of the sea, to sit on the rocks in the moonlight, while the great ships are sailing by; and then you will see both forests and towns." The youngest daughter longed for her turn to rise to the surface, but she had to wait. Meanwhile, each year one of her sisters returned from her journey with tales of wondrous sights. The littlest mermaid's sisters soon grew indifferent to the wonders they had witnessed but would frequently rise to the surface together and sing. They had more beautiful voices than any human being could have; before the approach of a storm, and when they expected a ship would be lost, they swam before the vessel and sang sweetly of the delights to be found in the depths of the sea, begging the sailors not to fear if they sank to the bottom. But the sailors could not understand the song; they took it for the howling of the storm. And these things were never to be beautiful for them; for if the ship sank, the men were drowned, and their dead bodies alone reached the palace of the Sea King.

Finally it was the turn of the youngest sister. Her grandmother placed a wreath of white lilies in her hair and ordered eight oysters to attach themselves to the tail of the princess to show her high rank. When she complained of the pain, her grandmother told her, "Pride must suffer pain." The little mermaid sighted a ship, and as the waves lifted her up, she could see through the windows the most handsome young prince. It was his sixteenth birthday. Through the glow of the fireworks display the mermaid watched the prince and the party until a dreadful storm approached. The ship floundered and the prince was thrown into the sea. The mermaid realized that he could not live under the sea, so she rescued him, holding his head above the water until she brought him to shore. "The mermaid kissed his high, smooth forehead, and stroked back his wet hair; he seemed to her like the marble statue in her little garden, and she kissed him again, and wished that he might live." The mermaid waited behind a rock and watched a young girl find the prince on the sand. The girl quickly summoned help and they took the prince away to safety.

The little mermaid returned home in a melancholy mood and stayed that way for a long time because she could not find her prince again. She spent a great deal of time in her own garden with her marble statue that was very like the prince. Finally her sisters discovered her longing and took her to the surface to a place near the prince's palace. She returned to that place many times to watch him and the other humans. She went to her grandmother and asked: "If human beings are not drowned, can they live forever? Do they never die as we do here in the sea?"

Her grandmother explained that the humans had a much shorter term of life; mermaids often lived 300 years and then became foam on the surface of the water. The humans, on the other hand, had souls, and they rose above the earth to reside in a glorious region that the mermaids can never see. The mermaid determined to obtain a soul. Her grandmother explained that the only way a mermaid can obtain a soul is to have a human male love her so much that he could give a soul to her while retaining his own. But, the grandmother reminded her, this could never happen because she had a fish's tail, which humans think is ugly, preferring legs instead.

That night there was a wondrous ball at her father's court, but the mermaid could only think of the world above her. She left silently, first to sit in her garden, but then, with much courage, to journey to the home of the sea witch.

The sea witch tried to discourage the little mermaid, but to no avail. She prepared a potion for her to drink on land the next morning before sunrise. This would give her legs, but she would feel great pain, as if a sword was passing through her. Although she would appear graceful, she would always feel as if she were stepping on sharp knives. The witch also told her that the change was irreversible; she would never be able to return to her mermaid shape. If the prince did not marry her, her heart would break, and the first morning after he married another, she would become foam on the crest of the waves. The mermaid agreed to the conditions, and when the witch asked for payment of her voice, she agreed to that as well. She would be left with her "beautiful form, [her] graceful walk, and [her] expressive eyes; surely with these [she could] enchain a man's heart." She was never pressured to make the decision but did so willingly.

Once her tongue had been cut from her mouth, the little mermaid took the potion and traveled to the marble steps of the prince's palace. She drank and fell back in tremendous pain. The prince found her, but she could not tell him who she was or how she got there, naked and silent. He took her to the palace, where her beauty and expressive eyes enchanted the court. The prince kept her by his side; she slept at his door on a velvet cushion and wore a page's dress that he had fashioned for her. She enjoyed his company, although her feet hurt and bled always. Time passed; her sisters came to the shore to visit and even her grandmother and the old Sea King swam close to the surface so they could see her. But the prince did not love her as a woman. She discovered that the prince loved the image of the woman who had saved his life, never realizing that the little mermaid was the one. One day he told her that he must voyage to a neighboring kingdom to meet a princess who was to become his future wife. She traveled with him, only to find that the princess was the same girl who first came to the prince's aid when the mermaid left him on the shore. This was the image that the prince had fallen in love with, and he was pleased to marry her as soon as possible. The mermaid's heart was heavy, but she attended the wedding and traveled on the ship with the new bride and groom. She knew that she would not complete the voyage, for she would become sea foam. Late that evening her sister came to the mermaid with a sharp knife given to her by the sea witch in exchange for her long and beautiful hair. The mermaid was to plunge the knife into the heart of the prince, and when his warm blood fell on her feet they would grow together again and she would once again regain her mermaid form. The mermaid took the knife and entered the bridal chamber. "She bent down and kissed his fair brow, then looked at the sky on which the rosy dawn grew brighter and brighter; then she glanced at the sharp knife, and again fixed her eyes on the prince, who whispered the name of his bride in his dreams." The mermaid flung the knife aside and threw herself into the sea. She felt herself being taken above the water and found herself among the daughters of the air who, although they do not possess an immortal soul, can by their good deeds procure one for themselves after 300 years. The little mermaid looked below her at the prince and his bride looking frantically for her in the water, kissed the bride on the forehead, fanned the prince, and rose with the other daughters of the air.

"After three hundred years, thus shall we float into the kingdom of heaven," said she. "And we may even get there sooner," whispered one of her companions. "Unseen we can enter the houses of men, where there are children, and for every day on which we find a good child, who is the joy of his parents and deserves their love, our time of probation is shortened. The child does not know, when we fly through *the room, that we smile with joy at his good conduct, for we can count one year less of our 300 years. But when we see a naughty or a wicked child, we shed tears of sorrow, and for every tear a day is added to our time of trial!"*

A History of "The Little Mermaid"

Andersen's correspondence with Henriette Hanck shows that this story, at that time entitled "Daughters of the Air," was planned at the latest at the beginning of 1836, and the manuscript was completed by January 1837. Mermaids were popular in the literature of Denmark at that time.

> By using a currently popular theme Andersen apparently felt he was able to insert actual emotions and moods: a recently renewed acquaintance with childhood regions that seemed far away, isolated just as though on the bottom of the sea, and a relentlessly dissatisfied yearning back and forth between two poles—a romantic, but at the same time deeply personal emotion; it is reflected in the play, but in the fairy tale it had been replaced by a more determined striving towards a goal, that of eternal life." (Dal, 10)

This story was Andersen's favorite, and in a letter to his friend B. S. Inglemann, he stated that it was the only one of his works that affected him while he was writing it (Stirling, 163).

Fouque's narrative, *Undine* (1811), a minor classic, was influenced by Paracelsus's (1494–1541) treatise about the four soulless nature spirits, one of which is the undine. Through marriage with mortals, the elements seek that spiritual competition that shortens their life span on Earth but grants them everlasting salvation. In *Undine*, the King of the Sea, Undine's father, sends her to land to gain a husband. She marries her knight but then loses him to a mortal woman. Ironically, Undine wins him back at the moment he is to join his new wife on their wedding night but, alas, he dies at her hand. Fouque's tale was adapted by Jean Giraudoux, entitled *Ondine*, and made into an opera by E. T. A. Hoffman in 1812.

Andersen did not approve of the ending provided by Fouque. In a letter to Inglemann in February 1837, he expounded: "I have not, like de la Motte Fouque in *Undine*, allow[ed] the mermaid's acquiring of an immortal soul to depend on an alien creature, upon the love of a human being. I'm sure that's wrong! It would depend rather a lot on chance, wouldn't it? I won't accept that sort of thing in this world. I have permitted my mermaid to follow a more natural, a more divine path" (Sax, 157). However, the difference between these two tales is perhaps not as great as Andersen envisioned. Both authors use the attainment of a soul to mean the fulfillment of a destiny. "For Undine, this calling is the ultimate union with a beloved, accomplished not in this world but in the next. For the mermaid, her ethereal existence after death suggests artistic transcendence" (Sax 1998, 157).

Andersen's tale was made into a ballet in 1913. After seeing it danced by Jonas Collin's great-granddaughter, Ellen Price, art patron Carl Jacobson gave Copenhagen a statue of the mermaid to sit in the harbor. It was sculpted by Edvard Eriksen and set on a rock at Leangeline, in the promenade where in Andersen's youth the eastern defenses of the city extended to the sea. On April 4, 1964, when someone sawed off the head of the statue, contributions to recast the head and restore the statue came from all over the world. Decapitation of the statue occurred again in January 1998. Danish television stations received a statement from the unknown group, Radical Feminist Faction, claiming responsibility for the action. The statue, apparently, was a symbol of hostility to women and of men's sexually obsessed dreams of women's bodies.

Overview of Critical Interpretations of "The Little Mermaid"

1959: Erik Dal summarizes Professor Hans Brix's interpretation of the tale as follows: The mermaid's unrequited love for the prince symbolized Andersen's unrequited love for Louise, the daughter of his benefactor Jonas Collin. Brix also identified the bottom of the sea with the world in which Andersen originated and the dry world above with the one in which Andersen sought to gain acceptance. "And Louise's love in return, which would create for him a place in the home and a status of fraternal equality towards his friend Edvard Collin, is the objective for which the struggle is being made, but not attained—the whole narrative being adorned with the bright and splendid colours of the south" (10).

1961: P. M. Pickard, examining Andersen's life and its effect on his writing, states that "The Little Mermaid" was written as a reaction to Edvard Collin's engagement to Jetta and his dissatisfaction with his own reality. "Nothing ever moved him so much, for he was the little mermaid and had to lose his prince to Jetta. Himself lacerated by doubts about eternity, he ends the story in a mist of mysticism utterly unsuitable for children" (88).

1967: Dorothy Dinnerstein discusses the relationship between general features of human adolescence and that of Andersen's mermaid in regard to three crucial images in the tale. The first, and most ambivalent, image is the replacement of the mermaid's tail for human legs. The pain the mermaid experiences when walking with her newly acquired legs has a double meaning: the pain of independence and loneliness and the "special female pain of traditional sexual initiation" (107). The second image is the sacrifice of her tongue and her voice. To become adult, the girl must relinquish her right to communicate her opinions and experiences as well as her creative talent. It also can refer to the image of emasculation; the tongue can connote the fantasy of an internal penis. (107). The final image is the mermaid's search for immortality through marriage to the prince. Procreation is the only way that a female can achieve immortality. Her refusal to kill the prince is in fact an "unshakeable, fearless, non-dependent generosity to a chosen love, giving without expectation of receiving, the death-defying heroic deed of an autonomous being" (109).

1967: Christine Fell compares Gerta from "The Snow Queen" and the little mermaid and their quests for the "fulfillment of an ideal, in which the hero may be hindered and almost overcome by the indifference of his environment or by the destructive forces of evil" (84). The quest for reciprocal love is also one of Andersen's major themes, and Fell contends that it is loneliness that drives both Andersen and his characters. The mermaid's first test is the journey to the sea witch's house, which is fraught with danger and horror. His descriptions make it clear that the horror is real and not just the mermaid's emotional perception (85). The loss of her voice, according to Fell, emphasizes her complete aloneness: "When she had her voice she could not communicate with her own people because her ways of thinking were remote from theirs. Now that she has lost the means of communication she finds the prince, and it is indicated that he had the degree of understanding to share and respond to the little mermaid's thoughts and hopes, if the machinery of communication were not absent" (85).

1972: Maureen Duffy considers "The Little Mermaid" a castration story. There has been total disregard of the traditional sexual nature of the mermaid in Andersen's story. Duffy contends that she is a gentle, loving, made-up creature who wants, as real mermaids never do, to leave the water. Her longing for immortality symbolizes a desire for a child, and to be able to reproduce she must give up her tail and her voice. "She becomes dumb after a second castration of the tongue which symbolizes the writer's fear of the loss of words" (309). The attempt to "castrate" or kill the prince is "an elaborate narrative of a male homosexual fear recognized by psychiatrists, that the two partners castrate each other. One can only get back his tail at the other's expense, that is by forcing him to play a passive role" (309). The universality of this fear, for both heterosexuals and homosexuals, is the reason for the wide appeal of this tale. Duffy claims that Andersen's version places blame on the sea witch (the mother figure), for she is the one who, in folk belief, determines the child's gender either by her will or by what she eats or does during the pregnancy. The sea witch also symbolically castrates the mermaid's sisters by the cutting of their hair in return for the dagger. Therefore, this mermaid becomes an image of all our fears of castration in a sexual relationship that must be overcome before the relationship can be positive and loving. The mermaid sacrifices herself because the prince does not love her, but she gains immortality by a device "that echoes the nature of the author's own, by becoming a singing airy spirit and visiting children as he did by writing stories for them" (310).

1972: Barbara Fass explores the recurrent motif of the hero's identification with Andersen's "Little Mermaid" in Thomas Mann's *Doctor Faustus*. She traces the mermaid's history and progress through the work of John Keats, William Yeats, and Jean Giraudoux before discussing the utilization of Andersen's version in Mann's work. "In *Doctor Faustus* the soul is lost as a price for artistic greatness (the Faust legend) or won at the expense of aesthetics (the mermaid's fate)" (299).

1975: Kay Stone includes "The Little Mermaid" in her examination of persecuted heroines. She concludes that the mermaid is harshly punished for her unselfish love, suffering great physical pain and eventually death. Although she obtains an immortal soul along with her death, it does not seem like much compensation (122).

1978: Roger Sale maintains that "The Little Mermaid" is one of Andersen's most popular tales because its pathos has found a responsive echo in people who identify with the mermaid; "but it is really a chaotic desperate piece of work, very much out of touch with itself" (66). Andersen is driven, Sale contends, "to make the mermaid naturally inferior to the prince as a way of expressing his own sense of social or sexual inferiority" (66). However, the mermaids are beautiful and the prince "a dense and careless man," so it is difficult for the reader to understand the "natural" inferiority of the mermaid. It is the fact that mermaids have no immortal soul that renders them inferior for Andersen. The sea witch, in fact, reduces the mortal soul to a romantic and sexual prize. "To make socially inferior into sexually inferior and to make sexually inferior into naturally inferior, is bad enough, but to make naturally inferior into religiously inferior is sheer desperation" (67).

1979: P. L. Travers states that Andersen is in need of forgiveness for the last three paragraphs of the story. She might forgive him for the mermaid's wish, her sacrifice of her tail, and her graduation to life in the air, "But—a year taken off when a child behaves; a tear shed and a day added whenever a child is naughty? Andersen, this is blackmail. And the children know it, and say nothing. There's magnanimity for you" (93).

1983: In Ailene Goodman's discussion of the folklore roots of the mermaid, she contends that Andersen's version is true to the motif of mermaid as ominous portent. This is exemplified by the storm at sea that kills the prince's companions and sets the mermaid's course and the fatal desire of which the mermaid herself is the ultimate victim (34).

1983: Jack Zipes takes a concentrated look at Andersen's life and work to explore the popularity of the tales when they were first published and today. Zipes points out that Andersen was familiar with the folktales of sea creatures and Goethe's *Melusine* and Fouqué's *Undine* before embarking on his story of the little mermaid. His tale is different, Zipes maintains, because the focus is more on the torture and suffering that a member of the dominated class must undergo to establish true nobility and virtues (84). The mermaid's greatest failing is that she was attracted to a class of people who would never accept her as one of their own. Zipes claims a paradox in that the lessons Andersen seems to be preaching (true virtue and self-realization can be obtained through self-denial) are not virtues practiced by the nobility that she is striving to join. The message, however, is not a paradox because it is "based on Andersen's astute perception and his own experience as a lower-class clumsy youth who sought to cultivate himself: by becoming voiceless, walking with legs like knives, and denying one's needs, one (as a non-entity) gains divine recognition" (85).

1984:   Robert Solomon's analysis of the theme of the unappreciated, devoted, and silenced prairie wife in North American fiction and nonfiction leads him to Andersen's tale of the mermaid. He first considers the antecedents to Andersen's tale, which Andersen had always maintained was his own invention. Solomon states that Andersen "adopts the bloody feet and the sea-foam of Aphrodite and the singing of the sirens. . . . [H]is mermaid is silenced, as were the sirens when Odysseus closed the ears of his men to them" (144). Solomon also points to contemporary influences on Andersen's tale: Victorian fears about the dangers of female passion (144). Solomon states that by constructing the tale for children, Andersen "retreats from the problems presented by sexual maturation and the pressures that force women to be devoted to callous lovers" (145). He enumerates the basic components of the prairie mermaid motif:

> an authoritarian, insensitive and foolish husband; a young wife, full of old ideas of female subservience and submissiveness; a cold, arid, isolated land where there are no female friends; a homestead as old as the marriage and equally unsatisfying in terms of the women's needs for companionship, beauty and recognition; a storm or a move, which crystallizes the situation and challenges the man's sympathies for his wife, as well as her ability to express her desires to him; and a testing moment, when the wife accepts all that she has learned and silences her desires for beauty, companionship, and understanding. (150)

Andersen, Solomon concludes, identified female sexual maturation with suffering, marriage with coldness, and devotion with wordless submission (151). And he was not alone! Solomon's examination of pioneer fiction and historical accounts of life on the Canadian and U.S. prairies shows that, at least for a short period of time, the little mermaid lived as a prairie wife (151).

1986:   Wolfgang Lederer voices his conviction that the plot follows the familiar theme of redemption, not the "proper princely" method of redemption through heroic action but rather a woman's method of redeeming through love (170). Lederer points to similarities between the mermaid and Andersen: "Andersen made his debut on the Copenhagen stage as a dancer; and he too was always speechless—tongue-tied—when it came to declaring his love" (171). Like Andersen the mermaid had a beautiful voice, and lost it. She remains insubstantial, like her creator, and Lederer concludes that the mermaid is Andersen himself accepting the fact that he had the ability to project himself into his tales in the shape of either sex (172).

1989:   In his review of the Disney film, Charles Champlin discusses the number of interpretations that can be made from one source. " 'The Little Mermaid' is not about feminine consciousness or about the possibility of living in two different worlds. But obviously it is, or it can be made to be" (F6).

1990:   Pil Dahlerup refers to the basic dualism of this story that other researchers have discussed: life versus death, culture versus nature, and high status versus low status. Dahlerup claims that the mermaid does not want the prince or eternal life but that "confusion concerning the theme of the story mainly reflects the reader's conflict in handling a symbolic way of thinking and the author's conflict in the strategy of symbolizing" (420). It is, in fact, a story about the opposing values of innocence and sexuality, told in a melancholic mood. This mood is established by the use of the word "little" and by the narrator's method of argumentation and use of passive logic (424). The main difficulty is the choice of the mermaid symbol. In universal tradition, mermaids are regarded as sexual symbols, but Andersen's mermaid is anything but sexual. She therefore symbolizes the "a-sexual being" attempting to become sexual and transform her sexual situation into a spiritual one (426).

1990:   Rumer Godden correlates Andersen's pain and isolation with that of his most famous heroine. "When his Little Mermaid walked among humans, invisible knives pressed into the feet she had bought so dearly; she too, was always different from the humans around her, though they loved her" (557). Godden comments that the statue of the Little Mermaid, her face turned away from the people of the land, looks lonely and "might be called the statue of Andersen's heart" (557). Godden decries the bad translations, abridgments, and adaptations of Andersen's tales. "The Little Mermaid" may have dark elements, but the ultimate feelings of joy and tenderness make the tale one of the most loved tales in the world (562).

1990:   Niels Ingwersen and Faith Ingwersen (Dahlerup 1990) consider the four tests that the mermaid faces in Andersen's tale. First, she strives for transcendence, rejecting the seductive and destructive nature of mermaids when saving the prince from the storm, and, second, willingly makes a sacrifice of her tail and her voice. "It should be noted . . . that our heroine is miserably failing her nature as a mermaid, but splendidly passing her tests as someone attempting to transcend her present level of existence" (Dahlerup 1990, 413). Her third test is to secure the love of the prince without the use of her voice, and her final test is that of the dagger. "In Andersen's tale the protagonist also learns what is the real goal of her quest. . . . By sacrificing herself, she has again rejected a soulless life, and as she assumes spirit form, she regains her voice and can finally express her love of the heavenly, just as she has acquired the independence to achieve it" (Dahlerup 1990, 44). The authors state that the tale of a soul's longing for transcendence is completely ignored by the Disney version but that the film is truer to the folktale struggle between good and evil than Andersen's tale is (Dahlerup 1990, 415). However, Disney only shows the negative side of feminine rule and the positive side of masculine rule.

1990:   Gregory Nybo claims that the story is not about unrequited love as much as it is about death and our subterfuges in trying to deny its existence (Dahlerup 1990, 416).

1990:   Sabrina Soracco (Dahlerup 1990) takes a psychoanalytic approach to the tale and concludes that the desire of the mermaid to leave the world of the pre-Oedipal mother dominates the initial part of the story. Her sacrifice of her voice and tongue can be interpreted as a form of castration, with the sea witch as castrator. "One might venture to say that H. C. Andersen's tale thus thematizes the suppression of female and maternal subjectivity in the patriarchal order" (Dahlerup 1990, 409). The mermaid sacrifices the matriarchal order further by refusing to kill the prince and by directing the dagger toward the sea. Soracco concludes that the mermaid's castration may represent Andersen's own fear of losing his ability to express himself as an artist, and her persistent attempts to gain access to a different world may reflect Andersen's own entrapment in the position of outsider (Dahlerup 1990, 412).

1990:   Ulla Thomsen (Dahlerup 1990) turns to structuralism to examine the tale of the mermaid and the preconditions that must be satisfied to achieve her desire to become human, to marry the prince, and to achieve immortality. Several approaches are discussed in reference to the story. According to the contract model, the mermaid breaks a contract and is ostracized by the community, moving to a world of different rules. She cannot return to the old world because she is ultimately too good and different from the raw and destructive power of the sea witch (Dahlerup 1990, 405).

1990–
1991: Roberta Trites admits that although this story contains many patroniz-
ing, nineteenth-century attitudes toward women, "a value system that at
least acknowledges the legitimacy of femininity shapes the fairytale"
(145). Her article explores the ways in which the Disney film eliminates
the values that affirm this femininity. She states that much of Andersen's
imagery symbolizes the burgeoning sexuality of the little mermaid.
Andersen depicts human love as a product of maturity and the pain that
the mermaid endures as the only way the mermaid knows to achieve her
quest: the gaining of an immortal soul (148). There are strong overtones
of Christian allegory in Andersen's tale: "grace through a man's love is
not the only means to salvation. Although it takes longer, salvation can
also be achieved through the self-sacrifice of good works" (151).

1992: Susan C. Roberts considers this tale to be an unmitigated tragedy that is
better suited to dour Scandinavian temperaments than those of optimistic Americans. "It is," she claims, "Andersen's stark confession of the betrayal of his feminine soul" (19). The mermaid represents the anima, a
figure from the unconscious depths, who saves the life of the prince and
sacrifices her own for love of him. The only way that she could have entered real life was if the man would have given her a voice.

1993: A. Waller Hastings contends that the mermaid's willingness to sacrifice
the happiness she has painfully pursued through real danger provides a
second chance at immortality. "Even though the romantic/erotic narrative is frustrated, the 'higher' narrative of moral progress remains a possibility—is, in fact, enhanced by the mermaid's refusal to destroy
another life" (85). Hastings contends that the mermaid's erotic pros-
pects were destined to failure. This failure may be seen as "the inevitable
heartache of human love," one that Andersen was intimate with himself
(88). The mermaid was destined not only to be rejected but to be ignored
by the object of her desire.

1993: In her note to her essay about the film version of the tale, Susan White
points out that Andersen was writing in the same atmosphere that produced Kierkegaard's meditations on the nature of Christianity. She
states that the history of the mer-world in Andersen's writing included
two failures on the stage of his poem *Agnete and the Merman,* first written in 1834. In this poem, as in the more successful "The Little Mermaid,"
the focus is on a girl's separation from home and parents. Kierkegaard
included the "Agnete and the Merman" story and uses it, as Andersen
did, as an allegory of their broken engagements, although Kierkegaard
clearly identified himself with the merman (285).

1994: Marina Warner considers the tale both morbid and powerful. She states
that Andersen's telling it specifically for children intensifies its moral
preachiness about feminine love and duty, self-sacrifice and expiation

(398). Warner examines the silencing of the mermaid and the pain and resulting blood of the acquisition of legs and reflects that the chilling message of the tale "is that cutting out your tongue is still not enough. To be saved, more is required: self-obliteration, dissolution" (398).

1995: Rachel Bennett contends that Charles Dickens's *Little Dorrit* displays patterns of romance similar to those in "The Little Mermaid." She discusses the fact that Dickens was familiar with Andersen's tale and in fact had met the author. Bennett discusses various similarities between the two stories. The loss of her voice denotes, in terms of romance, the descent of the mermaid into the upper world, and each step she takes after that increases her pain until she makes the ultimate sacrifice (188).

1995: Laura Sells continues Roberta Trites's argument that the Disney film subverts Andersen's mermaid's self-actualization process, but also offers Zipes's interpretation that Andersen's reward was never power over one's own life but rather the power of servitude to God.

1996: Jorgen Johansen claims that his interest in the tale is the result of the tension between a powerful, almost heartbreaking representation of the merciless tragedy of human love and desire on the one hand, and a perhaps unconvincing and sentimental religious reparation on the other (203). He discusses the topography of the story and the opposition between land (here) and sea (down there).

Johansen states that the tale is conceived with the salvation of the little mermaid as the plot's finale and claims that Andersen established continuity between the earthy and the sacred by making the fulfillment and happiness of human love a precondition for the acquisition of heavenly love (208). The tests and sacrifices the mermaid must undergo are to this end. "To man mermaids represent seduction, animality, and death. To be accepted by man—i.e. the prince—the little mermaid must negate these three attributes; indeed, she must transform them into precisely their converse" (215). Johansen discusses the conditions of love and its fulfillment that are presented multidimensionally in the tale. He acknowledges that, on the narrative level, a major focus is on the question of the conditions of love during the passage from childhood to adolescence (232). "The cruelty of Andersen's story, but also its sublime tragedy, is due to the fact that it tells the story of someone who had an intense longing to make this passage [from nature to culture], who willingly made sacrifices to do so, and who perished" (240).

1997–1998: Rhoda Zuk considers Andersen's tale to be a wedding of two disparate genres: the male *Bildungsroman* and the female marriage plot. The story exposes the unresolved contradiction in political theory and practice between women's sexualized role and the normative (masculine) value of autonomy (166). It affirms the longing to escape the boundaries of racial, cultural, and sexual identity while at the same time exposing the relationship between that desire and the lonely agony of the alienated outsider (167).

1998: Rosellen Brown considers Andersen's tale a challenging story in its non-Disney version. The mermaid "is deprived of her voice, of her personality, her *self,* left only with her looks, which are captivating but (to the prince's eternal credit) insufficient compared to the pleasure of a complete speaking woman. The mermaid is a beautiful and loving husk and her longing is forever unrequited" (57). Brown states that it was the mermaid's inability to explain herself that both fascinated and panicked her: "The threat is always there for children that they will be inadequate, possibly even speechless, when it's urgent that they be heard. So the idea that the mermaid, for love, would volunteer to lose her voice and thus yield up any chance to make her case—ah, that was so terrible to me that I could hardly look it in the eye. And so, of course, I looked and looked" (59). Andersen captured one of humanity's primal terrors: voicelessness. "He suggested that too much wanting can change the one who desires (whatever her object) to the point of deformity. He reminded us how difficult, perhaps even how impossible, it is to try to leap certain barriers and successfully become something we are not" (62).

1998: Lucy Grealy speculates that if she had been allowed to read the unabridged versions of the Grimm tales and the "darkly punishing tales" of Andersen with "mermaids who give up everything magical for an unrequited and lacklustre reality," she would have been able to better understand the people around her (171).

1998: Vigen Guroian states that the Disney film version betrays Andersen's tale while it also exploits society's obsession with physical beauty and romantic love (70). Guroian contemplates the role of romantic love and concludes that the tale does not make it into an idol but rather issues a serious warning about the harm such an idol can bring (77). The discussion takes issue with Roger Sales's criticism of the tale and concludes that this is a great and profound fairy tale that "challenges every reader to contemplate his or her fate if love does not endure and personal immortality is just an illusion" (86).

1998: Meri Lao states that this is a cruel fable for children, particularly in the way it involves the audience by assuring them that the time of the mermaid's final test would be shortened or lengthened according to the number of good or bad children the daughters of the air found along their way (142).

1998: Joyce Carol Oates finds Andersen's tale "a disturbing parable of woman's place in the world of men" (253).

1998: Lissa Paul analyzes "The Little Mermaid" in the light of active and passive heroines. Traditionally, Andersen's tale is "read as a story about self-lessness, silence, self-sacrifice, patient endurance and suffering in the face of monumental injustice" (37). But we prefer an active heroine, do we not?

1998: Neil Philip introduces Andersen as a poet of human suffering. He was driven to write "The Little Mermaid," a tale that only adults could understand the deeper meaning of but that children will enjoy for the story's sake. It was the first fairy tale in which Andersen attempted to explore his own spiritual beliefs. "The story is now perhaps best known in Disney's more optimistic version—but the deeper meaning resides in Andersen's bleak and painful original" (15).

1998: Boria Sax claims that with Andersen's publishing of "The Little Mermaid" the motif of the animal bride entered popular culture. He considers the mermaid's tale to be an autobiographical one. "Like Andersen, the mermaid failed to obtain happiness in the new home but was granted some consolation. Andersen achieved his immortality not through deeds but through poetry" (156). The muse for the mermaid is the prince, but he may play another symbolic role as well: that of the adult Andersen.

1998: Marina Warner considers Andersen's mermaid very briefly in her examination of watery dangers. When Warner discusses the differences between single-tailed and double-tailed mermaids, she reminds her readers that the double tail of the little mermaid suggests the onset of menarche and sexual maturity (90).

1999: Sheldon Cashdan explores the role of the witch (Sea Hag) in this tale and concludes that the Disney version provides a closer approximation of a fairy tale than does Andersen's original story. After all, there is a happy ending and the wicked witch gets her just deserts in the film. According to Cashdan, Andersen's story is about the necessity for young girls to await maturation before embarking on sexual "adventures." At the same time, Cashdan celebrates the Disney version of Ursula, the personification of lust and sexual gratification. It is natural that the story requires the gaining of legs (to engage in sexual intercourse) and the loss of the voice (to add to the witch's store of sexuality) to demonstrate this point:

> A purist might argue that changing Andersen's tale corrupts the story by diluting the spiritual message of self-sacrifice the author intended to convey. But fairy tales are products of their time and constantly tale new form.... It may be that the Disney's studio's transformation of *The Little Mermaid* is the next evolutionary step in fairy tales. Although Walt Disney's early undertakings altered age-old stories to make them conform to his vision of

what a fairy tale should be, current norms regarding sex and violence may bring fairy tales closer to what they originally were meant to be. (171)

1999: Margaret Starbird considers Ariel, from the Disney film, to be "a powerful metaphor for the plight of the 'Sacred Feminine'." Starbird points to various indications that Ariel can be considered a Magdalen figure: the painting by Georges de la Tour, "Magdalen with the Smoking Flame," which is in Ariel's underwater collection; the mirror and the book Ariel carries, which have strong symbolic meanings in medieval art; and the ancient connection of Mary Magdalene with the mermaid and the "Queen of the Sea."

2000: Niels Ingwersen's entry in Jack Zipes's encyclopedia states that the story is based on the Christian-inspired folk belief that supernatural creatures do not have souls and will disappear into nothingness upon death. The story glorifies suffering and self-denial (300).

2000: Maria Nickolajeva states that "The Little Mermaid" is "based on a medieval ballad, eagerly exploited by romantic poets. Andersen, however, reversed the roles and toning down the ballad's motif of the Christian versus the pagan, created a beautiful and tragic story of impossible love, which certainly also reflected his personal experience" (14).

Reworkings of "The Little Mermaid" in Novel Form

There is only one reworking of the story in novel form at the time of this writing. The mer-child in question is actually the son of the famous Andersen heroine.

The Mer-Child

1991. Morgan, Robin. **The Mer-Child: A Legend for Children and Other Adults**. New York: Feminist Press.

This is a contemporary fable in novel form about two outsiders, the mer-child and a young girl of mixed racial heritage. The girl is ostracized because of her appearance but also because her legs are paralyzed. She is taken to the beach and left there in the sunshine each day of the summer and eventually makes friends with the mer-child. Both look forward to these summer visits. "That was the summer she read to him the Hans Christian Andersen story *The Little Mermaid*. He found it marvelously sad and was astounded to discover that his mother was so famous as to be in a human's book—even if the storyteller did get some of the facts wrong" (1991, 37). This slight novel explores issues of acceptance and identity.

Short Stories

There are many more short story adaptations of the tale than novel adaptations. As evidence of reawakened interest in the tale, more reworkings have been published since the release of Disney's *The Little Mermaid* than before it came out.

1985. Yolen, Jane. **"The Undine."** In *Dragonfield and Other Stories.* New York: Ace, 199–203.

Yolen "emphasizes the notion of male betrayal and female autonomy in an implicit critique of Hans Christian Andersen's 'The Little Mermaid'." Here the mermaid leaves the prince, who beckoned her, to return to her sisters in the sea that "opened to her, gathered her in, washed her clean" (Zipes 1994, 156).

1993. de Lint, Charles. **"Our Lady of the Harbour."** In *Dreams Underfoot.* New York: TOR, 358–403.

A statue on Wolf Island is a reproduction of the famous one that stands in the harbor in Denmark. Matt, an intense musician, often goes to Wolf Island to sing, and one day the young mermaid overhears him. She has kept herself hidden because she knew she had no soul, but eventually she makes a bargain to gain legs to find Matt. Her voice is the price she must pay, and she has only eight days to fulfill her yearning. Unfortunately Matt has problems with relationships, and time passes much too quickly. "It's like that legend about the little mermaid," she said as she finished up. She glanced at the statue beside them. "The real legend—not what you'd find in some kid's picture book" (400).

1995. Galloway, Priscilla. **"The Voice of Love."** In *Truly Grim Tales.* Toronto: Lester, 60–73.

Beginning with a summary of the Andersen tale, this story follows the voyage of the prince and his bride after the wedding. He suddenly realizes that he has not seen his silent companion and begins to miss her. His melancholy takes him to the sea, where he converses with the mermaid's sister and discovers the price she had paid to be his companion. He has a statue built in the harbor in her memory, and this time, when a storm washes him over the side of his ship, he does not resist but follows the voice to the one he loves. But she no longer possesses her voice, does she?

1995. Gardam, Jane. **"Pangs of Love."** In *The Armless Maiden and Other Tales for Childhood's Survivors,* edited by Terri Windling. New York: TOR, 173–81. [Originally published in *Close Companies: Stories of Mothers and Daughters.* London: Hamish Hamilton, 1983].

This is the story of the little mermaid's younger sister who, having been raised on the stories of her sister's heroic sacrifices, decides to go to the surface to check out this other world for herself. She meets with the lovelorn prince and informs him of the price of her sister's relationship with him. When he professes his love for her, this mermaid asks him to sacrifice his legs and to get himself a singing voice. He contemplates it but cannot, at the last moment, agree to such terms. The sister is not disappointed, she claims, but as the sea-witch gently points out, "So now—unclench that fist" (181). A breezy tone does not diminish the seriousness of the theme of choice and freedom in relationships.

1995. Garner, James Finn. **"The Little Mer-Person."** In *Once Upon a More Enlightened Time.* New York: Macmillan, 29–39.

This is a role reversal, ecologically correct version, in which the "prince" is transformed into a sea creature to prove his love for the mer-person. They, of course, live happily ever after.

1995. Sickafoose, Munro. **"Knives."** In *The Armless Maiden and Other Tales for Childhood's Survivors,* edited by Terri Windling. New York: TOR, 155–71.

Mathilde's father kept her helpless in her room. When she became too curious about the outside world, he kept her drugged and then made sure she could never walk on her own. After he dies in a car accident, she is found and taken to the hospital. After reconstructive surgery her motor responses are working again but she finds it too painful to try to walk and retreats within herself. Through the reading of Andersen's tale, she discovers that someone else has had to suffer a similar pain and that the choice for recovery is up to her. A sad and bleak tale that ends with a promise of hope.

1995. Smeds, Dave. **"Foam."** *Realms of Fantasy* (December): 54–61.

On her fifteenth birthday, her father warns Coral that the sea witch has always hated her. "To kill you, she must actively break the magic which formed you, with your consent" (56). But Coral disregards the warning when she is desperate to be with the prince she loves. She is made human for only three days, and if she does not succeed in winning her prince, she will die. It is not her actual voice that is taken but rather the power to communicate in human speech. This one fares no better than Andersen's mermaid, but when she dissolves into foam she discovers her true nature and place in the wider scheme of the gods.

1996. Walker, Barbara G. **"The Littlest Mermaid."** In *Feminist Fairy Tales.* New York: HarperSanFrancisco, 77–188.

It seems as if this little mermaid is following in her great-great-great aunt's footsteps by falling in love with a terrestrial she has rescued from the storm. After acquiring legs through the help of the sea witch, she is towed to shore and makes her way to the palace. During her unclothed journey a man driving a wagon accosts her. She soon unseats him, devises clothing from leaves, and enters the palace gate. Once she meets the prince, the romance is played out; perhaps it does not proceed too smoothly and painlessly at first, but every one is happy at the conclusion.

1997. Donoghue, Emma. **"The Voice."** In *Kissing the Witch: Old Tales in New Skins.* New York: Joanna Cotler, 185–204.

This is a first person account of a not-so-young fish seller and her bargain with a witch. For the price of her voice and physical pain, she travels to the city and begins a relationship with the man of her dreams. When she is betrayed, she retreats to the streets until she makes it back to the home of the witch. There she discovers who is really in charge of her fate: herself.

1999. Shaw, Melissa Lee. **"The Sea Hag."** In *Silver Birch, Blood Moon,* edited by Ellen Datlow and Terri Windling. New York: Avon, 100–121.

This story "originated as Shaw's rebellion against the dearth of strong, sympathetic adult female characters in animated Disney films. She noticed a disturbing trend for positive female characters to be either adolescent heroines or bumbling grandmothers, with women in between usually portrayed as villains" (Datlow and Windling, 100).

Coral, the youngest mermaid, begs for assistance from the old sea hag to find her human sailor-prince. Although she wants to stop Coral from leaving the sea, the sea hag cannot deny the request. Coral's sisters also come to the sea hag to convince her to help them in getting Coral to return, but they receive more than they bargained for. The sea hag tells them the story of their births and her origin as a hag. With the power of love, the sea hag finds Coral but leaves her there with her prince when she discovers that, unlike the former human she had fallen in love with many years ago, Coral's prince truly loves her.

Feature Films

Ingwersen's entry for "The Little Mermaid" in Zipes's encyclopedia states that none of the film versions "is interested in the metaphysical ideas of that story; instead, they concentrate on exploring the comic and tragic potential of beautiful voices, tails versus legs, cross-species relationships, and slippery sex" (317). When we think of film adaptations of this story, the Disney animated version immediately springs to mind. However, it was neither the first film adaptation made in the 1980s and 1990s nor the only one made by Disney Studios.

Faerie Tale Theatre's The Little Mermaid

1984. **Faerie Tale Theatre's The Little Mermaid.** Directed by Robert Iscove and starring Pam Dawber, Treat Williams, Karen Black, Helen Mirrien, and Brian Dennetry. 50 minutes.

A fun, fast, and furious romp with the Faerie Tale Theatre's trademark irreverence for Andersen's tale.

Splash

1984. **Splash**. Disney Studios. Starring Tom Hanks, Daryl Hannah, and John Candy.

This film received an Oscar nomination for "Best writing, screenplay written directly for the screen" and a Golden Globe nomination for "Best Motion Picture in a Comedy or Musical." In this adaptation of Andersen's tale, the heroine loses her voice temporarily and acquires the ability to walk. The traditional ending is reversed as the mermaid, Madison, saves Allen from drowning twice. The first time he was only eight years old; the second time was 20 years later.

Madison goes to New York to find Allen, gaining legs in the process and learning English by watching television. Allen falls in love without realizing she is a mermaid. When she reverts to her original form, he follows her into the sea. "Instead of dying in an attempt to become human, she has caused a human to renounce humanity and become aquatic" (Ingwersen 2000, 317).

Walt Disney's The Little Mermaid

1989. **Walt Disney's The Little Mermaid**. Directed by John Musker and featuring the voices of Jodi Benson, Samuel E. Wright, Pat Carroll, Christopher Daniel Barnes, Buddy Hackett, Kenneth Mars, Rene Auberjonois, Ben Wright, and Jason Marin.

We selected this tale for discussion in this book partly on the basis of the popularity of the Disney studio's adaptation of "The Little Mermaid." The film, first released in 1989, has preempted the original authorship of the story in the minds of a decade of viewers. Perhaps this is just as well because the Disney movie has only a surface resemblance to Andersen's unhappy tale.

History of *The Little Mermaid*

The film marked the first time the Disney Studios had produced a feature film adapted from a fairy tale since *Sleeping Beauty* (1959). It grossed $76 million in its initial release and won two Academy Awards, for Best Song and Best Original Score, the first Oscar awarded to an animated film since *Dumbo* in 1942. The musical score was actually written before any of the animation began, so the plot and characters were substantially developed through the film's music (Sells 1995, 183). The idea of Disney making an animated movie of "The Little Mermaid" actually dates back to the late 1930s, when Walt Disney mulled over a feature that would be composed of vignettes based on several Andersen tales. Kay Nielsen, art director for segments of *Fantasia*, created storyboards and artwork for "The Little Mermaid" at that time, but the Andersen project was abandoned. Some of Nielsen's artwork appeared in the shipwreck scene 50 years later in the movie (Thomas, 119). In an uncharacteristic move for the studio, the film was released as a video within a year of its appearance in movie theaters as the company's increasingly savvy marketing division responded to the comments of people leaving the theater after viewing the film (Hastings, 89).

The first commercially successful animated film from the Disney Studios since Walt Disney's death, *The Little Mermaid* was hailed as a forerunner in a new wave of animated films featuring "acceptable" role models for young girls. However, regardless of this claim, it is still the male characters who defeat the sea witch and return Ariel to the human world. The little mermaid is actually a more active character in Andersen's tale because she is the one who conceives of the transformation into human form herself and must pass through deadly obstacles to reach the sea hag, who then warns her of all the dangers involved. Undeterred, the mermaid takes the potion from the sea hag to land, where she undergoes her transformation safely. In the film, Ariel is merely a pawn for Ursula's evil devices. In fact, Ursula acts the role of the devil; the mermaid, and later Triton, must sign a contract (pact) with her (Hastings, 87).

Andersen's tale is adapted to appeal to the children and teenagers of the 1980s while maintaining the core patriarchal family values on which the Disney Studios based all their products (O'Brien, 170). Disney replaced the nineteenth-century religious ideals with twentieth-century goals for adolescents: the need for individuality and the desire for independence from the constraints of society. At the same time, because for many young women there was an increasing movement away from the feminist thought that had flourished in the previous decades, confusion arose about these traditional female roles and gender ideology. There was also firm pressure from the press and the political arena to return to basic values during the 1980s.

> At the beginning of the film, Ariel's curiosity is intellectual, and she collects artifacts from sunken ships to further her education, although this marks the beginnings of her materialism. Her intellectual interests quickly turn to emotional dependency once she sees Eric. Changing the reason for the mermaid's initial curiosity reflects Disney's attempt to make the character's motivation understandable to modern children and teenagers, and does not reflect any new-found Disney feminist ideology. . . . Andersen's limited feminism is replaced by patriarchal images of a helpless Ariel who must turn to her male animal friends for both intellectual and physical support in times of difficulty. (O'Brien, 172–73)

The film also replaces many of Andersen's philosophical concerns with contemporary sociological ones. Ariel's stern but loving father is now a major character in the drama, while her biological mother is noticeably absent. The mermaid is from a one-parent family, and after becoming estranged from that parent must rebuild harmony through a happy marriage. The traditional American faith in the power of the individual is affirmed by the happy ending of the film (Sax, 168).

The marketing of the film in North America took two directions simultaneously. The advertisements both highlighted the animation and the characters that appealed to children and focused attention on the romance, songs, nostalgia, and magic to appeal to the adult population. "Ads for adults will focus on the studio's heritage, playing up the nostalgia and magic associated with other Disney animated films like *Snow White*" (Magiera, 24). In Germany the film is known as *Ariell* rather than *The Little Mermaid*. There has been speculation that the difference in title was to lessen the offense that Andersen aficionados may feel in response to the changes to the well-loved Andersen story. The second "l" may have been added to differentiate the film from the brand name of a popular detergent, "Ariel" (Bendix, 280). The name "Ariel" has other connotations as well. To some critics, it denotes the magical island and reconciliatory themes of Shakespeare's *The Tempest* (Zuk, 171). Indeed, is Disney's *Little Mermaid* not a story of reconciliation between father and daughter?

The Disney Differences

Andersen's bleak romantic tale was tinkered with for the film; "real or symbolic loss of virginity, social failure and death" are not the usual fare offered by the Disney Studios (Bendix, 284). Andersen's nineteenth-century audience would have found the emphasis on the virtue of the mermaid's silent self-sacrifice attractive but would not understand the contemporary "willful American high-school junior" who actively and defiantly disobeys her father, portrayed in Disney's reworking of the tale; today's audience would have had problems with Andersen's religious overtones (Paul, 25). At the same time, "embedded within this classic narrative about an adolescent girl's coming of age is a very contemporary story about the costs, pleasures and dangers of women's access to the 'human world' " (Sells, 176).

Table 5.1 shows how the film adaptation differs from Andersen's original tale.

Table 5.1. Comparison of Andersen's "The Little Mermaid" to Disney's *The Little Mermaid*

ASPECT	ANDERSEN	DISNEY
Quest	Immortal soul	A mate
Parental influence	She experiences no parental repression because the story does not center on her growth for maturity but rather on her quest for a soul (Trites, 146).	Triton, her father, is overprotective and portrayed as tyrannical. The movie centers on a young girl gaining autonomy from her father.
Value system	Religious overtones to the quest	Ariel must choose between her father and a potential mate.
Reason for human form	To gain an eternal identity	So her identity can be defined by mortal love: "The underlying message creates a startling incongruity: Children, especially girls, can gain an identity independent from their parents by becoming dependent on someone else" (Trites, 146).

(Table 5.1 continues on p. 196.)

Table 5.1—Continued

ASPECT	ANDERSEN	DISNEY
Love	Equated with "soul"	Equated with "marriage"
Terms of bargain	Can live as human until the prince marries someone else; has the leisure to develop her love slowly	Only rewarded if prince kisses her within three days
Decision to become human	Self-determined	Depends on characters who are stronger than her to shape her destiny for her (Trites, 148)
Other characters:		
Sea witch	Willing to help even though she does not agree with the mermaid's decision; bond created between the two; repulsive	Ursula, a mature woman who is predatory and menacing: "Disney gives its sea-witch an interest in the mermaid's relationship with the prince that the original witch does not have . . . an opportunity to compete . . . for the possession of the mermaid's soul, which Ursula perceives as a weapon to use against Triton" (Trites, 149). She is "an elegant octopus, exuding the charm, allure, and power of evil" (Bendix, 286).
Prince	Never imagines that he has been rescued by the mysterious, mute girl who appears soon after he escapes the shipwreck (Hastings, 87); rather melancholy	Immediately suspects Ariel's identity; fun-loving, attractive; rescues the mermaid and marries her
Conflict between good and evil	None	Centers on evil's attempt to conquer good

The film has changed the role of the setting quite substantially from the role Andersen had given it, but critics do not always agree about the importance this change has had in the interpretation of the story. For one critic, "the realm under the sea is then simply a replica of the realm above the sea, and the otherness so important to Andersen's tale is obliterated in Disney" (Bendix, 288). But to another, the film's sea world reflects a Third World environment, "the colonized space of marginalized or muted cultures, often invisible to the inhabitants of the white male system" (Sells, 178). The motivation and gender roles of Andersen's characters have been greatly altered as well (see Table 5.2).

Table 5.2. Changes in Cast: Schematic Comparison of Dramatis Personae
(Adapted from Bendix 1993, 284)

ANDERSEN	DISNEY
Sea king (father, widower)	Triton, king of the mer-people
Sea king's mother (grandmother)	Sebastian, the crab (Triton's right hand, musical director, guardian to Ariel)
Six daughters, among them the Little Mermaid	Triton's six older daughters Ariel (seventh daughter) Flounder, Ariel's fish companion Scuttle, a well-meaning seagull
The prince	Eric, the prince
Royal parents, court	Grimm, the royal chancellor Max, the prince's dog
Crew of the ship	Sailors
Young maidens of the temple, one of whom becomes the bride	"Since Eric's infatuation is so shallowly based on beauty rather than on personality, he is easily deceived by Ursula's disguising herself as the raven-headed ingenue who possesses the little mermaid's voice" (Trites, 148).
Sea witch	Ursula, the witch Flotsam and Jetsam, Ursula's barracudas
Additional sea people	Additional mer-people Scores of water species, birds, and mammals French cook Matron maid
Slave girls	Washer women Peasants, priest, wedding guests

These alterations are particularly noticeable in regard to the little mermaid herself: In the Disney film she is acquisitive, flirtatious, and not required to sacrifice anything. "While Andersen's tale centers on the little mermaid's pure and principled nature. . . . Disney's heroine is relieved of the necessity for conscious struggle on finding herself magically and painlessly transformed into a new person in the human world, a marvellous land of adventure and opportunity, where she progresses by employing her childlike charm" (Zuk, 171). She is not interested in acquiring a soul but in collecting things. Andersen's mermaid, rather than simply passing from the domain of her father to that of a husband, attains an independent destiny and is rewarded by her continuing capacity to give love whether or not she receives it. She even bestows affection on the prince's chosen bride (Cravens, 641). (See Table 5.3.)

Table 5.3: A Comparison of Andersen's Little Mermaid and Disney's Ariel

ASPECT	ANDERSEN	DISNEY
Personality	A dreamy child who does not fit into either world (Bendix, 286)	A spirited, spunky teenager who is basically a spoiled child and who escapes her obligations and the wishes of her father (Bendix, 286)
Reason for ascent to surface	A rite of passage undertaken at age 15	A tabu, a rule that she breaks with great regularity (Bendix, 286)
Meeting with prince	Rescues prince when on her rite of passage	Sees him on one of her forbidden expeditions, rescues him, then discovers statue
Relationship with father	Only mentioned in initial paragraph	A visually and psychologically imposing figure (Bendix, 286)
Relationship with family	No conflict	Generational conflict with father
Self-actualization	Ordeal undertaken alone	Accompanied by Sebastian, Flounder, Scuttle, and Max
Relationship with prince	Treated as a sister and a pet	Marries the prince

Even though the focus in the Andersen tale is not on maturation or female roles, the many positive female figures in his tale provide a more accurate portrait of what it is to be a woman than the movie does (see Table 5.4).

Table 5.4. Female Characters and Their Roles in Andersen's "The Little Mermaid"
and Disney's *The Little Mermaid*

FEMALE CHARACTERS	ANDERSEN	DISNEY
Information source	Grandmother (also as a positive role model and kind authority figure)	A male bird that misinforms the mermaid. The authority of the grandmother has been transferred to the father. Sebastian also becomes a major information source but he is ineffectual and basically performs as comic relief and musical director.
Sea witch	Supports the little mermaid's search for an immortal soul; contributes blood from her own breast to make the transforming potion	Major conflict and personification of evil
Sisters	Sacrifice their only treasure (hair) to help their sister	Do not take any action; their friendship role is replaced by a male character, Flounder.
Prince's beloved	Someone whose femininity the mermaid respects. She also finds the prince on the beach and ultimately becomes his bride. Her role is eliminated in the film to provide a vehicle for a happy ending. (Bendix 1993, 285)	An illusion: "Eric falls in love with his memory of the physical beauty and the voice of the maiden who rescues him. Eric never considers this girl's personality" (Trites 1990–1991, 148).
Daughters of the Air	Teach the mermaid about charity and exist only as females	Not present
The mermaid: both agree to be voiceless, to give up their physical forms, and to separate themselves from their cultures. Because they have no verbal communication skills and are illiterate, they can express their personalities only by relying on their appearance. (Trites 1990–1991, 152)	Prince regards her as an object of beauty rather than a person to be loved.	Disney subverts the mermaid's process of self-actualization. Ariel effaces herself and gets her man.

Influences of This Film on Future Generations

There has been widespread speculation about the effects of this film on its viewers and on the generations of viewers to follow. A major focus has been on the image of the female body. "Disney's gender images stress body stereotypes that play right into the hands of plastic surgeons, diet programs and the fitness and clothing industries" (Bendix, 287). Another concern has been implied racial overtones about the mer-people. "This racist and colonialist perspective (Mer-people just sing and dance, while humans work) reinforces the human/nonhuman and culture/nature dichotomies by associating the merpeople, and by implication Caribbean and other equatorial people, with a closer-to-nature, live-off-the-land indigenous lifestyle inferior to the industrial life style"(Murphy, 132). Sebastian the Crab is an obvious caricature of a black Caribbean, a symbol of the limited access to power of minority groups in North America (Bendix, 288).

Poetry

There seem to be few poetic reworkings of the tale, and both examples that we found predate the Disney film.

1981. Viorst, Judith. "**. . . and although the Little Mermaid sacrificed everything to win the love of the prince, the prince (alas) decided to wed another.**" In *If I Were in Charge of the World and Other Worries: Poems for Children and Their Parents*. New York: Atheneum, 30–31.

In this poem the mermaid tells young women that there is no need to change who they are to attract the person of their choice. After all, he might have liked her better with her tail.

1985. Yolen, Jane. **"Undine."** In *Dragonfield and Other Stories*. New York: Ace, 204–5.

The poem is a lament about the fate of this mermaid and others who fall for a prince of the land folk.

Picture Books

There are no appropriate reworkings of the tale in picture book format at the time of printing.

Internet Resources

Niels Ingwersen, whose entry in the Zipes's encyclopedia has been quoted in this chapter, has posted his course syllabus for "The Tales of Hans Christian Andersen" on the World Wide Web at www.scandinavian.wisc.edu/hca/. There are countless Web sites dedicated to Ariel and the Disney film and to Andersen himself. However, few of these offer anything but praise for both subjects under consideration. A simple search for "The Little Mermaid" will locate all the current Web sites.

Classroom Extensions

The following classroom extensions may be adapted for use with other fairy tales as well.

"Andersen Murdered?"

Rumer Godden discusses Andersen's writing style and the desecration of his stories to make them "suitable" for children:

> The idea that children should be given books without shadows—books of brightness and lightness and laughter, nothing else—seems to be wrong; perhaps the reason why such books are so lifeless is that living things have shadows. This sheltering has led to what can only be called a desecration of Andersen's work; judicious editors have cut it, changed the endings, in some cases simply taken the plot away from the story and told it again, until, as Mr. Elias Bredsdorff, professor of Scandinavian Studies at Cambridge and expert on the *Tales* [Andersen's fairy tales], said, "What we have is Andersen murdered." (Godden, 561)

Do you agree or disagree with Godden's sentiments? Discuss, using examples from Andersen's "The Little Mermaid" and other renditions of his story.

The Loss of Voice

"The significance of the mutilation points up the intimate connection between the witch's character and the mermaid's sexual longings. In folklore, a woman's voice is traditionally associated with seductiveness and thus symbolizes lustful feelings" (Cashdan, 167). As discussed in Chapter 3, the sirens in the *Odyssey* use their seductive singing voices to lure men to their doom. Is this a major theme in Andersen's tale? Why was it so important that the mermaid sacrifice her voice?

The motif of the physical loss of voice in this tale and the silencing of the voice in "The Wild Swans" provides an interesting comparison of the roles of the female in the traditional tales. How many of the reworkings in both chapters focus on this aspect, and why?

The Prince

Lissa Paul reminds us of the mermaid's sacrifices of her voice and tail for the man she loves. In Andersen's story, she loses him to another woman regardless of her sacrifices. "And he suffers no pangs of conscience or guilt because he had no idea what the mermaid suffered for him" (9). What is the role and responsibility of the prince in regard to the mermaid's fate? Is he really as oblivious as Paul claims?

The Little Mermaid Movie

Because so much of the discussion in this chapter focuses on the Disney film, we have provided classroom extensions specific to it.

Access, Autonomy, and Mobility

Laura Sells discusses the song "A Part of Your World," sung by Ariel in the movie. Sells states that the song expresses Ariel's desire to run, walk, and dance, all synonyms for mobility. While she sings, Ariel absentmindedly caresses a book that she cannot read. This symbolizes her longing for knowledge. Her desire for access is characterized by her hunger for and fascination with another world in which she believes she can be independent and have autonomy (Sells 1995, 179). What do these terms mean to you? Do they mean the same thing to the young intended viewers of the movie? Is there any problem with Ariel's longing for these things? Does she fulfill her desire for them by the end of the movie?

Consequences

The original complexities of the story were eliminated in the Disney adaptation. "The child who reads Andersen's fairy tale has experienced a world in which desires have consequences that may be painful, where wanting something badly enough to suffer for it may not make it happen; the child who views the Disney film experiences a world in which bad things only happen because of bad people, where desire is always fulfilled" (Hastings, 90). Hastings continues his lament, claiming that this moral simplification increases the possibility that the viewers will become adults who do not accept the consequences of their actions but rather blame the causes of their unhappiness on personalized evil outside of their control. Do you agree with Hastings? Could a popular movie have such power to influence generations of children and adults?

Disney's Patriarchal Point of View

Many of the criticisms directed against the film focus on the patriarchal worldview that critics think it promotes.

> Women who begin the film as strongly independent and self-empowered are brought back into the patriarchal fold when they fall in love. Disney's films' affirmation of patriarchal values also is strongly evident in the persistent absence of matriarchal support in animated fairy tales. Disney's princesses and princes do not have mothers or grandmothers and the princesses do not have sympathetic sisters. Thus the only system in which Disney

characters can potentially find happiness is a patriarchal one because that is the only option. (O'Brien, 180)

Why do so many females identify with a heroine that some critics term a cross
between a typical rebellious teenager and a fashion model from Southern California? "Although children might be delighted by Ariel's teenage rebelliousness, they
are positioned to believe in the end that desire, choice, and empowerment are
closely linked to catching and loving handsome men. . . . Ariel becomes the metaphor for the traditional housewife-in-the-making narrative" (Giroux, 58).

Is this true of all of Disney's animated fairy tale films? Has there been a
marked change since the first of these films was made? Why do you think this has
happened? What does it tell us about our society? What will this mean to future
generations of viewers?

Drag Queens?

Laura Sells claims that:

> according to the directing animator, Ruben Acquine, Ursula was
> modeled on the drag queen Divine, while the voice and ethos be-
> hind Ursula belonged to Pat Carroll. Both of these character ac-
> tors are known for their cross-dressing roles. . . . A composite of
> so many drag queens and camp icons (Joan Collins, Tallulah
> Bankhead, Norma Desmond, Divine), Ursula is a multiple cross
> dresser; she destabilizes gender (1995, 182)

Do you agree with Sells? Why or why not? Was the portrayal of Ursula effective? Did her "camp" personality make her more evil? More fun? More "other?"

The Silencing of Women

The loss of voice or the right to speak is a motif in numerous folktales around
the world. It is a focus of two of the tales in this book, "The Little Mermaid" and
"The Wild Swans," both written by Hans Christian Andersen. Many critics have
focused on the loss of voice in the film version of *The Little Mermaid* as well. What
do you think of the following quote in respect to the Disney version? To Andersen's tale? What sacrifice is made in "The Wild Swans?" Does it have the same
repercussions as those alluded to here?

> Articulating one's own dreams and wishes—possessing an
> autonomous voice—is a strong indicator of the development of
> selfhood. Little wonder, then, that alarms sound for feminists
> concerned with the psychological development of girls' and
> women's sense of self when Ariel literally sacrifices her voice and
> mermaid body to win Eric's love. What is gained by females who
> silence themselves in a masculine society? (Henke, Umble, and
> Smith, 237)

Ursula's Demise

Trites laments the fact that it is Eric, rather than Ariel, who kills the evil Ursula. Ariel has suffered much more at Ursula's hands than Eric has, but he is given the satisfaction of destroying her power nonetheless. "This is Disney's most annoying reworking of Andersen's plot . . . can't the maid kill the witch herself? . . . Nice girls are not supposed to have that much power" (Trites, 150).

What do you think about this statement? Why is Eric, and not Ariel, the agent of Ursula's defeat? Would it have changed your perception of the mermaid if she had been ultimately responsible for the death? Explain.

References

Bendix, Regina. 1993. "Seashell Bra and Happy End." *Fabula* 34 (3/4): 280–90.

Bennett, Rachel. 1995. "Hajji and Mermaid in *Little Dorrit.*" *RES New Series* 46(182): 174–90.

Brown, Rosellen. 1998. "Is it You the Fable Is About?" In *Mirror, Mirror On the Wall: Women Writers Explore Their Favorite Fairy Tales*, edited by Kate Bernheimer. New York: Anchor, 50–63.

Cashdan, Sheldon. 1999. *The Witch Must Die: How Fairy Tales Shape Our Lives.* New York: Basic Books.

Champlin, Charles. 1989. "Diving into the 'Little Mermaid' Sexism Issue." *Los Angeles Times* (December 5): F1, F6.

Cravens, Gwyneth. 1992. "Past Present." *Nation* 254(18): 638–41.

Dahlerup, Pil. 1990. "Splash! Six Views of 'The Little Mermaid'." *Scandinavian Studies* 62: 403–29. [Includes Ulla Thomsen's "A Structuralist Approach"; Sabrina Soracco's "A Psychoanalytic Approach"; Niels Ingwersen's and Faith Ingwersen's "A Folktale/Disney Approach"; Gregory Nybo's "A Synopsis"; and Pil Dahlerup's "The Little Mermaid Deconstructed"].

Dal, Erik. 1959. *The Little Mermaid by Hans Christian Andersen.* Copenhagen: Host & Son.

Datlow, Ellen, and Terri Windling, eds. 1999. *Silver Birch, Blood Moon.* New York: Avon.

Dinnerstein, Dorothy. 1967. " 'The Little Mermaid' and the Situation of the Girl." *Contemporary Psychoanalysis* 3: 104–12.

Duffy, Maureen. 1972. *The Erotic World of Faery.* New York: Avon.

Fass, Barbara F. 1972. "The Little Mermaid and the Artist's Quest for a Soul." *Comparative Literature Studies* 9: 291–302.

Fell, Christine E. 1967. "Symbolic and Satiric Aspects of Hans Andersen's Fairy-Tales." *Leed Studies in English* 1: 83–91.

Giroux, Henry A. 1997. "Are Disney Movies Good for Your Kids?" In *Kinderculture: The Corporate Construction of Childhood,* edited by Shirley R. Steinberg and Joe L. Kincheloe. Boulder, CO: Westview Press, 53–67.

Godden, Rumer. 1990. "Hans Andersen, Writer." *Horn Book* (September–October): 554–62.

Goodman, Ailene S. 1983. "The Extraordinary Being: Death and the Mermaid in Baroque Literature." *Journal of Popular Culture* 17(3): 32–48.

Grealy, Lucy. 1998. "Girl." In *Mirror, Mirror on the Wall: Women Writers Explore Their Favorite Fairy Tales,* edited by Kate Bernheimer. New York: Anchor, 168–77.

Guroian, Vigen. 1998. *Tending the Heart of Virtue: How Classic Stories Awaken a Child's Moral Imagination.* New York: Oxford University Press.

Hastings, A. Waller. 1993. "Moral Simplification in Disney's 'The Little Mermaid'." *The Lion and the Unicorn* 17: 83–92.

Henke, Jill Birnie, Diane Zimmerman Umble, and Nancy J. Smith. 1996. "Construction of the Female Self: Feminist Readings of the Disney Heroine." *Women's Studies in Communication* 19(2) (Summer): 229–49.

Holbek, Bengt. 1990. "Hans Christian Andersen's Use of Folktales." In *The Telling of Stories: Approaches to a Traditional Craft: A Symposium.* Odense: Odense University Press, 165–82.

Ingwersen, Niels. 2000. "The Little Mermaid." In *The Oxford Companion to Fairy Tales: The Western Fairy Tale Tradition from Medieval to Modern,* edited by Jack Zipes. New York: Oxford University Press, 300.

Johansen, Jorgen Dines. 1996. "The Merciless Tragedy of Desire: An Interpretation of H.C. Andersen's 'Den lille Havfrue'." *Scandinavian Studies* 68: 203–41.

Lao, Meri. 1998. *Sirens: Symbols of Seduction.* Translated by John Oliphant. Rochester, VT: Park Street Press.

Lederer, Wolfgang. 1986. *The Kiss of the Snow Queen: Hans Christian Andersen and Man's Redemption by Woman.* Berkeley: University of California Press.

Magiera, Marcy. 1989. " 'Mermaid' Aims to Reel in Adults." *Advertising Age* (October 16): 24.

Murphy, Patrick. 1995. "The Whole Wide World Was Scrubbed Clean:" The Andocentric Animation of Denatured Disney." In *From Mouse to Mermaid: The Politics of Film, Gender and Culture,* edited by Elizabeth Ball, Lynda Haas, and Laura Sells. Bloomington: Indiana University Press, 125–36.

Neff, Heather. 1996. "Strange Faces in the Mirror: The Ethics of Diversity in Children's Films." *The Lion and the Unicorn* 20(1): 50–65.

Nickolajeva, Maria. 2000. " Hans Christian Andersen." In *The Oxford Companion to Fairy Tales: The Western Fairy Tale Tradition from Medieval to Modern,* edited by Jack Zipes. New York: Oxford University Press, 13–15.

Oates, Joyce Carol. 1998. "In Olden Times, When Wishing Was Having: Classic and Contemporary Fairy Tales." In *Mirror, Mirror on the Wall: Women Writers Explore Their Favorite Fairy Tales,* edited by Kate Bernheimer. New York: Anchor, 247–72.

O'Brien, Pamela Colby. 1996. "The Happiest Films on Earth: A Textual and Contextual Analysis of Walt Disney's *Cinderella* and *The Little Mermaid.*" *Women's Studies in Communication* 19(2) (Summer): 155–83.

Paul, Lissa. 1998. *Reading Otherways.* Stroud, Glos, UK: Thimble Press.

Philip, Neil. 1998. *The Little Mermaid and Other Fairy Tales of Hans Christian Andersen.* New York: Viking.

Pickard, P. M. 1961. *I Could a Tale Unfold: Violence, Horror & Sensationalism in Stories for Children.* London: Tavistock.

Roberts, Susan C. 1992. "Fractured Fairy Tales." *Common Boundary* (September/October): 17–21.

Sale, Roger. 1978. *Fairy Tales and After from Snow White to E. B. White.* Cambridge, MA: Harvard University Press.

Sax, Boria. 1998. *The Serpent and the Swan: The Animal Bride in Folklore and Literature.* Blacksburg, VA: McDonald & Woodward.

Sells, Laura. 1995. "Where Do the Mermaids Stand?" Voice and Body in 'The Little Mermaid'." In *From Mouse to Mermaid,* edited by Elizabeth Bell, Linda Haas, and Laura Sells. Bloomington: Indiana University Press, 175–92.

Solomon, Robert H. 1984. "The Prairie Mermaid: Love-Tests of Pioneer Women." *Great Plains Quarterly* 4 (Summer): 143–51.

Starbird, Margaret. 1999. "The 'Little Mermaid' and the Archetype of the 'Lost Bride'," http://members.tripod.com/~Ramon_K_Jusino/littlemermaid.html.

Stirling, Monica. 1965. *The Wild Swan: The Life and Times of Hans Christian Andersen.* London: Collins.

Stone. Kay. 1975. "Romantic Heroines in Anglo-American Folk and Popular Literature." Ph.D. dissertation, Folklore Institute, Indiana University.

Thomas, Bob. 1991. *Disney's Art of Animation: From Mickey Mouse to Beauty and the Beast.* New York: Hyperion.

Travers, P. L. 1979. "The Primary World." *Parabola* 4(3): 87–94.

Trites, Roberta. 1990–1991. "The Little Mermaid." *Journal of Popular Television and Film* 18: 145–52.

Warner, Marina. 1994. *From the Beast to the Blonde: On Fairytales and Their Tellers.* London: Chatto & Windus.

———. 1998. *No Go the Bogeyman: Scaring, Lulling and Making Mock.* London: Vintage.

White, Susan. 1993. "Split Skins: Female Agency and Bodily Mutilation in 'The Little Mermaid'." In *Film Theory Goes to the Movies,* edited by Jim Collins, Hilary Radner, and Ava Preacher Collins. New York: Routledge, 182–95.

Wilmington, Michael. 1989. " 'Little Mermaid' Makes Big Splash." *Los Angeles Times* 15(1): F1, F8.

Wood, Naomi. 1996. "Domesticating Dreams in Walt Disney's *Cinderella.*" *The Lion and the Unicorn* 20(1): 25–49.

Zipes, Jack. 1983. "Hans Christian Andersen and the Discourse of the Dominated." In *Fairy Tales and the Art of Subversion: The Classical Genre for Children and the Process of Civilization.* New York: Methuen, 1983, 71–95. [Reprinted in Zipes' *When Dreams Came True: Classical Fairy Tales and Their Traditions.* New York: Routledge, 1999, 80–110].

———. 1994. *Fairy Tale as Myth, Myth as Fairy Tale.* Lexington: University Press of Kentucky.

Zuk, Rhoda. 1997–1998. "The Little Mermaid: Three Political Fables." *Children's Literature Association Quarterly* 22(4): 166–74.

CHAPTER 6

THE
WILD SWANS

ndersen crossed a bridge when he transferred a number of tales from folklore to literature, but we, the scholars, investigate either one or the other side of the bridge and we have not quite succeeded in describing the crossing itself. (Holbek 1990, 177)

In Chapter 4 we discussed the fact that very few of Andersen's tales were actually based on traditional folklore. There is one story, however, that is well known as Andersen's own and that shows up in the Grimms's collection of tales not only once but three times under three separate titles. All four of these titles are identified under the same tale type number: Andersen's "The Wild Swans," and "The Twelve Brothers," "The Seven Ravens," and "The Six Swans" by the Brothers Grimm.

Andersen's "The Wild Swans" personalizes the heroine by giving her a name.

&

Eliza lived happily with her 12 older brothers and their father until their father brings home a new wife who does not like any of the children. She transforms the boys into swans and banishes Eliza into the forest. Eliza returns home when she is 15 years old and her stepmother once again manages to banish her, but not before we realize Eliza's essential goodness. Eliza meets an old woman in the forest who informs her of her brothers' plight and the method for breaking the spell that keeps them in their swan form. While Eliza is working hard, weaving the nettles into coats for her brothers, she is discovered by a king, who brings her to his home. Captivated by her beauty, he ignores the fact that she does not speak, but eventually he can not ignore the charges of witchcraft that are brought against her by the Archbishop when she goes to the graveyard to gather more nettles. Her brothers attempt to speak to the king in their human form, but their efforts are thwarted. They do, however, manage to rescue their sister before she is burned at the stake. She throws the coats of nettles over her brothers so they can retain their human form. Alas, the

209

last coat is not completely finished, and Eliza's youngest brother is left with a swan's wing instead of an arm. She and her brothers return to the home of the king, and all live in peace and contentment the rest of their days.

Of the three Grimm variants, "The Six Swans" is the closest to Andersen's reworking of the tale. In this tale, the king realizes at the beginning that his new wife is a danger to his children.

🐦 ───

He hides his children away, but his new wife follows him and, using his own magic yarn, makes six shirts for the brothers. The young sister is not noticed at the time and the stepmother does not realize she exists. The sister witnesses the transformation but cannot convince her father that his wife had anything to do with it. Her brothers tell her how to break the spell, and she sets to work sewing shirts of starwort. She is discovered by the king's huntsmen, who bring her before him. She also captures the heart of the king and together they produce three children. It is her mother-in-law who denounces her, claiming that she is an ogre who ate her own children. The last day of the spell coincides with the day of the execution, and her brothers arrive just in time. As in the above tale, the last shirt has not been completed, and the girl's youngest brother is left with a swan's wing.

The other two variants involve the father as the agent of the transformation instead of the stepmother. In "The Seven Ravens" the father is disgusted with his sons' clumsiness on the day of the baptism of their ill sister. He curses them, they become ravens, and he immediately forgets about their existence. Their sister thrives and eventually hears the gossip about her brothers and their fate and goes searching for them. She finds them in a glass mountain and transforms them simply by showing them their parents' ring. Once they are transformed, they all return home to their parents. The king in "The Twelve Brothers," on the other hand, decides to murder his 12 sons if his thirteenth child is a female, so he can assure her inheritance. The mother hides her sons to protect them from their father. When the sister asks about them, her mother tells her the truth, and the sister eventually finds them and befriends them. However, she unwittingly picks 12 lilies by the house, causing her brothers to transform into ravens. She discovers that to break the spell she must not utter a sound for seven years. She, like the heroines in the first two variants, is found by and married to a king. His mother lays charges of wickedness against the girl but is foiled when the spell is broken at the end of the seven years. The brothers regain their human form and forgive their sister, and all, with the exception of the mother-in-law, live peacefully the rest of their days. Incidentally, of all the Grimm variants, the only character who is given a name is the youngest brother in this tale, who initially recognizes his sister and convinces his brothers to accept her. His name is Benjamin.

This chapter is dedicated to crossing the bridge mentioned at the beginning of this chapter and to traveling beyond into the world of other writers who, like Andersen, transferred tales from folklore to literature.

Tale Type: AT 451

The Maiden Who Seeks Her Brothers. The 12 brothers are changed into ravens.

I. *The Brother and Their Sister.* (a) Seven (twelve) brothers have a younger sister. (b) The parents have promised the death of the brothers if a daughter is born; the brothers discover this; the mother lets them know by a sign if a girl is born; the brothers flee; the sister finds them; or (c) the boys leave home out of fear of their father or stepmother.

II. *Transformation of Brothers to Ravens.* (a) Through a wish of their father or (b) stepmother or (c) because their younger sister has plucked 12 flowers from an enchanted garden, the brothers are transformed into ravens.

III. *The Sister's Quest.* (a) The sister seeks for them and asks direction of sun, moon, and stars and finds them on a glass mountain (and they are thereby disenchanted) or (b) the sister must remain speechless for years and make shirts.

IV. *The Calumniated Wife.* (a) A king sees the speechless girl and marries her. (b) On the birth of her children they are stolen and she is accused of killing them.

V. *Disenchantment.* (a) As she is about to be executed her period of silence is over, the ravens fly down, are disenchanted, and all is cleared up.

Motifs:

I. Z71.5.1: Seven brothers and one sister. P253.0.5 One sister and six (seven, eleven, twelve) brothers. P251.6.7. Twelve brothers. S272. Sacrifice of brothers promised if girl is born. T595. Sign hung out informing brothers whether mother has borne boy or girl. N344.2. Wrong sign puts out leads to boys' leaving home. S. 272.1 Flight of brothers from home to avoid being sacrificed.

II. S11: Cruel father. S31. Cruel stepmother. D521. Transformation through wish. D515. Transformation by plucking flowers in enchanted garden. C515. Tabu: touching (plucking) flowers. D151.5 Transformation to raven. D161.1. Transformation to swan.

III. P253.2: Sister faithful to transformed brothers. H1385.8.Quest for lost brothers. H1232. Directions on quest given by sun, moon, and stars. H1114. Task: climbing glass mountain. D783. Disenchantment by being found when lost. D753. Disenchantment by accomplishment of tasks. D753.1. Disenchantment by sewing shirts for enchanted brothers. D758.

Disenchantment by maintaining silence. Z72.2 Seven years, seven months, seven days.

IV. N711: King (prince) accidentally finds maiden in woods (tree) and marries her. K2116.1.1. Innocent woman accused of killing her new-born children.

V. H215: Magic manifestation at execution proves innocence.

(Thompson, 153)

Comparison of the Four Tales

Table 6.1 compares the four tales in type AT 451.

Table 6.1. Comparison of Tale Type AT 451

ELEMENT OF STORY	THE WILD SWANS	THE SIX SWANS	THE 7 RAVENS	THE 12 BROTHERS
Main Character	Princess Eliza	King's young daughter	Peasant's daughter	King's young daughter
Beginning of Story	The 12 children lived happily with their widowed father.	Lost king comes upon an old woman in the forest who offers her daughter as his wife in return for directions out of the forest.	Man and his wife have sickly daughter who needs to be baptized immediately. Her 7 brothers go to the well to fetch water for the ceremony. They accidentally break the jug and their father is furious with them.	King decides that if his 13th child is a girl he will assure her inheritance by murdering his 12 sons. He has 12 coffins made and locks them in a secret room. Mother sends the sons far away and organizes a signal for them. If it is a son, a white flag will be flown, if a daughter, a red flag. Only return if white flag.
Agent of Transformation	Stepmother	Stepmother	Father	Sister
Reason for Transformation	Stepmother did not like the children; Eliza banished from home as well.	Father hides the children from his new wife. She follows him on one of his frequent visits and discovers that he finds the hidden place with the help of a magic ball of yarn.	Father curses in anger; he does not remember saying it and has no idea what has happened to his sons.	She unwittingly picks 12 enchanted lilies.

ELEMENT OF STORY	THE WILD SWANS	THE SIX SWANS	THE 7 RAVENS	THE 12 BROTHERS
How They Are Transformed	"Fly like great birds, who have no voice."	Stepmother finds the yarn and makes 6 shirts from the yarn, sewing a transformation charm into each of them. Sister is not with them at the time and stepmother does not know of her existence.	"I wish the boys were all turned into ravens."	The picking of lilies transforms the brothers and causes the house to disappear as well.
Manner in Which the Sister Discovers the Fate of her Brothers	Returns home at age 15; stepmother has 3 frogs try to turn Eliza into something ugly so her father would not recognize her. The frogs changed into poppies instead. "She was too good and too innocent for witchcraft to have any power over her." However, second ploy worked and Eliza banished again. Old woman in forest tells her about her brothers as swans.	Sister witness to the transformation and tells her father, who does not believe his wife had anything to do with the deed.	Local gossip, which is confirmed by her parents when she questions them.	The first time, Mother tells the girl about her brothers when she asks about 12 shirts she finds. She is the cause and the witness of the transformation into ravens.
Regaining Human Form	Each night they turn back into men; have permission to return to homeland once each year for 3 days.	Only for one-quarter of an hour each evening do they regain their human form.	Not mentioned in the story.	Cannot regain human form unless spell is broken.
Dwelling Place for Girl and Swans	They create a net and fly her over the water to another land.	She makes her home in a tree in the forest.	Not mentioned	In a small house in the forest. She finds them there but is warned that they have vowed to kill her or any maiden they see. The youngest brother, Benjamin, gets them to change their minds.

(Table 6.1 continues on page 214.)

Table 6.1—Continued

ELEMENT OF STORY	THE WILD SWANS	THE SIX SWANS	THE 7 RAVENS	THE 12 BROTHERS
Method for Breaking Spell	Gather nettles from graves in a graveyard; break them into pieces with her hands and feet; spin and weave 11 coats with long sleeves; she cannot utter a sound throughout ordeal	"For six years you may neither speak nor laugh, and in that time you must sew together six little shirts of star-wort for us."	Travels the world looking for them. The morning star gives her a chicken drumstick and tells her to use it to open the glass mountain to find her brothers.	Must not utter a sound for seven years.
Character Who Gives the Information	Fairy who appears in a dream	Brothers	Morning star	Old woman in the forest
Character Who Finds Her	King out hunting finds her in a cave.	Huntsmen find her in her tree and bring her to the king.	She finds a dwarf in the glass mountain who welcomes her until her brothers return.	King who was out hunting. He climbs the tree and brings her down.
Antagonist	Archbishop	King's mother	None	King's mother
Charge Against Her	Witchcraft (She has to gather more nettles for the shirts and is followed to the graveyard and surrounded by ghouls.)	Man-eater (Her mother-in-law took their three children one by one and smeared blood over the mouth of the sleeping mother.)	None	Wickedness (because she cannot laugh)
Punishment	Death by fire	Death by fire	None	Death by fire
Action of the Brothers	Attempt to speak with king in their human form but transform into swans before they can. Swans arrive while she is still in the cart on the way to the fire. She immediately throws the coats over her brothers and reclaims them as human.	Last day of the six years corresponded to the day of the execution. While she is tied to the stake her brothers arrive, and she places the shirts upon them to reclaim them as human.	They find their parents' ring, which their sister has left in the bottom of one of their glasses and state: "God grant that our sister may be here, and then we shall be free."	Last day of the 7 years corresponds with the timing of the fire at the stake. They regain their human form and quench the flames, saving their sister.
Fate of Youngest Brother	Left with swan's wing	Left with swan's wing	All ravens transformed	All ravens transformed

ELEMENT OF STORY	THE WILD SWANS	THE SIX SWANS	THE 7 RAVENS	THE 12 BROTHERS
Ending	All the pieces of firewood transform into roses as Eliza and her brothers proclaim her innocence and they all return to the castle in peace and contentment.	The three children were found; the mother-in-law was burned at the stake; and the king, queen, and her six brothers lived happily in the castle.	They all returned to the home of their parents.	Brothers, king. and queen all lived together happily. but wicked mother-in-law died miserably. (The actual method of this death is not mentioned.)

History of "The Wild Swans" in Print

Scholars have not been as fascinated with the history of this tale in any of its manifestations as they have with others in the Grimm canon. There appears to be consensus, however, that it was widespread as an oral tale in both Germany and Denmark before any of the variants were captured in print.

The Brothers Grimm

"The Twelve Brothers" was originally titled "The Twelve Brothers and the Little Sister," in the manuscript. Jacob Grimm recorded the original handwritten version, but it was his brother Wilhelm who prepared the tale for the 1812 publication. "Wilhelm's reworking of the tale emphasizes two factors: the dedication of the sister and brothers to one another and the establishment of a common, orderly household in the forest, where they live peacefully together" (Zipes 1988, 40). The first edition of this story presents a king whose horror at the idea of having a daughter is very extreme. "If the thirteenth child that you bear is a girl, I'll have the twelve brothers killed. But if it's a boy, they can all stay alive and live together." By the second edition, the situation is reversed and the king is so pleased with the idea of having a daughter that he is willing to sacrifice his sons for her to be financially secure. "If the thirteenth child you are about to have is a girl, the twelve boys must die, so that her wealth may be great and that she alone may inherit the kingdom" (Tatar 31). Jack Zipes feels that Jacob and Wilhelm were particularly drawn to this tale type because of its theme of several brothers and one sister who overcome adversity after separation from their parents. The brothers and the sister, whose reputation is restored by the end of the tales, create a new home together and are content (Zipes, 40). This theme apparently appealed to the brothers so much that they included three variants of it in their collection of tales.

"The Twelve Brothers" was apparently collected by Jacob from the Ramus family and a second version of the tale from Dorothea Viehmann. He was also responsible for collecting "The Seven Ravens" from the Hassenpflug family. An informant added an introductory section to this tale from Vienna. Wilhelm gathered "The Six Swans" from Dortchen Wild. This tale, according to Ruth Bottigheimer, owed a great deal to the story "Die Sieben Schwane" in the collection *Feemarhrchen,* published in 1801 (Bottigheimer 1987, 37).

Hans Christian Andersen

Andersen's tale was based on stories he had heard as a child in Denmark. I could not find any documentation about his source of this tale, but it has been acknowledged as an adapted folktale. "The Twelve Wild Ducks," in Peter Christen Asbjørnsen and Jorgen Moe, *Norske Folkeeventyr (Popular Tales from the Norse)* is an analogue of the Grimms's "The Twelve Brothers," first published in 1845. Andersen's version of the tale was published several years earlier, in 1838, two decades after the Brothers Grimm first published their tales.

Overview of Critical Interpretations of "The Wild Swans"

1975: Kay Stone, in her dissertation on romantic heroines, states that in comparison to the other heroines in her research, the heroine in Andersen's "The Wild Swans," is extremely aggressive. "She does go in search of her lost brothers and decides to save them, but accomplishes this in the persecuted manner of her Grimms' counterparts in 'The Six Swans' and 'The Twelve Brothers' " (1975a, 122).

1975: In her article on folktale heroines, Kay Stone reminds the reader that the innocent heroine of "The Six Swans" is the victim of a scheming and ambitious woman (1975b, 43).

1976: Bruno Bettelheim refers to the tale of "Seven Ravens" only in a note. He contends that it is possible to consider the brothers as "representing that which had to disappear for Christianity to come into being" and that their sister represents the new religion, which can only succeed if the old paganism does not interfere with its development; they only return once she has liberated them through self-sacrifice (12–13n). He does not address any of the other tales under discussion in this chapter.

1978: Roger Sale claims that the woman who gave Eliza, the heroine in Andersen's version, the raspberries and whose voice told Eliza how to disenchant her brothers was "a substitute for the good mother who has died bearing children and in effect [she] pass[es] on the hopes attendant upon birth or puberty" (43). The fact that the Grimms did not have such a figure in their version of the tale demonstrates that this magical and benign woman was too much even to wish for (43).

1979: Pierre Bange submitted a semiotic analysis of "The Twelve Brothers," comparing the 1810 manuscript with the version published in the second edition (1819). He touched upon the presence of a veiled theme of incest (McGlathery 1993, 80).

1981: Peter Taylor and Hermann Rebel consider the Grimm tales "The Twelve Brothers," "Brother and Sister," "The Seven Ravens," and "The Six Swans" as historical sources for their research on the draft, the private family, and the larger Hessian society. They discuss the brothers' sources for these tales and maintain that for these peasant women, "storytelling was a craft which involved remembering accurately, telling, and teaching what one knew repeatedly to those who could learn it" (355).

"The Seven Ravens" involves the transformation of the brothers into ravens and their subsequent departure from the family and their sister, who grows up without knowing them. In this tale the sister does not travel to a forest, nor is there a king to marry her, and in the end the brothers are not integrated into another family but return to the family of origin. "The girl's entry by baptism into the family, the boys' loss of the baptismal vessel, and the father's misinterpretation of their delay make up the first symbolic complex of the story" (360). This probably reflects the nature of the social relations within the family where the sons are afraid of their father's reactions to the accident, and it is the next aspect of the tale that interests Taylor and Rebel more: the transformation of the boys into ravens. The association of the ravens with Odin as the scavengers of the battlefield and the messengers of war and death is noted. Taylor and Rebel connect this association with the symbolism of direct dispossession in German imperial law. "To be declared *Vogelfrei* (free as a bird) meant one was in essence declared socially dead: his wife became a widow, his children became orphans, and he lost inheritance, honor, and protection of the laws" (360). The second important symbol complex of this tale is the sister's journey and the successful integration of the brothers into the family. Taylor and Rebel discuss the nature of the articles the sister takes along on her journey and the bone key she receives to unlock the glass mountain. "This is the only story in which the sister gives up a claim to her patrimony without gaining access to another through marriage" (361).

"The Twelve Brothers" and "The Six Swans" have an additional complex of symbols that concern the difficulties of the period of exile and transformation, the loss of the original patrimony, and the risks the sister runs in restoring her brothers to the social world (361). The social themes in these tales are similar to those addressed in "The Seven Ravens" and include "the birth of a female, the breach in family life, the explicit dispossession of the sons, the transformation by social exile, the sister's difficult task and renunciation of her patrimony, the elimination of a rival, and the final social reintegration" (362). In "The Twelve Brothers," the female characters trigger changes in both the ordinary social world and the symbolic world of power. The mother acts to save her sons, the "old woman" provides the magic formula for the disenchantment, the sister enters a magical world with her vow of silence and her spinning, and the sister's rival undermines her struggle to release her brothers (362). According to Taylor and Rebel, the symbolism in this tale is concerned explicitly with war and concerns of patrimony. They consider forests as "places where people have been disinherited and expelled from the normal social life of families" (363). The trees themselves function as places between transformation of the ordinary and the magical worlds in this tale.

Taylor and Rebel claim a much clearer association between the avian forms (expressions of social disconnection) and military service (a consequence of such disconnection) in "The Six Swans." The swans represent the transformation experienced by the Norse goddesses of the battlefield, the Valkyries (364). The shirts are made of asters, "the 'star' flowers whose name is derived from *aster*, the morning star of the ancient Greeks. The only evidence that remains of the power struggle to bring about the transformation of the brothers is the crippled arm of the youngest son. This swan wing is a reminder of the pain and loss he has experienced when losing his original patrimony in the system of ultimogeniture" (365). This system involves the inheritance of the estate by the last born sibling, and in three of the tales under consideration in this essay the youngest brother makes special appearances in this disinheritance struggle (366). Taylor and Rebel conclude their study by stating that for a significant proportion of eighteenth-century Hessian peasant society, "it was advantageous to transmit property to girls and to dispossess sons whose claims would interfere with the reconstitution of property" (372). These sons could be absorbed into the army. In the tales under discussion, however, the sisters were not "rational" because they rejected their role as heir and rescued their brothers (373):

> In all of the four tales examined, the sisters sought to bring their brothers back into the world of people. Into the social world of families; and in all but one of the four, sisters had to reject the role of "advantaged heir" to accomplish this. In all but one of the tales—in which the simple act of renunciation suffices—reconnection is accomplished by emigrating with a husband through whose family the brothers reacquired their human social shape. (375)

1986: Ruth Bottigheimer discusses the silent heroine in both "The Twelve Brothers" and "The Six Swans." They are "powerless against the world," not speaking a word or laughing for six or seven years (depending on the tale) to save the lives of their transformed brothers (120). These tales demonstrate that there is a close relationship between language and power as both sisters face burning at the stake because they refuse to speak. Speechlessness also occurs in conjunction with the archetypal female occupations of spinning and sewing and reflects the society's image of the quiet woman (129).

1986: In his notes, Wolfgang Lederer states that the incomplete transformation of the last swan in "The Wild Swans" renders him "a not-quite-human creature—like Andersen" (248).

1986: Gerhardo Mueller comments on fairy tale crimes and their punishments in "The Six Swans" and "The Twelve Brothers." The historic punishments for the charge of witchcraft in the first tale and perversion of justice causing false execution (attempted) in the second tale are death by fire. In both tales, the heroine is condemned to burn at the stake or be boiled by oil. Thus, the tales accurately reflect the judicial system in which they were formulated.

1987: Ruth Bottigheimer explores several other aspects in these three Grimm tales, including the moral and social vision of the tales. She claims that the specific wording of the tales demonstrates that good female characters are not allowed to manipulate fire, including the domestic fire of the hearth. One of her examples is "The Twelve Brothers," in which the sister "sought for the wood for cooking and herbs for vegetables, and put the pans *on the fire* so that the dinner was always ready when the eleven came" (28). She infers that it is the youngest brother, Benjamin, who actually lights the fire for his sister; the girl, along with her counterparts in countless other tales, is not allowed to control the flames at any time.

The fact that the three tales are homologous offers Bottigheimer an opportunity to focus on the shifting functions and patterns of motifs, because together they illuminate the mechanics of alternate tellings of the same plot (37). The tales, despite their similarities, offer diverse views of women and power, and the individual assembly of the motifs in each tale "suggests a consistent ordering of symbols congruent with assessments of women ranging from inherently powerful to utterly enfeebled" (37). The father's responsibility for the transformation in each tale reveals the daughter's shifting value. The father in "The Twelve Brothers" intends to murder his sons to guarantee his daughter's inheritance; the father in "The Seven Ravens" curses his sons for their apparent carelessness; and in "The Six Swans" the father is not involved at all in the transformation of his sons, unless his marriage to a wicked stepmother figure is taken into account.

The shirts also perform different functions in each of the three tales. They provide the first clue for the sister to the existence of the brothers in "The Twelve Brothers." The sister is much more independent and aggressive than her counterparts in the other two tales (38). There are no shirts in "The Seven Ravens," but in "The Six Swans" the shirts are the means of transformation into the birds and the method of redemption in the end.

Each of the three stories incorporates a star, but in varying degrees of importance. The girl in "The Twelve Brothers" actually has a star on her forehead, and the girl in "The Seven Ravens" journeys to the stars to seek her brothers. The star resides in the starwort plant that the sister uses to make the shirts in "The Six Swans":

> The astral image consistently retreats from intimate association with the sister figure, changing from an integral part of her body to the material of a task she fails to complete. The manner in which each sister sets off on a quest to save her brothers similarly corroborates the general tenor of each tale: in the first she sets off openly, and in the second and third she resorts to subterfuge, departing secretly. (38)

The role of the father and mother diminishes from tale to tale as well. Once the father and mother set the action in motion in "The Twelve Brothers," they are not heard of again. The mother's role also changes from an active queen in the first tale, to a passive non-royal mother in "The Seven Ravens," to the wicked stepmother of the third story. Likewise, the role of the hunting king, or the girl's husband, also changes from tale to tale. He finds her himself in "The Twelve Brothers" and asks her to marry him, to which she assents by nodding her head. The motif of the king in the woods appears twice in "The Six Swans." First it provides the rationale for acquiring the stepmother; second, a different king's huntsmen discover the girl in the tree (39).

Bottigheimer once again addresses the large role of silenced females in the tales with reference to these three tales. She points to a major difference between the Grimms's tales and the Norse "The Wild Ducks," stating that the sister saves her own life in the latter, but in "The Twelve Brothers" it is the youngest brother who must plead for her both to her brothers and then to her husband after the brothers have been reclaimed (80).

1987: Maria Tatar refers to the "folkloric cousins" in "The Twelve Brothers" and "The Six Swans" who spin and sew their way to salvation, finding deliverance by withdrawing from the world and retreating into the world of silent domestic activities (114). Tatar points out that although the transformation spells in all these tales are equally effective, it is only the one uttered by the stepmother that arises from a willful act of premeditated evil (141). She also states "that brothers and prospective bridegrooms are turned into animals by older women may be read as a telling commentary on women's attitudes toward male sexuality" (146).

1988: Jack Zipes dissects the theory proposed by Taylor and Rebel (1981) in their discussion of "The Twelve Brothers," "Brother and Sister," "The Seven Ravens," and "The Six Swans." They claim that the social development depicted in the four tales is related to ultimogeniture and the attitude of sisters to their brothers who were drafted into the army (Zipes

1988, 48). The tales, therefore, represent the defense of a new non-patrimonial inheritance system in which the youngest daughter is allowed to inherit the family property. However, they continue, by inheriting property the youngest daughters were placed under greater stress to marry the right kind of man and produce the right kind of children. Zipes bolsters his argument that their theory is faulty by pointing to a problem of narrative perspective. Taylor and Rebel assumed the tales were gathered from the German peasant population, whereas it is known that "The Twelve Brothers" was collected from the daughters of a French pastor; "The Seven Ravens" and "Brother and Sister" from the Hassenpflug family, who had French origins; and "The Six Swans" was from Dortchen Wild, Wilhelm Grimm's future wife. Zipes points out that this latter tale had been printed in a collection of literary fairy tales at that time (1988, 49). Taylor and Rebel also do not take into consideration the constant editing of the various versions of the tales: "[T]he vision of the family in the Grimms tales becomes more and more bourgeoisified from 1812 to 1857" (Zipes 1988, 50). They do not take into account that these tales are tale types that are found in other countries and are not particularly Hessian. These tales do, however, demonstrate signs of matrilineal initiation and marital rites that may be pre-Christian (Zipes 1988, 50).

1989: Joyce Thomas's analysis focuses on enchanted animal-human siblings. The test in these tales is usually one of duration and endurance—of length rather than feeling itself—because the love bond had been achieved previously when the siblings were in their human form (153). She contends that because the reader already knows that the brothers will be disenchanted, the interest in the story lies in the type of test the sister must face and the new form of her siblings. Thomas states that the brothers are typically transformed into some type of fowl, "always something pleasant, which further underscores the tale's overall pleasant cast and sense of positive relationship" (154). There are six, seven, or twelve brothers, which necessitates using a communal creature such as a flock-grouped bird (154). She also discusses the role of absolute silence in these tales. Silent suffering is the term of the girl's heroine status and her brothers' disenchantment (237).

1990: Bengt Holbek considers Andersen's use of folktales in his literary fairy tales. Holbek states that Andersen found "The Wild Swans" in a book of Danish fairy tales written by Matthias Winther. This collection appeared in 1823 and contains 20 tales he apparently heard from his nurse or local peasants. Winther's tale is "The Eleven Swans" and, according to Holbek, not well told (168). Holbek considers Andersen's writing talent to be dramatic and lyrical rather than epic (172). He states that although Andersen expanded the Winther tale, he did not add anything that would point to Andersen's awareness of other variants of the tale, of which at least 15 are known in Danish folklore (175). Andersen's expansions include a different type of heroine from the others. The sister is shown to be devoted to her brothers through her selfless acts of spinning thistles and maintaining silence in the face of great obstacles. Andersen's Elisa possesses an innate goodness that is demonstrated through her struggles with her witch stepmother. The stepmother "uses toads (the most abominable creatures Andersen can think of); her kissing of the toads is an obscene act with overtones of perverted sexuality; but to no avail" (176). The toads are transformed into red poppies. Holbek maintains that the flowers are not roses because, in Andersen's universe, roses symbolize perfection, and even this heroine cannot create perfection out of such wickedness (176). In Andersen's universe, and quite different from the world of genuine folklore, the qualities of good and evil have become absolutes, and innocent goodness always triumphs over evil (176). In the appendix to this article, Holbek includes an English translation of Winther's tale for comparison with Andersen's literary treatment.

1991: Martin Hallett and Barbara Karasek begin their section on Andersen with "The Six Swans" by the Brothers Grimm. Although "The Wild Swans" is actually derived from a Danish version of Tale Type 451, the similarity to "The Six Swans" is unmistakable and illustrates Andersen's debt to folklore. They point out that Andersen was well acquainted with the work of the Grimms (152).

1991: Jack Zipes refers to "The Twelve Brothers" in his discussion on the reconstitution of home and the creation of a new type of family. He states that the original manuscript was entitled "Twelve Brothers and the Little Sister," and the reworking of the tale for the 1812 edition emphasizes the dedication of the siblings to each other and the establishment of a common, orderly household in the forest.

1992: Christa Kamenetsky alludes to the Grimms's "The Seven Ravens" and states that these ravens may evoke the mythical image of Odin's talking ravens, Hugin and Munin (Thought and Memory) (82).

1993: James McGlathery summarizes his previously published thoughts about "The Twelve Brothers." He had stated in *Fairy Tale Romance: The Grimms, Basile and Perrault* (University of Illinois Press, 1991) that the devotion between the sister and her brothers was the point of the entire story. "The brothers' transformations into ravens and their resulting disappearance effectively remove them from the sister's presence 'as tangible objects of forbidden love' " (McGlathery, 80). The brothers are restored to their human form only after their sister is married and no longer lives alone with them in their little hut. He restates his theory that "the father's mad desire for a daughter introduces the underlying theme of incestuous attachment" (80). This in fact is a case of "like father, like son."

1993: Marie-Louise von Franz compares "The Six Swans" and "The Seven Ravens." At the end of both tales, the number of characters equals eight. She discusses this factor in light of number symbolism; the number eight carries "the meaning of the Self, the totality aspect; it steps out of the process of evolution into an eternal static state" (134). Both the raven and the swan are birds of Apollo. She refers to the *Pocket Dictionary of German Superstitions*, stating that the word "swan" has the same root as the Latin word *sonare*, meaning "sounding" or "sound," and the swan is reputed to know the future, particularly in forecasting its own death (137). In many mythologies, the raven was originally a white bird and is often regarded as a creator trickster with many powers. The silent sister, in both tales, is involved in the task of getting a bewitched person back into human life and worked for many years in the deepest introversion and concentration to find the human way to let irrational content—swans and ravens—reappear in a way that does not shock the rational world (143).

1994: Elizabeth Barber's exploration of women's work includes a chapter on the connections between the manufacturing of all aspects of clothing and traditional myth and folklore. She considers the magical shirts made of nettles an example of the real turning into the fantastic when people misunderstand the process. "Everyone knows that nettles sting the skin painfully; therefore, to make a soft and handsome shirt from such a plant would clearly take nothing short of magic. Or at least it must have seemed to peasants who were vaguely aware that such objects had once existed" (ch 10, 3d p.). Barber explains that laboratory studies have shown that all the Scandinavian archeological finds of fabric thought to be linen actually consist of nettle fiber. The nettles had been picked in the wild, then retted, spun, and woven exactly like flax. Elderly peasant women practiced the process during World War I when domestic supplies of the common fibers were scarce (ch 10, 4th p.).

> It turns out that nettles can be picked comfortably if one is careful always to move the hand in the direction in which the stingers will lie flat (up the stalk), and the process of retting rots away the stingers, so there is no problem at all after that. The resulting fiber is finer and silkier than flax, giving a much nicer chemise. Magic indeed! (ch 10, 4th p.)

1994: Marina Warner deliberates briefly on the heroine who "suffers in silence and is eventually triumphantly vindicated" (391). Warner, summarizing the basic story as told in "The Twelve Brothers," "The Six Swans," and "The Wild Swans," declares that this was her favorite tale as a child. For her, the tale seemed to tell a story of female heroism, generosity, staunchness; I had no brothers, but I fantasized, at night, as I waited to go to sleep, that I had, perhaps even as many tall and handsome youths as the girl in the story, and that I would do something magnificent for them that would make them realize I was one of them, as it were, their equal in courage and determination and grace. Sewing was a skill my mother possessed—as did the nuns who taught the more nimble pupils at my school invisible mending—so it was easy to identify with the descriptions of the heroine's finger as she spun the nettles or the thistles or the flax, whatever cruel stuff the witch insisted she used to weave for her brothers' shirts. (392)

Warner, referring to Ruth Bottigheimer's study of speech patterns in the Grimm tales, states that the equation of silence with virtue and forbearance with femininity met certain sociocultural requirements for family balance in the early nineteenth century of the tellers of these tales. However, the irony is that, to transmit the tales, the female tellers must transgress these values: "[T]hey are flouting, in the act of speaking and teaching, the strictures against female authority they impart: women narrators, extolling the magic silence of the heroic sister in 'The Twelve Brothers,' are speaking themselves, breaking the silence, telling the story" (1994, 394). Warner also contemplates the environment in which the tales may have been told. The heroine's bleeding fingers would be very familiar to an audience of textile workers in the Huguenot community of Hesse. Her silence could be a stratagem of survival for women and disadvantaged workers struggling for their livelihood (395).

1997: Several entries in David Leeming's *Storytelling Encyclopedia* contain references to "The Seven Swans," which is proclaimed a variant of Grimms's "The Six Swans," in which the brothers are originally transformed into swans by the stepmother, who throws swan shirts over them. The symbol of the swan is "a living epiphany of light, incarnating both the solar male and the lunar female" (440). The entry on swans culminates by stating that swans are common in the fairy tales of both Andersen and the Brothers Grimm; the Andersen tale referred to is "The Ugly Duckling"; the Grimm tale is "The Wild Swans" (441).

1997: Julie Sinn's abstract of her study of women in fairy tale woods suggests that "wood" in these tales is not only a refuge from patriarchal authority but also a place where this authority is more easily expressed. When the woman is found, she is plucked from her tree branch and presented to the king; the wood that is a refuge from one king becomes the expression of patriarchy for another king. She states that the girls in "The Twelve Brothers" and "The Six Swans" were comfortable in their trees and left them reluctantly at the request of the king. He plucks each of them out of the tree in the same fashion by which he plucks an apple, pear, or other piece of fruit from a tree. This Grimm image of a female being plucked from a tree dates back to when Wood wives, spirits who lived in the forest and protected the trees, were captured by the Wild Huntsman.

1998:   Margaret Atwood speaks of birds in the fairy tales. She makes reference to "The Six Swans," "The Seven Ravens, " and "The Twelve Brothers," stating that it is the latter of the three tales that is the most complex. It is "noteworthy because the brothers are to be killed by their parents—who are having twelve creepy little coffins made in secret, each with a little death pillow in it—if the expected thirteenth baby is a girl, because the king wants her alone to inherit. So much for the supposed universal sexism of fairy tales" (27). Atwood also states that those who were changed into birds in these tales were in fact dead. The swan brothers were imprisoned in the bodies of an alien species, a coffin of another sort. The act involved in changing them back to humans was not only an act of metamorphosis but also one of resurrection. "The white feathery swan bodies are shed like shrouds as the brothers step back into the ordinary light of daily life" (30).

1998:   Terri Windling also explores the role of birds in traditional myth and tales. She recounts briefly the Irish myth "The Children of Lir" and thematic links to "The Six Swans" and "The Seven Ravens." Windling also points her reader to "two entertaining accounts of what may have happened to the younger brother" in the first two novels discussed later in this chapter.

2000:   Graham Anderson claims that this tale has ancient antecedents in the myth of Chione, the daughter of Boreas and Oreithuia (Northwind and Mountainmaid). Their two sons, Zetes and Calais, change into birds, and "there is the possibility that she was able in some form of the story to search for them and disenchant them" (59).

2000:   Maria Nickolajeva declares that Andersen's version of this tale "acquires an unmistakable individuality and brilliant irony" (14). Unfortunately she does not elucidate this statement.

Reworkings of "The Wild Swans" in Novel Form

There are currently five novel-length reworkings of this story. It is interesting to note a slight trend in their focus. The first two novels, published in the 1960s and 1980s, explore the fate of the youngest brother, the one who is not completely transformed into his human form. The novels by Kerr and Marillier, both published very recently, contemplate the testing of the sister and tell her story instead. The fifth novel is described as a lusty fractured tale marketed as a romance novel.

Charles de Lint's reworking of "Jack the Giant Killer" (see pages 67–68) also includes a character from this tale type:

> As his captors dragged him closer and the creatures already present began to howl, one of those old fairy tales she'd been trying to remember came back to her. It was the one about the seven brothers who were turned into swans. At the end of the story, after their sister had woven nettle shirts for each of them, they had all turned back into men. All except the youngest. He was left with a swan's wing because his sister hadn't had time to finish one sleeve of his shirt. This swan man was like that, she thought. Except his sister hadn't finished off either one. (108)

The Seventh Swan

1962. Gray, Nicholas Stuart. **The Seventh Swan**. New York: Tempo Books. Reprinted by Dobson in 1984.

A note on the contents page of the 1984 edition states: "A wonderful version of the 'Wild Swans' legend is among the stories of Hans Christian Andersen." John Clute and John Grant describe this novel, a prose edition of Gray's play of the same name, as a poignant tale of a man's bondage as a swan "told with pleasing wit, but the drama under which he learns better how to be a man is strongly conveyed" (432).

Gray's reworking of Andersen's tale takes place in the Highlands of Scotland in the beginning of the sixteenth century. The story begins with a young man, Alasdair, having problems adjusting to having a wing instead of an arm. He is residing at Kinrowan, the home of his sister Agnes, and is both terrified and mesmerized when he hears the call of the swans. Alasdair was only three years old when the first transformation took place. Agnes never knew the fate of her brothers until she was 16; aided by the words of an old woman, she managed to find them. She then had to make shirts from nettles that she gathered in the dead of night from the edges of a graveyard and be silent the entire time. She married the chief, and one day, while he was out hunting, was accused of witchcraft for her inability to speak and her nocturnal activities in the graveyard. Her brothers returned in time to save her and to have their spell broken, but the final shirt had not been completed. Alasdair has spent the last two years trying to come to terms with his disability and his perception of himself.

Young Fenella, who is listening to Agnes's story, accepts the challenge of making Alasdair whole once again. She decides to study sorcery and, along with Alasdair's mercenary bodyguard, Ewan, prepares to break the spell entirely. She is aided by a bard, who sends her and Ewan to the well in the haunted thorn wood. They are joined there by Alasdair. Fenella pulls some weeds from the soil and sees something in the well that the men cannot until they too touch the weeds. A person looking into the well will see "whatever he most dreads to see. His own fear—his own shame—his own nightmare. Alive in the well—moving, and speaking, and being" (Gray, 51). Fenella, who has drunk the water, disappears, and the men are told to find her at Kinrowan if they can. At the same time, a young hedgehog arrives at Kinrowan. The reader knows that this is Fenella, but Alasdair does not. Fenella is transformed further into a toad, but thankfully her brain functions with clarity. Meanwhile, the plot thickens, and Alasdair and Ewan have been captured and kept in a cave. It is up to Fenella to help them escape. Eventually they all do escape from prisons of their own making and desolate futures.

The story of "The Wild Swan" is told at the beginning of the tale and provides the motivation for the novel. However, this is not a reworking of the story as much as it is a continuation of it. Several reviewers on amazon.com remark that they read this book as young adults and have never forgotten it. It is lighthearted, a great romp with a strong female character and plenty of plot twists. Recommended for all ages.

Swan's Wing

1981. Synge, Ursula. **Swan's Wing**. London: The Bodley Head.

Matthew, the narrator, intertwines his life story with that of the eleventh prince from Andersen's tale, the one who receives the unfinished shirt. The first section of the book is Matthew's origin story: the tale of the foundling child, thought to be the spawn of the devil by the superstitious villagers but saved by the parish priest, who recognizes Matthew's talent as a carver of wood and stone. During his early journeys, Matthew sees the newlywed duchess, who "had been a girl chance-met at the roadside" and who was "dumb as a post" (27). He also has a chance meeting with Gerda the goose girl when the two of them experience a marvelous sight: "Eleven swans were flying from the east, their wings beating in unison, rising and falling in the same slow rhythm, and it seemed to Matthew as though they dragged the blanket of the dark behind them, it followed so quickly on their passing" (33). Not too long after this a disgruntled Matthew begins his aimless traveling and sees a hunchback whose "cloak had gaped as he turned, showing what was concealed beneath it. . . . this man was *winged*" (44).

The second part of the story follows Matthew and Gerda as they attempt to help Prince Lothar find an antidote to complete his transformation into a complete being. Along the road they meet with uncertainties of their own and of others. The others, it seems, they could help. "Even if Lothar had met again with the witch-queen who had married his father, and had she consented to unsay her spell, I think he would still have carried to his grave the shadow of a swan" (72). Lothar meets and is attracted to the Countess at one of their stops along their frustrating journey. His lengthy stay with the Countess and his loss of memory are highly reminiscent of Kay's sojourn with the Snow Queen. Eventually, through the agency of one of Gerda's geese, Lothar regains his senses. At the same time Gerda receives a blessing, a walnut, and a riddle from an old peddler woman, and the three decipher the riddle, find the crossroads, and complete the transformation between human and swan until Lothar is whole once again.

Poetically written, the story is told in two distinct sections. The first part is written in first person narration, interspersed with journal entries. The rest of the novel, although it continues Matthew's story, is written in the third person. Full of allusions to fairy tales, saints, and Arthurian tales, this medieval reworking of Andersen's tale offers an exploration of religious expectations as well as faith, love, and friendship.

The Wild Swans (Kerr)

1999. Kerr, Peg. **The Wild Swans**. New York: Warner.

This novel is a complex weaving of parallel stories about two adolescents from two distinct time periods. Eliza's story is the traditional tale, set in the seventeenth century. She is the daughter of the Earl of Exeter. To disenchant her 11 brothers, she travels to the New World and a Salem-like village. Elias's story is much more current. He is a young gay man living in New York City in the early 1980s. The novel alternates between their individual stories; the substantial similarities are striking: Both are rejected by their families, are persecuted for being different from other members of the community, and discover the importance of love and loyalty. The two stories are linked in other ways as well, and these minute details brought an additional depth to the narratives. Both narratives are well researched and brought to life with authentic historical detail and characterization.

Eliza's story is the one we are concerned with in this discussion. After she is taken to North America in a net carried by her swan brothers, Eliza discovers in a dream the method to break the spell that their stepmother has cast. While she undergoes her trials of silence and weaving coats from nettles, she meets and marries the local magistrate, Jonathan Latham. Her presence and her relationship with Latham are resented, and eventually challenged, by William, the local clergyman. She is accused of witchcraft, tried, and sentenced to be hanged. Jonathan's despair and helplessness are a focus of this novel. This is a husband who loves his mute wife but is equally condemned to be silent in her defense. William's underlying motivation for his distrust and hatred of Jonathan's wife is also explored. Kerr has followed Andersen's storyline significantly. She has stripped it of its religious overtones and fleshed it out with characters whom the reader grows to care about. Through her careful reworking of this story, the parallel story gains in clarity as well.

In the author's note, Kerr states that:

> Some people claim that fairy tales have nothing to tell us anymore, that stories full of heroes battling evil may be amusing but they're mostly a waste of time for all but the very young. I don't agree, because in the course of writing this book I've discovered that real heroes and heroines still exist in this world, racing against time while combating betrayal and bigotry, just as Eliza did—and their actions have meant the difference between life and death for millions. (391)

John Charles's review of the book in *VOYA* asserts that: "This beautifully-written, magical book is perfect for sophisticated teens" (192).

Daughter of the Forest

2000. Marillier, Juliet. **Daughter of the Forest**. Book One of the Seven-waters Trilogy. New York: Tor.

Marillier combines a vivid and earthy picture of ancient Ireland, Britain, and Denmark with two traditional tales of the transformed swan: the Celtic myth of the Children of Lir and the fairy tale of "The Six Swans." Sorcha is the youngest child and the only daughter of a Celtic lord. She and her six brothers are extremely close although they are all different in temperament. Their father is distant and demanding, but all is well until Sorcha, the narrator of this novel, and her brother Finbar intervene in the capture and torture of a young Briton prisoner. This leads to Sorcha's first meeting with the Lady of the Forest. Soon after, their father is bewitched by and quickly marries the Lady Oonagh who, like her fairy tale counterpart, detests her new stepchildren and does everything in her power to cause them great harm.

The underpinning of Sorcha's travail is the Grimms's story "The Six Swans." Her brothers are transformed before her eyes into swans. The Lady of the Forest plays the role of the old woman, informing Sorcha of the method of disenchantment, to gather the caustic starwort plant and weave the fibers into shirts while remaining silent:

> From the moment you leave this place till the moment of your brothers' final return to humankind, no word must pass your lips, no cry, no song, no whisper must you utter. Nor will you tell your story in pictures, or letters, or any other way to living creature. You will be silent, mute as the swans themselves. Break the silence, and the curse remains forever. (118)

They can regain their human form only at midsummer and midwinter's eve. Only Sorcha's brother Conor retains his human consciousness and can communicate with her when in the form of a swan, although Sorcha and Finbar often communicated telepathically before the transformation. While secluded in the forest, learning how to handle the starwort and the physical and emotional pain thrust upon her, Sorcha is discovered by a trio of ruffians, who rape her. This propels her farther on her adventure as she runs blindly from her sanctuary into the arms of the Briton, Red. He personifies the king of the fairy tale and, with the blessing of the fairy folk, he takes her home to Britain. He soon realizes that she has been harmed and gives her the latitude to heal herself and finish her puzzling task of weaving shirts.

Red's family does not receive Sorcha kindly. Not only is she the enemy, she also is silent and strange. She is disliked particularly by Red's uncle Richard who, after she marries Red and while Red is away looking for his brother once again, orchestrates a trial and a funeral bier for Sorcha. She calls to Conor, and five of her brothers arrive in time for their shirts to be thrown over them. Finbar is late, and before he arrives the wind takes the shirt out of her hands. At this precise moment she notices someone is trying to kill Red and screams out a warning to him. The spell is broken, and Sorcha and her brothers explain the situation and immediately leave for home to confront Oonagh. They find their father and his home in disarray but do not find their stepmother. They begin to rebuild Sevenwaters, but things have changed. Red arrives to find Sorcha and she realizes how much they love each other. He has given up all claims to his own country and settles in with the family. But one by one the brothers begin to leave their home. Finbar, although not the youngest brother, was the last brother to be transformed, and he is left with one wing. He too soon disappears. It is at this time that Sorcha discovers that all her troubles and adventures were orchestrated by the fairy folk to bring her and Red together to produce the next generation of inhabitants at Sevenwaters, who are the focus of the next book in the trilogy.

In an online interview, Juliet Marillier explains why she incorporated the fairy tale into this first novel: "With this story I wanted to explore how it would be for a real family, with their individual and collective strengths and weaknesses, if these extraordinary events really happened to them. How would they cope? How would it change them? That's what this story deals with." All the characters in the novel are well rounded, complex, and compelling. The landscape and both the ancient Druid belief system and the newly introduced Christian religion are genuinely depicted. Recommended for young adults; the narrator herself is only 16 by the end of the novel. The book was short-listed for the Aurealis Award for Best Fantasy Novel of 1999 and for the Romantic Book of the Year 2000.

The Wild Swans (Holmes)

2000. Holmes, Kate. **The Wild Swans**. New York: Love Spell.

Kate Holmes introduces her novel by stating that the inspiration for her story is the "Fractured Fairy Tales" on the old *Rocky and Bullwinkle Show*. However, she heated up the overall "fractures" for her reading audience. James Richard Henry Michael Bledgabred Taillefer is fed up with women who talk too much. He jests that if he can find a woman who won't talk his ears off, he would marry her immediately. Enter the Royal Highness Princess Arianne of Montavia, who cannot speak until she breaks the spell cast upon her 12 brothers. This novel follows the story to its predictable ending, but it is a lighthearted, tongue-in-cheek journey for those who like their romance novels with a large dash of locker room humor.

Short Stories

When we first began the research for *New Tales for Old*, there was not enough available reworked material to write a chapter about this tale. Since that time, the number of novels has more than doubled and, although the increase is not as dramatic, there are more short stories as well. But the focus of the short story authors seems to be quite different than that of those who wrote the novels.

1993. Stevermer, Caroline, and Ryan Edmonds. **"The Springfield Swans."** In *Snow White, Blood Red,* edited by Ellen Datlow & Terri Windling. New York: Avon, 271–80.

The Swenson family was absolutely crazy about baseball, so much so that Mr. Swenson tried to produce a team all by himself. It was unfortunate that his death just before his youngest son's fourteenth birthday (when he would be eligible to play with his brothers) prevented him from realizing his dream. It was doubly unfortunate that his second wife disliked the game so much that she cursed the boys at their father's funeral. "If I hear another word about baseball from any of you ever again. . . . I hope you all grow wings and fly away to hell" (274). Well, it wasn't as if she really meant it. But you know how it is with stepmothers and curses. Before anyone could do anything, the oldest child, Anne, made a comment, and her brothers all became white swans, After a few abortive calls to the university, Anne finally got in touch with the right department, which told her she had to sew shirts for the boys, and to do this without smiling or speaking. Anne, who was not much of a seamstress, managed to do so just as the big baseball game was about to begin. She also managed to acquire a husband in the process. And the youngest brother? Well, he became a very famous pitcher—what an arm he had! A tongue-in-cheek rendering of the tale.

1998. Lutz, John. **"Swan Song."** In *Once Upon a Crime,* edited by Ed Gorman and Martin H. Greenberg. New York: Berkley Prime Crime, 211–24.

A hot new country and western band is taken over and renamed the Swan Brothers as a result of a blackmail scheme, but things go vastly awry in this tongue-in-cheek reworking of the tale featuring a young singer who saves the lives of the members of the band from her wicked mother.

1999. Edghill, India. **"Wild Swan."** *Marion Zimmer Bradley's Fantasy Magazine* 44 (Summer): 6–9.

The sister's story begins after the disenchantment of her brothers. Although the princes and the others in the kingdom are grateful and jubilant, the sister can't throw off her own sorrow and silence. She refuses all the hopeful suitors, to the dismay of her family. She climbs a deserted tower, passing lifeless rooms. "One held straw, and a spinning wheel. Another was empty save for an elaborate gilded bed, its velvet hangings rotting with dust. On the landing below the rooftop, the room held only a pile of rope, its length coiled sleek, and golden beneath the open window" (8). At the top she calls out to a lone swan, but although he circles around her, he does not stay. What remains, however, is a single feather, and she realizes that her next task is to weave herself a gown of swan feathers.

2000. Link, Kelly. **"Swans."** In *A Wolf at the Door and Other Retold Fairy Tales,* edited by Ellen Datlow and Terri Windling. New York: Simon & Schuster, 74–92.

Emma Bear, the narrator of the story, has already been silenced by the death of her mother before the story begins. Her fairy godfather, Rumpelstiltskin, had been a friend of her mother's and, along with him, Emma has inherited her mother's skill as a seamstress, vowing to finish the quilts her mother started for herself. The quilts for her older brothers, covered with images of Elvis, Star Wars, and other icons of modern popular culture, were completed before her mother's death. But everything changes on the day her father brings home a new wife. Emma's stepmother cannot abide noise, and one by one she changes Emma's noisy brothers into swans. This does not upset Emma too much, but finally she must step in and take control. After all, the entire school assembly, her father, and her schoolmates have been transformed as well. After researching her problem in the school library and discovering the scope of the disenchantment, Emma decides to create a large quilt, large enough to cover the school gymnasium. The quilt has swans on one side of it and shirts on the other.

Poetry

2000. Miner, Carrie. **"The Seven Swans."** http://www.endicott-studio.com /cof7swan.html.

The poem reflects the sister's thoughts as she ponders her brothers' position and hers. Do they realize, she wonders, that one of her brothers will have to live with "a token wing in trade for time spent sewing [her] own shirt—of feathers."

Picture Books

Although this book is not technically a picture book in the usual sense and defies categorization, we felt this was the most appropriate place to discuss it. Other picture book versions of the variants of this tale follow the traditional stories and are not considered reworkings.

1996. Dinter, Ingrid. **How I Grew with Wild Swans**. New York: Colophon.

This book of photographs and drawings is not a reworking of the tale itself but rather an assemblage of seemingly arbitrary excerpts of Andersen's text of "The Wild Swans" and Mary McCarthy's "How I Grew." The artist's photographs sometimes perfectly illustrate the text but at other times seem incongruent. McCarthy's text carries allusions to Andersen's tale. Her father had died before he finished reading her "a long fairy tale about seven brothers who were changed into ravens, and their little sister." She writes that she has not been able to find that particular story since, just its cousins, such as "The Seven Ravens" and "The Six Swans."

Graphic Novels

1999. Adlard, Charles. **"The Twelve Brothers."** In *The Big Book of Grimm: Truly Scary Fairy Tales to Frighten the Whole Family!, by the Brothers Grimm as Channeled by Jonathan Vankin & Over 50 Top Comic Book Artists.* New York: Paradox Press, 18–21.

This version follows the main elements of the storyline, with the illustrations showcasing facial expressions.

Internet Resources

Several sites have been concerned with "The Six Swans" in many of its guises. An interesting chart depicting the meaning of the symbols in this tale can be found at http://www.acs.appstate.edu/~davisct/symbols/tales/six_swans_MA .htm.

A discussion of the meaning of the tales can also be found on the message board of the Web site "Fairy Tales: Origins and Evolution," www.geocities.com/surlalunefairytales/boardarchives/jul2000/insearch_swans .html. The discussion is initiated by Carrie Miner, who states that she is trying to write a poem about this tale. (Her poem is cited under "Poetry" in this chapter.") There are also numerous Web sites that reproduce the texts of the four tales. They can be found using any competent search engine.

Classroom Extensions

Many of these suggestions can be adjusted for use with other tales as well. The first suggestion is an echo of other approaches to silence and voicelessness in previous chapters.

The History of Silence

The heroine's development, through silence and sewing, is very different from earlier depictions of spinning and weaving as communal tasks shared among women that allowed them to talk while their hands were busy. Find some of these myths and tales and contrast their heroines and the role of speaking with the sister's silence.

> Silence in connection with girls and women, an occasional element of other traditions, seems to have become so ingrained in the German fairy tale tradition that it grew into a narrative necessity in newly revised or composed nineteenth-century fairy tales. (Bottigheimer 1987, 75)

Is this true of the twentieth-century reworkings of the tale? Discuss.

Manipulation of Motifs

Ruth Bottigheimer discusses how the manipulation and reordering of the same motifs in the three Grimm versions of the tale type 451 modify "the figure of the independent princess as she appears in 'The Twelve Brothers' and result in the personally ineffectual little sister in 'The Six Swans' " (1987, 39). The heroine in the last tale is "abandoned in a forest treed, silenced, pursued by a malevolent witch, married to a king, accused of cannibalism, and tied to the stake" (1987, 39). Compare the treatment of the girl in these three tales with Elise in "The Wild Swans" and the sister in the Norse variant, "The Twelve Ducks." Does the restructuring of the motifs account for the varied tones of these tales? Why or why not?

The Weaving of Nettles

There have been numerous references found that attest to the theory that Northwest Native Americans and peasants in some areas of Europe used stinging nettle (Urtica dioica) stem fibers for papers, woven cloth, mats, and baskets. Why would the girls in these tales have so much pain and agony making the shirts from nettles if others could do so effectively? Why is starwort the plant of choice in the one story? What is starwort, and how does it compare to nettles? What might the symbolic meaning of nettles be?

References

Anderson, Graham. 2000. *Fairytale in the Ancient World*. London: Routledge.

Atwood, Margaret. 1998. "Of Souls as Birds." In *Mirror, Mirror on the Wall: Women Writers Explore Their Favorite Fairy Tales*, edited by Kate Bernheimer. New York: Anchor, 22–38.

Barber, Elizabeth Wayland. 1994. *Women's Work: The First 20,000 Years*. New York: W.W. Norton.

Bettelheim, Bruno. 1976. *The Uses of Enchantment*. New York: Alfred A. Knopf.

Bottigheimer, Ruth B. 1986. "Silenced Women in the Grimms' Tales: The 'Fit' Between Fairy Tales and Society in Their Historical Context." In *Fairy Tales and Society: Illusion, Allusion and Paradigm*, edited by Ruth B. Bottigheimer. Philadelphia: University of Pennsylvania Press, 115–31.

———. 1987. *Grimms' Bad Girls & Bold Boys: The Moral & Social Vision of the Tales*. New Haven: Yale University Press.

Charles, John. 1999. "Review of *The Wild Swans*." *VOYA* (August): 191–92.

Clute, John, and John Grant. 1997. *The Encyclopedia of Fantasy*. London: Orbit.

De Lint, Charles. 1995. *Jack of Kinrowan*. New York, TOR.

Hallett, Martin, and Barbara Karasek, ed. 1991. *Folk and Fairy Tales*. Peterborough, ONT: Broadview Press.

Holbek, Bengt. 1990. "Hans Christian Andersen's Use of Folktales." In *The Telling of Stories: Approaches to a Traditional Craft: A Symposium*, edited by Martin Ojgaard. Odense: Odense University Press, 165–82.

Kamenetsky, Christa. 1992. *The Brothers Grimm and Their Critics: Folktales and the Quest for Meaning*. Athens: Ohio University Press.

Lederer, Wolfgang. 1986. *The Kiss of the Snow Queen: Hans Christian Andersen and Man's Redemption by Woman*. Berkeley: University of California Press.

Leeming, David Adams, ed. 1997. *Storytelling Encyclopedia: Historical, Cultural, and Multiethnic Approaches to Oral Traditions Around the World*. Phoenix: Oryx Press.

Marillier, Juliet. n.d. "Interview," www.slowglass.com.au/interviews/j-marillier.html.

McGlathery, James M. 1993. *Grimms' Fairy Tales: A History of Criticism on a Popular Classic*. Studies in German Literature, Linguistics, and Culture: Literary Criticism in Perspective. Columbia, SC: Camden House.

Mueller, Gerhardo W. 1986. "The Criminological Significance of the Grimms' Fairy Tales." In *Fairy Tales and Society: Illusion, Allusion ad Paradigm*, edited by Ruth B. Bottigheimer. Philadelphia: University of Pennsylvania Press, 217–27.

Nickolajeva, Maria. 2000. " Hans Christian Andersen." In *The Oxford Companion to Fairy Tales: The Western Fairy Tale Tradition from Medieval to Modern*, edited by Jack Zipes. New York: Oxford University Press, 14.

Sale, Roger. 1978. *Fairy Tales and After from Snow White to E. B. White*. Cambridge, M.A.: Harvard University Press.

Sinn, Julie. 1997. "How She Came to be in a Fairy Tale Wood: A Study of Women and Nature in the Collected Tales of the Brothers Grimm," *Kansas McNair Journal*, www.ksu.edu/mcnair/abstr96.htm.

Stone, Kay. 1975a. "Romantic Heroines in Anglo-American Folk and Popular Literature." Ph.D. dissertation, Folklore Institute, Indiana University.

———. 1975b. "Things Walt Disney Never Told Us." In *Women and Folklore: Images and Genre*, edited by Claire R. Farrer. Prospect Heights: Waveland, 42–50.

Tatar, Maria. 1987. *The Hard Facts of the Grimms' Fairy Tales*. Princeton, NJ: Princeton University Press.

Taylor, Peter, and Hermann Rebel. 1981. "Hessian Peasant Women, Their Families, and the Draft: A Social-Historical Interpretation of Four Tales from the Grimm Collection." *Journal of Family History* 6 (Winter): 347–78.

Thomas, Joyce. 1989. *Inside the Wolf's Belly: Aspects of the Fairy Tale*. Sheffield, England: Sheffield Academic Press.

Thompson, Stith. 1961. *The Types of the Folktale: A Classification and Bibliography. Antti Aarne's Verzeichnis der Märchentypen*, translated and enlarged by Stith Thompson. 2d revision. FF Communications, no. 184. Helsinki: Suomalainen Tiedeakatemia.

Von Franz, Marie-Louise. 1993. *The Feminine in Fairy Tales*. Rev. edition. Boston: Shambhala.

Warner, Marina. 1994. *From the Beast to the Blonde: On Fairytales and Their Tellers*. London: Chatto & Windus.

Windling, Terri. 1998. "One Is for Sorrow, Two Is for Joy: The Magical Lore of Birds." *Realms of Fantasy* (October): 28–35, 81.

Zipes, Jack. 1988. *The Brothers Grimm: From Enchanted Forest to the Modern World*. New York: Routledge.

———. "Dreams of a Better Bourgeois Life: The Psychosocial Origins of the Grimms' Tales." In *The Brothers Grimm and Folktale*, edited by James McGlathery. Urbana: University of Illinois Press, 1991, 205–19. [Zipes, Jack. 1988. *The Brothers Grimm: From Enchanted Forest to the Modern World*. New York: Routledge].

CHAPTER 7

UPDATES TO NEW TALES FOR OLD

In the few years since the publication of *New Tales for Old* there has been a steady stream of reworkings of the tales we discussed in that book. This chapter is an attempt to update that volume. Of course we realize that by the time you are holding this volume in your hands, another update could be forthcoming.

"Cinderella"

Novels

1992. Pratchett, Terry. **Witches Abroad.** London: Corgi.

An attempt to describe any book by Terry Pratchett is likely to lead to a surfeit of adjectives and a string of quotations. Pratchett is a best-selling writer in Great Britain because his work is funny in so many different ways—clever, hilarious, witty, slapstick, intertextual—and at the same time full of intelligent insight into what it is to be human and to tell stories:

> Stories exist independently of their players. If you know that, the knowledge is power.

> Stories, great flapping ribbons of shaped space-time, have been blowing and uncoiling around the universe since the beginning of time. And they have evolved. The weakest have died and the strongest have survived, and they have grown fat on the retelling . . . , twisting and blowing through the darkness. (8)

In this complicated version of the Cinderella story, fairy godmothers come in twos. The good ones are kind, and the bad ones are powerful. Cinderella's good godmother dies, but she leaves her responsibility for the girl to Pratchett's trio of witches: hapless Magrat Garlick, earthy Nanny Ogg, and cantankerous Granny

Weatherwax, who is by far the most powerful of the three but uses "headology" instead of magic, except as a last resort. The three set off for Genua, a place rather like New Orleans, full of strange swamp magic, to save Cinderella from marrying the prince.

1998. Loggia, Wendy. **Ever After: A Cinderella Story**. New York: Dell.

A novelization of the 1998 film *Ever After,* which is described elsewhere in this chapter. The book is faithful to the movie.

1999. Haddix, Margaret Peterson. **Just Ella**. New York: Simon & Schuster Books for Young Readers.

The ball is over, Ella is engaged to Prince Charming, and she's living at the palace to be trained in the graces of royalty. The problem is that she's really just plain Ella Brown, a bookworm and a tomboy, and none of this suits her. Spunky enough to get to the ball on her own in her dead mother's wedding dress (no fairy godmother needed), she's disgusted by the false passivity expected of ladies and the endless artificiality of court life. Worse, she comes to realize that when she met Charming she lost not her heart but her head. He's a brainless lout, and she can't marry a man she doesn't love or respect. There is one person at the court who interests her: Jed Reston, who wants to end the long war with a neighboring kingdom and alleviate the suffering of the common people on both sides of the border.

When Ella tries to break her engagement to Charming, she's locked up in the dungeon, but she tunnels her way out with the help of a servant girl. After stopping by her old home to collect a few books and some clothes, she makes the dangerous journey to Jed's refugee camp on the border and the happily-ever-after that's right for her: meaningful work and Jed.

Ella's feisty feminism is a little too heavy-handed and clichéd, and there's more than a touch of Harlequin romance to this novel. Haddix has traded the magic of the fairy tale for adolescent wish-fulfillment.

1999. Jukes, Mavis. **Cinderella 2000**. New York: Delacorte.

At first this piece of realistic fiction for teens seems disappointingly banal: another young adult shopping mall novel about adolescent problems with parents, siblings, and boyfriends. Will Ashley get to go to the December 31, 1999, New Year's Eve ball at the country club? It's being given by the rich in-crowd of kids at school, not her usual group, and the boy she has a crush on will be there. Her loving but embarrassing stepmother wants her to babysit her impossible twin half-sisters instead. Her visiting step-grandmother solves all Ashley's problems with understanding and a lot of money she won in a lottery. Ashley, the Cinderella figure, never does become an interesting character, but the story gradually develops some of the emotional depth one looks for in Mavis Jukes's work.

1999. Maguire, Gregory. **Confessions of an Ugly Stepsister.** New York: ReganBooks.

There may be a trace of magic in this complex novel; it's hard to be certain. It is set in Holland at the time of Rembrandt, in the seventeenth century, and questions about beauty and its opposite, about painting, and about the nature and power of images shape the story. The Cinderella plot is there, but the focalizing character is Iris, a painfully plain child who flees from England to Holland with her mother and her grotesque, apparently retarded sister. The mother, Margarethe, finds work first in the house of a painter and later in the house of a rich tulip broker and his wife, who have a strangely beautiful daughter, Clara. Margarethe poisons the tulip broker's wife and marries him. When the tulip bulb market crashes, and with it the family's fortune, Margarethe promises Clara both to their main creditor and to her dressmaker. She hopes that if she can take Iris, properly dressed, to the ball the Dowager Queen of France is giving, Iris will captivate the visiting Prince and save them all. However, Clara wins the Prince and sends money to support her stepfamily after she is married. Iris marries the painter's apprentice, who loves her, and becomes a painter herself. The prologue and epilogue of the story are the reflections of the second stepsister, Ruth, spoken years after all these events happened.

2000. Pullman, Philip. **I Was a Rat!** New York: Knopf.

What if one of Cinderella's footmen wandered away while she was at the ball and therefore didn't get turned back into a rat when the magic vanished at midnight? He remains a boy but has only a young rat's experience of the human world, so none of it makes sense to him, and most of it is dangerous. Bob and Joan, a kindly old shoemaker and his wife, who grow to love him and want to keep him, take him in. But the boy, Roger, gets lost and into a great deal of trouble. The heartless Philosopher Royal, a greedy freak show owner named Tapscrew, and the gutter press complicate matters almost fatally. Finally Bob goes to see the Princess—the gift of a pair of small red slippers is his entrée—and asks her to help. In the end, it all comes right. But both the Princess and Roger are stuck with the consequences of Cinderella's wish.

Pullman's exploration of those consequences is unusual and clever. Pages of *The Daily Scourge,* a tabloid newspaper that twists reality to suit its need for sensation, tell part of the story. The visual contrast between these hard-edged, screaming pages and the soft, funny sketches that illustrate the book is part of the complex mix of fairy tale, social commentary, and adventure that makes this story so interesting.

Short Stories

1994. Garner, James Finn. **"Cinderella."** In *Politically Correct Bedtime Stories,* by James Finn Garner. New York: Macmillan, 31–37.

The ball turns into a brawl when the men begin to fight over who gets Cinderella. When midnight strikes in the middle of the fuss and Cinderella's grand clothes turn back into rags, the "womyn" realize how oppressed they have been by their finery. The men fight until they've killed each other, and the women take over the kingdom and "set up a clothing co-op that produced only comfortable, practical clothes for womyn" (36–37).

1995. Harlan, Annita. "Princess in Puce." In *The Armless Maiden*, edited by Terri Windling. New York: Tor, 71–84.

The introductory comment by the editor says that this Cinderella "is a quick-witted and angry young woman, determined to reclaim her life" (71). Actually, she's a good deal more passive than Cinderella in the Grimms's version on which this story is based. The birds of the air have all the initiative. But the modern tongue-in-cheek tone is amusing: "Priscilla had Mom's brain, so she knew she was getting the shit end of the stick. Dad's brain was where it had always been, so he didn't notice her plight" (72). Harlan makes some lively changes to the Grimm tale, replacing the slipper with a glove, expanding the characterization, and giving Cinderella/Priscilla and the prince an extra encounter. The framing thoughts of the putative storyteller raise two interesting questions: Is retelling an old story just an easy way to meet a deadline, and is the ending of the story too easy on Cinderella's father?

1995. Lisle, Holly. "Armor-Ella." In *Chicks in Chainmail*, edited by Esther Friesner. Riverdale, NY: Baen, 66–88.

An antidote to every weepy, passive Cinderella, El is six feet tall and has "shoulders like a blacksmith from swinging a two-handed sword for hours on end" (66). She knows the handsome prince is "an avaricious, land-grabbing, double-crossing" sneak, but she wants him anyway, for his beautiful body and for the luxurious life she would have as a princess. She makes a contract with the Folk of the Enchanted Forest (her father was a lawyer), and with their help bags her man. Luckily, the prince loves women who know how to use a whip. So everyone lives happily ever after, because they all got what they wanted.

1996. Fisher, David. "Kingdom v. Prince Charming: Summation of Mr. Clarion (Prosecution for the Kingdom)." In *Legally Correct Fairy Tales*, by David Fisher. New York: Warner Books, 67–76.

Prince Charming is accused of sexual abuse. The prosecution argues that the search for the owner of the improbable glass slipper was a con job, a ruse to let the Prince indulge his foot fetish by fondling as many women's feet as possible. The surprise witness for the defense is clearly not credible: "Cinderella, she calls herself. A woman who works by day as a poor stepsister, who has nothing to her name and so has nothing to lose by claiming to be the mystery woman" (74). After all, what woman in the world would publicly admit to wearing a size 14 shoe?

1996. Huth, Angela. "Another Kind of Cinderella." In *Another Kind of Cinderella and Other Stories*. Boston: Little, Brown, 1–23.

In this extraordinarily bleak tale, the Cinderella figure is Reginald Breem, second violin in the Winterstown Concert Orchestra. He is a disappointed man tied to his grotesquely fat, domineering mother. Rehearsals are under way for the

Christmas pantomime, which is going to be "Cinderella," and Reginald falls in love with Valerie, the girl playing the title role. He knows it's hopeless, but he asks her out for coffee and confesses his love. He can't understand her response that she's "another kind of Cinderella": he's too naive to see what the reader sees, that she's trapped in an abusive lesbian relationship with the tough woman who plays Prince Charming. After the performance, Reginald goes home and kills his mother with his violin case.

1998. Cooper, Louise. **"The Glass Slip-Up."** In *The Mammoth Book of Comic Fantasy*, edited by Mike Ashley. New York: Carroll and Graf, 177–96.

It turns out that Cinderella's father and stepmother had a good reason to keep her hidden in the kitchen. Although she's beautiful, she's also appallingly vulgar, a serious embarrassment to the royal family. Prince Charming insists that the opportunistic and inept fairy godmother undo the mess she's created. Divorce is out of the question, so her solution is to go back in time and make the slipper fit someone else. This time around, she makes it fit herself, which isn't much of an improvement for Charming.

1998. Peterson, Audrey. **"Anniversary Ball."** In *Once Upon a Crime*, edited by Ed Gorman and Martin H. Greenberg. New York: Berkley Prime Crime, 322–41.

It's a year after Cinderella and Prince Charming met at the ball. The young married couple are deeply in love, and Princess Cindy is four months pregnant. But disaster threatens; someone is trying to kill Charming. Who is the villain? And is the Prince really the target?

1998. Roberts, Gillian. **"After Happily Ever."** In *Once Upon a Crime*, edited by Ed Gorman and Martin H. Greenberg. New York: Berkley Prime Crime, 2–17.

Fairyland is being logged over, unicorns have become dray horses, and Cinderella is an ambitious schemer, a "professional cutie" with no family feeling at all. The narrator is one of Cinderella's stepsisters (and victims), whose purpose is to point out the number of ways in which the human world has got the story all wrong. She's writing from the castle dungeon; Cinderella framed her for the murder of Prince Charming.

1998. Rusch, Kristine Kathryn. **"Love and Justice."** In *Once Upon a Crime*, edited by Ed Gorman and Martin H. Greenberg. New York: Berkley Prime Crime, 361–72.

Cinderella and her children live apart from Prince Charming because he beats her. When Cinderella and a friend are found murdered, all the clues point to Charming. But the King loves his children even more than he loves justice, so the palace sheriff and the King reluctantly conspire to cover up the crime.

1999. Bedford, Jacey. **"Baron Boscov's Bastard."** In *Twice Upon a Time*, edited by Denise Little. New York: Daw Books, 204–27.

After a serious beginning, this story turns into a sequence of funny bits that seem more cobbled together than developed. Ella, the base-born daughter of Baron Boscov and a servant, is herself a servant in his household. The stable lad, Jimmy Buttons, tells her to take her future into her own hands instead of waiting for a fairy godmother to come along. To everyone's surprise, a fairy godmother does turn up. She's overworked and underequipped, but she does her best with a recycled Sleeping Beauty spell. Thanks to her ingenuity, Ella gets to marry Jimmy, and her beautiful but nasty half-sister gets the degenerate prince.

1999. Fahnestock, Todd, and Giles Custer. **"True Love (or The Many Brides of Prince Charming."** In *Twice Upon a Time*, edited by Denise Little. New York: Daw Books, 157–75.

Prince Charming marries Cinderella, but the hordes of singing, dressmaking mice she brings with her drive him crazy, and her spendthrift fairy godmother nearly bankrupts the kingdom. So Cinderella winds up in the dungeon, and Charming meets and marries Snow White. The seven dwarfs are not only "horrible houseguests" (169); they're all having an affair with Snow White. The Prince has all eight of them beheaded. Sleeping Beauty, the next bride, is into kinky sex with sharp objects. She's burned at the stake. Charming, having renounced romance, becomes increasingly withdrawn, unkempt, and generally beastly, until one day a girl named Beauty comes along.

1999. Mayer, Gloria Gilbert, and Thomas Mayer. **"Cinderella."** In *Goldilocks on Management: 27 Revisionist Fairy Tales for Serious Managers*, by Gloria Gilbert Meyer and Thomas Meyer. New York: American Management Association, 141–49.

Cinderella cleans the offices of a corporation in Luxembourg where her sisters are vice-presidents. Cinderella is just as bright and talented as her sisters, but she never puts herself forward or asks for more than a cost-of-living raise. She doesn't get invited to a ball given by the royal family, although her sisters do. While she's glooming at home wishing she could go, Joan Rivers reaches out of the television set to give her rented clothes, a limo and driver, John Travolta as a dance teacher, and the encouragement she needs to crash the party. The midnight tabu is the deadline for returning the rentals. The prince, who declares himself "unattached, heterosexual, and emotionally available" (143), turns out to share many of Cinderella's interests. After the ball he advertises for the owner of the slipper on milk cartons. Cinderella does have the sense to call the 800 number on the carton; they marry, and "she never has to empty a wastebasket or vacuum a carpet again" (144).

Basic lesson: "High Performers should be given the opportunity to succeed" (144). The bottom line: "As an employer, it is your job to provide [the right] opportunities for the people in your organization who deserve them" (148–49).

2000. Block, Francesca Lia. **"Glass."** In *The Rose and the Beast: Fairy Tales Retold*, by Francesca Lia Block. New York: Joanna Cotler Books, 55–70.

This story is so lyrically written that it is difficult to understand and impossible to summarize. It's about finding the courage to tell the story of your life truly, about self-doubt, and about the danger of hiding yourself to be safe. "All the things that girls feel they are not when they fear that if they become, if they are, they will no longer be loved by the sisters whose hearts they have not meant to break" (66).

Graphic Novel

1999. **"Aschenputtel, or Cinderella."** In *The Big Book of Grimm: Truly Scary Fairy Tales to Frighten the Whole Family!, by the Brothers Grimm as Channeled by Jonathan Vankin & Over 50 Top Comic Book Artists.* New York: Paradox Press, 8–12.

The printed text says that Cinderella's stepsisters are beautiful. The pictures show stout, tall, bosomy blondes with snub noses, a strong contrast to the dark-haired, wraith-like Cinderella. After the first and second nights of the ball, the prince follows Cinderella home, and he sees the girl smeared with ashes at the hearth. So after the stepsisters are exposed as frauds (the pictures show close-ups of the toe and heel being cut off, with lots of blood), the prince himself remembers that there's a third daughter and insists she try on the slipper. The last frame has the birds attacking the eyes of the stepsisters in the foreground.

Feature Films

1998. **Ever After.** Directed by Andy Tennant. 20th Century Fox.

Set in sixteenth-century France, this enjoyable version of Cinderella is pure historical fiction and worth the attention of adults as well as teens. The PG 13 rating rightly indicates that this is not primarily a children's film.

The role of the fairy godmother is taken by Leonardo da Vinci, traveling with an entourage of dainty boys and the canvas of the *Mona Lisa* in his baggage in lieu of a name tag. His famous ingenuity, rather than any magic, gets Cinderella to the ball. Drew Barrymore as Cinderella is a sturdy, loving, competent child, deeply influenced by Thomas More's *Utopia* and sensible of her responsibilities to her father's estate and its people. Anjelica Houston as the stepmother is nasty enough to pull the wings off butterflies, but tragically human all the same. One is made to wonder how differently this story might have played itself out if Cinderella's dying father had given his last words and love to his new wife instead of to his daughter. The Prince (played by Dougray Scott) is a gorgeous hunk who has a lot of growing up to do, very conscious of his *noblesse* but with no sense of *oblige*. He rejects Cinderella after the ball because his pride has been hurt by her deception, but by the end he has learned a great deal from her, including the fact that she's perfectly capable of saving herself.

The film begins and ends in the early nineteenth century. The Brothers Grimm are interviewing Cinderella's many-times-great-granddaughter to get the true story (they mention that they find Perrault's fairy godmother and pumpkin unbelievable). This framing device gives an opportunity for some clever references to the fairy tale tradition, including a wise statement by Cinderella's descendant that can be understood in several ways: "They lived happily ever after but that isn't what matters. What matters is that they lived."

Internet Resources

Shen's Books and Supplies, "Home of Cinderella Tales from around the World," offers a number of Cinderella versions at http://www.shens.com.

"The Frog King"

Novel

1999. Mitchell, Stephen. **The Frog Prince: A Fairy Tale for Consenting Adults**. New York: Harmony.

Mitchell refers to the traditional version of this tale as the "condensed version" and fleshes out the missing motivations and thoughts of the characters in this short novel set in Renaissance France. He discusses, as part of his story, the reasons behind the motifs in this traditional tale; makes numerous references to other popular traditional tales (quickly summarizing their main motifs but never naming them); and provides a rather philosophical and, at times, pedantic extension of the story.

Short Stories

1997. Jacobs, A. J. **"The Frog Prince."** In *Fractured Fairy Tales as Featured on Jay Ward's The Adventures of Rocky and Bullwinkle and Friends*. New York: Bantam, 11–16.

The witch decides to cast a spell on a frog and turn him into a handsome prince. This does not sit well with him, so he sets off to find the witch to reverse the spell. On his journey he meets a princess whom he marries against both their wishes since he still insists he is a frog. Finally one day a witch comes along who turns him back into a frog. Before he can enjoy himself too much, the original witch arrives and changes him into a chicken. (She's a little rusty with her spells these days.) He complains to the local union of witches and ultimately, both he and his princess live happily ever after . . . as frogs!

1998. Clark, Simon. **"Now Fetch Me An Axe."** In *Once Upon a Crime*, edited by Ed Gorman and Martin H. Greenberg. New York: Berkley Crime, 64–86.

The princess of crime, author Rebecca St. Taine, writes about her experiences as she awaits the arrival of her murderer at her home. She muses on the first time she met the vagrant, who wanted nothing more than to dine with her as his reward for pushing her car out of the snow. She concentrates on how her publicist insisted that she honor her promise to the vagrant for great news coverage, and she focuses on the fact that there had been no footprints in the snow! This provides the clue to the real culprit: one of identical triplets. The title of the story is from a stanza of a verse in the Scottish version of the tale, "The Well at the End of the World."

1999. Kilworth, Garry. **"The Frog Chauffeur."** In *Silver Birch, Blood Moon,* edited by Ellen Datlow and Terri Windling. New York: Avon, 122–31.

This contemporary story opens with the transformed frog sleeping beside the middle-aged princess. He offers himself to her as a lover, husband, or man and is accepted first as her lover and her chauffeur and then as her husband. During the next several years she notices that her husband is regressing, eating flies and other bugs. In her desperate research to discover what is happening, she re-reads the fairy tale "The Frog Prince" and realizes that it was not a kiss that caused the transformation. "What if the frog had been out of the pond that day, hopping by Isabel's sleeping form, when she suddenly thrashed in her dreams, struck out and hit the passing frog a blow, causing it to change into John?" (129). What if John was a descendant of that ancient prince before his transformation? With great trepidation she tells John of her theory and is dismayed to find his lifeless body floating in the pool the next day. Her life is less fulfilling, but she is comforted by her three famous children: a long-jumper, a swimmer, and a poet!

1999. Lee, Tanith. **"Kiss Kiss."** In *Silver Birch, Blood Moon,* edited by Ellen Datlow and Terri Windling. New York: Avon, 7–24.

This is a story of transformation and irony. The princess takes a long time to make friends with the slimy frog that follows her home, but eventually a strong friendship develops. When the frog begs her to kiss him, she has no hesitation because she would do anything for her gentle companion. Unfortunately, although the transformed frog is indeed handsome, he begins to shed some of his former humanity and gentleness.

1999. McKillip, Patricia A. **"Toad."** In *Silver Birch, Blood Moon,* edited by Ellen Datlow and Terri Windling. New York: Avon, 354–61.

Toad, the narrator, maintains that the princess, although spoiled and conniving, really knew all along what the toad represented.

1999. Sherman, Josepha. **"Feeding Frenzy or the Further Adventures of the Frog Prince."** In *Twice Upon a Time,* edited by Denise Little. New York: Daw Books, 260–69.

It is very sad indeed that when a couple marries they are not left alone to live happily ever after. If it wasn't activists against animal cruelty (she did throw him against the wall, did she not?), then it was environmentalists who worried about the ecological effects of a prince living as a frog or reporters looking for exclusive interviews. Finally, evidence is collected against the original transgressor, Dame Gruesome, who is taken to court and ultimately banished to the Realm of Science. As for the reporter who did not know when to leave well enough alone, he now has his own exclusive article to write, once he no longer is a frog!

"Hansel and Gretel"

Short Stories

1997. Jacobs, A. J. **"Hansel and Gretel."** In *Fractured Fairy Tales as Featured on Jay Ward's The Adventures of Rocky and Bullwinkle and Friends*. New York: Bantam, 49–53.

Hansel and Gretel leave home to find food for their impoverished family. Unfortunately they get lost, run into a witch, and Hansel gets turned into an aardvark. Gretel saves the day by teaching the witch how to fly her broom, and the two return home on the back of a French-speaking duck. There they find their father has changed his career; he is no longer a woodchopper but a hunter, and they have plenty to eat.

1998. Dawson, Janet. **"Invisible Time."** In *Once Upon a Crime*, edited by Ed Gorman and Martin H. Greenberg. New York: Berkley Crime, 342–59.

Greta and Hans are living on the streets of San Francisco because they were evicted from their apartment after their mother abandoned them. Three squatters find them, one of whom decides to sell them to the highest bidder once they have been "fattened up." However, this Greta is even more resourceful than her namesake and, although there is not an oven in the story, an open elevator shaft works a "treat."

1998. Enstrom, Elizabeth. **"Harvest Home."** In *Once Upon a Crime*, edited by Ed Gorman and Martin H. Greenberg. New York: Berkley Crime, 100–116.

In this horrifying tale, the father plays no role in the disappearance of his children. In fact, he desperately wants them back and arranges for a badly needed heart transplant for the stepmother just to find out where she left them. The tale is an unusual blending of the traditional folktale and a contemporary urban legend.

2000. Nix, Garth. **"Hansel's Eyes."** In *A Wolf at the Door and Other Retold Fairy Tales*, edited by Ellen Datlow and Terri Windling. New York: Simon & Schuster, 108–23.

The contemporary setting of this tale makes the events of the traditional tale more plausible than ever before. Rather than a gingerbread house, the two children find themselves in a Sony Playstation shop, where Hansel becomes mesmerized and imprisoned by the video games he is encouraged to play. The witch recognizes that Gretel has power and offers her a choice: She can become the witch's apprentice or she can be taken slowly apart as a source for organ donations. The major prize, however, is Hansel's eyes for the witch herself. The upright freezer is an intriguing substitution for the oven!

2000. Stableford, Brian. **"Chanterelle."** In *Black Heart, Ivory Bones,* edited by Ellen Datlow and Terri Windling. New York: Avon, 102–35.

This tale begins with the story structure of "Hansel and Gretel" and incorporates elements of two literary fairy tales, "Luscignole," a novella by Catulle Mendes, and Gerhardt Hauptmann's play, "The Sunken Bell." "The link between fairies and magic mushrooms was appropriated from Maureen Duffy's book on *The Erotic World of Faery*" (135).

Poetry

2000. Cash, Debra. **"Witch."** In *Black Heart, Ivory Bones,* edited by Ellen Datlow and Terri Windling. New York: Avon, 100–101.

This poem is a sorrowful introspection on the function of the witch in the traditional tale, from her point of view.

"Little Red Riding Hood"

Short Stories

1998. Crider, Bill. **"It Happened at Grandmother's House."** In *Once Upon a Crime,* edited by Ed Gorman and Martin H. Greenberg. New York: Berkley Crime, 43–63.

The reminiscences of a werewolf about a high school experience formulate this inversion of the traditional tale. Redheaded Marie Grayson asks our hero for help for her grandmother when she discovers he is a werewolf. However, it is Marie who saves the "wolf" and kills the "huntsman" serial rapist killer in this lightly sardonic reworking.

1998. Helfers, John. **"The Better to Eat You With."** In *Once Upon a Crime,* edited by Ed Gorman and Martin H. Greenberg. New York: Berkley Crime, 225–42.

Henry, an elderly photographer, misses the perfect shot at a wolf near his cabin in the woods. He is cold and uncomfortable but not in as much trouble as the people in a small plane that crashes soon after. He rescues the young woman in the red hooded parka and brings her to his cabin. During the rescue he is aware of being watched by a wolf pack. The woman insists, at gun point, that Henry lead her out of the woods, and once again the pack of wolves are on the periphery, but not for long. It is the woodsman who is the survivor in this chilling rendition of the tale.

1999. Helfers, John. **"Savior."** In *Twice Upon a Time,* edited by Denise Little. New York: Daw Books, 176–79.

In this taut, concise report narrated by the huntsman, the reader feels his anguish as Little Red's lover is forced to kill her when the wolf's stomach is opened. Although the wolf did swallow her whole, too much time had passed to prevent the damage done by the stomach acid.

2000. Block, Francesca Lia. **"Wolf."** In *The Rose and the Beast: Fairy Tales Retold.* New York: Joanna Colter Books, 101–29.

The young protagonist runs away from sexual abuse at home and the resulting argument between her mother and stepfather when her mother discovers what has been happening. The girl flees toward sanctuary with her grandmother in the desert. When she arrives she finds her stepfather has traveled faster than she has and is being held at gunpoint by the grandmother. When the girl discovers the fate of her mother, she takes the shotgun and uses it effectively. This powerful and disquieting story reads like a stream of consciousness dialogue.

Poetry

2001. Miner, Carrie. **"Wolf,"** http://www.endicott-studio.com/cofwolf.html.

Told from the point of view of the wolf, in this poem the ravaging of the girl is something he cannot resist. He loves her so much he has to "gobble [her] up."

"Rapunzel"

Short Stories

1992. Woods, Máiríde. **"Happy Ever After and Other Obsessions."** In *Ride on Rapunzel: Fairytales for Feminists.* Dublin: Attic Press, 96–102.

In this romp of a story, Rapunzel is adopted by a woman who increasingly feels the need to protect the child—from television, food contaminated by additives and preservatives, the education system, and men. Rapunzel accepts it all with equanimity, falls in love with a bald man who has a hair fetish, and makes a successful career as a psychotherapist.

1994. Garner, James Finn. **"Rapunzel."** In *Politically Correct Bedtime Stories,* by James Finn Garner. New York: Macmillan, 23–30.

The witch has a back-up set of hair and so is able to catch Rapunzel and the prince together. While the prince and the witch discuss record contracts and video deals for Rapunzel's beautiful singing, Rapunzel, realizing that "her hair had been exploited for the transportational needs of others" (29) for years and that she's about to be exploited some more, sneaks out the window, climbs down the second set of hair, and rides away on the prince's horse. Later she sells her hair for a charity auction.

1997. Cashorali, Peter. **"Romaine."** In *Fairy Tales: Traditional Stories Retold for Gay Men*, by Peter Cashorali. New York: HarperSanFrancisco, 53–64.

Rapunzel is a boy named Romaine, and the sorcerer is a dim-witted ogre who tries to bring up the boy to be an ogre like himself. Unfortunately, Romaine just doesn't like football, toy trucks, and guns. When he lets a "sissie-boy" go instead of cooking him for supper, the ogre is fed up and locks him in a tower. When he wants to visit, he calls up "Hey, Romaine, Romaine up there! I want to come up—throw down your hair" (57).

Unaccountably, the ogre has never gotten around to giving the boy a crew cut. A passing prince, Sean, is captivated by Romaine's long black hair. When the ogre discovers their dalliance, he takes Romaine far away, and then beats Sean up. The ogre's words ("you're sick!") are more wounding than his blows. Sean wanders the world, cynical and heartless, and when he again meets Romaine, who is working as a trash collector, he can't recognize him. The tears Romaine weeps for his poor friend clear Sean's vision of the world; the two of them go to Sean's kingdom, where the king welcomes them; and the ogre turns to stone at the end.

1998. DuBois, Brendan. **"Rapunzel's Revenge."** In *Once Upon a Crime*, edited by Ed Gorman and Martin H. Greenberg. New York: Berkley Prime Crime, 177–97.

The connection to Rapunzel is so thin that it shouldn't really count, but the story is good. A U.S. cop goes to Quebec City to rescue her husband, who is being held by mobsters in the Chateau Frontenac until he works the last bugs out of a computer program that reliably predicts the winners of horse races. When he finishes, he'll be killed. The cop and her husband communicate through coded e-mail. The message she sends to tell him the plan of escape is "Rapunzel, Rapunzel, let down your hair," a reference to a family joke. He climbs down out of the window on a braid of power cords, cable connectors, and surge suppressors to the escape car waiting below.

1998. Haddam, Jane. **"Rapunzel."** In *Once Upon a Crime*, edited by Ed Gorman and Martin H. Greenberg. New York: Berkley Prime Crime, 137–62.

This dark reworking is the extreme opposite of a children's story. Rapunzel's tower is a stack of cages in a sleazy carnival sideshow in Waterbury, Connecticut. Each cage holds a woman who can be won for sex by throwing dice. Rapunzel is in the top cage and is the most expensive to play for. All the men want her, but no one ever gets the prize. Fifteen-year-old Daniel is just a high school loser. His rich friend Bobby, who takes him to the carnival, however, is seriously twisted by drugs and a vicious fear of women. Bobby tries to sneak up to Rapunzel's cage and winds up dead. The story is permeated with despair, rage, and horrifying fantasies of sexual violence.

1999. Goldstein, Lisa. **"The Witch's Child."** *Realms of Fantasy* (December): 66–69, 89.

In this fine reworking, the witch took Rapunzel because "she had long wanted a girl, someone who would be herself, her other self, someone who could start over again and not make the same mistakes she had made" (66). She is a miserable, disappointed woman who fears the world outside her small, dark room, and all she can teach Rapunzel is her own unhappiness. Every story she tells Rapunzel begins well but ends "in a welter of despair and loose ends" (68). Although Rapunzel escapes from the tower, she is still trapped by the way of seeing the world that she learned from the witch. True freedom comes when she realizes that the witch taught her one good thing, to tell stories, and that Rapunzel can tell her own story a different way. This creative, well-written interpretation of the old tale is about mothers who try to make their daughters extensions of themselves and about daughters who must take responsibility for the stories of their own lives.

1999. Parks, Richard. **"Thy Golden Stair."** In *Twice Upon a Time*, edited by Denise Little. New York: Daw Books, 139–56.

What happens when a character in an old story breaks the usual pattern? Rapunzel climbs down from her tower and into confusion. The world doesn't work as it should, and a buzz of voices surrounds her, trying to push her back into the tower. She doesn't know what they are until the witch explains that they are the people who remember the story:

> Eventually the people doing the remembering change. Their *idea* of what your life was changes. The idea of what a life *should* be changes. It takes time, but eventually it happens. The story changes. That's why you were able to leave the tower. Those who remember are out of agreement. They're fighting over you now, though they don't really know that. (151)

Rapunzel lives her own life for a while, but then she encounters the voices again, this time embodied in a fox. It's time to get on with the story, they agree. They also agree that Rapunzel will "find the new story, the one that makes sense for all of us now" (155). This metafictional treatment of the tale is puzzling but worth reflecting on.

Graphic Novel

1999. **"Rapunzel."** In *The Big Book of Grimm: Truly Scary Fairy Tales to Frighten the Whole Family!, by the Brothers Grimm as Channeled by Jonathan Vankin & Over 50 Top Comic Book Artists.* New York: Paradox Press, 56–59.

Notable only because of the graphic novel format, this story is told straight, except for two changes that weaken its coherence. The wife isn't pregnant when she begins to crave the rapunzel in the witch's garden, and the text explains why the witch locks Rapunzel up in the tower: The girl is so beautiful that the witch can't stand to look at her. This motivation unfortunately makes nonsense of the witch's subsequent visits to the girl ("Rapunzel, Rapunzel, let down your hair"). The pictured witch is middle-aged at most, with a white streak in her thick hair, a mole, long fingernails like claws, and pointed teeth.

Picture Book

1998. Vozar, David. **Rapunzel: A Happenin' Rap**. Illustrated by Betsy Lewin. New York: Doubleday.

The characters are pictured as dogs, the text is rap, and the setting is the big city. Rapunzel is a spoiled, greedy teenager more interested in her hairstyle than in Fine Prince. The witch zaps the prince downtown and throws Rapunzel out of the tower when she whines just once too often. But all ends happily. Rap finds her parents and opens a beauty shop with Fine Prince, and they have twins. Published for children as a Doubleday Book for Young Readers, but cool enough for young teens.

"Rumpelstiltskin"

Novel

1999. Napoli, Donna Jo, and Richard Tchen. **Spinners**. New York: Dutton.

The opening sequence is a love scene between the maiden and the tailor, her lover. He has given her a necklace made of shells. She is quite sure that her father will agree to their marriage, but her father is not impressed with the tailor at all and vows that she will be his wife only if he can make her a gold wedding dress by the next full moon. If he cannot do so, the girl will marry the miller. The tailor gets a spinning wheel from an old woman. This wheel spins straw into gold, and he sets to making a wedding dress for his beloved. Unfortunately, the spinning process also cripples him, and when his pregnant sweetheart sees him, she rejects him and marries the miller. When she rejects him but accepts his gift of a ring, the tailor leaves town, taking the spinning wheel with him.

The story jumps ahead to the miller's daughter Saskia, who does not have a mother but has a shell necklace and ring that once belonged to her mother. Her father is not a happy man and spends too much money and time on drink. Saskia grows to be a fine spinner and it is her earnings that keep the tiny family afloat.

The tailor returns to town unnoticed and unrecognized several years later. When he discovers the existence and identity of his daughter, he has Elke, a woman he has met in the woods and who works in the castle, exchange the girl's spinning wheel for his own. This is advantageous when her father's boasting takes her and the spinning wheel to the castle. When she meets the king, "Saskia feels as though she is a skein of yarn herself, lying on a table in the market, helpless against anyone's hands" (108). This king is as heartless as her father, and the girl finds herself in a room filled with straw. All her attempts to spin the straw into gold are useless, and she finally gives up in despair. Meanwhile, Elke smuggles the tailor into the room where Saskia, under the impression he is magic, gives him her necklace in return for his spinning. Following the pattern of the traditional tale, she exchanges her ring on the second night, and on the third night, since she has nothing else to give, offers herself. This gift, however, he is not interested in taking, and his unreasonable anger about her failure to realize that he is her father makes him demand her first-born child.

Although she spurns the advances of the king, he forces her to marry him, and several years later she becomes pregnant. The tailor comes for the child when it is a year old but allows his daughter three chances to guess his true name, the hateful name her mother called him. Saskia discovers that he is her father, confronts the miller, and discovers by chance the tailor's name. The tailor is so upset when she utters the name that his leg, which never stopped pumping since he first spun straw into gold, drives him into the floor and is finally still. The tailor's lonely life of torment is at an end.

Short Stories

1997. Jacobs, A. J. **"Rumpelstiltskin."** In *Fractured Fairy Tales as Featured on Jay Ward's The Adventures of Rocky and Bullwinkle and Friends.* New York: Bantam, 18–22.

One day Gladys, the miller's daughter, meets up with a PR agent, a little man who could spin out the truth. She does well with her new found fame until the day she meets a king who believes all the publicity. He threatens her, and the story follows the traditional pattern set by the Brothers Grimm. As for the little man, well, there are unconfirmed reports about a girl who can make diamonds out of turnips in another kingdom!

1997. Jacobs, A. J. **"Son of Rumpelstiltskin."** In *Fractured Fairy Tales as Featured on Jay Ward's The Adventures of Rocky and Bullwinkle and Friends.* New York: Bantam, 151–56.

Rumpelstiltskin's son leaves home to make a name for himself, but after meeting the miller's daughter and spinning straw into gold, he discovers his name for himself when he puts up a mailbox. He doesn't like it and so leaves every one at peace. He also changes his name!

1999. Briggs, Patricia. **"The Price."** In *Silver Birch, Blood Moon,* edited by Ellen Datlow and Terri Windling. New York: Avon, 28–47.

Briggs chooses one of her least favorite tales and reworks it to deflect some of the problems she found with the tale: What was a common miller doing talking to a king anyway? In this telling, the narrator is a weaver who notices and meets the strange man at market before the storyline begins to unravel with a fateful meeting with the king. Other than this previous meeting and the fact that the dye she uses in her work is made from the rumpelstiltskin plant, this story follows the story structure of the traditional tale. And, oh yes, most of the characters are worthy as well!

1999. Miller, P. Andrew. **"One Fairy Tale, Hard-Boiled."** In *Twice Upon a Time,* edited by Denise Little. New York: Daw Books, 240–59.

The hard-boiled private eye knew trouble when it looked him in the eye, and the young woman in his office was definitely trouble. The case was fairly straightforward: find the missing person, a little man, and discover his name. One major problem was the tight turnaround time: three days. A second major problem was the fact that the detective was an urban sort and, unfortunately, got lost easily in the woods. He was also very soft inside his hard-boiled shell and managed to bring satisfaction to all concerned: the woman, the little man and his wife, and the two orphan children living in a house made of candy.

1999. Nye, Jody Lynn. **"Spinning a Yarn."** In *Twice Upon a Time,* edited by Denise Little. New York: Daw Books, 4–29.

Forced by the tax auditor and to save his grandson, the miller sets out to discover the name of the helper. During his journey through the enchanted wood he encounters other characters from familiar tales as well. Tongue-in-cheek reworking of the tale. If only the miller's wife had been home to advise him!

"Sleeping Beauty"

Novel

1999. Card, Orson Scott. **Enchantment**. New York: Del Rey.

"The old tale of Sleeping Beauty might end happily in French or English, but he was in Russia, and only a fool would want to live through the Russian version of any fairy tale" (71). But this is exactly what Ivan, the protagonist, does. The European tale of "Sleeping Beauty" is superimposed on the Russian landscape and a wealth of folklore to create a novel of beauty and strength. As a child, Ivan sees the sleeping beauty in the woods and cannot forget her. He immigrates to the United States but feels himself being drawn back to Russia as a young adult. But this is a variant of "Sleeping Beauty" that he has problems recognizing:

> Yet even as he recognized and admired the medieval village he had expected, Ivan had to wrestle with a completely different set of expectations, courtesy of Walt Disney. Wasn't it Sleeping Beauty he had kissed? Then where was the magnificent palace? Never mind that Disney's movie version of the story was set in some weird combination of the 16th and 19th centuries—Ivan couldn't help being let down seeing—and hearing, and smelling—such a course reality instead of a magical dream. (83)

Ivan and Katrina, the princess, have to face a greater menace than Disney's evil witch. They have to confront the fierce Baba Yaga, the ravages of anti-Semitism, and the horrors of Russian history. Card's commentary on the nature and role of folklore throughout the novel adds a further dimension to this complex and tightly orchestrated novel. It is a pleasure to follow the foreshadowing of the folklore and the intertwining of the old world with the modern to the satisfying end of Card's story. "He knew the origins of the tales of Baba Yaga's house that stood up on chicken legs and ran from place to place at her command. In all his years of study, he had never seen a single speculation from a folklorist or a literary historian that the origin of the witch's walking hut might be a high-jacked 747" (353).

1999. Levine, Gail Carson. **Princess Sonora and the Long Sleep**. The Princess Tales. New York: HarperCollins.

Being the cleverest baby in the world may not seem to be difficult to handle, but once the fairies bestow their gifts on the baby princess, Sonora is beset with numerous problems. Of course, the primary concern is controlling the advent of the long sleep that she understands is inevitable. She was quite adamant about this because "Sonora loved her mind, and she wanted to know where it was at all times" (38). However, a twist of fate removes this aspect of control from her and she succumbs ungraciously. Levine has played with the major motifs of this tale to create a blithe caricature of the traditional tale. "Princess Sonora knows, but don't ask her . . . ."

2000. McKinley, Robin. **Spindle's End**. New York: Putnam.

Although the first chapter of the book is difficult to enter because of McKinley's choice of voice, her version of "Sleeping Beauty" takes flight in a grand and satisfying manner. Selected to be a witness to the baby's christening, young Katriona becomes embroiled in the princess's life when the wicked fairy curses the child. Urged by the other fairies, Katriona returns home to her aunt in her remote village with the child and they raise her as their own kin. Rosie grows up in secret to be a delightful child, overflowing with all the beauty and gracious, basically useless, gifts bestowed upon her before she was taken away. It is when she reaches her majority that she is found and returned to the royal residence to face the fate her guardians had so tried to avoid. But she does not return alone or helpless. McKinley does great justice to this traditional tale about a passive princess and her long sleep.

Short Stories

1999. Bishop, Anne. **"The Wild Heart."** In *Silver Birch, Blood Moon*, edited by Ellen Datlow and Terri Windling. New York: Avon, 203–14.

Two aspects of the princess, "the Gentle Heart" and "the Wild Heart," are separated by the queen after the princess has been raped by the queen's lover. Once the Wild Heart escapes, the princess falls into a coma and remains as if asleep until the time that the two are joined once again. A strong reworking of the traditional tale, told from the point of view of the returning "Wild Heart."

1999. York, Pat. **"You Wandered Off Like a Foolish Child to Break Your Heart and Mine."** In *Silver Birch, Blood Moon,* edited by Ellen Datlow and Terri Windling. New York: Avon, 215–30.

Responding to the manuscript of the story by Anne Bishop, this version of the tale revolves around the anguish of a mother as she tends to her son trapped in the briers surrounding the castle. It takes five years for the "right" prince to come along, and with the dying of the hedge itself comes the death of all those left hanging among its brambles.

2000. Block, Francesca Lia. **"Charm."** In *The Rose and the Beast: Fairy Tales Retold.* New York: Joanna Colter Books, 73–97.

Cursed by being too beautiful, young Rev has turned to the prick of a needle to gain oblivion from her life and the photographers and lovers that have made it intolerable for so long. When she meets Miss Charm, she finds a place to sleep, to heal, and to finally find solace and peace. Block offers a disturbing look at exploitation in contemporary North American society.

2000. Costikyan, Greg. **"And Still She Sleeps."** In *Black Heart, Ivory Bones,* edited by Ellen Datlow and Terri Windling. New York: Avon, 63–89.

This discovery of a lifetime was not what the narrator, an archeologist, expected at the dig of an eighth-century castle in Northumbria, but indeed, that is what the uncovering of the sleeping girl became. A local variant of "Sleeping Beauty" tells about Arthur and Guinevere's daughter Margaret and the curse placed upon her by Morgana. Even Merlin could not counter the spell, although he altered it so that she could be awakened by the kiss of her own true love. Although the sleeping girl did not date back as far as the Arthurian myth, the Royal Thaumaturgical Society in London, while identifying the strength of the magic enchantment the girl lay under, could not awaken her either. There were numerous attempts to kiss her awake and plans to make money to do so, but neither the kisses of Edward, the Prince of Wales, nor the various scientists who studied her predicament could cause even a flutter in her shallow and measured breathing. When pondering on the nature of love, the narrator realizes how much he loves his wife. "How could I have loved her, never knowing her? And how could I have known her, merely looking?" (81). He then realizes that if the spell is to be broken by her true love, this person is centuries dead, and no one else can break the spell. She is donated, as a living artifact, to the British Museum, and sleeps there still. This reworking offers an interesting exploration of the nature of love.

Picture Book

1999. Craddock, Sonia. **Sleeping Boy**. Illustrated by Leonid Gore. New York: Atheneum.

A rather didactic reworking of the story that focuses on Germany from the beginning of the twentieth century to the tearing down of the Berlin Wall. The young boy and his family sleep through World War II and its aftermath as a result of the blessing of an aunt.

Poetry

1999. Sherman, Delia. **"Carabosse."** In *Silver Birch, Blood Moon,* edited by Ellen Datlow and Terri Windling. New York: Avon, 25–27.

The tale is told from the point of view of the twelfth fairy (there was never a thirteenth!). When bestowing her gift upon the young princess, Carabosse gave the gift of being a monarch without the necessity of being wed. The entire court was so horrified that Carabosse amended her wish so that the princess could sleep protected for 100 years and awaken in a more enlightened time.

2000. Cash, Debra. **"Briar Rose."** In *Black Heart, Ivory Bones,* edited by Ellen Datlow and Terri Windling. New York: Avon, 98–99.

The sleeping princess speculates on the images she receives while sleeping for a century.

"Snow White"

Novel

2000. Lee, Tanith. **White as Snow.** New York: TOR.

The three aspects of a woman, maiden, mother and crone, are incorporated in this interwoven and multilayered tale of Snow White and Persephone and Demeter. The story begins when the child is seven years old and it incorporates several other elements from the traditional folktale: the two faces of the mother, the huntsman and the boar, the seven dwarfs, and the mirror. However, this is not a straightforward reworking of these elements: The dwarfs are lusty (they also represent the seven sins in a theatrical performance), and there are rape and illicit love affairs between the queen and her huntsmen. The child (and the queen) find themselves in lengthy comas during which they lose touch with reality and the people around them.

The second part of the book begins ten years later, when the queen discovers that her daughter is still alive. The manifestations of the plot against the child's life are not as simple as laces, a comb, or a poisoned apple. And the need for the mother to find her child is not as strictly tied to the loss of beauty. "And Arpazia went through into the hill, after her daughter who was her own self, through into the Underworld of Hell, armed only with a basket of dead apples" (249). The third part of the book ties the search for her child and herself together and incorporates much more of the Elysian mysteries of Greek myth.

This is a complex tale and aimed at a mature reading audience.

> Soon, the watching mirror saw in the East, that always-rising place of renewals, advents, brightness like itself. The mirror offered neither question nor reply. The mirror's dialogues were done. And when the sun rose, it rose blood-red. (319)

Short Stories

1999. Kiernan, Caitlin R. **"Glass Coffin."** In *Silver Birch, Blood Moon,* edited by Ellen Datlow and Terri Windling. New York: Avon, 48–66.

A gritty, contemporary worldview of drug peddlers, scrap scavengers, and other assorted outsiders of mainstream society explodes in this dark reworking of the tale. The imagery is very visual: "[N]ew cracks at her feet, as the razor wire grows around her like brambles, wriggles up from the dead soil and metal writhes against the tarmac" (56). For mature readers.

1999. Rodgers, Alan. **"Fifi's Tail."** In *Twice Upon a Time,* edited by Denise Little. New York: Daw Books, 107–38.

Fifi is a wolf. Fifi is not her preferred name, but since Snow White bespelled the wolf after the fiascos with Little Red Riding Hood and the Three Little Pigs, Fifi had very little choice in the matter. The adventures that beset Fifi as bodyguard to the little "witch" take her into the hut of Hansel and Gretel as well as the seven dwarfs. This story could not get too much more fractured. Needless to say, it all gets sorted out in the end to most of the characters' satisfaction, especially Fifi, who is "very choosy about which pigs the butcher slaughters for him" (138).

1998. Hess, Joan. **"Heptagon."** In *Once Upon a Crime,* edited by Ed Gorman and Martin H. Greenberg. New York: Berkley Crime, 32–42.

Narrated by Miss Neige's psychiatrist, the story embraces all the elements of the Disney version of the tale. From the patient's states of mind—"grumpy," "bashful," "dopey," "sleepy," "happy," and "sneezy"—to her familiar addressing of the narrator as "doc," her story relates the suicide of her mother, the arrival of a stepmother, the murder of her "prince," and Miss Neige's six known personalities. Unfortunately for the doctor, there is one personality that he was not aware of, and it is very "nasty" indeed! Written in a breezy style, this story is fun to read and compare to the more traditional renditions.

1998. Hoch, Edward D. **"Snow White and the Eleven Dwarfs."** In *Once Upon a Crime,* edited by Ed Gorman and Martin H. Greenberg. New York: Berkley Crime, 198–210.

When Anne's beauty and potential career as a model threaten her aging stepmother's modeling career, the threats and nasty comments become more than Anne can handle, and she runs away from home. She finds herself in an abandoned motel occupied by migrant workers from Cuba. She asks if she can hide there for a while, perhaps clean up the place a little. "She giggled at a sudden thought. . . . 'Something like Snow White and the Seven Dwarfs.' 'Eleven . . . . There are eleven of us' " (203). She names them after the dwarfs in the film and four of Santa's tiny reindeer, and she cooks and cleans for them until she hears the news that her father has been found murdered and a warrant for her arrest has been issued. She and her new allies set a successful trap for the stepmother so Anne's name can be cleared. Unfortunately for the stepmother, the 11 dwarfs and one Snow White make up the 12 members of the jury.

2000. Block, Francesca Lia. **"Snow."** In *The Rose and the Beast: Fairy Tales Retold*. New York: Joanna Colter Books, 3–31.

Snow's young mother felt that she could not raise her baby properly. To counter the fear that the child would devour her, she gave her to the gardener to raise. He, in turn, gave her to seven brothers who would look after her. With them, Snow grew to maturity and was given "the belief in herself, instilled by seven fathers who had to learn it" (11). Everything changes on the day the gardener returns for a visit. He is enchanted by her and unwittingly communicates this to the girl's mother, whom he has been living with all these years. The mother decides to get rid of her daughter for good and decides to poison her. "She had read about it—simple recipe—too messy with razor blades" (21). Snow falls into a coma and awakens to the kiss of the gardener, but her first reaction is to call for the seven brothers. "In her sleep she had seen love. It was poisoning. Devouring. Or was it seven pairs of boots climbing up the stairs to find her" (31).

2000. Maguire, Gregory. **"The Seven Stage Comeback."** In *A Wolf at the Door and Other Retold Fairy Tales,* edited by Ellen Datlow and Terri Windling. New York: Simon & Schuster, 136–49.

Seven poetic dialogues, each in seven measurements, some repeated, relate the point of view of the seven dwarfs about their emotions about Snow White, the Prince, and the awakening. The strongest images evoked are the poison apple and the glass coffin. The final voice is that of Snow White herself; she is now a mother and remembers her former experiences only as a fragment of a dream.

2000. Yolen, Jane. **"Snow in Summer."** In *Black Heart, Ivory Bones,* edited by Ellen Datlow and Terri Windling. New York: Avon, 90–96.

The setting of this reworking has been moved to a rural community in the United States. When Snow is set upon by the young snake worshipper her step-mama has introduced her to, she runs away into the forest. There she is found and given a home by seven miners. One day, her step-mama arrives in disguise. Snow invites her in, feeds her deep-dish apple pie, and brains her with the frying pan. Everyone lives happily after . . . well, not step-mama, but no one misses her.

# APPENDIX

Child Ballads

#1 "Riddles Wisely Expounded"

Novel

> 1998. Dean, Pamela. *Juniper, Gentian, and Rosemary.* New York: TOR.

#2 "The Elfin-Knight"

Short stories

> 1997. Oates, Joyce Carol. "In the Insomniac Night." In *Black Swan, White Raven,* edited by Ellen Datlow and Terri Windling. New York: Avon, 80–101.

#3 "False Knight on the Road"

Graphic novel

> 1997. Gaiman, Neil. "False Knight On the Road." In *Ballads.* Illustrated by Charles Vess. Abingdon, VA: Greenman Press, 8–16.

#32 "King Henry"

Graphic novel

> 1997. Yolen, Jane. "King Henry." In *Ballads.* Illustrated by Charles Vess. Abingdon, VA: Greenman Press, 17–27.

#45 "The Three Ravens"

Short story

> 1998. de Lint, Charles. "Twa Corbies." In *Twenty 3: A Miscellany*, edited by Anna Hepworth, Simon Oxwell, and Grant Watson, Infinite Monkeys/Western Australian Science Fiction Foundation. [Also in *The Year's Best Fantasy and Horror: Twelfth Annual Collection*, edited by Ellen Datlow and Terri Windling. New York: St. Martin's Griffin, 1999].

Graphic novel

> 1997. de Lint, Charles. "Twa Corbies." In *Ballads*. Illustrated by Charles Vess. Abingdon, VA: Greenman Press, 78–87.

#84 "Barbara Allen"

Graphic novel

> 1997. Snyder, Midori. "Barbara Allen." In *Ballads*. Illustrated by Charles Vess. Abingdon, VA: Greenman Press, 38–46.

#243 "James Harris" ("The Daemon Lover")

Graphic novel

> 1997. Sherman, Delia. "The Daemon Lover." In *Ballads*. Illustrated by Charles Vess. Abingdon, VA: Greenman Press, 69–77.

Andersen Tales

"The Flea and the Professor"

Short stories

> 1999. Jacobs, Harvey. "The Vanishing Virgin." In *Silver Birch, Blood Moon*, edited by Ellen Datlow and Terri Windling. New York: Avon, 67–80.

"The Little Match Girl"

Short stories

> 1995. Bishop, Anne. "Match Girl." In *Ruby Slippers. Golden Tears*, edited by Ellen Datlow and Terri Windling. New York: Avon, 247–71.

> 1999. Mayer, Gloria Gilbert, and Thomas Mayer. "The Little Match Girl." In *Goldilocks on Management: 27 Revisionist Fairy Tales for Serious Managers*. New York: American Management Association, 51–56.

> 2000. Oates, Joyce Carol. "You, Little Match Girl." In *Black Heart, Ivory Bones*, edited by Ellen Datlow and Terri Windling. New York: Avon, 212–33.

Graphic novel

> 1997. O'Connell, Michael, and Jeff Curtis. "The Little Match Girl." In *Mythography* 2 (February): unpaged.

Poetry

> 1997. Tem, Steve Rasnic. "The Little Match Girl." In *Black Swan, White Raven*, edited by Ellen Datlow and Terri Windling. New York: Avon, 102–3.

"The Nightingale"

Novel

> 1988. Dalkey, Kara. *The Nightingale*. New York: Ace.

"The Red Shoes"

Short stories

> 1995. Wade, Susan. "Ruby Slippers." In *Ruby Slippers. Golden Tears*, edited by Ellen Datlow and Terri Windling. New York: Avon, 8–14.

> 2000. Cutter, Leah. "The Red Boots." In *Black Heart, Ivory Bones*, edited by Ellen Datlow and Terri Windling. New York: Avon, 181–97.

"The Steadfast Tin Soldier"

Short stories

> 1997. Kress, Nancy. "Steadfast." In *Black Swan, White Raven*, edited by Ellen Datlow and Terri Windling. New York: Avon, 330–49.

> 1999. Braunbeck, Gary A. "A Leg Up, or The Constant Tin Soldier (Gonzo Version)." In *Twice Upon a Time*, edited by Denise Little. New York: Daw Books, 270–78.

> 1999. Mayer, Gloria Gilbert, and Thomas Mayer. "The Steadfast Tin Soldier." In *Goldilocks on Management: 27 Revisionist Fairy Tales for Serious Managers*. New York: American Management Association, 107–14.

"The Tinder Box"

Short story

> 1997. Frost, Gregory. "Sparks." In *Black Swan, White Raven*, edited by Ellen Datlow and Terri Windling. New York: Avon, 142–77.

"Thumbelina"

Short stories

> 1993. Jacobs, Harvey. "Persimmon (After *Thumbelina* by Hans Christian Andersen)." In *Snow White, Blood Red*, edited by Ellen Datlow and Terri Windling. New York: Avon, 214–27.

> 1997. Friesner, Esther M. "No Bigger Than My Thumb." In *Black Swan, White Raven*, edited by Ellen Datlow and Terri Windling. New York: Avon, 61–79.

> 1999. Wade, Susan. "Ivory Bones." In *Silver Birch, Blood Moon*, edited by Ellen Datlow and Terri Windling. New York: Avon, 193–202.

> 2000. Block, Francesca Lia. "Tiny." *The Rose and the Beast: Fairy Tales Retold*. New York: Joanna Cotler, 35–52.

"The Ugly Duckling"

Short story

> 1999. Mayer, Gloria Gilbert, and Thomas Mayer. "The Ugly Duckling." In *Goldilocks on Management: 27 Revisionist Fairy Tales for Serious Managers*. New York: American Management Association, 83–90.

Poetry

> 1982. Hay, Sara Hendersen. "Local Boy Makes Good." In *Story Hour*. Fayetteville: The University of Arkansas Press, 24.

General Folktales

Three of the following folktales have never been designated as tale types because of the lack of variants found by Antti Aarne and Stith Thompson when they were compiling their indexes of tale types. Because "Dead Moon," "Goldilocks and the Three Bears," and "The Shoemaker and the Elves" are well-known tales, we have included them in this appendix.

"Bearskin" (Tale Type 361)

Graphic novels

> 1998. Hines, Gareth. *Bearskin: A Grimm Tale*. Cambridge, MA, Thecomic.com.

> 1999. Wilson, Gahan. "Bearskin." In *The Big Book of Grimm: Truly Scary Fairy Tales to Frighten the Whole Family!, by the Brothers Grimm as Channeled by Jonathan Vankin & Over 50 Top Comic Book Artists*. New York: Paradox Press, 150–53.

Short film

> 1982. *Bearskin*. (From the Brothers Grimm by Tom Davenport and Gary Carden). Delaplane, VA: Davenport Films, 20 minutes.

"Bluebeard" (Tale Type 312)

Short stories

1986. Atwood, Margaret. "Bluebeard's Egg." *Bluebeard's Egg: Stories*. New York: Anchor [1998 reprint].

1992. Oates, Joyce Carol. "Blue-bearded Lover." In *Caught in a Story: Contemporary Fairytales and Fables*, edited by Christine Park and Caroline Heaton. London: Vintage, 182–84. [Reprinted in part In *Mirror, Mirror on the Wall: Women Writers Explore Their Favorite Fairy Tales*, edited by Kate Bernheimer. New York: Anchor, 1998, 69–271].

1996. Jackson, Shirley. "The Honeymoon of Mrs. Smith, Version I." In *Just an Ordinary Day*, edited by Laurence Jackson Hyman and Sarah Hyman Stewart. New York: Bantam, 70–79.

1996. Jackson, Shirley. "The Honeymoon of Mrs. Smith, Version II: The Mystery of the Murdered Bride." In *Just an Ordinary Day*, edited by Laurence Jackson Hyman and Sarah Hyman Stewart. New York: Bantam, 80–88.

2000. Block, Francesca Lia. "Bones." In *The Rose and the Beast: Fairy Tales Retold*. New York: Joanna Colter, 151–66.

Poetry

1982. Hay, Sara Hendersen. "Syndicated Column." In *Story Hour*. Fayetteville: The University of Arkansas Press, 27.

"The Brave Little Tailor" (Tale Type 1640)

Short story

1998. Roberts, Les. "The Brave Little Costume Designer." In *Once Upon a Crime*, edited by Ed Gorman and Martin H. Greenberg. New York: Berkley Crime, 275–89.

"The Bremen Town Musicians" (Tale Type 130)

Short stories

1994. Waldrop, Howard. "The Sawing Boys." In *Black Thorn, White Rose*, edited by Ellen Datlow and Terri Windling. New York: William Morrow, 217–44.

1998. Crowther, Peter. "The Musician of Bremen, GA." In *Once Upon a Crime*, edited by Ed Gorman and Martin H. Greenberg. New York: Berkley Crime, 303–20.

1999. Mayer, Gloria Gilbert, and Thomas Mayer. "The Bremen Town Musicians." In *Goldilocks on Management: 27 Revisionist Fairy Tales for Serious Managers*. New York: American Management Association, 189–200.

"Brother and Sister" (Tale Type 450)

Short story

> 1995. Steiber, Ellen. "In the Night Country." In *The Armless Maiden and Other Tales for Childhood's Survivors*, edited by Terri Windling. New York: TOR, 300–344.

Graphic novel

> 1999. Sutton, Tom. "Brother and Sister." In *The Big Book of Grimm: Truly Scary Fairy Tales to Frighten the Whole Family!*, by the Brothers Grimm as Channeled by Jonathan Vankin & Over 50 Top Comic Book Artists. New York: Paradox Press, 76–80.

"Clever Hans" (Tale Type 1696)

Short story

> 1998. Breen, Jon L. "Clever Hans." In *Once Upon a Crime*, edited by Ed Gorman and Martin H. Greenberg. New York: Berkley Crime, 19–31.

Graphic novel

> 1999. Emerson, Hunt. "Clever Hans." In *The Big Book of Grimm: Truly Scary Fairy Tales to Frighten the Whole Family!*, by the Brothers Grimm as Channeled by Jonathan Vankin & Over 50 Top Comic Book Artists. New York: Paradox Press, 95–97.

"The Dead Moon"

Short story

> 1993. de Lint, Charles." The Moon Is Drowning While I Sleep." In *Snow White, Blood Red*, edited by Ellen Datlow and Terri Windling. New York: Avon, 50–79.

"Donkey Skin/Allerleirauh" (Tale Type 510B)

Novel

> 1993. McKinley, Robin. *Deerskin*. New York: Ace.

Short stories

> 1995. Snyder, Midori. "Tattercoats." In *Black Thorn, White Rose*, edited by Ellen Datlow and Terri Windling. New York: Avon, 173–202.

> 1995. Windling, Terri. "Donkeyskin," In *The Armless Maiden*, edited by Terri Windling. New York: Tor, 295–99.

> 1995. Yolen, Jane. "Allerleirauh." In *The Armless Maiden*, edited by Terri Windling. New York: Tor, 36–39.

1997. Donoghue, Emma. "The Tale of the Skin." In *Kissing the Witch,* by Emma Donoghue. New York: Joanna Cotler, 143–63.

1998. Allynn, Doug. "Thousandfurs." In *Once Upon a Crime*, edited by Ed Gorman and Martin H. Greenberg. New York: Berkeley, 385–97.

1999. Wilson, Barbara. "Suit of Leather." In *Salt Water and Other Stories.* Los Angeles: Alyson Books, 206–30.

Film

1970. *The Magic Donkey (Peau D'Âne).* Directed by Jacques Demy. France: Mag Bodard/Marianne.

Poetry

2000. Snyder, Midori. "Donkeyskin," http://www.endicott-studio.com/cofskin1.html.

Graphic novel

1999. "Alleleirauh" In *The Big Book of Grimm: Truly Scary Fairy Tales to Frighten the Whole Family!, by the Brothers Grimm as Channeled by Jonathan Vankin & Over 50 Top Comic Book Artists.* New York: Paradox Press, 90–94.

"Diamonds and Toads" (Tale Type 480)

Novel

1999. Levine, Gail Carson. *The Fairy's Mistake.* New York: HarperCollins.

Short stories

1999. Cadnum, Michael. "Toad-Rich." In *Silver Birch, Blood Moon*, edited by Ellen Datlow and Terri Windling. New York: Avon, 251–57.

1999. Hoffman, Nina Kiriki. "How I Came to Marry a Herpetologist." In *Twice Upon a Time,* edited by Denise Little. New York: Daw Books, 30–39.

1999. Hopkinson, Nalo. "Precious." In *Silver Birch, Blood Moon*, edited by Ellen Datlow and Terri Windling. New York: Avon, 92–99.

Poetry

1982. Hay, Sara Hendersen. "The Flaw." In *Story Hour.* Fayetteville: The University of Arkansas Press, 35.

"The Fisherman and His Wife" (Tale Type 555)

Short stories

1997. Cadnum, Michael. "The Flounder's Kiss." In *Black Swan, White Raven*, edited by Ellen Datlow and Terri Windling. New York: Avon, 6–13.

1997. McClaughlin, Mark. "Prince of the Dark Green Sea." In *Bending the Landscape: Fantasy*, edited by Nicola Griffith and Stephen Pagel. Clarkston, GA: White Wolf, 55–59.

Poetry

> 1982. Hay, Sara Hendersen. "New England Tragedy." In *Story Hour*. Fayetteville: The University of Arkansas Press, 36.

"The Gingerbread Man" (Tale Type 2025)

Short story

> 1994. Cadnum, Michael. "Can't Catch Me." In *Black Thorn, White Rose*, edited by Ellen Datlow and Terri Windling. New York: William Morrow, 120–28.

Graphic novel

> 2000. Kelly, Walt. "The Gingerbread Man." In *Little Lit: Folklore and Fairy Tale Funnies*, edited by Art Spiegelman and Francoise Mouley. New York: Joanna Cotler, 39–44.

"The Girl with No Hands" (Tale Type 706)

Novel

> 1973. Oats, Joyce Carol. *Do With Me What You Will*. New York: Vanguard.

Short story

> 1995. Snyder, Midori." The Armless Maiden." In *The Armless Maiden and Other Tales for Childhood's Survivors*, edited by Terri Windling. New York: TOR, 17–30.

Poetry

> 1971. Sexton, Anne. "The Maiden Without Hands." In *Transformations*. Boston: Houghton Mifflin, 81–86.

Graphic novel

> 1999. DuBurke, Randy. "The Girl with No Hands." In *The Big Book of Grimm: Truly Scary Fairy Tales to Frighten the Whole Family!, by the Brothers Grimm as Channeled by Jonathan Vankin & Over 50 Top Comic Book Artists*. New York: Paradox Press, 30–33.

"Godfather Death" (Tale Type 332)

Novel

> 1996. Pollack, Rachel. *Godmother Night*. New York: St. Martin's Press. (For mature readers).

Short stories

> 1994. Zelazny, Roger. "Godson." In *Black Thorn, White Rose*, edited by Ellen Datlow and Terri Windling. New York: William Morrow, 245–80.

> 1997. Yolen, Jane. "Godmother Death." In *Black Swan, White Raven*, edited by Ellen Datlow and Terri Windling. New York: Avon, 350–58.

Poetry

> 1971. Sexton, Anne. "Godfather Death." In *Transformations*. Boston: Houghton Mifflin, 31–34.

Graphic novel

> 1999. Mannion, Steve. "Godfather Death." In *The Big Book of Grimm: Truly Scary Fairy Tales to Frighten the Whole Family!, by the Brothers Grimm as Channeled by Jonathan Vankin & Over 50 Top Comic Book Artists*. New York: Paradox Press, 169–71.

"Goldilocks and the Three Bears"

Short stories

> 1995. Goldstein, Lisa. "Brother Bear." In *Ruby Slippers. Golden Tears*, edited by Ellen Datlow and Terri Windling. New York: Avon, 124–33.

> 1996. Fisher, David. "Kingdom v. Goldilocks." In *Legally Correct Fairy Tales*. New York: Warner, 107–16.

> 1999. Friesner, Esther M. "Case #285B." In *Twice Upon a Time*, edited by Denise Little. New York: Daw Books, 56–66.

> 1999. Mayer, Gloria Gilbert, and Thomas Mayer. "Goldilocks and the Three Bears." In *Goldilocks on Management: 27 Revisionist Fairy Tales for Serious Managers*. New York: American Management Association, 3–14.

> 2000. Bradfield, Scott. "Goldilocks Tells All." In *Black Heart, Ivory Bones*, edited by Ellen Datlow and Terri Windling. New York: Avon, 143–53.

> 2000. Cadnum, Michael. "Bear It Away." In *Black Heart, Ivory Bones*, edited by Ellen Datlow and Terri Windling. New York: Avon, 136–42.

Poetry

> 1982. Hay, Sara Hendersen. "The Grievance." In *Story Hour*. Fayetteville: The University of Arkansas Press, 13.

> 1995. Vande Velde, Vivian. "All Points Bulletin." In *Tales from the Brothers Grimm and the Sisters Weird*. San Diego: Harcourt Brace, 36.

> 1999. Gaiman, Neil. "Locks." In *Silver Birch, Blood Moon*, edited by Ellen Datlow and Terri Windling. New York: Avon, 313–18.

"The Goose Girl" (Tale Type 533)

Short stories

> 1994. Wynne-Jones, Tim. "The Goose Girl." In *Black Thorn, White Rose, edited* by Ellen Datlow and Terri Windling. New York: William Morrow, 151–72.

> 1999. Springer, Nancy. "Gilly the Goose Girl." In *Twice Upon a Time*, edited by Denise Little. New York: Daw Books, 94–106.

2000. Farmer, Nancy. "Falada: The Goose Girl's Horse." In *A Wolf at the Door: and Other Retold Fairy Tales*, edited by Ellen Datlow and Terri Windling. New York: Simon and Schuster, 44–53.

Poetry

1982. Hay, Sara Hendersen. "The Goosegirl." In *Story Hour*. Fayetteville: The University of Arkansas Press, 37.

Graphic novel

1999. Langridge, Roger. "The Goose Girl." In *The Big Book of Grimm: Truly Scary Fairy Tales to Frighten the Whole Family!, by the Brothers Grimm as Channeled by Jonathan Vankin & Over 50 Top Comic Book Artists*. New York: Paradox Press, 34–37.

Short film

1983. *Goose Girl*. (From the Brothers Grimm by Tom Davenport and Gary Carden). Delaplane, VA: Davenport Films, 18 minutes.

"The Juniper Tree" (Tale Type 720)

Short story

1995. Straub, Peter. "The Juniper Tree." In *The Armless Maiden and Other Tales for Childhood's Survivors*, edited by Terri Windling. New York: TOR, 96–119.

Graphic novel

1999. Rogers, Wm. Marshall. "The Juniper Tree." In *The Big Book of Grimm: Truly Scary Fairy Tales to Frighten the Whole Family!, by the Brothers Grimm as Channeled by Jonathan Vankin & Over 50 Top Comic Book Artists*. New York: Paradox Press, 13–17.

"Little Poucet"

Short story

1993. Tem, Steve Rasnic. "Little Poucet." In *Snow White, Blood Red*, edited by Ellen Datlow and Terri Windling. New York: Avon, 228–47.

"King Thrushbeard" (Tale Type 900)

Short story

2000. Glassco, Bruce. "Thrushbeard." *Realms of Fantasy* (December): 64–69, 99.

Short film

1982. *Bristlelip*. (From the Brothers Grimm by Tom Davenport and Gary Carden). Delaplane, VA: Davenport Films, 19 minutes.

"Mr. Fox" (Tale Type 955)

Poetry

> 1995. Gaiman, Neil. "The White Road." In *Ruby Slippers. Golden Tears*, edited by Ellen Datlow and Terri Windling. New York: Avon, 358–71.

"Old Sultan" (Tale Type 101)

Short story

> 1998. Coward, Matt. "Old Sultan." In *Once Upon a Crime*, edited by Ed Gorman and Martin H. Greenberg. New York: Berkley Crime, 88–99.

Graphic novel

> 1999. Chiappetta, Joe. "Old Sultan." In *The Big Book of Grimm: Truly Scary Fairy Tales to Frighten the Whole Family!, by the Brothers Grimm as Channeled by Jonathan Vankin & Over 50 Top Comic Book Artists*. New York: Paradox Press, 182–83.

"Puss 'n Boots" (Tale Type 545)

Short stories

> 1979. Carter, Angela. "Puss-in-Boots." in *The Bloody Chamber and Other Stories*. London: Penguin, 68–84.

> 1993. Friesner, Esther M. "Puss." In *Snow White, Blood Red*, edited by Ellen Datlow and Terri Windling. New York: Avon, 303–37.

> 1999. Hirsch, Connie. "Puck in Boots, the True Story." In *Twice Upon a Time*, edited by Denise Little. New York: Daw Books, 40–55.

> 1999. Mayer, Gloria Gilbert, and Thomas Mayer. "Puss in Boots." In *Goldilocks on Management: 27 Revisionist Fairy Tales for Serious Managers*. New York: American Management Association, 99–106.

Graphic novel

> 1999. Geary, Rick. "Puss in Boots." In *The Big Book of Grimm: Truly Scary Fairy Tales to Frighten the Whole Family!, by the Brothers Grimm as Channeled by Jonathan Vankin & Over 50 Top Comic Book Artists*. New York: Paradox Press, 116–18.

"The Robber Bridegroom" (Tale Type 955)

Novel

> 1942. Welty, Eudora. *The Robber Bridegroom*. 1942. San Diego: Harcourt, Brace & World. Reprinted in 1987 with illustrations by Barry Moser.

Graphic novel

1999. Beroy, J. M. "The Robber Bridegroom." In *The Big Book of Grimm: Truly Scary Fairy Tales to Frighten the Whole Family!, by the Brothers Grimm as Channeled by Jonathan Vankin & Over 50 Top Comic Book Artists.* New York: Paradox Press, 104–7.

"The Shoemaker and the Elves"

Short stories

1995. Cadnum, Michael. "Naked Little Men." In *Ruby Slippers, Golden Tears*, edited by Ellen Datlow and Terri Windling. New York: Avon, 116–23.

1995. Lannes, Roberta. "Roach in Loafers." In *Ruby Slippers, Golden Tears*, edited by Ellen Datlow and Terri Windling. New York: Avon, 97–115.

1997. Jacobs, A. J. "The Elves and the Shoemaker." In *Fractured Fairy Tales*. New York: Bantam, 61–66.

1997. Schimel, Lawrence. "The Shoemaker and the Elvis." In *Elf Magic*, edited by Martin H. Greenberg. New York: DAW, 139–49.

1999. Mayer, Gloria Gilbert, and Thomas Mayer. "The Elves and the Shoemaker." In *Goldilocks on Management: 27 Revisionist Fairy Tales for Serious Managers.* New York: American Management Association, 161–70.

"Snow White and Rose Red" (Tale Type 426)

Novel

1989. Wrede, Patricia. *Snow White and Rose Red.* New York: TOR.

1999. Bodger, Joan. *The Forest Family.* Toronto: Tundra.

Short story

2000. Block, Francesca Lia. "Rose." In *The Rose and the Beast: Fairy Tales Retold.* New York: Joanna Colter, 133–49.

Poetry

1985. Colby, Joan. "Rose Red to Snow White." In *Disenchantments: An Anthology of Modern Fairy Tale Poetry*, edited by Wolfgang Mieder. Hanover: University of Vermont; University Press of New England, 186. [Originally published in 1976].

1985. Levertov, Denise. "An Embroidery." In *Disenchantments: An Anthology of Modern Fairy Tale Poetry*, edited by Wolfgang Mieder. Hanover: University of Vermont; University Press of New England, 183–84. [Originally published in 1967].

1985. Unger, Barbara. "Breasts." In *Disenchantments: An Anthology of Modern Fairy Tale Poetry*, edited by Wolfgang Mieder. Hanover: University of Vermont; University Press of New England, 185. [Originally published in 1973].

2000. Nadel, Cory-Ellen. "Rose Red," http://www.endicott-studio.com/cofrosrd.html.

Graphic novel

1999. Draughtsman, D'Israeli D'Emon. "Snow White and Rose Red." In *The Big Book of Grimm: Truly Scary Fairy Tales to Frighten the Whole Family!*, by the Brothers Grimm as Channeled by Jonathan Vankin & Over 50 Top Comic Book Artists. New York: Paradox Press, 146–48.

"The Story of the Youth Who Went Forth to Learn What Fear Was" (Tale Type 326)

Short story

1995. Collins, Nancy A. "Billy Fearless." In *Ruby Slippers. Golden Tears*, edited by Ellen Datlow and Terri Windling. New York: Avon, 154–77.

Graphic novel

1999. Benton, Gregory. "The Boy Who Learned to Shudder." In *The Big Book of Grimm: Truly Scary Fairy Tales to Frighten the Whole Family!*, by the Brothers Grimm as Channeled by Jonathan Vankin & Over 50 Top Comic Book Artists. New York: Paradox Press, 60–64.

"The Three Billy Goats Gruff" (Tale Type 123)

Short stories

1993. Gaiman, Neil. "Troll Bridge." In *Snow White, Blood Red*, edited by Ellen Datlow and Terri Windling. New York: Avon, 281–94.

1995. Vande Velde, Vivian. "The Bridge." In *Tales from the Brothers Grimm and the Sisters Weird*. San Diego: Harcourt Brace, 72–76.

1999. Mayer, Gloria Gilbert, and Thomas Mayer. "The Three Billy Goats Gruff." In *Goldilocks on Management: 27 Revisionist Fairy Tales for Serious Managers*. New York: American Management Association, 211–20.

2000. Waldrop, Howard. "Our Mortal Span." In *Black Heart, Ivory Bones*, edited by Ellen Datlow and Terri Windling. New York: Avon, 303–16.

"Three Little Pigs" (Tale Type 124)

Short stories

1996. Fisher, David. "USA v. Wolf: Deposition of Mr. Wolf." In *Legally Correct Fairy Tales*. New York: Warner, 33–44.

1999. Mayer, Gloria Gilbert, and Thomas Mayer. "The Three Little Pigs." In *Goldilocks on Management: 27 Revisionist Fairy Tales for Serious Managers*. New York: American Management Association, 29–34.

1999. Shepard, Lupita. "Wolf at the Door." In *Twice Upon a Time*, edited by Denise Little. Daw Books, 180–97.

Poetry

1982. Hay, Sara Hendersen. "The Builders." In *Story Hour*. Fayetteville: The University of Arkansas Press, 10.

"Tom Thumb" (Tale Type 700)

Short story

1997. Jacobs, A. J. "Thom Tum." In *Fractured Fairy Tales*. New York: Bantam, 67–73.

Poetry

1982. Hay, Sara Hendersen. "Only Son." In *Story Hour*. Fayetteville: The University of Arkansas Press, 12.

Graphic novel

1999. Fingerman, Bob. "Tom Thumb." In *The Big Book of Grimm: Truly Scary Fairy Tales to Frighten the Whole Family!, by the Brothers Grimm as Channeled by Jonathan Vankin & Over 50 Top Comic Book Artists.* New York: Paradox Press, 47–51.

"The Twelve Dancing Princesses" (Tale Type 306)

Short stories

1981. McKinley, Robin. "The Twelve Dancing Princesses." In *The Door in the Hedge*. New York: Ace, 137–216.

1998. Wingate, Anne. " 'The Twelve Dancing Princesses' Revisited." In *Once Upon a Crime*, edited by Ed Gorman and Martin H. Greenberg. New York: Berkley Crime, 374–83.

1999. Mayer, Gloria Gilbert, and Thomas Mayer. "The Twelve Dancing Princesses." In *Goldilocks on Management: 27 Revisionist Fairy Tales for Serious Managers.* New York: American Management Association, 65–74.

2000. McKillip, Patricia A. "The Twelve Dancing Princesses." In *A Wolf at the Door: and Other Retold Fairy Tales*, edited by Ellen Datlow and Terri Windling. New York: Simon and Schuster, 150–66.

Poetry

1971. Sexton, Anne. "The Twelve Dancing Princesses." In *Transformations*. Boston: Houghton Mifflin, 87–92.

Picture book

1999. Allen, Debbie. *Brothers of the Knight*. Illustrated by Kadir Nelson. New York: Dial.

"The Twelve Months" (Tale Type 480)

Short story

2000. Sherman, Della. "The Months of Manhattan." In *A Wolf at the Door: and Other Retold Fairy Tales*, edited by Ellen Datlow and Terri Windling. New York: Simon and Schuster, 1–16.

Author/Illustrator Index

Motif Index

Tale Index

These references are to pages where tales have been mentioned outside of their individual chapters or are mentioned in passing.

Title Index